D1108062

INTRODUCTION TO PSYCHOTHERAPY

BY J. A. HADFIELD
Psychology and Mental Health

INTRODUCTION TO PSYCHOTHERAPY

ITS HISTORY AND MODERN SCHOOLS

BY

J. A. HADFIELD

Late Lecturer in Psychopathology and Mental Hygiene
University of London

London
GEORGE ALLEN AND UNWIN LTD
RUSKIN HOUSE MUSEUM STREET

FIRST PUBLISHED IN 1967

This book is copyright under the Berne Convention. Apart from any fair dealing for the purpose of private study, research, criticism or review, as permitted under the Copyright Act, 1956, no portion may be reproduced by any process without written permission. Enquiries should be addressed to the publishers

© *George Allen & Unwin Ltd.*, 1967

RC480
H25

PRINTED IN GREAT BRITAIN
in 10pt Times Roman type
BY J. W. ARROWSMITH LTD
BRISTOL

CONTENTS

CHAPTER I

INTRODUCTORY

Psychotherapy is the treatment of disorders of mental and emotional origin by mental means.

Most people in these days have some idea of the subject although this knowledge is usually vague. They have an idea that Freud 'put it all down to sex'. They may know that Jung believed in what he called the Archetypes, though what those are they have but the vaguest idea. Adler they may not have heard of, but they are at least conversant with his discovery, the 'Inferiority complex', for this is the one complex which people boast of having. The reason for its popularity is obvious, for when you say you have an inferiority complex it means that you are a much finer fellow than you think you are!—a back-handed compliment to yourself.

The purpose of this book is to give the intelligent reader some idea of what it is all about.

It is a subject that concerns everybody, for there is no one who has not got some form or another of neurotic disorder, be it only a tendency to depression, or defeatism, jealousy or irrational suspicions, or a dislike of travelling away from one's base, or some sexual aberration. Some people are aware of these aberrations in themselves and wonder what is the cause. Others have them but do not recognize them as abnormal. I have had people say 'I have a dislike of travelling by underground, but everyone has that!' 'I have dreams of being chased (or of suffocation), like everybody else.' A cleric of high repute once said to me 'I should like to be analysed, for I am sure I have not a single complex!' My immediate thought was 'That is the first one to start off with!'

The *disorders* with which Psychotherapy deals are the psychogenic disorders, that is to say those disorders which are of psychological origin. They are the psychoneuroses.

It does not rightly deal with diseases of organic origin such as pleurisy, coronary thrombosis or a fractured leg; nor does it treat mental disorders of constitutional and physical origin, such as melancholia, delusions of the paranoic or hallucinations of the alcoholic and drug taker. All these, being physiological, are better treated along physiological lines.

It does treat anxiety states, phobias, obsessions and sex perversions, for these are mainly psychogenic. It also treats disorders of a physical nature like hysterical paralysis and nervous indigestion, for these, though physical in manifestation, originate in mental and emotional causes.

The *methods* used in Psychotherapy are varied. Some resort to treatment by *persuasion* which is an appeal to reason, and try to convince the patient of the unreasonableness of his fear of crossing the road or travelling by underground. Others treat by *hypnotic suggestion*, which appeals not so much to the reason as to the subconscious mind. *Analytic treatment* goes deeper and tries to discover and treat the underlying causes of the disorders. It is far more radical than treatment by suggestion. There are others who have no belief in the psychological origin of disorders and therefore treat mental conditions of all kinds by *drugs* and other physical, means; but they are not psychotherapists, for though they treat mental disorders, it is not by mental means. All these methods of treatment and their advocates will be fully discussed.

Classification. We may then divide the disorders which affect man into four groups.

1. *Physical* disorders which have a *physical* origin, like pleurisy or cancer. These are the concern of the general practitioner, the physician and the surgeon.

2. *Physical* disorders which have *psychological* causes, like hysteric paralysis of the leg. These are the concern of the psycho-therapist.

3. There are *mental* disorders like delusions of the insane or melancholia, which are *physically* caused and are the work of the psychiatrist and not specifically of the psychotherapist.

4. There are *mental* and emotional disturbances like sex perversions and phobias, which have a *psychological* origin and are also the task of the psychotherapist, including psycho-analysis.

We observe from the foregoing account that when we are presented with any disorder, say a headache, we have first to decide whether it is psychogenic, that is to say originates in mental and emotional causes, or whether it is organic, due to physical causes. For a physical disorder, such as a paralysed leg may have either a physical or a mental cause, and a mental symptom like depression may originate in either mental or physical causes. The treatment in each of those cases is quite different from the others, and they must be clearly distinguished if treatment is to be effective.

A correct diagnosis is the first essential. An acquaintance of mine, suffering from acute depression, was first diagnosed as a psychoneurotic case, for which there was strong evidence since he had always suffered from an inferiority complex and was having troubles in his profession. He went to another psychiatrist who diagnosed his case as cyclo-thymia, a constitutional disorder and gave a poor prognosis. It was ultimately discovered that he was suffering from recurrent benign tertiary malaria, and received the proper treatment. This case confirms the teaching of my professor of medicine in Edinburgh, who stressed that almost all false diagnoses were sins of omission, something we did not think of. He therefore taught that when presented by a patient with any symptom we should call to mind all possible causes, and then by a process of elimination as well as by positive signs and symptoms come to a correct diagnosis.

The difference in point of view may be illustrated by a story, no doubt apocryphal, told of a woman who had a copious flow of tears. The physician, making a chemical analysis of the tears, found an excess of salt and water, so put her on a saltfree diet and cut down her fluid intake. The tears continued. A surgeon was consulted and he decided to stop the flow of tears by excision of the lachrymal duct. The tears came as before but even more copiously over the cheeks. Ultimately she went to a psychotherapist who found that she had recently lost her husband and diagnosed that her sadness was the cause of her tears. He gave her suggestion treatment which restored her confidence to face life, and behold her tears automatically disappeared!

History. It is a general principle in science that we cannot understand its present day status without knowing something of its development in the past. When we do delve into the past we meet with some surprising results. For instance, we find that the Negritos of the Philippine Islands, a primitive pigmy tribe, practise precisely the same methods which Freud originally used, that is to say they hypnotize their patients, get them to go back to infantile experiences, and release their repressed emotions in the form of abreaction! The patient emerges from his trance with his symptoms cured.

We shall then start our study with a brief glance at the methods used in primitive societies.

This book sets out to be *comprehensive*, that is, to take an all-round view of the subject. But it would be impossible in an introduction of this kind to deal with all those who have made contributions to this science, it is only necessary to our aim to give the reader a working knowledge of the subject. Still less is it necessary to describe the offshoots of the various schools. I have therefore chosen only those contributors who have made specific advances in the development of the science, such as when the belief in the intervention of spirits as a cause of disease gave place to Mesmer's theory of the 'magnetic fluid', and when that in turn gave place to the theory of hypnotism as a purely subjective phenomenon: again, when treatment of symptoms by suggestion gave place under Janet to investigation of *causes*, which Freud further found went

A*

back to infantile experiences, and which Jung found to be in yet deeper layers of the collective consciousness, a residue of ancestral traits.

Furthermore, I have particularly set out to emphasize the *positive contribution* of each rather than to describe those of their theories which are of dubious speculation. This I am the better able to do since I do not belong to any of the established schools, so that I am able to appreciate the contributions of all. Moreover, as Director of Studies at the Tavistock Clinic for thirteen years I had the privilege of inviting and of entertaining men of high repute, such as Jung, Adler, Stekel, Coué, McDougall, Myers, Rivers, Gesell and Groddeck, but unfortunately not Freud. In such personal converse one is often able to get a view of their theories which one could not always obtain by reading their books.

That does not mean that I have refrained from criticism altogether, for without criticism we cannot sift fact from speculation to arrive at the truth. For this reason and the need for brevity, I fear that those who belong to those schools will find, in the unlikely event that they read the book, many shortcomings and omissions. But as the book is intended for the general reader, that is a risk that I must take.

In fact, I have never been particularly enamoured of 'schools' of thought in psychotherapy. We do not have 'schools' of orthopaedic surgery! Why of psychotherapy? It shows a weakness in our science. Such schools have the advantage that they can pursue to the utmost some particular aspect of science, as Freud did with sex and Jung with the collective and racial unconscious, but not only does this sometimes lead to absurd extravagances (as when during the First World War some Freudians said that the reason why we feared the Zeppelins was that they were phallic symbols), but specific schools are apt to discount and discard the findings of other schools. So truth is stifled in controversy. There is truth in all these schools.

In judging of the various schools, I have therefore had to emulate the example of the newly appointed magistrate in the North of England, who, on taking up office, declared that he would always seek to maintain a proper balance between partiality and impartiality!

Whether it is of advantage to be oneself a practising psychotherapist, as I have been for over fifty years, is doubtful, for one is apt to be prejudiced in favour of one's findings. But at least it does make one's interest in the subject more living; and also enables one to check the theories of others by one's own experiences.

My experience of treating cases of psychoneuroses has led me to views differing from the other schools in many respects which I have described in the last chapters of the book. Whether they are right or not remains for future investigators to decide: but at least they have come from experience and are not simply theoretical. They are also, I claim, common sense!

I trust that the book may be of some value not only to the intelligent public who are interested in human nature and its disorders, but also to medical students who will later be confronted with numerous cases of this kind, and to general practitioners who would like a comprehensive account of what it is all about, without wading through numerous volumes; finally to ministers and clergy who are constantly confronted with these problems in their 'cure of souls'.

TERMS

It cannot be assumed that every reader is conversant with the terms used in this science, for they are sometimes bewildering, and even experts are not always agreed about them. I may perhaps be permitted to explain some of those terms.

Psychology may be defined as the 'scientific study of mental states and processes'. It is a pure science; that is to say its aim is none other than the discovery of truth about the mind. It is sometimes said that 'We are all psychologists nowadays'. That is not strictly true! Most people including playwrights and novelists, are now interested in the workings of the mind and of behaviour but only those who study it scientifically can be called 'psychologists'!

Psychotherapy is different; it is an applied science, the application of psychology to the problem of treating disease. As already stated it is properly applied only to the treatment of those disorders which are psychogenic, of psychological origin.

Psychoneurosis. Such disorders are called psychoneuroses or simply 'neuroses'. They used to be called 'functional nerve disorders', since they were disorders in the functioning of the mind without there being any perceptible change in bodily structure. We use the term 'psychogenic' when we refer to their origin; we use 'psychoneuroses' when we refer to the condition itself; we use the term 'psychopathology' when we refer to the study of the disease itself, just as in medicine the pathologist studies diseased conditions without reference to treatment; and we use 'psychotherapy' when we refer to their treatment.

The term *psychotherapist* is used in general of those who treat disorders by mental means of whatever kind. They are not necessarily medical men and women, and many distinguished psychotherapists, like Professor Flügel and Melanie Klein (who for some years dominated the London Institute of Psychoanalysis), were not medically trained. But the term should be applied only to those who deal with these disorders by scientific means; not to faith healers for instance.

The term *medical psychologist* is often used as synonymous with psychotherapist, but it should be confined to medical men and women and should, strictly speaking, be used only of those with an academic training in psychology. It is the term I apply to myself. A medical psychologist may use all methods and is not confined to analysis.

Psychoanalysis. The term 'psychoanalyst' should be applied only to those who have gone through a specified course of training at a recognized institute of psychoanalysis. It is a term particularly reserved for Freud's methods of investigation and treatment. It is also applied to the body of truth he thus discovered, so that we say 'psychoanalysis teaches . . .'.

The term *analysis*, however, covers a wider field. It is a term used in many sciences, in chemistry for instance, as when we speak of a 'chemical analysis of the contents of the stomach'. In our science it is mainly used as a method of investigation of the unconscious causes of neurotic disorders.

The Freudian is one form of analysis. Jung also is analytical, but to distinguish this method from Freud's he calls it 'analytical psychology'. Adler's method which he calls 'individual psychology', is analytic in that he investigates the causes of the inferiority complex, though he has little truck with the 'unconscious mind' used by Freud or Jung.

Psychiatry is a more comprehensive term used in relation to the study and treatment of mental disorders of all kinds, whether of physical or mental origin, and does so largely by physical means such as the use of drugs. The term 'alienist' used to be applied to those doctors who dealt with people whose minds were 'alienated' in other words, the 'insane'. The term 'psychiatry' used to be confined to the treatment of such insane persons and mental deficients, whereas psychotherapy was used for the treatment of the so-called 'functional nervous disorders'. They are now all lumped together under 'psychiatry', oblivious of the fact that the psychiatrists were among the chief opponents of psychotherapy and psychoanalysis at the time when these methods came to the fore in the First World War—indeed some of them still are opposed to psychological treatment. They may be called the Canutes of psychological medicine.

The extension of the term 'psychiatry' to all emotional disorders is unfortunate, for there are many psychiatrists, well trained in the treatment of psychotic disorders like schizophrenia or melancholia who know little or nothing about the treatment of emotional disorders, yet try their hand at the latter with unhappy results. They get psychotherapy into disrepute. The term 'psychiatrist' should be used only of those medically qualified.

Mental hygiene is particularly concerned with prevention. It has as its aim the maintaining of mental health and the prevention of mental disorders—just as ordinary hygiene is concerned with keeping the body in good health and good working order, such as the work of the Medical Officer of Health which is preventive. The term mental hygiene, however, is often used to cover the treatment of early cases, with a view to preventing them developing further. Mental hygiene is not a pure science but a normative science, having as its norm or standard that of mental health. The National Association of Mental Hygiene is devoted to that work.

Similarly ethics is a normative science, but whereas mental hygiene is concerned with standards of health, ethics is concerned with standards of behaviour, in other words with morals. The two, however, are closely linked—as in delinquency—and the psychotherapist is often confronted with moral problems and sometimes lays down the law concerning problems for which he is not trained, with unfortunate results.

Psychological Medicine. To be precise we must distinguish this term from medical psychology. The former is a *branch of medicine*, that branch of medicine which is concerned with disorders of the mind of whatever nature, whether of psychological or of constitutional origin. The diploma in this subject is therefore rightly called the 'Diploma of Psychological Medicine' (D.P.M.). The term is almost synonymous with psychiatry, as broadly used, except that in the latter the emphasis is upon healing, whereas in psychological medicine the emphasis is upon the study of the subject. Both are confined to medically trained persons.

Medical psychology, strictly speaking, is a *branch of psychology*, a branch which concerns itself with the study of medical problems. It is equivalent to 'educational psychology' or 'industrial psychology' which are the applications of psychology to educational and industrial problems. There would be nothing to prevent a psychologically trained person from making a study, say, of jealousy or even the motives which lie behind a neurosis, without being medically trained, or treating such disorders.

Apart from psychotherapists and medical psychologists there are many others like faith healers, spiritual healers, like those at Lourdes, and Christian Scientists, who treat mental disorders, but they do so by other than scientific means. They usually make no distinction between psychogenic and organic diseases, and set out to cure cancers and pneumonia by their means as well as hysteric conditions. They are mainly, but not always, religious.

We cannot afford to neglect these in our study, for they undoubtedly get results in many cases.

PART 1
PRE-SCIENTIFIC

CHAPTER II

THE PRIMITIVE PERIOD

Psychotherapy, the treatment of ills by mental means, is to be found in all parts of the world and amongst the most primitive people. The principles underlying their practice are basically the same as in modern communities.

It is also interesting to find that in primitive societies there was the same division of function into three groups; medical, surgical, and psychiatric. Then, as now, each of these groups had its distinctive method of treatment; and each comprised a different group of men, each with its own speciality.

To illustrate these practices and differences I cannot do better than describe the conditions in one corner of the globe which was my birthplace, namely the Loyalty Islands, South Pacific, the anthropology of which was contained in a book, now out of print, by my mother: *Among the Natives of the Loyalty Group* by E. Hadfield.

Primitive medicine. In those islands there were the orthodox physicians, the 'medicine men' who cured by herbs and the leaves of bushes which grew all over the island, and by sea water. The leaves would be soaked in water, and sometimes bucketfuls were drunk at a time. Children had the liquid poured down their throats, and also into eyes, ears and noses for good measure. These medicines would obviously have some cleansing and purgative properties.

To take sea water the children's heads were held under water till they gulped it down. In one case at least this led to drowning the child.

It was the orthodox form of cure for adults also. You might see, almost any day, men and women standing waist deep in the sea, whilst a friend with a funnel-like container made of banana leaves poured sea water down their throats till they had taken one or two gallons. Then they would wade ashore, lie down in the shade of a tree until the water was vomited or acted as a purgative. This stomach wash-out was given for all diseases; but as biliousness from eating bad fish was one of the commonest diseases, it proved to be most effective. It was also most popular because they got it cheap, a ready-made health service, without the patient having to pay a fee to a private medicine man. But there were cases in which the stomach was so distended that the patient died, but they always ascribed this to other causes so that the remedy is as popular today as ever, and with good cause.

11

Wax in the ear, producing deafness, was cured by putting a very small insect like the lady-bird into the ear and closing the orifice with cotton. The insect would eat the wax and the deafness was cured.

The remedies of the medicine man however, were quite ineffective as medicine unless administered by the right person: the doctor's prestige must be maintained. Even when the medicine had been given by the right doctor, its effects could be neutralized or a relapse caused, if the compensation given by the friends of the invalid were below the doctors expectations. Reverberations of these conditions are not unknown in modern medical practice.

The power of healing was 'hereditary', passing from father to son, as so often is the case in modern practice.

Primitive surgery. Primitive man also had his surgeons, a body of men quite separate from the physicians, who performed serious operations like trepaning, and without an anaesthetic. If a man had a severe head ache, the surgeons cut a slit in his forehead and inserted a bit of coconut shell. A servant of ours had his forehead covered with scars from such operations. Whether it cured the headache by bloodletting or whether the pain of the crude cutting with a sharp stone masked the headache, we are left to guess.

A boy of twelve who suffered from headaches had incisions of the scalp made from ear to ear and from forehead to occiput, with a sharp shell, but with no anaesthetic. The scalp was then folded back, water (probably sea water, an antiseptic) being poured over it to remove the blood. The skull was then scraped at the painful spot, a piece of coconut shell was inserted, and the scalp stitched up over the coconut shell with native twine and a needle made of the bone of the flying fox. The operation took about an hour, after which he walked away, leaning on his mother, to his home a hundred yards away. Not only did he survive the operation but the fact that the operation did him no harm was proved by the fact that he grew up to be a very intelligent teacher and could speak four or five languages. These natives were very stoical with regard to pains they understood; but not with internal pains like colic or neuralgia the cause of which they did not understand, and which they therefore put down to evil spirits.

For all kinds of bruising, lancing with a long sharp thorn, tapped over the wound gently to avoid the bone, was used, with the object of letting out 'bad blood'; and the patient would boast afterwards how very black the blood was, just as patients nowadays brag to their friends of the seriousness of their operation in hospital!

The surgeons, then as now, specialized. Some were orthopaedic surgeons, such as those in the village of Josep, who practised bone grafting. If a femur was fractured, the surgeon would make an incision and insert pieces of bone from the flying fox alongside the fracture—a method of transplantation practised by orthopaedic surgeons of the present day, who however have better materials, better conditions and also have anaesthetics.

Other surgeons of the Loyalties were not above resorting to chicanery. If a person suffered from headache, such a surgeon would diagnose it as due to a foreign body in the head which would have to be removed (they never ascribed a headache to digestive disorders!). Even here they specialized: with some surgeons the foreign body was hair, with others a stone with others a shell. There was reason for this, for with the instruments the surgeon would also bring the prescribed object wrapped up in a bunch of leaves. He got the patient to kneel down and close his eyes (this was very necessary!) and then smote him on the head—and, lo and behold! the stone or shell fell to the ground to everyone's amazement, and the headache was cured.

But there were sceptics even then. One woman of our acquaintance suffering from headaches, went to such a practitioner but without much faith. The little confidence she had was shattered when she saw that he had some hairs secreted in his fingers before the operation. Alas! she was not cured of her headache. But what could be expected of such a sceptic? She even refused to believe that the moon could restore good teeth! All modern doctors know of such troublesome women, who not only disbelieve in the doctor's pills, but shake the faith of others who have confidence in him. They are a pest in the modern consulting room!

I mention these more orthodox practices of medicine and surgery to point out that not all primitive treatment was due to quackery or sorcery; indeed what strikes one about these remedies like sea water and bone grafting is their efficiency.

Primitive psychiatry. But our special interest is in the sorcerers or wizards who were the psychiatrists of primitive society. They cured people of their ills whether mental or physical by psychic means.

Even the primitive surgeons and physicians were not altogether independent of magic, for pain was sometimes supposed to be the work of malignant spirits, and not to have local origin. Thus a headache could be caused either by evil spirits or by something in the head; in other words they recognized that, as we would say now, the headache could have a psychological as well as a physical origin. That is why to cure the headache the surgeon would open up the scalp to let out the 'black blood', the sorcerer let out the evil spirits.

There were also some diseases like tuberculosis, introduced by the white man, which were beyond the skill of doctors, surgeons and sorcerers alike. The patients were regarded as being possessed by devils, so that in one case such a man was buried alive to get rid of his devil—a most effective remedy.

As they considered that illnesses were due to malign spirits, so they relied upon the mediumship of spirits to cure, although they used material symbols in their practice. The spirits were contained in certain fetishistic objects, usually stones, but also trees and pieces of wood. The man who came into possession of one of these fetishistic objects, however humble his origin might be, became a man of great importance and could be greatly feared. The object itself was not able to do the work, nor on the other hand could the man do without the object; but the possessor, by virtue of possessing the stone and the spirit in the stone or tree, could have this power. It corresponded to the modern diploma.

How it was decided that a stone which looked no different from any other stone possessed this magical quality the natives themselves could not say. I possess many of the fetishistic objects and they look harmless enough.

Idiots and deaf mutes were supposed to bear the penalties of the shortcomings of their parents. This was not at all a bad shot considering that many forms of insanity and mental deficiency are inherited.

These sorcerers could produce diseases as well as cures. If you wanted to harm an inconvenient relative you brought something of his, such as a toe-nail (much as we now take a 'specimen' to the laboratory), and by a curse on that they laid a curse on the man even at a distance. Holding the toe-nail or bit of hair, the sorcerer simply uttered the name of the victim (the name being an integral part of the person), together with an incantation; but the incantation had to be very correctly recited to produce the effect—like the modern prescription.

One young man in our Islands suspecting an old man of causing his headaches, charged him with it and implored him to stop doing so, but when the old man made no answer the young man killed him.

When a 'sorcerer' was suspected of producing illness or failure of crops, the villagers would beg him to destroy his fetishistic stone. By so doing he would destroy the power of the evil spirit— and incidently his own power. If in a village a tree was suspected of harbouring evil spirits it would be cut down and destroyed.

Let it be noted that the sorcerer got his results by magic, and not by religion. That is to say he himself, not the god, produced the results by virtue of his possession of the stone. Magic was therefore the precursor of science; for the scientist has the belief that certain results will automatically follow certain actions without outside interference, whereas religion depends on divine intervention—for God or gods to do the work.

Religion in the sense of a belief in an all-powerful deity did not exist amongst the Loyalty Islanders. But they did believe in the spirits of the departed who could be invoked by the sorcerer. This could hardly be called ancestor worship, for the spirits of the departed were not held in any great awe, and they were subject to the sorcerer and so had their uses.

Whilst these Islanders had no belief in one supreme being they seem to have had a vague belief in two or three beings who had an oversight over districts of the Island. But these played no important part in the life of the community, and there was no 'divine healing' as understood in the Church today. There was 'spirit healing' as there is at the present day, but no 'spiritual healing'—the difference being that the spirits were subject to the sorcerer, but did not heal on their own initiative.

There were, however, two distinct types of spirit: the spirits which were contained in the stone or tree were almost universally evil, whereas the spirits of the departed were kindly. In the Church today the same idea persists: the counterpart of the departed spirits being the saints—who also have their specialities; St Michael cured scurvy; St Clair, diseases of the eye; St Francis specialised in pets; St Ouen in deafness; St Petravelle in fevers; St Cloud in boils; whilst St Christopher, with little effect, is the guardian saint of motorists.

As the savage took a tree to be the abode of spirits, so in these days there are numerous 'healing wells', the most notorious of which is at Lourdes, for the healing of diseases, (See p. 103). How the use of holy wells originated I do not know, but perhaps because these wells were usually springs whose waters were much cleaner than surface water and contained more of the healing salts of the earth. The drinking of the spring water might well cure illnesses, including those due to the drinking of the contaminated water of the ordinary surface wells.

It is probable that many curses as well as diseases had a materialistic interpretation. There was a curse laid on a small uninhabited island off Uvea, (one of the Loyalty Islands), that whoever visited it would die. A young man of our acquaintance anxious to get some of the manure deposited by innumerable sea birds for centuries, defied the curse and did die, although he stoutly maintained he had no pain. This might be put down to the well-known fact that if a native expected to die he often did die. But the true explanation may be otherwise; namely that he died neither from the curse nor from expectation of death, but from phosphorus poisoning—for he would probably not wash his hands between gathering the manure and eating—just as plumbers in our country may get lead poisoning if they are not scrupulously clean.

There are those at the present day who practice spirit healing (as distinct from spiritual healing) and deliberately work by the mediumship of certain spirits of the departed, such as the spirit of Pasteur, of Lister, of Christ and others. What these eminent persons would have thought of their names being used in this way one shudders to think!

As science advances man is more and more capable of curing diseases himself, and the call upon the gods, spirits or magical powers declines. 'Quite early', says Janet, (Psychological healing, p. 22) 'the gods lost interest in the treatment of fractures and dislocations and handed over these elementary matters to the surgeon.' 'If miracles have not ceased today, this is simply because medical science has not yet advanced to a stage at which miracles will become needless.' (ibid., p. 26).

CHAPTER III

BASIC PRINCIPLES OF PRIMITIVE PSYCHOTHERAPY

This brief review of the medical service in a primitive community defines for us the basic principles of psychotherapy which are the same nowadays as in primitive life.

The foregoing illustrations show the belief:

(a) that mind has an influence over the bodily functions,
(b) that both mental and physical disorders can be produced by mental means,
(c) that these disorders can be cured by mental means.

Moll points out in his book on hypnotism that these primitive forms of treatment may again be divided into three groups. In some cases the person is all-important; in others the method; whilst in a third the condition is self-induced. They often overlap.

Emphasis on the person. In ancient times the cure depended largely on the prestige of the person administering the cure. Such was the sorcerer, who had powers which the ordinary man did not possess: by virtue of his possessing the fetishistic stone he was regarded with great awe. A sheik could cure by breathing on the patient or by touching his foot. The Roman Emperor Vespasian, King Francis of France, Queen Elizabeth I and Queen Anne, could, by their touch, cure scrofula or scurvy. They all did so by virtue of their authority: hence the name "Kings Evil" for that disease.

Queen Elizabeth the First enhanced her prestige by this means and though she was most fastidious about personal cleanliness and the beauty of her hands, she would not hesitate to touch the filthy sores of the sick, most of whom it is said on good authority were healed. Samuel Johnson was one of Queen Anne's patients.

One wonders, however, if there is not a materialistic explanation to this. Scurvy is a disease of Vitamin C deficiency, and the sufferers coming from long distances would *en route* live largely on such vegetation and leaves as they could gather, so that by the time they reached the king or queen it may be surmised that their scurvy was well on the way to cure! The queen put the finishing touch on Vitamin C.

During his voyages in the South Seas, Captain Cook's first action on anchoring at an island was to send a party ashore to collect green vegetables. He knew nothing of Vitamin C, but he did know what saved the sailors from scurvy. The American nick-name for the Englishman 'Limey' derives from this addiction to lime juice as a preventive of scurvy.

In the First World War, so we are told, the army psychiatrists in Germany, though only of the rank of Lieutenant, were given the title of Major to boost their authority in the eyes of the patients and so increase the patient's suggestibility.

In modern psychoanalysis we have the same phenomenon occurring in the transference situation. The patient analysed may endow his analyst with superhuman qualities, even omnipotence, and regard him with awe, so that he swallows any interpretation of symptoms or dreams that the analyst suggests.*

The same emphasis on the 'person' appears in the Church to-day. It is only the archbishop who by virtue of his office can consecrate a bishop: and only a bishop who can ordain the clergy, which confers on them powers not possessed by others, so that they alone can pronounce the forgiveness of sins. When therefore an army colonel, in the Great War, taking a drum-head service before his regiment, inadvertently recited the Absolution, he suddenly realized what he had done and corrected himself, shouting 'As you were!', thus restoring the soldiers to their state of sin!

It is also only a priest, by virtue of his office, who can exorcise evil spirits or a ghost haunting a house. But he has to recite the correct formula, as given in the Book of Common Prayer.

In all these cases the prestige of the *person* is the essential feature.

Emphasis on the method. The sorcerer, apart from his prestige, had to use a certain formula and incantation to produce his result. As a rule these had to be very accurately repeated. They were also secret; for anyone else who had the secret formula might have the same power.

The Dervishes of the East produced insensibility to pain by the monotonous beating of drums, just as the modern hypnotist some-times uses the metronome for the same purpose. In this case the prestige of the person does not come into the picture; it is the method which counts. The Abyssinians practised putting people to sleep, a hypnotic sleep, by the same method of drums and monotonous sounds.

The recital of prayers in the Liturgy, given in a monotonous tone, and many sermons drolled out in the same fashion, have the effect of putting people into a state of somnolence and perhaps by these means increases their suggestibility. Possibly in this the clergy are right, and the businessman in the congregation who says he can listen better with his eyes closed may be right; and the sermon may

---

* In other cases, however, the patient sees his analyst as the most degraded, cruel and despicable person alive, which is a great hindrance to treatment.

have a greater effect when the worshippers are in this suggestible condition. A clergyman was described as 'a good shepherd' for 'he kept watch while his flock slept!'

The secrecy of the formula has its counterpart at the present day in the hieroglyphics of the medical prescription, a formula sacred to the doctor and the chemist alone—sometimes only to the doctor —which must not be questioned nor even understood by the patient. It would never do for the patient to know what it was the doctor really prescribed, for the formula might lose its potency if an interfering neighbour could read the prescription and declared, 'That is only Epsom salts'. It remains a mystery, and the medicine becomes more effective the more mysterious it is, for everyone likes a mystery.

In the Temple of Aesculapius recourse was had to the interpretation of dreams as a means of treatment. The sick were laid down and put to sleep (a hypnotic sleep), and were told in their dreams by the gods, of the remedy that would cure them—incidentally an illustration of the problem-solving function of dreams (see p. 243).

Galen also wrote that many cures were brought about in the Temple solely by the administration of shock treatment to the mind—an anticipation of cure by electric shock at the present time; or when, for instance, a man subjected to a car accident recovers the use of his paralysed legs, or when a man confronted by his brother whom he thought killed in the war, suddenly recovers his speech.

How are we to explain this? In every neurosis there is repressed emotion, the symptom being due to the repression. When the patient gets a shock, he is thrown off his guard, the repressing force is removed, all the repressed emotion is suddenly released and the symptom disappears.

In the Church the sacrament of Baptism is a striking illustration of the efficacy of a formula—for even the Roman Catholic Church accepts the validity of the Sacrament *by whomever performed*, provided the correct formula—'In the name of the Father, the Son and the Holy Ghost'—is used. In this case it does not require a priest to repeat the formula, any father can do so for his dying child and it is accepted as valid. Here the person is unimportant; the formula is all-important. There were therefore strong protests both by Catholic and Protestant priests when the daughter of the President of the United States was re-baptized into the Roman Church, it was considered quite unnecessary by both sides.

Self-induced states. What we should in these days call auto-suggestion was practised more in early times than at the present time. Crystal gazing was a common practice amongst the early

Egyptians. Fakirs in India, practising Yoga can almost suspend animation, and can produce insensibility to pain. One such Fakir whom I had the privilege to investigate years ago was able to put the point of a sword behind his gullet until it came out on the other side of his neck. He did this by bunching up all the organs in the front of the throat and with great caution and deliberation pushed the sword behind these strictures till the point protruded on the other side. This was a most dangerous proceeding since structures like that of the carotid artery, jugular vein and vagus nerve, were in the region, but beside being a Fakir he was also a qualified medical man and knew what he was doing. To do this he obviously rendered himself insensible to pain.

The method employed by many Fakirs included fixed gazing—a method later introduced by Braid (p. 37) and used till the present day to induce hypnosis.

Indeed there was an early Christian heretical sect known as the Montanists who produced insensibility to pain by gazing at their own umbilicus—not a very thrilling object to concentrate upon. But that is the very point; it is important that the object concentrated upon should be of no intrinsic interest, or else the mind would wander. Some people put themselves to sleep by concentrating on sheep jumping over a wall: this method would be useless to a farmer for he would begin to worry about that fence which needs mending.

There was also a heretical Christian sect called the Taskodrugites (finger to nose) who produced insensibility to pain by bringing the forefinger to the nose.

Coué-ism with its formula—'Every day in every way I am getting better and better', is a form of auto-suggestion, depending on the use of a formula. Coué always insisted that the patient cured himself—it was self-induced, whereas in fact the patient was first put into a state of suggestibility. We shall have something to say about that later (p. 79).

Insensibility to pain can be self-induced. Seligman the anthropologist reported that in an Indian tribe, the natives would induce in themselves a condition of frenzy in which they would cut themselves with knives with complete insensibility to pain.

We may also refer here to a curious state which may be classified as self-induced although it might be better termed 'contagion hypnosis'. An illustration of this is *Latah*, in Malay, mentioned by Wm. McDougall. When a person's attention is suddenly called to another person he will immediately begin to imitate him in every action. Imitation, suggestibility, and hypnosis all belong to the same sphere of the mind, the subconscious, the subcortical area of the brain.

Another illustration of such contagion, is 'speaking with tongues' mentioned in the *Acts of the Apostles* (chap. 2, verse 4). I have witnessed a similar exhibition at a religious camp meeting in the back woods of Maine, U.S.A. when one person got up and started babbling incoherently, another followed, till hundreds of people were on their feet all babbling away. The suggestive effect was such that it required quite an effort to keep one's seat! Under such conditions it was said that healing 'miracles' took place, although I saw none—but I can well believe it, since everyone was reduced to a state of suggestibility by the emotional atmosphere.

Reference may here be made to the miracles of the New Testament. The prevailing view at the time, accepted by Jesus, was that diseases were due to evil spirits, which were capable of entering men and animals alike, and had to be 'cast out'. When cast out they could enter into others as they did from 'Legion' into the Gaderine swine (Mark 8, v. 3; Luke 8, v. 33).

Many diseases were considered to be due to sin. (Thy sins are forgiven thee! Arise and walk!) At the present day modern psychotherapy confirms this for it is recognized that one of the most potent factors in the production of neurotic disorders is that of guilt. It is repressed guilt which underlies obsessional propitiations. Thus sin and neurotic disease were closely associated.

But as a principle, the idea that all disease was due to sin was rejected by Jesus. To the question 'Who did sin, this man or his parents?', He gave the answer, 'Neither this man nor his parents.'

R. Micklem in his book on *The New Psychology and Miracles* came to the conclusion that apart from the miracles of the raising of the dead (Lazarus and Jesus Himself), all the diseases cured in the New Testament *could* be psychological in origin and so amenable to suggestion. We ask 'What of leprosy?' In those days there was no clear diagnosis and some skin diseases cured might have been other than leprosy as we know it. A false diagnosis often accounts for the claim of supposed cancer and other organic diseases by spiritual cures healing at the present day (p. 108).

Although the miracles of Jesus are often cited as proof of His divinity, He Himself discouraged this idea, for He had resisted that temptation to power long before, in the wilderness. Indeed, he went further and did not claim exclusive power to heal: for when he was charged with casting out devils in the name of Beelzebub, he replied, 'If I by Beelzebub cast out devils, by whom do your sons cast them out?'—implying that they also succeeded in doing so. He also gave His disciples the same injunction to heal the sick and to cast out devils. His motives in healing were humanitarian, not to boost his prestige.

Indeed in the miracles of the New Testament we have a good illustration of the three approaches to the cure of diseases. The Roman Centurion (Math. 8, v. 5) who wished his son healed, appealed on the grounds of *prestige*, 'I also am a man of authority. I say, Come, to one and he cometh; Go, to another and he goeth,' and he ascribed the same authority to Jesus as a force in his cure of disease. But also there is the emphasis on the method, '*Only say the word*, and my son shall be healed'! In other cases the cure comes from the patient himself, 'Thy faith hath saved thee; go in peace', (Luke 7, v. 50) such a cure being *self induced*.

PART II
EARLY SCIENTIFIC PERIOD

CHAPTER IV

ANIMAL MAGNETISM

This brings us to the age of Astrology and Animal Magnetism.

'Paracelsus' was a pioneer in this movement. It was the pen-name of one who rejoiced in the name of Aurelius Phillippus Theophrastus Bombast de Hohenheim.* He lived in 1493–1541, and worked up his observations on the influence of the stars on humans into a quasi-scientific system known as astrology which was described as a 'sympathetic system of medicine'. Stars and planets were able to emit rays and to influence men's minds and bodies with subtle emanations. 'As the moon wanes', it was said, 'so warts disappear'. The word 'lunatic' perpetuates the belief that the moon (luna) has an effect upon men's personality, even inducing madness.

This belief in the magical power of heavenly bodies then extends itself to magnets by means of which disease could be cured—and even to plants, which were conceived as emitting rays and emanations affecting man.

The early Egyptians regarded precious stones as charms, possessing special qualities and affecting the destinies of men and women—as people do at the present day—so that we speak of 'my lucky stone'. Certainly the possession of a precious stone in these days gives a girl an ecstatic thrill and no doubt increases the bodily metabolism: it cures many of despondency!

It was inevitable that if stars, planets, plants and stones could affect men's lives by their subtle emanations, the same potency should apply to animals and men.

Helmont maintained that subtle fluids emanated from men, so that they could cast their magnetic influence upon others and so heal them of their diseases. Maxwell went further and held that these rays which could influence men were also to be found in the excreta of men. He was also the first to speak of the 'vital spirit of the universe', a view very like that of Bergson's *élan vital*. He advanced the theory that diseases were due to the withdrawal of vital fluid from the organs, an anticipation of Janet's views (p. 47) that neurotic disorders were due to the lowering of psychological tension. Maxwell maintained therefore that health could be restored by applying the excreta of healthy animals and men to wounds, to replace the 'vital spirit'.

* It is tempting to suggest that the word 'bombastic' came from him, especially as this word was first used in 1565, soon after the man. It meant stuffed with raw cotton and so came to be used of inflated language and behaviour.

This belief in the healing force of excreta is perpetuated in some country places where they put excreta, as they do cobwebs, on wounds. The action of cobwebs may have the effect of stopping the bleeding by producing coagulations of the blood.

Astrology, of course, is still widely practised, forming a regular feature in our Press. 'What the stars foretell' has brought many people a most lucrative practice, and even scholars like Jung believe in the value of casting one's horoscope—the idea being that one's life is greatly influenced by the planets under which one was born. The various predictions regarding Hitler's death, however, lamentably failed in their accuracy, so that obviously their principles require revision.

Odic force. A modification of these theories was that of Reichenbach with his theory of the 'Od', or 'Odic force', which was defined as 'an imponderable force, analogous to electricity and to magnetism'. It was conceived as a material force (like the magnetic fluid of Mesmer), and was administered by contact and the laying on of hands to transmit the odic force from the healthy healer to the patient.

There are reputable people in these days who believe in the 'odic force' as a means of cure. Whilst as far as I know there is no proof of its existance as such, we cannot rule it out altogether. For we do know that some people produce a considerable amount of electricity in their bodies (some women spark when they remove their silk underclothes), and there is no reason why some of this should not be transmitted. Probably however, any curative effects of the contact comes about as the result of suggestion not of the odic force.

The idea of transmission of a mysterious force by contact is perpetuated in the laying on of hands in ordination, in which some gift is 'conferred' on the young priest, so that 'once a priest always a priest'. However evil a life he may later live, its effects, once produced, cannot be eradicated (as with vaccination).

Since healing forces could be transferred from a healthy person to a sick person, it could not be long before the theory arose that diseases also could be transferred from a sick person to a healthy person or animal. One 'cure' of nasal catarrh or common cold was to blow one's nose on a coin, wrap this in paper, throw it over your shoulder (the right ritual had to be observed, as with the medicine man), and the cold would be transferred to the person who picked it up, no doubt lured by the bait of the coin.

This practice is not without its scientific basis. The transmission of the common cold by sneezing or contact is common enough, even without the lure of the coin, and the person transmitting the cold would get better in a day or two anyway, without performing that ritual or going to that expense. But the theory was different; in animal magnetism the transmission was put down to emanations and rays from the nasal contents; we now know it is an infection from living organisms.

As is so often the case in scientific investigations, the facts are fairly established; it is only the theory to explain the facts that is at fault.

It is interesting to find in the Old Testament an instance in which not diseases but sins are transferred in this way. The sins of the people of Israel were once a year transferred to an unfortunate goat, who thereupon was driven into the wilderness, carrying their sins away, (Lev. 16, v. 9). A famous picture by Holman Hunt depicts such a 'scapegoat' weighed down by the burden of the iniquities of the whole people. This term 'scapegoat' is still used of those often innocent persons upon whom is placed the onus of some disaster.

These theories of astrology and animal magnetism cannot, strictly speaking, be regarded as 'psychotherapy', for according to these theories the cures were brought about by physical rays and emanations, not by mental means. But we include them for two reasons. In fact what cures took place were probably the result of suggestion, so that the animal magnetists were practising psychotherapy without knowing it. The second reason is that the theories though false led to Mesmer, and Mesmer's theories and practice led to hypnotism, and hypnotism was the means whereby analytic methods were first discovered.

CHAPTER V

MESMERISM

It was the work of these pioneers in animal magnetism which gave the impetus to Mesmer. In fact it was seeing a man produce cures by means of a magnet which aroused his interest. But he concentrated on the influence that persons could have upon other persons, by means of magnetic fluid, for curative purposes.

Mesmer, an Austrian physician, born in 1734, who subsequently settled in Paris, is often regarded as a charlatan; and his showmanship gave support to this view. He practised in a large darkened room in the centre of which was his famous *baquet*, a box or tub in which were water, powdered glass and iron filings, which was supposed to contain his magnetic fluid. He entered the room wearing a silken robe of pale lilac, holding a long thin rod. Plaintive music was played as he passed amongst the patients, whom he touched either with his hand or with his rod. Out of the *baquet* protruded rods which the patients applied to the painful spot. Many of the patients got convulsions whilst others had hysterical crises. This release of emotion was no doubt salutary and, as we now see it, cured the patients of their ills by a process we call 'abreaction'. Again, the facts were correct, the explanation wrong.

His theory, like that of the previous animal magnetists, was a physical one, namely that a fluid passed out from the physician to the patient—the so-called mesmeric fluid. That is why contact was necessary, by hand or by rod. But curiously enough, Mesmer did not make 'mesmeric passes' over the human body, nor indeed, was he acquainted with 'mesmeric sleep'!

'The magnetic fluid' said Welenze, 'is an emanation from ourselves guided by the will—he who magnetises for curative purposes is aiding with his own life, the failing life of the sufferer'. The same explanation was accepted in New Testament times as a form of healing, when Jesus said, 'who touched me?', knowing that virtue had gone out of Him' (Luke 8, v. 46).

Mesmer further held that man is himself like a magnet, the right side of his body being opposed to the left side. Disease was due to the disharmony between the two, which could be rectified by the application of magnetism.

Mesmer's theories were not so out of the way, for the principles of his 'magnetic fluid' were very similar to the laws of electricity then being discovered. Electricity, it was found, could be transferred from one object to another, (Greg, 1729); so Mesmer said the magnetic fluid could be transferred from one person to another. Electricity could be stored in Leyden jars (1748)—just as the magnetic fluid in Mesmer's *baquet*. Both could have an effect on persons. It was therefore quite a tenable theory, though it proved to be wrong.

The cures that he effected probably had nothing to do with either electricity or magnetic fluid, but were due to two facts, first the release of repressed emotions in the convulsions and 'hysteric crises', and secondly to the effect of suggestion. Nor need we condemn him for his darkened room, purple robes and plaintive music, for, as we now see it, all these were means calculated to put the patient in a state of suggestibility, an atmosphere conducive to healing.

In any case his reputation depended on his cures and these he certainly obtained.

There is this also to be said for Mesmer, that though we may regard his theories as false, he did, after all, attempt a scientific explanation, and if this has proved to be inadequate it shares this with many other theories of the present day, for hardly a year passes without some well-established scientific explanation being proved wrong and some medical theory discarded.

What probably occurred was that mesmerism got rid of the patient's pain by the use of suggestion and that having got rid of the pain Mesmer may be excused for thinking he had cured the disease itself. In any case to get rid of the pain of an incurable disease is most welcome to the patient, who can at least die in peace. We do it every day with morphia.

The trouble with Mesmer was that he claimed too much: but how was he to know? It is always a mistake to exaggerate. Many just causes are dammed because of exaggerated claims—for opponents will invariably seize upon the exaggeration, attack this effectively and so condemn the main truth. We may criticize Mesmer, but if it had not been for him and his cures, all modern theories of hypnotism and of psychogenic disorders including Freudian psycho-analysis would hardly have evolved.

Such popularity and success of an unorthodox healer was bound to bring its opponents—just as during and after the First World War there was violent opposition to all psychological forms of treatment, particularly from the neurologists of that time (not now), whose practice had consisted very largely of neurotic patients. One cannot help recalling the story of the silversmiths of Ephesus in olden times, who made graven images. When St Paul was making his converts to Christianity, there was an inevitable slump in graven images, and the silversmiths, 'seeing that their hope of gain was gone', shouted 'Great is Diana of the Ephesians!' (Acts 19, v. 28).

So there were two commissions on mesmerism, one held by the Faculty of Medicine in Paris in 1784, and another in 1831. The first offered no opinion as to cure (thus side-tracking the main issue); it said it did not find any evidence of magnetic fluid (probably correct), but enjoined that 'In future no doctor will be allowed to write favourably of animal magnetism nor practise the same on penalty of losing his professional privileges' (quite an illogical inference).

The later Commission in 1831 was more open-minded; it was more favourable as to cure, but said it was all imagination and therefore of no importance! Nevertheless the French Government, being of a practical turn of mind, offered Mesmer 20,000 francs to reveal his secret, but he refused the offer. (Flügel, *One Hundred Years of Psychology*, p. 67). In the same way the British Government in the First World War established neurological hospitals for the psychological treatment of patients, on the purely practical grounds that it was the psychologists who got the results with 'shell-shock'.

In France, therefore, the practice of animal magnetism and mesmerism tended to fall into the hands of laymen, whereas in Denmark, Prussia and Germany it was officially recognized. In Germany, Wolfart was sent to Mesmer to study under him, returned to practise magnetism in the hospital in Berlin and became Professor. Indeed theological students were instructed in its principles. It was, however, rejected in Mesmer's native Austria: he was no prophet in his own country.

But the adverse criticism of the two French commissions were a serious blow to Mesmer, and mesmerism began to fall into disrepute. It was further crushed by ridicule, for people resort to ridicule when they lack logical reasons for their objections. One patient, a Count, died at the moment his case was being published as a cure. 'Monsieur Conte de Gebelin', the cynic said, 'has just died, cured by animal magnetism.'

PART III
LATER SCIENTIFIC PERIOD

CHAPTER VI

SUBJECTIVE THEORIES OF HYPNOTISM

This phase, following Mesmer, was characterized,
(a) by the discovery of new phenomena under hypnosis, such as somnambulism, and
(b) by an important change in theory; from the physical theory of mesmeric fluid or magnetism to a psychological explanation, namely of hypnotism.

(a) *New phenomena observed. Somnambulism.* Although mesmerism, and hypnotism for that matter, is associated in the popular mind with being 'put to sleep', it is probable that Mesmer himself was quite unaware of 'mesmeric sleep'. The animal magnetists, it is true, sometimes observed that the patients went to sleep, and recorded the fact, but they took no more notice of the fact than if they had gone to sleep listening to the band in the park. After all if you are concentrated on imparting the mesmeric fluid to the patient, it matters little whether or not the patient goes to sleep. Nor in fact, is sleep in the ordinary sense necessary to the hypnotic state (see p. 37).

Mesmer's disciple, however, the Marquis Chastenet de Puységar, in 1784 stumbled across a most interesting fact. As a landowner, he was accustomed to mesmerize the patients on his estate. One youth, a shepherd, instead of having the usual 'hysterical crisis' went to sleep. Nothing at all could wake him. After a while another astounding thing happened: the shepherd spontaneously got up without waking and proceeded to walk and to converse in that state. Not only this, but, what was even more astonishing, he obeyed all that the Marquis told him to do. Then, after he woke up, he had completely forgotten all that had happened in the trance. Puységar further noted that when the patient was mesmerized, he was in a peculiar relationship with the mesmerizer, for whilst he was indifferent to everyone else, he replied and obeyed only the person mesmerizing him—and not others.

He discovered from this one case:

(i) *Artificial somnambulism:* induced sleep-walking;

(ii) *Suggestibility:* the automatic response and obedience of the patient to the mesmerist's commands;

(iii) *Amnesia:* forgetfulness, following the mesmeric state; and

(iv) *Rapport:* the exclusive attention and response of the patient to the physician.

All these are characteristic of hypnotism as we understand it at the present day.

Such shrewd observations as these were not the work of cranks; they were very closely observed, and by many doctors of high repute, who kept very full and careful notes of the behaviour of their patients under the influence of magnetism. Those who scoff at these early investigations do themselves an injustice.

That was nearly 200 years ago, yet some people speak of hypnotism as though it were something new! Nor was this the first instance of somnambulism observed. 'This spectacle', says Janet (*Psychological Healing*, p. 34), 'of a person with their eyes shut and in a state of trance, obviously recalled the priestesses of the temple of Apollo at Delphi who were entranced and made prophecies'. These priestesses, we are informed, were often simple farm girls, who were put, or put themselves, into this somnambulic state.

These newly discovered facts were taken as though confirming the mesmeric theory. In fact they did demonstrate an extraordinary state of mind but in theory they pointed in the opposite direction, for it is difficult to see how the passage of a physical magnetic fluid brought about such extraordinary results. These discoveries take us far beyond the influence of the magnetic fluid, and made a new theory necessary.

(b) *Change in theory*. The credit for the complete change from a physical to a psychological explanation belongs to the Abbé Faria, who in 1814–15 gave the final blow to the mesmeric theory. He advanced the view that 'No unknown force was necessary to explain the phenomena'. 'All was subjective'. The cause was in the person himself. He demonstrated his theory scientifically by experiments designed to exclude all physical influence; he proved that no contact was necessary as it was in the 'fluid' theory. He was the first to hypnotize a person by simply saying 'sleep!'. His method was to arrest the patient's attention and then suddenly to call out 'Dormez!' (Sleep). No fluid there!

Later on the Abbé, a thoroughly honest man, was accused of fraud and was set down as a swindler because of a trick played on him by his traducers. They induced an actor to pretend to submit himself to the process of hypnotism, and to feign sleep, and then accused Faria of fraud. To such meanness can men stoop to discredit the honest. Not one scientist came forward to defend the Abbé.

It is, however, the theory of the Abbé Faria that has been accepted by modern scientists, and his name should be honoured for what was at the time a most daring innovation.

Janet claims that the honour is due to Bertrand. Probably both Faria and Bertrand made the discovery independently.

Bertrand (1820), indeed, advanced the modern theory of hypnotism, saying that artificial somnambulism could be explained on psychological grounds alone, and he went further than Faria in explaining it. He did so simply by the laws of imagination, attention, will and desire. The patient, says Bertrand, goes to sleep because he *thinks* he is going to sleep, and wakes because he has the *idea* of waking (Janet, *Principles of Psychotherapy*, p. 20). 'Among these persons, an idea fills the mind so exclusively that they can pay no attention to any other thing than that represented by particular images'. How better could the hypnotic state be described, for such concentrated attention to the exclusion of all else is one of the essential features in the state of hypnosis. We shall see later that this was the view adopted by Pavlov (p. 62).

There is a great deal of truth in this theory, for expectation plays an important part in hypnotizing, and focusing the attention on some object before the eyes, with the suggestion that the patient will go to sleep, are methods used in modern hypnotism.

But Bertrand's views are a little sweeping. For under the old magnetists their subjects sometimes went to sleep although there was nothing to suggest that they went to sleep; nor was it expected by either the magnetizer or the subject. Certainly the suggestion of 'sleep' sends a patient to sleep; but that is not to say that everyone who is sent to sleep did so from the expectation of sleep. But the statement was in the main correct in that it explained hypnotism in mental and no longer in physical terms. Imagination and attention certainly play a very important part in hypnosis (see p. 61–62).

Experimental phenomena. But theory apart, Bertrand extended the phenomena observed in the hypnotic state. He was able to produce experimentally symptons such as hallucinations—seeing someone who was not there—and even negative hallucinations—making the subject not see objects which were there. He could also make the subject forget some fact which he knew perfectly well. Also he produced post-hypnotic actions to take effect after the subject was wakened. He thus applied the experimental method, which is an essential stage in scientific proof of any phenomena.

The notion of Bertrand concerning imagination and attention was developed by his pupil Norget (1854) (Janet, ibid. p. 157), who claimed that the phenomena were in accordance with the popular principle of idio-motor action—namely that 'every idea tends to work itself out in action'. If the patient under hypnosis was given the idea that he was paddling in the sea, he would act on this notion, taking off his shoes and stockings and turning up his trouser legs.

So in treatment: if you hypnotize a person with say, paralysed legs, and put the idea into his mind that he can walk—provided you exclude all other conflicting ideas, as you do in hypnosis—this idea will dominate his mind and make him walk. Attention according to some, is therefore the key-note of hypnotism.

Malebranche developed the idea of suggestion. He noted what he called 'the contagious communication of powerful imaginings, how ideas passed from one person to be accepted by another,' and described this as a common feature of everyday life. This was in the seventeenth century. This we now call suggestibility. It is essentially an attitude of passivity, of dependence, of receptivity.

He discovered also how symptoms were often the results of suggestion, mentioning the case of a servant maid who had to hold a candle whilst the foot of an old man was lanced for bleeding, and thereafter suffered from a piercing pain in her own foot for several days. He also discovered and described the importance of attentive concentration in producing what we now call the hypnotic state.

The facts of hypnosis are by these experiments well established— and very strange they are! As for the theory, we have passed clean away from the physical theory of magnetic fluid as an explanation of these facts, to a purely subjective psychological explanation of them, though the term 'hypnotism' was not yet invented.

CHAPTER VII

BRITISH CONTRIBUTIONS TO HYPNOTISM

James Braid (1795–1866). So far, Animal magnetism was confined to the Continent. Then Lafontane of France gave demonstrations of mesmerism in England, including Manchester, where a medical practitioner, by name James Braid, became interested, took it up, and finished by making several contributions of note.

At first he adopted a physiological theory, not, it is true, that of magnetic fluid, but, using the method of fixed gazing, he thought that the 'sleep' was induced by fatigue—the fatigue of the eyes. This is probably a contributing factor, but certainly not the essential one.

He experimented first with members of his family and very successfully; but when he found that they went into a hypnotic sleep simply by telling them they were going to sleep, he could hardly continue to maintain the view that this was due to fatigue, but was forced to accept the view of Faria and Bertrand, that all was subjective and psychological. This made a great change in the approach to the problem, for the emphasis was no longer on the external means (namely the magnetic fluid) but subjectively, on the state of mind induced in the patient. To this state of mind Braid gave the name 'Hypnotism,' that is to say 'sleep', for he considered sleep to be its main feature and the essential characteristic of the hypnotic state. We know that this is not the case: sleep in the ordinary sense is by no means a necessary accompaniment of hypnosis, for persons hypnotized, say by stage hypnotists, may be fully aware of their surroundings, of what they are told to do and of what they are doing, but they are quite incapable of resisting the orders of the hypnotist. We shall see however that the notion of sleep cannot altogether be discarded, for according to Pavlov (p. 62), sleep and attention were cognate phenomena.

The method of fixed gazing which Braid introduced is the most commonly used in medical practice at the present day and is perhaps the most effective, no longer as a means of tiring the eyes, but of arresting the attention.

Braid also first used the word 'suggestion' which, he said, 'is a method of producing an effect by calling the imagination into play.' Credit is commonly given, not to the discoverer but to the person who first gives the discovery a name. Malebranche described this state of suggestion very lucidly but failed to give it a name. Freud was an adept at giving names to mental processes, as in his use of the words 'identification' and 'sublimation', the facts of which, however, were known long before; but by giving names to processes

37

persons certainly gave clarity to the *ideas*, so that they are better understood and therefore more fully accepted.

On the question of how many people can be hypnotized, Braid could hypnotize ten out of fourteen. On one occasion in London he hypnotized sixteen out of eighteen. This is a very good average, especially as it would mean, according to his theory, that he puts them into a state of 'sleep', for amnesia, which is what sleep implies, requires a fairly deep stage of hypnosis.

We may then consider that James Braid with his *method* of fixed gazing, which is a definite and successful technique, and with his establishment of Hypnosis as a *theory* supplanting that of animal magnetism, put the whole subject on a firm and scientific foundation.

Hypnosis in surgery. To James Esdaile (1808–59), a British Government surgeon in Calcutta, must be given the credit, more than anyone else, of performing numerous painless operations, and major ones at that, such as amputation of the leg, with no other anaesthetic but hypnosis. There was indeed a Government Hospital in Calcutta devoted to the performing of these operations. (It is, however, claimed that he was not the first to do so; priority has been claimed in the case of Adam; for it has been suggested that it must have been in a hypnotic sleep that God put Adam 'in a deep sleep' when he removed a rib to make woman; otherwise it is said Adam would have strenuously resisted any such idea!)

Esdaile was hounded out of the medical profession for his great discovery and his services to humanity; as was Elliotson, on the staff of University College Hospital, London, who was forbidden to practise it by the Hospital authorities. In France (1829) Cloquel also used hypnotism for painless operations and related his experiences to the French Academy of Medicine only to be met with the displeasure and opposition of the celebrated surgeons, who put him down as an imposter! It all shows how prejudiced scientific man can be with a subject they do not understand and when their preconceived ideas are threatened!

The argument which one eminent surgeon brought forward against the abolition of pain by hypnotism for operations, was that is was not God's will that the patient should be relieved of pain. When, however, ether and chloroform were discovered and used for the same purpose, it was apparently no longer the will of God that patients should suffer pain!

It is in a way unfortunate that it was just when hypnotism was being established as an analgesic that ether and chloroform were discovered. They were much easier to administer and were more certain, for not all people would be sufficiently hypnotized for that purpose. On the other hand hypnosis not only abolished the pain but apparently most of the shock, and also any pain or nausea after the operation. It can also abolish any feeling of apprehension about the operation which the patient may have, and produce in him a calm and peaceful state of mind before and after, which no doubt aids recovery. It is undoubtedly the best form of anaesthetic —if only we could find an easy method of hypnotizing.

It is also curious and significant that the wound in such operations apparently heals more rapidly. I found this in an experiment I made, described in *The Lancet* for November, 1917. With the patient's permission I burnt him in two places on the arm with a hot thermometer case, as equally as possible. In one case I suggested there would be no pain afterwards, in the other case ordinary pain. The wound without pain had very little inflammation and healed much more rapidly than the one with pain, suggesting that pain, having done its work in calling attention to a disorder is detrimental to cure. Pain in ordinary illness is very wearing and gets one down. The abolition of pain in all illness would be of incalculable value. *If we could discover some certain way of hypnotizing, it would have the effect of the abolition of all pain.*

Another discovery of Braid was that under hypnosis one could revive long-forgotten memories, an anticipation of analytic methods, but he does not seem to have connected these with the *cause* of the neurosis (Blomberg, *The Mind of Man*, p.181–2). He used of this phenomena the phrase, 'The extraordinary re-vivification in memory of things long since forgotten', this phrase suggesting not only the recall of memory but the revival (re-vivification) of emotions connected with it. He did not, however, have the luck that Brewer had later in seeing his patients cured of their symptoms by that means. If they were cured, as possibly they were, he would put it down to his suggestions, not to the recovery of forgotten experiences with abreaction and the release of emotion.

CHAPTER VIII

THE SCHOOL OF PARIS
CHARCOT

The experimental method:

Charcot (1825–1893) was a renowned neurologist at the Medical School of Salpêtrière in Paris and made some original studies in the field of neurology. When he turned his attention to the problem of hypnotism, he brought to bear the same scientific precision to the subject as he had done to disseminated sclerosis and other purely physical disorders. It was a failure; for one cannot successfully apply the methods suitable to one branch of science like physiology to the phenomena of a different science like psychology.

Charcot did a great service in treating hysteria as a serious disease, and gave it a place in orthodox medicine. He also demonstrated that hysteria was a disease of men as well as women and therefore could not be due to the womb. The thousands of shell-shock cases in the First World War finally confirmed that.

The fact, however, that a distinguished neurologist should seriously study the phenomena of hypnotism was itself a score, for it brought the subject to the attention of the orthodox physician who was prepared to listen to one of such high repute. His reputation was still further enhanced amongst the orthodox when he proceeded to discredit it!

For his theory, as opposed to the 'normal' theory of the school of Nancy, was the 'abnormal' theory that hypnotism was a form of hystero-epilepsy. That was not difficult for him to establish since the only hypnotized persons he studied were hystero-epileptics from his clinic! His conclusions were entirely false; it has been proved beyond doubt that normal and intelligent people can be hypnotized, and often better, because they can co-operate more.

A further fallacy he perpetrated was that there were three distinct stages of what he called 'grande hypnotism'. For historical interest these states are described.

Catalepsy, which is produced by a sudden loud noise and other means. In this state the subjects eyes are open and his limbs are so flexible that you can move them any way you like—*flexibititas ceria.*

Lethargy, produced by fixed gazing (Braid's method), or by closing the eyes. In this state the subject is unconscious of what is taking place: he is 'asleep'.

Somnambulism or sleep-walking, produced by fixed gazing or by rubbing the top of the head, in which the patient moves about and can converse.

There is no truth whatever in these 'stages'. They are all, of course, phases commonly observed in hypnosis, but that they are produced in that way or in that order, is a pure fantasy. Janet, his co-worker, who hypnotized numerous people, never found these stages; on the other hand he could produce them and did, if he suggested them. I have hypnotized hundreds of people amounting to thousands of times, but have never once observed those 'classical stages' in that order in my patients.

Why then did they appear in Charcot's cases? The simple explanation was that the patients were schooled beforehand by Charcot's assistants (who did the hypnotizing) as to what was expected of them and they dutifully followed the pattern. In brief, these stages were themselves the result of suggestion. (Janet, *Psychological Healing*, p. 81.)

That does not mean that either Charcot or his assistants were charlatans any more than was Mesmer; it only means that they had no clear understanding of psychological principles and in particular of the importance of suggestion. If an assistant rubbed the top of a patient's head and told her she was becoming sleepy, she would become so. In later experiments rubbing the head alone would be enough to produce the hypnotic sleep—a pure conditioned reflex. But that does not mean that it is rubbing the top of the head itself which caused that result! You could get the same result by scratching the soles of her feet.

His application of neurological principles to psychological problems was ineffective for the simple reason that suggestion is not a neurological but a psychological phenomenon.

Janet says that 'Charcot had no notion of the proper way to study anyone's mental condition'.

One naturally assumes that when a distinguished neurologist advances theories of this kind, that he has made his deductions from numerous cases which he has hypnotized—and Charcot has the reputation of being a great hypnotist. What are the facts? We have it on the word of Janet who worked with him that Charcot never himself hypnotized anyone at all (Janet, *Psychological Healing*, p.187). And from how many cures did he draw his conclusions? Janet tells us from not more than a dozen cases in a decade! Compare that with the hundreds of cases carefully observed and reported by some early magnetists, so despised by Charcot, and of others like Liébault and Janet, who hypnotized hundreds if not thousands, and it is not surprising that Charcot's method and conclusions have been discredited and gone into decline.

It is not surprising, also, that Axel Munthe, who wrote *The Story of San Michele* and saw Charcot's demonstrations, makes great fun of him.

Why then, with all these mistakes, do we mention Charcot? Because there was one contribution he made regarding the origin of the psycho-neuroses which was of the greatest value. He was able, under hypnosis, to produce hysteric symptoms such as paralysis, *experimentally*. The symptoms thus produced were in all respects identical with the symptoms observed in hysterical paralysis. By experimentally producing these symptoms he established beyond doubt the psychogenetic nature of hysteric disorders.

This was a distinct stage further on in scientific procedure, for after the observation, collection and classification of the phenomena, the next phase in the process of scientific proof is to produce the phenomena experimentally under prescribed conditions. It is one thing to declare, as Faria did, that hysterical symptoms were subjectively produced; another thing to produce them experimentally as Charcot did.

Charcot would tell a hypnotized girl that she was paralysed, and she would find herself unable to move her arm. He pointed out that these manifestations of physical symptoms produced by hypnosis were in no way different from the hysterical symptoms presented by patients. This was of the greatest importance for treatment, for if we can *produce* a paralysis by mental means alone, by such means can they be cured. So Charcot concluded, 'Since the cause of these conditions is mental, it is by psychic means that we can cure them'. It is curious, incidentally, that the first person to establish experimentally the psychological origin of hysteric disorders was a neurologist!

It was also to Charcot's credit that whilst tracing the patient's symptoms back to shocks, he maintained, as Freud did later, that it was not the *physical* shock which caused the neurosis but 'the ideas, and the concern the patient maintained in this connection'. In other words it was the *psychic* shock, the shock to the mind, which produced the neurotic disorders (Janet, *Principles of Psychotherapy*).

We can therefore forgive Charcot his blind spots regarding the nature of hypnotism and the stages of hypnosis for the demonstration of these great discoveries.

CHAPTER IX

THERAPEUTIC SUGGESTION

SCHOOL OF NANCY

The School of Nancy: Liébault; Bernheim.
The School of Nancy was in opposition both in theory and in practice to the School of Salpêtrière under Charcot.

Liébault (1823–1904) may be said to be the father of therapeutic suggestion. Previously the mesmerists and hypnotists obtained cures, but Liébault made regular use of it in general practice.

He was a general practitioner in Nancy. Essentially a clinician, he set out to use hypnotism for humanitarian reasons, and for the relief of human suffering. At his clinic he worked in a large room where his patients, rich and poor alike, sat round the walls, while he went round hypnotizing them and giving them suggestions, each according to his needs. There was none of the showmanship of Mesmer.

Unlike his contemporary Charcot, he was very skilled at hypnotizing and out of one thousand people, in only twenty-seven cases did he fail to produce enough suggestibility for his therapeutic purpose. One-fifth of his patients he could get into a somnambulistic state. He wrote a book on his work, *Du Sommeil* (1866). He was laughed at, but that did not concern him for he had cures, and his theories and work have long outlived his critics.

He was greatly helped by Bernheim, the Professor of Medicine at the Medical School in Nancy. In his book *De la Suggestion* (1866) the professor made a very generous gesture to the general practitioner by saying that all his knowledge and interest in hypnotic suggestion was wholly derived from Liébault.

Bernheim had graduated at the Salpêtrière under Charcot, but he turned against Charcot's views that hypnotism was of a pathological nature. He experimented with the 'stages' of Charcot's *grande hypnotism* and found that none of these phenomena occurred under conditions which precluded suggestion and declared that Charcot's 'stages' were in fact due to suggestion. Liébault and Bernheim, indeed, devised a new theory of hypnosis which was in direct contrast not only with the mesmerists but with Charcot and his Parisian school, and a conflict raged between the two schools.

Their theory was a very simple one. Hypnosis, they said, was a form of suggestion, and suggestion was an ordinary constituent of everyday life. This is the *normal* theory of hypnosis as against Charcot's 'abnormal' theory that it was a form of hysteria and hystero-epilepsy. Quite normal people are open to hypnosis as they are to suggestion.

Hypnotic sleep was, according to the school of Nancy, nothing more than 'sleep, plus rapport'.

Rapport itself, like suggestability, is a normal condition of everyday life—for a person can be asleep to all else, but *en rapport* with one particular person, as in the case of the mother who is asleep and unaware of all the noises of the night, but is awake to the slightest move or cry from her infant. This theory of hypnosis as 'partial sleep' was previously held by Vogt, neurologist in Berlin, and later by Pavlov.

The School of Nancy maintained further that all the phenomena of hypnotism are due to suggestion. If we take that to mean that the phenomena are directly suggested, it is hardly true for in a hypnotic state there are physiological changes such as changes in circulation and cessation of bleeding (p. 71). But in general, the statement is true.

Bernheim was also interested in the question whether you could compel an ordinary person to commit a crime by hypnotic suggestion. He found that apparently you could, for a girl was given a pistol, told it was loaded, and instructed to fire at her mother, which she did. This was by no means conclusive, for it is now found that even under hypnosis a patient does possess some judgment and can see through the game.

Bramwell confirms this in a case in which a girl was given a lump of sugar, told it was arsenic and to put it into her absent mother's cup of tea. She did so and therefore gave the impression that she could be made to murder her mother. But questioned by Bramwell in a later hypnosis why she had done it, she said that she knew it could not be arsenic or else he would not have told her to do it!

Bernheim proceeded further with his investigation. He wanted to discover whether it was possible to cure organic diseases as well as hysterical symptoms. For that purpose he experimented and succeeded in producing blisters, as others have done.

Following on this Liébault made a very interesting observation regarding organic disease. He pointed out that many symptoms gave warning of their approach in dreams. For instance, a lady dreamt she was suffering from toothache. She had no pain during the day, and nothing wrong was found with her teeth on examination. But a few days later one of her teeth was found to be decayed. This suggestion of premonitory signs of organic disease was later taken up by Jung. After all it is quite understandable, (and we need not appeal to occultism for an explanation); it is simply that in sleep, when we cut out all extraneous stimuli, we are far more sensitive to sensations from within the body. We all have experienced that a pain which feels frightful at three o'clock at night turns out to be trifling when seen in the light of day, when it comes under the scrutiny of the conscious mind.

To summarize: the most notable contributions of the School of Nancy were in the sphere of therapeutic suggestion. They also provided us with a simple and common-sense approach to the whole subject of hypnosis, wresting it out of the realm of the magical and relating it to the ordinary suggestion of everyday life.

Moll (*Hypnotism*, p. 39) sums up the situation well: 'Faria formerly made use of a mental method to obtain hypnosis. Liébault subsequently developed and completed the process Bernheim made it universally known'.

Suggestion treatment can cure many cases, and many cure them radically by breaking a vicious circle. Its weakness is that it does not get down to root causes, so that the deep disorder of personality may emerge in a substitute form (p. 231). Hence the need for analysis.

CHAPTER X

THERAPEUTIC ANALYSIS

JANET

Pierre Janet (1859–1947) was Professor of Psychology in Paris. He was at first a colleague of Charcot and, as we have seen, was a critic of the latter's work and methods; for Charcot was a neurologist whose incursion into the field of psychology was not altogether successful, whereas Janet was a medical psychologist from the beginning, with a thorough grasp of the workings of the mind.

Janet's contribution both to psychotherapy and psychology was outstanding. His views as to the basic cause of neurotic disorders deserve far more attention than they have received. This neglect was perhaps because he did not found a 'school', but was concerned only with the truth.

In the first place he was a great clinician, having made a detailed investigation of hundreds of cases, which he tabulated, classified and recorded in many large volumes. Compare that with the very few cases on which both Charcot on the one hand and Freud on the other based their original theories.

He applied to these data all the requisites necessary to establish scientific proof—*observation* of data, *classification* of data, *experimentation* (with Charcot, producing symptoms experimentally under prescribed conditions) and finally *generalization* and drawing conclusions.

From these data he was able to reach conclusions as to (a) the nature and structure of the human personality, and (b) the nature, causes and cure of hysteric disorders, which mesmerism, the School of Nancy and Charcot had all failed to do.

(a) *Structure of the personality*. It is to the credit of Janet that he regards the whole personality as a unity; the mind and body are one; energy is not divided into mental energy and physical energy, but is of one source, one form, binding the whole personality together and enabling it to function as a whole.

The human personality, he said, is a synthesis, built up of all the sensations and experiences of our everyday life. These experiences are held together and unified by *psychological tension* and energy.

The source of this energy is to be found in the whole body; 'We think', he says, 'with our whole body, with our livers as well as with our brains'. (There is no doubt that the state of our livers affects our thinking.)

Janet says: 'From the scientific point of view the distinction (between organic and functional) has no meaning; it is inadmissible,

46

but the distinction does exist and has an important bearing for scientific theory'.

It may be observed in passing that Janet's concept of the personality combines the 'static' view of the personality (which regards the personality as 'built up'), with the 'dynamic' psychology (so popular with later psychologists like McDougall and Freud). For the very essence of this synthesis is that it is held together by psychological energy and tension, a dynamic concept.

The *quantity of energy* we possess depends on our general health and vitality. Some people constitutionally have far more energy and drive than others: they are successful people, capable of great achievement. Others are the 'weeds', poorly equipped, never capable of much.

But the quantity of our energy varies from time to time and from day to day in any individual. At any particular time we may have a larger quantity of energy available and our psychological tension is high, as after a good night's sleep. At other times it is at a low ebb, as after a tiring and worrying day: we are then lethargic, bored and may have little interest in life.

Neuroses are the result of the lowering of psychological tension.

Levels of mental energy. Janet, therefore, in his lectures, though not as far as I can discover in his writings, describes a hierarchy of human functions, the highest of which are operative when we are on a high level of psychic tension: and others, which are all we can manage when we are at a low ebb, fatigued from mental or physical exhaustion.

When we are at a low ebb of energy we are capable merely of the most primitive reactions. The more energy we have, the higher the functions we can perform.

The phases, then, are as follows, starting from the lowest.
Reflex action.
Perceptive functions.
Elementary social behaviour.
Elementary intellectual behaviour.
Affirmation and belief.
Deliberation.
Rational behaviour.
Experimental functions, and finally,
Organization and interpretation of results, which is the highest function of man.

If we may take a simple example; eating. When we are at a very low ebb of psychic tension, say with an illness, we have to be fed: all we are capable of doing is the reflex action of swallowing. At a higher level we are able to feed ourselves and even to complain about our food—a true sign of convalescence! Then we can converse with friends, but we soon get exhausted. When we have still more vitality we may entertain friends at a dinner party. We may go further, and if we are feeling particularly fit and top of our form, we may keep the conversation going with wit and humour. Finally, we may cope adequately with a situation at a dinner party when one of our guests gets drunk, starts to abuse another of the guests and makes amorous advances to the wife of another. To do that successfully requires a high degree of psychic tension!

The causes of the lowering of psychological tension, may be (a) constitutional or hereditary, or (b) due to environmental conditions.

(a) A person may be of poor material, inferior from the beginning, and never able to cope adequately with life. In other cases congenital factors play an important part; that is to say, although there is no hereditary trait, the child is born delicate, with defects either of mind or body—as in some dull and backward children. There are also certain times of life like the menopause, when, owing to changes in physiological adaptation, there is a lowering of psychic tension with consequent liability to fall into neurosis. (Treating menopausal women is a hard task).

(b) Environmental influences. Fatigue whether of mind or body, is an important factor in the lowering of tension, as we have all experienced. When we are tired we can't be bothered, slight things worry us, we become irritable and even our speech is inaccurate so that we use wrong words.

Other conditions producing a lowering of psychic tension are shocks of all kinds—physical shocks as in a street accident or mental shocks at receiving bad news. Shocks deplete our energy (and blood sugar) and render us helpless with depression of spirits.

Illnesses, particularly fevers of all kinds, lower our vitality so that we feel worried, anxious, become depressed and lose control over our emotions. Pain also has a devastating effect on our emotions sapping our energies. All these conditions are conducive to neurosis.

Emotional conditions, Janet says, are a wastage of energy and deplete our resources. For he has a curious conception of emotion; it is 'surplus behaviour'. It happens when you try to do more than you are capable of and fail; or when you overdo it and expend more energy than is demanded (cracking a nut with a sledge hammer).

In both cases there is a wastage of energy which results in fatigue. When we give up, and look for lesser achievements in life, we feel better and more energetic. So when a person finds things too much for him and gives way to tears, he feels better because there is no longer a wastage of energy in emotion.

In all this, it will be observed that Janet treats the whole organism, physiological and psychological, as one; physical and emotional shocks equally deplete our energy, and the source of energy being one, the exhaustion of this energy may bring about either physical or mental symptoms.

Effects of the lowering of psychic tension. Disorders of behaviour and neuroses arise from this cause.

Classification of the neurosis. Janet classifies the neuroses into various forms depending on the psychic energy available.

(a) *Psychasthenia:* When the psychic tension from whatever cause is low, the personality is feebly held together, and consequently the synthesis is poorly maintained. The result is 'psychasthenia', which is literally 'weakness of soul'.

(b) *Hysteria:* When on the other hand the energy is still further exhausted, the personality cannot hold itself together at all and splits apart. This is characteristic of hysteria, in which there is a splitting of the personality, (as distinct from mere weakness of the personality), such as we find in a paralyzed leg or in dual personality.

(a) *Psychasthenia.* We have seen that the synthesis of the personality is held together by psychological tension or energy. If that tension is low, the synthesis is poorly maintained, the will is feeble and the personality finds it difficult to cope, with the result that the individual suffers from anxieties, neurasthenia, poor digestion, weak respiration and circulation. We also may suffer from obsessions in which we have no proper control over our thoughts and actions; from aboulia or lack of will power; from indecision, doubts, reveries and day dreaming; from de-personalization and feelings of unreality.

Obsessions are one form of psychasthenia. They may be intellectual, the patient being obsessed with the *idea* say of suicide or killing without any impulse to do so nor with any intention of doing such a thing; he may be obsessed with the idea of failure although he is successful; or he may be obsessed by the thought of 'millions and billions'. A tune ringing in the head is a mild form of obsession.

We may also have obsessional compulsions to *act* in certain ways such as the impulse to stab or to hurt; or the obsessions may take a *moral* form of religious scruples, over-concientiousness; or of propitiations like hand washing and other rituals.

Anxiety states. The symptoms may take an *emotional* form like depression or fear. Janet originated the distinction between anxiety states and phobias. 'So far as they are attached to specific ideas they are *phobias;* so far as they are without relation to a determined thought or object they constitute *les angoisses*, anxiety states'.

Amongst the *phobias* he described are, (i) bodily fears such as fear of cancer, or of sexual impotence; (ii) fears of objects, such as knives; (iii) fears of situations, like agora-phobia and claustro-phobia, and (iv) fear of being obsessed by morbid fear.

Janet says that 'hypothetically we may say that such fixed ideas are dangerous because they are no longer under the control of the personality; because they belong to a group of phenomena which have passed beyond the domination of the conscious will.'

The main features characterizing all these psychasthenic states is the feeling of incompleteness, *le sentiment d'imcomplétude*, which is due to the lowering of psychological tension. There is incompleteness of action, of will, of thought. Some suffer from intellectual incompleteness, in which they cannot concentrate, cannot grasp things. In other cases, there is incompleteness of feeling; they complain they have lost all affection and all appreciation of things, or that they have lost their religious faith: or they suffer from headaches and tiredness. In all of these the patient as we say, is 'not himself'. The personality is not working fully owing to the lack of psychic tension and energy. In all of them there is 'a suppression of part of the personality' and consequently feebleness in coping with the problems of life. Such people are incomplete and inadequate.

So Janet sums up: 'The psychasthenic is characterized by a feeling more or less general, more or less deep, more or less permanent, of psychological incompleteness.'

This is well illustrated in a university patient of mine. She said, 'I don't know who I am. I have the feeling of being someone else. I think what everybody else thinks is true. They said at University that I was conceited. I think I can do things I can't—intellectual things, and can't do things I can. I passed the Intermediate exam but have often thought I hadn't.' One sees in such a case a complete inability to grasp reality, to cope with the intellectual and practical demands of life. She suffered, according to Janet's classification from Psychasthenia, weakness and inadequacy of personality.

Hysteria. If the psychic energy is further depleted the personality cannot hold together at all, and splits apart. *Hysteria is characterized by a splitting of the personality.* In a hysterical paralysis of the arm the function of the arm is 'split off' from the rest of the personality and therefore no longer under the control of the will: we have no power to move it.

We may illustrate the difference between the normal, psychasthenia, and hysteria by diagrams:

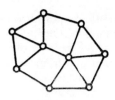 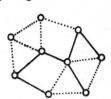 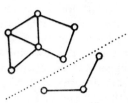

Healthy well co-ordinated personality good synthesis due to ample mental energy and tension

Psychasthenia: weakness of personality from lowering of psychological tension

Hysteria: splitting of the personality and dissociation

Dissociation. Janet originated the idea of mental dissociation. He says, 'Hysteria is a form of mental depression characterized by a retraction in the field of consciousness and by the tendency to the dissociation and emancipation of the system of ideas and functions, which by their synthesis constitute the personality.' In that statement he also states that the symptom is due to the release or emancipation of the dissociated complex, an anticipation of Freud's later views.

Amongst hysterical conditions which Janet describes are hysterical fits, paralyses, tics such as spasmodic blinking of the eyes, difficulties in swallowing, contractions, hysterical cramp, loss of breath, aphonia or loss of speech, mutism, (in which no sound is produced at all), stammering and stuttering. It has been said that stuttering is a movement we can't stop, and stammering a stoppage we can't move! (p. 330).

There are also dissociations of the senses as well as of feeling and action, like hysterical blindness, hysterical deafness, and anaesthesia of certain parts of the body, originally diagnosed as the 'witch's claws', which led many innocent women to be burned at the stake.

This dissociation or splitting of consciousness is well illustrated in a test invented by Janet which is still used in medical practice—the 'yes and no' test. A patient, shall we say, has sensations in his arm but is anaesthetic in his hand below the wrist. That in itself is an indication of a functional disorder because it does not correspond with the nerve distribution. To test it you tell him to close his eyes and to say 'Yes' whenever you touch him. You do so above the wrist and, of course, he says 'Yes. Yes'. Then you touch him on the hand he says 'No' each time you do so, indicating of course that he must have felt it, though he was not aware that he had, nor that he was giving himself away! That proves that the anaesthesia is not organic. There was a dissociation in consciousness, but not in the nervous system.

As to the specific symptom, Janet points out the importance of suggestion in the production of hysteric symptoms. One of the results of the lowering of psychic energy is that we become over-suggestible. Janet cites the girl who saw the father of a friend dead from anthrax and who thereupon got the idea that she had it, although she had never been exposed to it. Shock had obviously depleted her energy. A man seeing someone hanging by his heels from a railway carriage which was dragging him along, was seized with terror and instantly felt a sharp pain in his heels and limped for the rest of his life. Suggestion and identification obviously give rise to many such symptoms.

Psychopathology. Janet was, as far as I am aware, the first to study systematically and scientifically the specific causes of hysteria and neurotic disorders in his patients, which he found to lie in earlier experiences which had become dissociated. That is illustrated in the two cases just mentioned. Freud conceded this when he said 'It was ... Janet who first accepted a deeper approach to the ... processes present in Hysteria' (*Two Short Essays*, p. 44).

Take the case of Marie (Janet, *Psychological Healing*, p. 370), whom Janet treated in 1889. (Breuer and Freud's *Studies in Hysteria* were not published till 1893).

Marie suffered from convulsions and delirium at the time of menstruation, with shivering fits and anaesthesia of the left side and blindness of the left eye. This was traced back under hypnosis to her having had a cold bath at her first menstruation with consequent shivering (ibid., p. 595). Later the patient had a terrible fright through seeing an old woman fall downstairs, which covered the steps with blood. At nine she had to sleep with another child with loathsome scabs of impetigo, which gave her the blindness in the left eye. Marie could not bear to look so she 'turned a blind eye' to the horrible sight and developed the psychic blindness. Her left side, in which she had anaesthesia, was the side turned towards the loathsome girl. This is a very thoroughly investigated case.

Note the use of hypnosis not for suggestion but to discover the cause of the neurosis.

Take the case of another girl of twenty-one who had an obsessional horror about a tap. She kept crying 'What comes out of that tap is not water but blood,' and refused to drink from it. Janet, putting her under hypnosis, discovered that this related to the death of her mother whom she had nursed, and the horrifying drip, drip of blood from the mother's mouth as she died.

Indeed it was obvious in this and other cases that the symptoms were a revival and reproduction of part of a definite experience, now dissociated and forgotten.

Another case of Janet's, published in 1893, was of a girl of eighteen who had hysterical attacks in which she cried 'Thieves!' and 'Help, Lucien!' Under hypnosis she restored a memory of her house being burnt down, when the gardener Lucien had saved her from the flames. This event was later confirmed, and with the recovery of the event the hysterical attacks ceased.

A girl of twenty-two had serious contraction of the legs and inability to walk. At eighteen she had incestuous relations with her father with dread of the consequences. 'By modifying the patient's ideas, I was able', says Janet, 'to relieve her of all the symptoms, and then to confirm my theory as to its origin.' (*Psychological Healing*, p. 192–3).

Such cases as these might have been taken out of Breuer and Freud's *Studies in Hysteria*, except that they were described and published by Janet before those authors. It is to be observed, however, that Janet's cases all dealt with precipitating causes, as did Freud's earlier cases, not with infantile life where according to Freud's *later* work lay the predisposing causes.

Unless we analyse out all the predisposing causes the patient may be temporarily cured but is liable to relapse. There was the case of Irene, aged twenty, who had nursed her sick mother who died, leaving Irene completely exhausted. She then had crises of hysteria, hallucinations in which she kept re-living the scenes of her mother's last moments. In her waking state she had no memory of her mother's death nor for events three months before or two months after her mother's death. When ordinary treatment in hospital failed, Janet hypnotized her. This produced severe headache and vomiting—but at first no memory; but the memory was later recovered. In hypnosis she then became perfectly normal and said 'My true personality has returned.' From the moment Irene found herself able to remember her mother voluntarily, she ceased to see images of her mother in delirium; the crises and hallucinations vanished together with the terror. Nevertheless, she was not radically cured, for some years later (at twenty-eight) she had a relapse, but with different symptoms. As we now understand it, Janet had dealt with the precipitating causes, but not with the predisposing causes which probably belonged to earlier childhood.

Freud would probably interpret it that she wished her mother dead, yet could not bear to entertain the thought, and so repressed and forgot the whole experience.

Though Janet traced his cases down to actual experiences, he did not maintain the traumatic (shock) theory in all cases. He mentions fifty cases in which such a traumatic cause was discovered as one of the essential factors in the disease (ibid p. 992). But he maintained that there were many other neuroses in which there were no such traumatic experiences. 'Great care must be taken', he said, 'to avoid discovering traumatic memories when they do not really exist.'

Dual personality and fugue states are also due to dissociation of personality, but the extent of the dissociation is far greater. In hysteria the dissociation is limited, say, to one limb which is paralysed, or to deafness or blindness. In somnambulism there is a deeper and wider split, but still it is restricted to the performance of one act or episode which afterwards is completely forgotten, but which at the time absorbs the whole personality.

In dual personality and fugue states there is a much deeper cleavage in the personality, an imprenetrable crevasse separating the two almost complete personalities, each of which may act independently.

There is, however, a difference between the two: in dual personality there is a complete change in the *character* of the individual, for instance from a Dr Jekyll to a Mr Hyde, and then back. In fugue state there is a change in *environment*, in which the patient resorts to 'flight' (as the name implies) from an intolerable situation in life and forgets all about it.

Dual personality. A case of dual personality described by Janet in 1858 was that of Félida, who in her ordinary state (we cannot call it 'normal') was full of worries and pains, whereas in her other state she was happy and bustling. It is an essential in 'dual personality' that one state should be forgotten and unrecognized by the other. In Félida's case, in her miserable state she remembered nothing of her well state. She became pregnant during her euphoric state; but, when in the other state, wondered at the swelling in her abdomen. Morton Prince's case of Sally Beachamp is a classic instance (p. 101).

The only case of dual personality I have met was one well reported at the time in the Press, of a woman of ordinary education, the daughter of a jobbing gardener, who from time to time would go into a dissociated state in which she claimed to be 'controlled' by various persons in the past. In one of the unconscious impersonations, that of a 'Father Power', she conducted religious services at the Fortune Theatre in London, which I attended on several occasions, when she delivered sermons, in one case on Mithraic religions, which were quite beyond her ordinary comprehension and in which her whole character was changed. On other occasions she would be 'Father O'Flynn', in which she would talk away with a true Irish brogue (though she had never been to Ireland). On other occasions she was 'Little Sunshine', a happy little prattling child. She was accused of 'fraud' by the *Daily Mail*, and a court case ensued, under Justice McCardy. I gave evidence for her. The jury found for both sides, for they exonerated her on charges of fraud, but said the *Daily Mail* was justified on the grounds of its being a subject of public interest! My own theory of her performances is that she had in her childhood heard these sermons, which were indelibly registered in her brain, and that in her dissociated state she reproduced them just as they were given and received by her. However, the great physicist and spiritualist Sir Oliver Lodge, who also investigated her case, told me that when in a trance she discussed with him the atomic theory, which being a discussion could not have been a mere reproduction. It was a subject about which she knew nothing in her ordinary consciousness.

She would relapse into these personalities quite spontaneously.

In *fugue states*—described in the newspapers as 'loss of memory' —the person remains much the same, but changes his environment, with loss of memory of his past. I have had many cases of fugue, mentioned in *Psychology and Mental Health*. As to the cause of fugue states, I have found that the precipitating cause of the condition occurred when the person found himself in conditions which he loathed, yet had to endure. The revolt piles up until the subconscious mind solves the problem for him by saying, 'I'm off!'—and off he goes, obliterating his whole past life and its troubles: he may even forget who he is.

A strange feature of fugue states is that when people are in that state they behave like ordinary individuals. As Charcot says 'The police don't stop them!' They go into restaurants to eat, they book in hotels and nobody notices anything odd about them. That shows the extent of the dissociation; they act as a whole personality. It is not the personality that has changed, as in dual personality, but a change in environment which has obliterated from the mind his recent circumstances and fled from them.

So a clergyman patient of mine, who never wanted to go into the Church but was urged to do so by his mother, following his father's profession, found it irksome. After a service he suddenly 'lost his memory' and found himself in Cork, a city he had never before visited. A Major in the war, was put in charge of establishments, got into financial difficulties, disappeared, and a few days later was found in a public house, his clothes covered with mud, as he had been sleeping in ditches. He was court-martialled, but the court fortunately accepted my evidence that he was suffering from a genuine fugue state.

One of my most striking cases was of a tea planter in the East who was worried because of his inadequacy in controlling the workers. One day, while going round the plantation, he suddenly passed over a stile into the jungle and completely forgot all about the plantation. He was found twenty-one days later in an exhausted state by a stream. He recovered his memory of the whole experience under hypnosis. It transpired that he had lived for three weeks on three wild oranges but plenty of water from the stream. In his fugue he was in fact returning to childhood, when he so hated company, because of an inferiority complex, that when visitors came he always escaped into a wood at the bottom of the garden. The fugue reproduced this escape from intolerable social conditions.

A fugue state, being 'a flight' from intolerable conditions of life, is therefore of the same nature and serves the same purpose as does a hysteric pain or a paralysis, namely as a means of escape from the problems of life.

Treatment. Janet's method of treatment was (a) to discover under hypnosis what were the experiences which, being forgotten and dissociated, were the cause of the hysteric symptoms; (b) to bring these experiences back into consciousness and so to resolve the dissociation; (c) by the use of suggestion to improve the morale of the patient which had been lacking owing to the lowering of psychological energy and so to build up the personality once more.

His method, therefore, was analytic in so far as he went back to dissociated and unconscious causes, but he supplemented his analytic treatment by suggestion.

PART IV
HYPNOTISM

CHAPTER XI

WHAT IS HYPNOSIS ?*

The early scientific period has been largely preoccupied with hypnosis, first as a means of suggestion treatment and later, under Janet, as a means of investigation.

At this point, therefore, where the schools of hypnosis give place to the modern analytic schools, an assessment of hypnosis, what it is and its value in treatment, may not be out of place. Even now there are many misconceptions about it, some regarding it as dangerous, some as spooky, some as of great therapeutic value.

It is true that the phenomenon of hypnotism raises some very interesting problems, such as the curious fact that though we cannot by any exertion of the will affect the automatic functions of the body, like the rate of heart beat or the flow of gastric juices, we can affect these directly under hypnosis. There are numerous authentic cases in which blisters have been produced, and warts, rashes and other skin diseases have been cured by suggestion under hypnosis. That takes a bit of explaining.

The essence of hypnosis. The essence of hypnosis is the abolition of reason and of the critical judgment. In neurological terms it means putting in abeyance the higher, more recently developed layers of the cortex, which are concerned with reason and inhibition.

The results are (a) that, all criticism being abolished, the subject accepts without question whatever is presented to him, suggestibility being greatly increased; (b) that the mind operates on a lower, more primitive level of mental functioning. It is these lower functions which account for the strange phenomena displayed by a person in the hypnotic state.

Tell a person in his ordinary waking state of mind that he is paddling in the sea and he will of course criticize it and say 'Nonsense! I am sitting in your consulting room.' Say so to a hypnotized person and he will immediately take off his shoes, begin to roll up his trousers and gingerly approach the imagined water— all because his power of questioning has been removed and his critical judgment put in abeyance. He therefore accepts your statement without question: he is paddling in the sea.

This theory of hypnosis as being the result of the abolition of the critical judgment is confirmed by:

a. The methods of hypnotizing,

* The substance of this chapter is taken from my address as British President of the *International Society for Clinical and Experimental Hypnosis*, at the Royal Society of Medicine on February 6, 1961.

b. The conditions facilitating hypnosis,
c. Neurological evidence,
Chap. xii. The effects of removing higher cortical control.

A. *Methods of induction*

Most hypnotists would agree that the immediate aim in hypnotizing a person is to abolish the subject's criticism and so to put him into a state of passivity, the effect of this being that the patient becomes receptive, accepts whatever is said to him and obeys without question any command given him.

(i) *Relaxation method.* This is most obvious in the soothing relaxation method in which the patient is put into a comfortable condition, in a state of acquiescence, of drowsiness and even of sleep. In that state criticism is abolished. In the lighter stages he may hear what you say, he may even think what you tell him to do is silly; but he couldn't care less, accepts what you tell him without question and does what you command. His criticism, if present, is inoperative.

(ii) *The distraction method*, curiously enough, has the same effect. We get the patient to listen to the beat of a metronome, and he is given the suggestions while he does so. The rationale of this is that since his attention is distracted your suggestions evade his criticism and enter directly into the subconscious mind. Janet (*Psychotherapy*, p. 342) cured a case of flaccid paralysis of three months standing in one treatment, giving the suggestions to the patient, to the effect that she would make movements of her legs and then walk, whilst she was talking to someone else.

Automatic writing may be evoked in the same way—the conscious mind is attending to one thing while the subconscious attends to another. One soldier patient I had was telling me in hypnosis what he proposed to do in Oxford that afternoon while at the same time his hand was writing out an account of how he was blown up in the war. So, in hypnotizing with the metronome, the patient is attending consciously to the ticking, while subconsciously he is listening to the suggestions offered. The essence of that method is also the abolition of criticism.

(iii) *The authoritative method* is used by many hypnotists. Ferenczi calls this the 'father' method, whereas the calm soothing relaxation method is the 'mother' method. The natural reaction to authority is passivity and submission. 'Theirs not to reason why.' Many hypnotists therefore *command* the patient to close his eyes, to go to sleep, to tell him forcibly that he cannot open his eyes or move his arm or that he is an infant—and all these commands given authoritatively, are obeyed without question. It is this which makes it so easy to hypnotize soldiers and sailors. In the first World War I used to hypnotize twenty at a time each morning for therapeutic purposes, for soldiers and sailors are accustomed to laying aside their own opinions when under authority. Submission abolishes criticism.

(iv) *Shock*. Persons can be hypnotized by a sudden loud noise like the banging of a door. This puts them in a state of bewilderment, so that for the moment they 'cannot think'. Fear probably plays an important part in this, for subjects submitted to this kind of hypnotizing show signs of fear. Any emotion checks thought, and so renders the patient more passive and suggestible.

(v) *Fixed gazing*. This is the most commonly used method of all. The patient is instructed to keep his gaze fixed on a particular object, say a light, the end of your finger, a spot on the wall, and keep his attention concentrated upon it. This method is exactly the opposite of the relaxation method, for the whole attention is actively concentrated upon the object, and this requires a considerable effort of will. But it has the same effect of abolishing criticism; for as long as the patient's attention is concentrated upon that object, he cannot be criticizing what the hypnotist is saying, yet it enters into his mind. An illustration of subconscious appreciation while your conscious attention is elsewhere is when you are reading and the clock chimes. After the chimes are ended you can tell what the time was, for the counting of the strokes has taken place subconsciously even while your attention was concentrated on the reading.

The first explanation of this method of fixed gazing was that the sleep was due to fatigue of the eyes, a physiological explanation at first held by Braid (p. 37). But as we have seen, that explanation does not hold since you can hypnotize people simply by telling them to sleep.

We meet here the interesting fact that by a concentrated effort of attention a person goes to 'sleep'. How is this?

Attention and sleep. In spite of the fact that 'hypnosis' means 'sleep', a condition of sleep as we normally understand it is, as we have seen, by no means necessary to the hypnotic state. The stage hypnotist does not put his subjects to sleep; and a hypnotized person can be perfectly aware of his surroundings and of what he is told to do, yet he cannot resist carrying out the suggestions.

But we cannot so readily dismiss the idea of sleep; for there is a distinct connection between sleep and hypnosis. Pavlov, the great Russian physiologist, exponent of the conditioned reflex, maintained that attention *is* a form of sleep—they are both forms of inhibition. For when we are concentrating upon an object it means that we exclude, or are 'asleep' to, all other incoming impressions, being awake only to the object of our attention. Remove that and we are entirely asleep.

What happens when we hypnotize a subject by fixed gazing? He is told to fix his attention and concentrate upon a specific object, say a spot on the wall. In doing so he becomes asleep to all other extraneous impressions, and awake only to the spot on the wall, *and* the hypnotists voice. Then tell him to close his eyes, and the result is that he is now asleep to everything except the voice of the hypnotist. Since this is the only stimulus of which he is now aware, and there is nothing to counter it, he cannot do otherwise but accept without question, and implicitly obey, all that he is told to do. This constitutes the phenomena of rapport. Further, if the hypnotist departs the hypnotic sleep passes into a natural sleep.

Rapport. Rapport is a state in which the mind is asleep to all else, but awake only to a particular person or situation. In hypnotism it is to the voice of the hypnotist. Rapport is simply 'exclusive attention'. But exclusive attention to one person or object means being asleep to all others. Chastenet, as we have seen, discovered rapport (p. 33).

Rapport is found not only in hypnosis but in everyday life. It is a well known fact, that a mother may be fast asleep to all else, but *en rapport* with the slightest movement of her infant, whereas the husband, if he is a doctor, remains fast asleep at the howling of his infant, but is immediately awake at the sound of his telephone, whilst the mother, now returned to bed, sleeps soundly, indifferent to the telephone!

Rapport is a very primitive phenomenon, a function of the subconscious mind. We find it for instance in sub-human creatures like gulls. A gull may be apparently fast asleep on her nest, oblivious of the squawking of hundreds of gulls round about but when her mate returns from foraging, and even at a distance, makes what sounds to us exactly the same noise as the hundreds of others, she is immediately awake and welcomes him home! (Timbergen, *The Herring Gull's World*, p. 99).

In all these cases it is not the intensity of the stimulus which, for instance, wakes the mother, but the nature of the specific stimulus and the relationship of the person to the particular stimulus. She, like the gull, is awake to that stimulus alone. So the miller is said to sleep through the grinding of his mill, but wakes as soon as it stops with the lack of water. The subconscious mind, even in ordinary sleep, obviously has the power of discrimination.

It is possible to establish rapport with a deep sleeper; and we can produce even post-hypnotic suggestions in normal sleep, a method useful in children. In the dormitories at school we were often able to carry on a conversation with boys asleep and even extracted secrets from them, their inhibitions being removed; on waking they had no recollection whatever of these conversations, as in hypnotic amnesia.

So much for the methods of induction, all of which, from quite different angles, point to the fact that the central aim in hypnotizing and the essential feature in hypnosis is the abolition of criticism, so that whatever is presented is accepted without question and acted upon, since there is nothing to counter the suggestion.

B. *The conditions facilitating hypnosis*
These confirm us in this opinion:

(i) *Dependence* and passivity are the primary factors in hypnotism. There are some people who are by nature more dependent than others, and therefore more suggestible. This is temperamental, constitutional. It has nothing to do with intelligence: many very intellectual people are easily hypnotizable, whereas idiots and drunks cannot be hypnotized. Indeed, a man's intelligence may help in that he can co-operate more fully in concentrating and carrying out instructions, say in fixed gazing.

(ii) *Any strong emotion* tends to wipe out reason and therefore tends to suggestibility. If a man is in a panic and you shout out 'Run there!' he will run there. Even the angry person is amenable to suggestion, for if you speak quietly and calmly he will calm down. 'The soft answer', as everyone knows, 'turns away wrath'— but it is the softness of the answer and not the answer that does it.

Neurologists confirm this view. Babinski (*Hysteria or Pithiatism*, p. 41) says, 'Violent emotions obviously prepare the soil. They increase suggestibility at the expense of the critical sense.' He further says, 'I readily admit that a moral upset, *by weakening the critical sense*, may increase the patient's suggestibility.' Dupré, also a neurologist, says, 'Emotion, being an element in the distraction of the personality, favours suggestion.'

(iii) *The crowd.* Being a member of a crowd or mass of people also conduces to suggestibility. This is because in a crowd the individual merges his personality into that of the crowd; he is identified with the crowd and therefore withholds his own judgment.

For biological reasons of survival the herd must act as one, and so the individual in the crowd subjects his own opinions and is prepared to do whatever the crowd decides. The suggestibility of the crowd involves the suppression of personal criticism (Le Bon, *The Crowd;* and Trotter, *The Herd Instinct*). Bernheim admitted to Freud that 'his great therapeutic successes by means of suggestion were only achieved in his hospital patients (that is, in a crowd) and not with private patients.' (Jones, *Life of Freud*, p.238.) Or was it that the hospital poorer patients were more submissive?

(iv) *Personal relationship.* The hypnotic state is also facilitated by the personal relationship of hypnotist and subject. This may be a relationship of authority, or one of trust and confidence, or one of sex, or one of affection. It is essentially a revival of infantile dependence.

The Freudians have emphasized the sexual relationship as the essential one in hypnosis. This is one, but only one, of the factors and not the most important. The relationship in hypnosis between patient and hypnotist has been likened to the relation between child and parent. But that relationship is not primarily a sexual one; it is one of dependence—a biological necessity. An infant can do without sex; it cannot do without protection and security, and that means dependence on the parent. The duckling does not follow its mother around for sexual reasons but for security; its dependence on the mother is for protection, not to commit incest.

As the fundamental attitude of the child to the mother is one of dependence, so in hypnosis the attitude of the patient to the doctor whom he trusts is that of dependence, passivity and acquiescence.

Certain physiological agencies are also conducive to suggestibility and hypnosis.

(v) *Fatigue* is a contributory factor facilitating suggestibility, for fatigue, mental or physical, tires out first the higher cortical cells, whose inhibition is therefore removed, and so conduces to a non-critical state of mind.

(vi) *Drugs* such as cocaine and nitrous oxide are often used as an aid to hypnosis. The drug acts as a cortical depressant and produces the same phenomena as a hypnotically produced abolition of the cortical functions. It was in a cocaine addict that I was able to produce marked organic changes, including changes in temperature mentioned later (p. 72).

The use of cocaine would be a most valuable aid in inducing hypnosis for suggestion treatment or analytic investigation. The trouble with the use of such drugs is, of course, the danger of addiction.

All these conditions facilitating suggestibility and hypnosis have one feature in common. They all tend to abolish reason and criticism.

(c) *Neurological evidence*

It will help us to understand the phenomena of hypnosis if we turn for a moment to the anatomical and neurological aspects, to see what light this throws on our problem.

Our knowledge of the localized functions of the various parts of the brain is still very limited. But if we for the moment follow the orthodox text-book pattern, we have in the main three layers of cells in the cortex (see Brady, *Handbook of Physiology*, Vol. 3, p. 1546).

The highest, and latest developed, outer (supragranular or neo-cortical) layer is concerned with the highest functions of reason, intelligence and inhibition or control.

The lowest, (infra-granular, primitive, or paleo-cortical) layer of cells is concerned with instinctive activities and emotions on the one hand, and organic functions of the body on the other hand.

CORTEX OF BRAIN

Layers of cells	*Functions*
Surface granular	Reason: criticism: inhibition
Middle layer	?Intuition: association: conditioned reflexes etc.
Infra-granular	Instincts: emotions: bodily functions: digestion: circulation etc.

But there is a large number of mental functions of great importance in everyday life which come neither under the category of the primitive instinctive behaviour nor under that of reason and intelligence. We refer to functions such as intuition, imitation, suggestibility, aesthetic appreciation, sympathy, a sense of humour, recognition, a sense of time, and a number of others. Since these functions are of a higher order than the instincts like anger and sex, but lower than reason and intelligence, we may with some justification regard them as belonging to the *middle* layer of the cortex. This hypothesis, and I offer it as nothing more than a hypothesis, has some neurological backing. (Incidentally by 'higher' functions we mean the later, more recently developed, and therefore those making the individual better adapted to his environment. Thus intelligence is a later developed function than the instincts and it adapts the individual more effectively to his environment Therefore we call it a higher function.)

Consider then the results of removing cortical control. This produces effects both physiological and psychological.

Excision experiments tend to support this segregation of functions as Brady (ibid. p. 1538) has demonstrated:

Experiment (a). If you *excise the upper and middle layers of* the cortex in an animal, it exhibits a state of 'sham rage', biting and tearing. This seems to imply (i) that the inner layers of the cortex are concerned with primitive emotional states which are thus released; and (ii) that these emotions are normally kept in check by the middle or upper layers, which exercise a controlling influence over them, so that when these are removed the emotions become uncontrolled.

(b) if you remove the *outer* layers of the cortex, leaving intact the middle and inner layers, the opposite occurs: the animal becomes 'markedly placid'. This implies (i) that the middle layer, indepedently of the outer layer, has a controlling influence over the deeper emotional layers (for there is no sham rage now); and (ii) that the middle layer is associated with placidity and docility. This corresponds to what we call suggestibility, which is a state of passivity and acquiescence. Brady thus associates this state of docility with the middle layer of the cortex.

It is this middle layer of the cortex, with its passive suggestible state of mind, which comes into operation when the higher cortical cells are removed, either anatomically by excision or psychologically by producing passivity by hypnosis.

Since these subconscious, subcortical functions of the mind are so important for our daily living, it will be worth our while to have a look at them, for not only have some of them a direct bearing on the problem of hypnosis, but they have been woefully neglected by philosophers and psychologists alike.

Intuition (*p.* 272), is a case in point, it is not as 'high' a function as reason but not as primitive as the instincts. It is a primitive mode of drawing conclusions.

Dreams are also a function of a more primitive mind which functions even in sleep. Dreams have a very specific function, namely that of solving the unsolved problems of life when reason fails as we shall see later. They are of the same nature as intuition —indeed dreams may be said to be the language of intuition. They work out our problems subconsciously, as reason does consciously, and they do so not by reason and abstract ideas, but by the processes characteristic of the sub-conscious mind, namely by analogy, association and suggestion.

Analogy is a primitive method of drawing conclusions often resorted to in everyday life; and it is often more effective than reason. We say of a situation 'It is no use crying over spilt milk'

Or 'You don't hit a man when he is down.' 'There are plenty of other fish in the sea!' We use these modes of speech because they are more effective than reasoning, and they are more effective for the very reason that they appeal to a more primitive part of our mind—just as it is more effective to say, 'He has no guts!' than to say 'He has no intestines!'

Recognition is a subconscious process. We have not met a person for twenty years and yet when we meet him accidentally we recognize him! How? Certainly not by any reasoning process. By his eye? Yes! but how do we know by his eye!?

Time sense. We do not know what part of the brain registers the passing of time; but experiments prove that the subconscious mind, released from the inhibitions of the reason, has a time sense far beyond that which the fully conscious mind possessed. Many people have the power of waking up at a certain time in the morning, by concentrating on it before they go to sleep. It is quite beyond the power of reason, but not beyond the power of the sub-conscious mind, if left to itself.

Experimentally, I tell a man under hypnosis that he will carry out a certain action, taking a book from the table and putting it on the chair, in four thousand seconds after I wake him. He carries out this action within two seconds of the four thousand. No one in their senses could do this so accurately. Indeed, I read somewhere of a cock that crowed at six each morning irrespective of the time of year, and he had a son who had the same gift! They had no higher cortical sense to interfere with their perfect time-keeping!

Aesthetics also is a sub-conscious process. The meaning to us of a piece of music cannot be conveyed in words; nevertheless it has a meaning and we feel it as we do other aesthetic qualities. So-called 'pop' music and jazz carry us down to a very deep and low layer of the primitive mind and that is why it can put the young into a state of uncontrolled hysteria.

Humour. The sense of humour is also a sub-cortical process: it is certainly not a reasoning process; in fact, a lot of humour depends on its being so unreasonable and incongruous. Its biological function is to enable us to take not too seriously experiences in life which would otherwise overwhelm us. Wit, however, differs from humour in that it is more a matter of intelligence than of feeling or emotion.

Conditioned reflexes probably also belong to this middle layer of the cortex, as argued by G. R. Wilson in a paper on 'The Physiological Basis of Hypnotism' (*Proceedings of the Royal Society of Medicine*, February 4, 1927). He points out that one of the laws of

C*

reflex action, as defined by Sherrington ('*Integrative Action of the Nervous System*') is the Law of the common path.

Hypnosis and laws of the 'common path'. One of these laws is that if two presentations are given to the mind consecutively, it is the first given which secures the common path, to the exclusion of the second, and decides our actions. This operates in hypnosis.

In the First World War I made the following experiment with William McDougall at Oxford, which illustrates this. I had as a patient a regular sergeant whom I had often hypnotized. In waking suggestion I told him he could not walk across a handkerchief laid on the floor. He tried and failed. William McDougall then said, 'I am a major and Captain Hadfield is only a captain. I command you to cross that handkerchief.' The sergeant tried with all the exertion of his will, but he could not. He apologized with great embarrassment (for he was wide awake) for his failure to obey his senior officer, but there it was.

No regular sergeant would have behaved like this when in his full senses: he would certainly have obeyed the senior officer. But as his mind was operating only on a more primitive level my order got there first, and had siezed the 'common path' so that McDougall's later command could not oust it. The same idea is embodied in the saying that if you fling mud at a person some of it sticks, and it sticks even though there proves to be no truth whatever in the accusation. It is very difficult to get rid of a wrong impression once received.

This idea of the common path partly explains also why it is that once a hysteric gets the idea into his head that he has cancer, it is very difficult to get rid of it even by deep hypnotic suggestion. (There is however another reason, that this fear of cancer may come from a much deeper guilt complex deserving of punishment).

Another of the laws of the common path laid down by Sherrington is that if two presentations are made to the mind *at the same time* it is the stronger that wins. That is why many hypnotists give their suggestions very forcibly and repeat them frequently, and this is found to be effective.

My object in pointing out these various functions which are less highly developed than reason and intelligence, is that when the higher functions of reason and inhibition are in abeyance, it is these functions which become operative, and can for instance enable a drunken man to find his way home, a child to like or dislike persons, a somnambule whether naturally or in hypnosis to eat a meal, and for people to draw conclusions by analogy or association of ideas.

CHAPTER XII

EFFECTS PRODUCED UNDER HYPNOSIS

Having established, I hope, that the essence of hypnosis is the abolition of the critical judgment, as deduced from the methods of induction and the conditions facilitating, we have now to see how this thesis explains the phenomena found in hypnotism.

The results of putting in abeyance the higher cortical centres of criticism are in the main three:

(a) The first effect of removing the patient's criticism and cortical control is that he accepts without question all that is presented to him, his mind now being entirely passive, acquiescent and receptive: it reduces him to a state of suggestibility.

(b) It gives us direct access to the lower functions, even those of digestion.

(c) Thirdly, when the higher cortical function of the brain are removed, the more primitive forms of mental functioning come into play, functions which are normally kept in abeyance by the higher inhibiting layer of the cortex.

(a) *Suggestibility is psychic dependence*. As an infant in its help-lessness is physically dependent upon the mother for food, protection, comfort and for life itself, so it is *psychically* dependent on her. It takes over her actions—that is *imitation;* it takes over her feel-ings, so that if the mother is irritable the child is cross; if full of fun the child responds with laughter. That is *sympathy*. Finally it takes over her ideas, that is *suggestibility*. All these are manifestations of psychic dependence and all serve biological ends of self-preservation. For brevity we shall group them all three under the term 'suggestibility'.

But we must distinguish suggestion from suggestibility. Sugges-tion is the *process* by which propositions are introduced into the mind without question, whereas suggestibility is the *state of mind* which facilitates the acceptance of these ideas or propositions. It is suggestibility which we aim to secure in inducing hypnosis, for if a state of complete suggestibility can be attained the patient can be made to accept almost any suggestion we make without question. So if you tell a hypnotized patient he has a pain in the arm, since there is nothing to counter that idea, he has a pain in the arm; just as if we tell him he can't move his arm he finds it impossible to do so. Similarly we may induce therapeutic effects. If he has a pain we can abolish that pain; and if his arm is hysterically paralyzed because he thinks he can't move it, we tell him he can, and with any luck he will.

(b) Secondly, by the removal of the inhibiting processes of the higher cortical functions we can gain *direct access* to the subconscious and subcortical functions and so influence processes both psychological and physiological which we cannot affect by effort of will.

You cannot by willpower change the *rate of your heart beat;* nor can you increase or decrease your gastric secretions, for they are auto-nomic functions, that is to say they operate themselves without interference of one's will. But tell a person under hypnosis that his heart is beating faster and it will immediately do so; suggest to him that there will be an increase or decrease in his gastric juices, and the result will immediately follow.

(c) *Release of primitive subcortical activities.* A further result of withdrawing the higher functions of reason and critical judgment is that it automatically releases more primitive processes both of a physiological and psychological kind which are normally kept in abeyance, quite apart from any suggestion to that effect.

That is why when we remove by excision—or by alcohol—the higher functions of the cortex, the individual is activated by rage and other primitive emotions.

It is a neurological principle, first established by Hughlings Jackson, that if you abolish a higher nerve centre, it follows that the lower centres which have been kept in abeyance by the higher, come into play. They now take over, and dominate the thoughts and actions of the organism. Pavlov (*Conditioned Reflexes*, p. 289) confirms this, that the 'elimination of the cerebral hemispheres leads to the manifestation of the normal activity of the lower parts of the nervous apparatus'.

That then is what happens in hypnosis. Hypnotic phenomena (like catalepsy and suggestibility) are functions and activities of the lower brain when released from inhibitions of the highest cortical controls. These effects may be psychological or physiological.

A. *Psychological effects.* By the removal of cortical control we can affect psychological processes of the subconscious mind normally inaccessible to the will.

(i) *Memory revival.* Under hypnosis a patient may not only revive memories but re-live earlier experiences even to birth, by being told 'You are a child again!' That such memories may be true I shall demonstrate in a later chapter, XXXVIII.

This memory revival is used in discovering the causes of neuroses. This is not difficult to understand, for repression is an active process so that if it is removed under hypnosis or under drugs, and the inhibitions abolished, the repressed material emerges more readily. In any case the complexes which are repressed are emotionally

charged so that there is a natural tendency for this emotion to discharge itself into consciousness which it does the more readily if the
resistance can be removed. Indeed, as we have seen this occurs
nightly in our dreams. So in hypno-analysis we can revive memories
of childhood experiences.

(ii) *Emotions easily evoked.* Under hypnosis emotions can easily
be evoked. Simply by telling the subject that he is getting angry or
happy or afraid, he will express these feelings. If he is told he is
laughing he will laugh hilariously although there is nothing to
laugh at. Emotions belong to the lower centres of the brain, which
can obviously be reached directly under hypnotic suggestion even
in the absence of their natural stimulus. So in analysis we are able to
release long since repressed emotions.

(iii) *Post Hypnotic phenomena.* This is one of the most interesting
phenomena of hypnosis, but no more mysterious than most of its
manifestations. To take an instance; I was demonstrating hypnosis
to a group of doctors at Chatham Naval Hospital in the First World
War, and told the subject, an able seaman, in deep hypnosis, that
before he left the room he would turn on the light. (It was broad
daylight.) I wakened him and told him he could go. When he
reached the door he hesitated, looked at me and said, 'You don't
want me to turn the light on, do you?' I said 'No!' He hesitated
still, looked sheepish, then rapidly turned the light on and disappeared. Note in this case, that he felt what he was doing was
silly—he criticized his own action so far, but could not resist it; his
criticism was inoperative. Indeed, even when he was assured that I
did not want him to do it, the suggestion previously given possessed
the 'common path' and compelled him to do it.

McDougall (*Encyclopaedia Britannica*, 11th Edition, Vol. 14, p.
209) says that a post-hypnotic suggestion may be carried out
months after it is given. He also states that if the patient remembers
that he has been ordered to carry out a post-hypnotic action, he
may refuse to carry it out (ibid., p. 204). For in this case he links
up the order with his conscious reason and he now regards it as
stupid. My Chatham patient nearly remembered, for he asked me
whether I wanted him to turn on the light. As I said 'No!' the
suggested command was still left dissociated in his subconscious
mind. It is interesting to speculate what would have happened if I
had said 'Yes!' He might then have remembered being told, in
which case he might have refused to carry out so stupid an order!
Surely a topsy-turvy state of things.

Post-hypnotic suggestion is, of course, used in suggestion treatment: you not only tell a patient that he is full of confidence, but
that when he faces this difficulty or that examination or unpleasant interview, he will do so with complete reassurance. He may

afterwards remember nothing about it, but when the time comes he is surprised to find himself calm and full of confidence.

B. *Physiological phenomena* under hypnosis. Far stranger than the psychological effects are the physiological changes in bodily functions some of which can be produced under hypnotic suggestion, whereas others appear spontaneously.

The temperature of separate parts of the body can be raised or lowered by hypnosis and blisters can be formed. (Cases are mentioned in articles of mine in *The Lancet* November 1917, and July 16, 1920.) Blisters without pain heal more quickly.

It is possible to arrest and to produce *menstruation* by hypnosis. Indeed in my young days, before more effective gadgets were invented, young ladies would come to a hypnotist to have their periods postponed before a coming Ball. You cannot blush by trying to: but you can easily make a person under hypnosis blush by telling him he is blushing, although he has nothing to blush about.

Catalepsy. One of the most striking phenomena in hypnosis is that of rigidity, catalepsy. You hypnotize a patient, place him so that his neck is resting on one chair and his ankles on another, with no support between, and he can maintain that rigid posture for prolonged periods. No person in his senses could sustain such a posture, for discomfort, pain and fatigue would soon intervene and make him collapse. What is the explanation of this?

There is obviously in the mid-brain a centre for muscle tension. This capacity for rigidity is found in animals and is obviously of biological value, for when an animal is confronted with a sudden danger and cannot escape by the more sophisticated method of instinctive flight, its behaviour sinks to a lower neuronic level and its reaction is to stay stock still. This enables it to avoid detection— the phenomenon of 'shamming death'. The stick insect is a marked example, it prowls all night for prey, but in the day, when it is itself the prey of other animals, it remains still and evades detection. The same happens when a torch is shone upon it at night. Rabbits with the removal of their cerebral hemisphere exhibit such cataleptic phenomena (Pavlov, *Conditioned Reflexes*, p. 388). This implies that at that moment, the whole brain of the animal is inhibited except the centre of rigidity, with the result that the functions of this centre, released from all competing impulses from the rest of the mind, are intensely exaggerated.

Pavlov says, 'Catalepsy is thus a normal and habitual reflex which . . . manifests itself distinctly by virtue only of the inhibition of the action of the cerebral hemispheres.' Cut out these hemispheres, either by excision or by hypnosis, and the lower centres take over. 'In all these', he says, 'there is the elimination of the activity of the cerebral hemispheres without suppression of the lower parts of the brain.' This explains how it is that a hypnotized person can remain rigidly balanced on the two chairs for long periods. The whole of the brain is put to 'sleep' except the centre for muscle rigidity, which is called into action by our suggestions and is therefore alone operative.

Spontaneous changes. Catalepsy can thus be produced under hypnosis by direct suggestion; but it can appear under hypnosis spontaneously quite apart from specific suggestion to that effect—as it does in animals shamming death. There is however another spontaneous change under hypnosis which I have not found in books, but which I have often observed. In doing minor operations with no other anaesthetic than hypnotic suggestion (of which I did many in the First World War) I noticed that there was a marked diminution in bleeding as long as the patient was under hypnosis. I have taken out as many as thirteen teeth and there was not only no pain but practically no bleeding until the patient was awakened out of his hypnosis—and not then, of course, if he is kept under hypnosis long enough for the blood to coagulate.

We have then this remarkable fact: that under hypnosis, by the removal of the higher inhibiting functions of the mind and brain, we can gain direct access to the physiological functions of the autonomic nervous system, all of which are quite inaccessible to the ordinary will.

We are then confronted with some interesting conclusions:

(a) The first point to consider is that the voluntary nervous system has no direct effect on these organic functions. We cannot affect our circulation by effort of will. There appears to be some mechanism, or lack of mechanism, which prevents the voluntary nervous system from interfering with our visceral functions like gastric secretions.

It is well that it is so, for biologically speaking it would be undesirable that a girl should be able to upset at will the whole metabolism of the body by checking her menses. It is far better that these organic functions of the body should be allowed to work automatically and regularly: nothing must be allowed to interfere with them under ordinary circumstances. Nature provides for this guard.

(b) But there is an exception; for under extra-ordinary circumstances the higher brain can effect the organic functions *provided it goes by way of the emotions.* We cannot blush by willing to do so, but we can make ourselves blush if we think of some humiliation we have suffered, or past brick we have dropped. We can check the

gastric juices if we work ourselves up into a state of anger by thinking of some dirty trick someone has played on us; we can produce
peptic ulcers by constant worry. A girl cannot voluntarily stop her
periods, but the fear that she may be illegitimately pregnant may be
enough to do so. That means that whilst there is some guard preventing us from voluntarily affecting our organic functions, these
can be aroused in cases of emergency, for it is in such cases that the
emotions are aroused and required.

This is biologically necessary, for in any emergency, such as
meeting with a wild animal in the jungle, it is necessary that the
heart should immediately beat faster to replenish the muscles used
in the combat or in flight, and that the digestion should cease so that
all the blood possible should be at the service of meeting the danger.

(c) But there is another way in which these automatic functions
can be affected without even going by way of the emotions. The
strange thing is that when the conscious volition is put in abeyance,
as in hypnotic suggestion, we can produce exactly the same changes
in the organic functions as can be produced by the emotions, without arousing the emotions. You cannot blush at will, you can blush
if emotions of shame are aroused; but to a hypnotized person you
have only to say, 'You are blushing,' and he will blush without any
emotion and without having anything to blush about! You say to a
hypnotized girl, 'Your periods will stop!' and they do stop without
her either getting a legitimate or fearing an illegitimate baby. That
is to say that by hypnotic suggestions, when the highest centres of
the brain are put in abeyance, we can get direct access to the organic
functions of the body.

We may illustrate these processes by another example. Purdon
Martin ('Fits of laughter in organic cerebral diseases', *Brain*, Vol.
53, December 4, 1950) described cases in which the laughing centre
was stimulated by a tumour, so that the patient almost literally died
of laughing. Thus the laughing centres may be activated by
three stimuli; by something funny; by organic disease; or it can
also be evoked in hypnotic suggestion, the hypnotized person being
made to laugh uproariously when there is nothing to laugh at!

This has neurological support. Brady states that the middle
layer of cortical cells has anatomical connections with the deeper
and older structures, and with the thalamic and hypothalamic
nuclei, where are located the centres of various organic functions
such as muscle tension, body temperature and circulation.

Hypnotism of Animals. Animals can be hypnotized. A crayfish
can be hypnotized by gentle stroking; a hen can be hypnotized by
a straight chalk line or by putting its head under a wing and
swinging it round. A cobra, when in the striking position, if seized
at the back of the head suddenly turns rigid. No doubt Aaron knew

of this gimmick in his contest with the Egyptians, when he turned the serpent into a 'rod'. (Exodus, vii, 8–12.) A Freudian might interpret this serpent as a phallic symbol, but I hardly think this would have startled the Egyptians!

Pavlov (ibid., p. 294) says. 'The so-called hypnotism of animals is produced by some energic influence which suppresses every resistance; that is, it puts the animal in a state of passivity.' Again, 'With the wide spreading of the inhibition, all the above-mentioned reflexes gradually disappear, and the animal passes into a completely passive state, the state of sleep.' (ibid., p. 294–5). In both these quotations Pavlov supports the view that *hypnosis is essentially a state of passivity* not, as Freud says, of sex.

There are those who hold that animal hypnosis is not hypnosis at all. I can see no reason for this opinion—nor apparently did Pavlov. It depends, of course, on your theory of hypnosis. Those who assume that the basis of hypnosis is the Oedipus complex (incestuous desires towards the hypnotist) naturally find it difficult to explain how it is we can hypnotize a hen. So they solve the problem by saying that it is not hypnosis. But that should make us revise our theory, not discard the inconvenient fact! In such cases the exception proves (i.e. tests) the rule, to judge whether it is true or not. You cannot get rid of an unwelcome idea by denying it!

There are, of course, differences in animal and in human hypnosis. You cannot suggest things to an animal in words as you can do to a man, for that requires a higher development of cortical cells than the animal possesses.

But within these limitations the phenomenon is the same. In both animal and man, hypnosis can be produced by stroking—as in Mesmeric passes and in the crayfish. In both cases it can be produced by a sudden shock or strange stimulus—a noise or sudden movement. In both animals and man the cataleptic state may be produced spontaneously without any suggestion.

Dangers of Hypnosis. Hypnosis of course has its dangers, but they are greatly exaggerated. In expert hands I should say they are nil. I have never been convinced by these experiments which go to 'prove' that you can compel a person under hypnosis to commit a crime. Reference may here be made to Bramwell's experiment (p. 44) with the girl who 'poisoned' her mother with 'arsenic'.

Gilles de la Tonnette, before a distinguished audience of magistrates, professors and students, put a patient under hypnosis who thereupon displayed the most sanguinary instincts: she stabbed, she shot, she poisoned—the room was littered with corpses! The seance over, the professors departed, much impressed, leaving the girl still hypnotized with the students, who thereupon suggested to her that she undress and take a bath, telling her she was now quite alone. She, who had murdered all the magistrates without turning a hair, was seized with shame at the suggestion; and instead of acquiescing she now had a fit of hysterics. A person even under deep hypnosis can appreciate fact from play acting. She also retains her moral sense, which after all is a deep-seated subconscious process.

The generally accepted view therefore is that you cannot compel a person under hypnosis to do anything morally repugnant which you could not persuade him to do in ordinary waking life.

That does not mean that hypnosis, especially in inexperienced hands, is without its risks. In recent years, at a public performance, a lay hypnotist hypnotized a girl and got her to revert to childhood and behave like a little child. She afterwards suffered from depression and sued the hypnotist. What had happened? In returning her to childhood the hypnotist must have aroused depressing experiences of childhood, just as an analyst does; but not being an analyst the hypnotist was unable to deal with the situation thus produced. This case was largely instrumental in changing the law which now prohibits public hypnotic performances.

Can you hypnotize a man against his will? Normally one would not wish to do so. However I have hypnotized one man, a naval pensioner, against his will, by wearing him down, his refusal being for fear of getting well and losing his pension, and I suppose it might be possible to wear down a person's will to make him steal, but one can do that without hypnosis.

Therapeutic. Hypnosis may therefore be used (a) to abolish pain (b) to discover the deep-seated and unconscious motives of the neuroses (c) to release the emotions these repressed, (d) to re-adjust by suggestion the emerging material to the personality as a whole. For this process I invented the term "Hypno-analysis" (H. G. Miller *Functional Nerve Disorder*) in 1920.

CHAPTER XIII

AUTO-SUGGESTION: COUÉ

Auto-suggestion is giving oneself suggestion instead of having it given to you by another, which is hetero-suggestion. To receive suggestion the subject has to be in a state of quiescence, of relaxation, of passivity. How is this to be obtained if he is at the same time giving himself the suggestion?

One method is to prepare beforehand, by dwelling upon the positive suggestions one wants to give oneself, and then in a state of relaxation to concentrate upon these ideas.

This method is of the greatest value in one's ordinary daily life when, in anticipation of difficult situations, one gives oneself the suggestion for the coming event beforehand whilst in a state of relaxation—perhaps before you get up in the morning.

Say you have to give an after-dinner speech about which you are nervous. Relax yourself and then picture—not will—yourself before the people making the speech calmly, confidently, saying the things you want to say clearly and free from self-consciousness. It will surprise you to find that when the time arrives such an attitude of mind comes automatically and without any effort of will; you find yourself calm and collected. It is a post-hypnotic suggestion to yourself and is most effective. How different from the effect of being nervous beforehand and constantly giving yourself the morbid suggestion, 'I am sure I'll make an awful mess of it.'

It should be observed that this method of concentrating upon the situation you wish to bring about is very different from determining, say, to make a good impression at an interview, for that implies an effort of will and is strained, whereas suggestion is concentration in a state of relaxation. The only effort of will is in keeping the idea before the mind to the exclusion of all other ideas.

If you are faced with possible disappointment, say receiving an unfavourable verdict about a job, or from the doctor about your child's illness, you picture yourself in the situation taking it courageously and calmly. If you have an interview with a man likely to arouse your anger, picture yourself as very calm and collected during the interview however insulting he may be. If it is an unpleasant relative you have to entertain, you think of yourself doing so with consideration and interest in what she has to say. The principle underlying this practice of auto-suggestion is 'In time of peace, prepare for war!' We are calling to our aid the 'principle of the common path' (p. 67). By anticipating the situation before it arrives, the healthy thoughts have seized the 'common path' to the exclusion of other undesirable defeatist attitudes. If you wait till the moment arrives, then the undesirable emotions of anxiety, anger or disappointment have by this time seized the common path and dominate your behaviour. So, when you have an unpleasant task to perform, for instance spring cleaning your room, tidying your papers or getting that bit of digging done, if you think about it beforehand, while lying awake in bed in the morning, and picture yourself doing that task at a particular time, associating both time and job in your mind, you will find yourself getting up to do the job when the time comes without any effort, even without thinking. The process is subconscious and automatic. If on the other hand, you start off by saying, 'Oh! what an awful bore!' it will be!

This method may also be used to eradicate undesirable traits of character. If one is liable to be jealous, or depressed, apt to be bad tempered, or to be lazy—one can correct these minor faults by *anticipating* such situations that are liable to arouse such reactions during the day and imagine oneself with the *desirable* attitude of being friendly towards people, with confidence instead of timidity, even-tempered throughout however provocative the situation, and energetic instead of indolent. One can see from this the effectiveness of prayer on the psychological side, quite apart from any question of divine intervention.

On the other hand there are many people who, without realizing it, constantly subject themselves to morbid auto-suggestions. 'I'll *try*!' they say, but their thought is 'I have very little hope of succeeding!' This pessimistic expectation of failure is a morbid auto-suggestion which invites failure. How different the man who confidently says, 'I shall succeed this time!', and pictures himself succeeding.

This method of eradicating unfortunate habits is an alternative to the method already mentioned of exerting one's *will* to break a habit. Many people find the 'imaginative' method more effective.

Coué was the great exponent of auto-suggestion. The basic principle of Coué-ism was that 'when imagination and will conflict, it is imagination that wins.' As a simple experiment; if you clasp your hands together and concentrate on their being clasped, you may try to separate them but as long as you imagine them clasped you cannot unclasp them.

This works well in practice with many people, but in theory this antithesis between imagination and will is a fallacy. For what is it that enables you to keep your mind concentrated on your hands being clasped? It is of course your will that does so, and it may need a great effort of will to keep your mind concentrated on it. If your will is concentrated on your hands being clasped it cannot be exercising itself in unclasping them unless by feeble and sporadic efforts. Far from your will and imagination being opposing forces, your will is employed in concentrating your imagination on the hands being clasped. If on the other hand you concentrate less on your hands being clasped, perhaps from scepticism, the experiment fails, as it does with many people.

How then does it work in practice? Here again the explanation lies in the 'common path'. If you *start off* by thinking of your hands clasped, that idea has seized the common path to the exclusion of the effort to unclasp them: it got there first. On the other hand, if a person with whom Coué is trying the experiment starts off with the idea that 'this is all nonsense', then that idea occupies the common path, and it will be nonsense.

As in hetero-suggestion it is important that suggestions should be positive. Coué therefore never mentioned disease, only health. Betts Taplin of Liverpool, a clinical hypnotist of 50 years ago, told me he would never allow his patients to talk of their symptoms, but only to describe their improvements—'positive thinking'.

Another important feature of auto-suggestion is that of repetitiveness, even a parrot-like repetition of the formula 'Every day and in every way I am getting better and better!' It works! For the repetitiveness ousts any opposition or criticism, so that, as we have explained, (p. 59), the suggestion gets directly into the subconscious mind. William Brown of Oxford used the repetitive method even in hetero-suggestion repeating over and over again the suggestion he wished to convey to the patient.

Coué himself was essentially a clinician; and his therapeutic results were very often successful. He definitely disliked theorizing. It was Baudouin who was the theorist, and popularized this idea of the antithesis of will and imagination in his book *Suggestion and Autosuggestion*. But Coué, whom I knew well, told me that he himself did not think much of Baudouin and his theories on Coué-ism!

There is, however, a further criticism of Coué's methods. He was very insistent that the patient cured himself; it was *auto*-suggestion, the implication being that Coué himself had nothing to do with it. The patient, he said, by repeating the formula 'Every day and in every way I am getting better and better!' brought about his own cure. So it seems, and so it sometimes works. But Coué failed to distinguish suggestion and suggestibility. Suggestion, as we have seen is the process of transmission of an idea: suggestibility is the state of mind conducive to the acceptance of such ideas.

What Coué failed to realize was that although it was the patient who gave himself the suggestions, it was Coué who put the patient into a state of suggestibility, without which the suggestion which the patient gave himself would have little effect. Once the patient was reduced to a state of suggestibility, he could suggest to himself almost anything and it would be operative.

It was easy to see how this suggestibility was brought about by

Coué at his meetings. The conditions were precisely those we have described as conducive to suggestibility (p. 63). In the first place there were the crowded meetings, and crowds as we have seen induce the state of surrendering one's individual judgment in favour of a state of receptivity. There was Coué's reputation and his authority. Before he appeared on the platform, letters were read from previous patients who by his method had 'cured themselves' of various ills. Then he made a dramatic entry on to the platform amid great applause, this emotional atmosphere also abolishing criticism and encouraging suggestibility; and not least of all there was his kindliness and charm of manner—the personal relationship (p. 64) producing a rapport.

Coué's success therefore was largely his capacity to create a state of suggestibility in the patient, so that these auto-suggestions took effect. But when Coué returned to Paris many of his patients returned to their neurosis—of whom I had a number to treat! But many I have no doubt were permanently cured. Indeed I recently met by chance a man who was permanently cured of an obsession by reading Coué's methods.

CHAPTER XIV

CONDITIONED REFLEXES AND RE-CONDITIONING

This is a convenient point to consider treatment by conditioned reflexes, for the principles underlying such treatment are much the same as those employed in hypnotic suggestion, though the methods are quite different.

Nature provides us with certain innate reflexes or modes of response, which enable us to sustain life and guard against its dangers.

We automatically blink when a foreign object threatens the eye. When food is taken into the stomach it stimulates a reflex so that digestive juices flow to digest the food. These are innate, inborn and hereditary mechanisms.

But nature cannot supply us with reflexes to cope with every situation in life, so that she further provides us with the capacity to form new reflexes which also become automatic, to guard us against dangers for which nature has not provided innate reflexes. Most of our habits both of mind and action, such as manners of eating, driving a car and politeness on meeting people are conditioned reflexes.

These are so named because they are not innate, but 'conditioned' by new experiences.

Their formation was clearly described by Pavlov. In his well-known experiment he put meat on the tongue of a dog, and saliva flowed by a natural reflex. Then on another occasion he rang a bell, then put meat on the tongue, and of course saliva flowed. Then he found that the sound of the bell alone, without putting meat on the tongue, produced saliva. The innate response is now called forth by a new 'conditioned stimulus'. A conditioned reflex is an acquired reflex.

It is possible so to engineer these reflexes, that a dog could be made to wag its tail when beaten and bark angily when petted.

You go to the lake in the Park: the swans take no notice of you: you feed them: and thereafter they come flying towards you at the very sight of you, which has now become the conditioned stimulus of their flight. Thereafter they may do so without you feeding them; but if this happens several times the conditioned reflex dies out; they don't come. A conditioned reflex needs to be reinforced, by feeding in this case, or it fades away. That is why many morbid fears of the child such as the dark pass away.

Conditioning is used every day by mothers in the training of their children in useful social habits, although they do not call it that.

Punishment to deter the child from bad habits, rewards to encourage good ones, are forms of conditioning.

Purely physiological habits may be produced in this way. The infant is taught to pass motions each day at prescribed times, so that this becomes a habit. Even the stomach gets active as a meal time arrives.

Habit of mind can no less be developed by conditioning; such as habits of determination, of industry, of kindliness, courtesy and consideration for others, or of tolerating frustration and disappointment.

When these conditioned reflexes are once established in our minds, they form what we call 'dispositions:' so we have a disposition to be kind, to be cruel; to be generous or to be stingy; or we have a lazy or an industrious disposition.

These dispositions are the source of our habits and determine most of our behaviour; they are the springs of action. What we call 'complexes' are simply morbid dispositions (p. 135).

Disposition differs from temperament: *Temperament* is innate; disposition is acquired. Temperament is dependent on our physiological make up and is largely innate and constitutional. *Dispositions* are built up as the result of experiences. They are largely the result of conditioned reflexes; of repetitive actions. So we may have a melancholy temperament or we may have a depressed disposition, the latter being due to circumstances and upbringing.

Character on the other hand depends upon our aims and ideals in life. A person may have a kindly or grumbling disposition because he was brought up that way. He may however adopt, say, kindness or brutality as his standard and aim in life. This then constitutes his 'character'; good or bad.

Good habits are those which are conducive to adaptation to life; including social life. Bad habits are those which hinder rather than promote our adaptation. A good character depends on having right ends and standards of behaviour; a bad character is one who has poor standards in life.

Even so, 'good' or bad habits depend on our criterion: for by 'good' character we may mean good in the eyes of the community because it contributes to the welfare of the community like industry and honesty: being good is social conformity. On the other hand we may adopt a criterion of mental health. They are by no means the same. Ingratiation is approved by the community for it means conformity; but a person may be ingratiating out of a morbid fear, in which case it is the result of a conflict in his mind. For a youth may commit delinquencies which are disapproved by society; but it may be the only method he has to break away from the bondage to his domineering or doting mother, a bid for freedom.

Bad habits are as much the concern of the psychotherapist as are neuroses; but formed in this simple way, as conditioned reflexes they are often more effectively treated by suggestion than by analysis.

The formation of habits is of the greatest biological value for adaptation to life. We build up a system of habits by conditioning and the formation of dispositions.

They are in the first place a great saving of time, for instead of having to think out each time, what we should do, a great expenditure of both time and energy, we have already decided what to do in any given circumstances, and do it automatically and immediately, such as getting up at a certain time in the morning, paying one's bills promptly, behaving towards other people in a considerate way, or standing no nonsense when people start to make excuses. Habits are a short cut to efficiency.

Habits also have this advantage, that while we are doing them automatically we can be thinking and planning other things: we can thus do two things at once. For instance while we are shaving in the morning we can be thinking out our plans for the day; while we are walking to work, walking having now become a habit, so that we no longer need to think like the small child, of putting one foot before another, we can be considering how to deal with some unpleasant customer in an interview.

Habits of mind are built up in the same way as other conditioned reflexes. In the first instance, the habit has to be built up by conscious effort and then, by the repetition of the action or mode of thought, it becomes automatic. It takes quite a long time to teach a dog to 'beg', a conditioned reflex, and we do so by repeated actions. It takes a schoolboy quite an effort to be polite to others, but soon he is polite as a habit.

So it takes time in the first place to build up the habit of tackling problems as they arise instead of adopting the slogan 'Never do today what you can leave till to-morrow!' Soon it becomes easy and aids efficiency.

It is a hackneyed slogan which says 'Do it now!' but one necessary to efficiency. The trouble with putting things off is that our minds get cluttered up with worries till we do not know where to start. Clear the decks and you are ready for action—do that bit of carpentry right away, mend that garment or that fuse, go and face up to the unpleasant interview and immediately the mind experiences a great sense of freedom and is ready to go on to the next task.

Traditions are racial habits derived from racial experience; they are of great value and should not lightly be discarded although

it is the tendency of adolescents to do so in their urge for independence. But tradition must be abandoned if changed circumstances make it of no further value.

It is said that we should not be 'slaves of habit'. That simply
means that having formed a habit for one set of circumstances we
must not continue that habit when all reason for it has passed.
It is not a good motive for behaviour simply that we have always
done so before. That deadens initiative. Therefore, although we
must have a respect for tradition, we should try to discover why
such traditions are laid down and adopted; and revise them when
necessary.

Abnormal attachments. Conditioned reflexes are of the greatest
value but they also produce abnormalities. A child is not innately
afraid of the dark; but it is innately afraid of loud noises. If,
however, during the night it is suddenly wakened by a loud clap
of thunder or a drunken father, it may then become afraid of the
dark which is now attached to that fear. We may speak of this in
psychological terms as 'association of ideas', the dark being now
associated with fear; or we may speak of it in terms of 'conditioned
reflexes', that is to say, an acquired reflex of fear of the dark.
So if the infant associates sex feelings with a beating, this connection may persist so that it becomes a masochist, finding pleasure
in having pain inflicted upon it. If it associates feeding at the breast
with suffocation, then it has a conditioned horror of the breast,
and perhaps of women in general, so that it is left no option but
homosexuality (p. 322).

The great difference between the two theories is that the
'association of ideas' is a psychological term of consciousness,
whereas a 'conditioned reflex', strictly speaking, has nothing to do
with consciousness, but is described purely in terms of behaviour.
Nevertheless the term conditioned reflex has come to be used for
all such processes including the conscious.

This has the advantage that the laws of conditioned reflexes
have been studied much more precisely than those of association
of ideas and therefore can be more effectively applied in treatment.
On the other hand the fact that we are conscious of what we are
doing and can thus judge whether it is to our advantage or is
painful or dangerous, is of the greatest value in moderating and
even counteracting a conditioned reflex, but that makes use of the
higher function of intelligence. An older child with intelligence
might reason that there is nothing to be afraid of in the dark;
it was only the thunder which frightened it, and so avoid the morbid
reflex of fear of the dark. Indeed that is what usually happens so
that the child grows out of its fear. That is also what happens

when in analysis we discover the actual cause of the fear and re-condition it.

There are two main forms of bad or morbid habits both of which are automatic in their action.

(a) Behaviour disorders.
(b) Neurotic disorders.

(a) *Behaviour disorders.* Unfortunately many of the bad habits from which we suffer were produced for us by conditioning in childhood long before we had any say in the matter. Take the bad habit of procrastination or leaving unpleasant jobs in the hope that someone else will do them. This often arises from the fact that a mother did everything for the child instead of helping the child to clear up its own mess in order to develop a sense of responsibility.

On the other hand it may come from rebellion against a mother who is always chasing the child around till the child digs its heels in and refuses to do anything! It is indeed a strange fact in life that the same behaviour disorders may arise from two quite opposite forms of treatment.

Other people have a sense of defeatism which arises from another set of circumstances. If a child is always frustrated every time it shows any initiative and told not to, in the end it gives up before it starts because it knows it will never succeed. The world is half full of capable people who do nothing because they have no confidence in themselves: they have the ability but through the formation of a defeatist attitude they never give their ability a chance.

Bad habits of sulkiness, of jealousy, of suspicion, of distrust are all built up in the same way. If a child has felt badly let down by the mother who left him to go to hospital, he may be disillusioned about love and develop the attitude that you can't trust anybody. How socially hampering can this habit be in life!

We may get rid of bad habits in the same way as we can form good ones—in the first place by deliberately checking oneself each time the bad habit is treatening. It is important that we should make no exception, for as Wm. James says in his brilliant article on Habit in *Principles of Psychology*, it is like winding up a ball of string—let it once drop and you have to start all over again.

If we by exercise of the will persist in combating a bad habit of mind in this way, checking it every time, the bad habit after a time loses heart and dies a natural death!

(b) Neurotic habits have been formed in the same way and in many cases can be cured by re-conditioning. It may be used to treat morbid fears or sex perversions.

For many years it has been used as a cure for bed wetting. An apparatus is set up so that as soon as the sleeping infant begins to urinate, this sets off an alarm bell which wakens the child. After a time the very need to pass water wakes the child without the alarm. Many a case has been cured in that way. So with alcoholism.

Dr Dent of London was the pioneer in this field. He would ask the alcoholic what is his favourite drink—say champagne. The patient was then allowed to drink nothing except that drink. He was not even allowed to wash himself in case he drank some of the water. But each time he was given the drink he was also given an injection of apomorphine which made him sick. The association of drinking alcohol with vomiting was enough to put him off even champagne. But he was told to keep off alcohol altogether after-wards, or else the alcohol would drive him back to his old habits. I sent several cases of alcoholism to Dr Dent for such treatment with good results. Others have tried to carry out such treatment with less good results, for imitators do not always carry out the routine technique with precision and may miss important points.

There are certain conditions necessary to success in re-condition-ing. First, the new stimulus must come before the natural one—the bell in Pavlov's dogs must come before putting the meat on the tongue; the alcohol is given before the patient is sent sick by the apomorphine. The alcohol then becomes the 'conditioned stimulus' to sickness.

Secondly, it must be just before. If there is too great a gap, the connection is broken—just as it is little use for a boy to be thrashed by his father in the evening for a naughtiness he committed in the morning; he sees no connection. The association in time between the alcohol and the sickness, between the misdemeanour and the punishment, must be immediate.

Thirdly, Dent insisted that when cured, the patient must take no alcohol at all or there might be a relapse, for conditioned reflexes need to be re-inforced. It is, however, only fair to state that Dent's own explanation is not one of re-conditioning but that vomiting itself allays anxiety, which is at the root of the alcoholism. This explanation, however, is not favourably accepted.

This treatment has come to be called 'Aversion therapy'.

Many years ago (*British Medical Journal*, Feb. 28, 1942 'War Neuroses, a year in a neuropathic hospital'), I suggested that as neurotic disorders were of the nature of conditioned reflexes, it was surprising that no school of psychotherapy had sprung up to treat these disorders according to the laws of re-conditioning. Since then that omission has been rectified: work has been done along these lines by Professor Eysenck and his group at Maudsley

Hospital, who have, like some American workers, used this method.

Dr M. J. Raymond has mentioned a case of a fetichism for prams and handbags which was cured in that way. (Eysenck's *Behaviour Therapy*, p.303). Apomorphine was given, and just before the patient was nauseated he was confronted with prams and handbags. Thus these objects became associated with vomiting, and afterwards the sight of them would make him sick; so they lost their appeal. Previously he had sexual intercourse with his wife, but only by means of phantasies of the sexual pleasure aroused by these objects. After his treatment these objects gave him no pleasure, so that he could have intercourse without resorting to such phantasies. An excellent result. An analyst would go back to find out how he developed such a fetichism (see p. 321), which would be a more radical cure, but might take longer.

No doubt this method is successful in many cases and it is one which is worth while developing, because obviously it is far shorter than a prolonged analysis.

It will be observed how similar is this process to treatment by suggestion, in which under hypnosis a link-up or association of repugnance with an undesirable object and desire associated with the desirable object or situation is made.

Dent's treatment of alcoholism and Raymond's case of fetichism may be paralleled with a case of mine of cure of an addiction to laudanum by suggesting, under hypnosis, that every time he came to a chemist's shop he would have the urge to pass it. He had to come to me for further treatment because he found it impossible to buy a toothbrush.

There is the same objection to this kind of treatment as there is to treatment by hypnotic suggestion, which also is very effective in many cases. The objection is that (a) it deals with symptoms and not with causes, and (b) that it is superficial and is therefore inadequate for deep-seated neuroses.

Eysenck admits that conditioned reflexes cure symptoms only but justifies this, saying, 'Neurotic symptoms are simply learned habits: there is no neurosis underlying the symptom but merely the symptom itself. *Get rid of the symptom and you have eliminated the Neurosis.*' (*Behaviour Therapy*, p.9).

To put it otherwise, earlier conditioning has produced a kink in the person's behaviour, and it is that kink of behaviour which needs to be straightened out. How it was originally formed is of no significance. When the symptom is abolished that is the whole cure. Eysenck has therefore no use for unconscious motivation 'a learning theory does not postulate any such unconscious desires'.

Neuroses unfortunately are not *merely* bad habits. I wish it were so simple. Analysts find very often that the symptom disappears very early in treatment, but the patient is by no means cured of his neurosis, which shows itself in protean forms.

Let us take Lady Macbeth to the behaviourist. It is conceivable that her handwashing might be cured by compelling her to put her hands in water so hot that she develops an aversion to water and her handwashing may be cured! Is she cured? By no means, for her real illness was not her handwashing which was merely a symbol; but her sense of guilt as to the murders. Moreover, this guilt was unconscious for she refused to admit her guilt: one could not deal with this guilt by re-conditioning because neither she nor we knew of its existence. Her illness was far deeper than her behaviour of handwashing and would require far more radical treatment.

The objection then to treatment by re-conditioning the symptoms alone is the same as in most treatment by hypnotic suggestion, that we are not dealing with the real illness, but only with an outward manifestation of it, a mere symbol of the real disorder. We do not cure a case of measles by treating the spots.

To take a more recent case. A girl thief is sent to me. I might by re-conditioning or by hypnotic suggestion have stopped this. But why did she steal? For she did not want or require the things she stole. The stealing was an expression of something much deeper. She had had an illegitimate child which on pressure from her parents she immediately had adopted. In analysis it was revealed that the stealing was an expression of her lost motherhood. Consciously she told herself that she did not want the child: deep down it left this craving for something lost and missing—so she stole. What are we going to treat? We may cure the behaviour problem, the stealing, by re-conditioning or by suggestion, but it leaves the deep longing in her soul untouched. How could re-conditioning cure that, for even she did not know it was there till analysis revealed it, and if the stealing was 'cured' by re-conditioning this might come out in some other form such as depression.

Behaviourists claim that the conditioning therapy is concerned only with behaviour devoid of consciousness. Is it? Obviously this is not the case: for why should the alcoholic give up his alcohol and the fetichist his prams simply because it makes him vomit? Many drunkards vomit, but go on drinking. Obviously because vomiting is unpleasant and is associated with *feelings* of nausea and disgust. On the other hand the drunkard goes on drinking in spite of vomiting because it is an escape from life. If he is sick, so what! It would be just one of those things, and he goes on drinking! The motive is more important than the symptom.

Another interesting question arises. How is it, we naturally ask, that in some cases we can so easily cure some patients by suggestion or by re-conditioning and not others? How is it, indeed, that some cases of neurosis cure themselves?

In the first place, there are many cases which are simple habits which have no deep or unconscious motivation, but are produced by simple conditioning or association which can be cured by re-conditioning or by suggestion. The child who has a fear of the dark may be cured by giving it a night light, which is re-conditioning. It can be done more effectively by suggestions of reassurance: no analysis is necessary.

Even in some more deep-seated neurotic cases the original motive for the symptom may have long since disappeared; it no longer serves any purpose, but has become a pure habit. Such a person is ripe for cure and almost any form of cure, even a quack remedy, is sufficient excuse for the patient to give up his symptom. That may have been so in the case of the man with the fetich for handbags. A fetich is, we find in analysis, a breast-substitute going back to a fixation in childhood. With his experience of marriage this fixation has long since passed away.

In other cases only a very simple analysis is required. A patient was sexually impotent with his wife but not with others. It was discovered that the wallpaper in their bedroom was similar to that in a bedroom in which he was having an affair with a married woman when the husband, if I remember, unexpectedly burst in and gave him a beating. Removal of the wallpaper was said to have cured him. Maybe; and no doubt the patient would be grateful for this cure. But was this a cure by conditioning? It was surely a simple piece of analysis. He knew the two facts—the wallpaper and the previous humiliation: what he was not aware of, and what that very simple analysis revealed to him, was the connection or association between the two.

As likely as not, too, the benefit arose from his getting the whole thing 'off his chest' a well-known result of both confession and analysis. In any case it was not a serious case nor a complete perversion for it did not exclude sex relations, but only an aberration (p. 320).

Indeed there are some cases in which the patient gets well without any treatment at all. In my young days I had a friend who stammered. Years later I met him accidentally on the Canadian prairie and he had overcome his stammer. I asked him how? He replied that looking at it frankly he didn't think it was worth while. He knew that as a boy the stammer started when on the way back from

India, he watched a major and a colonel who both stammered. He thought it was fine. So he started to stammer. He had now lost his original motive to impersonate them!

Result of cure. It has been claimed that as many neurotic people are cured by the routine methods of the general practitioner as by psycho-analysis, and that prolonged treatment by psycho-analysis is unnecessary. I have no brief to defend the Freudian psycho-analysts, but the argument is false. It is a false comparison. The people who go to a psycho-analyst are the worst cases; they are the people whom the general practitioner has failed to cure, or knows he can't cure. You may as well argue that the G.P. cures as big a proportion, say two thirds, of his cases in general medicine as does the hospital and therefore hospitals are redundant— oblivious of the fact that the hospital, like the psycho-analysts, deal only with the worst cases which the G.P. cannot cope with. If the psycho-analyst, like the hospital, cures as large a proportion of these most difficult and otherwise incurable patients as does the G.P. with his milder cases, I would consider that they did very well.

To summarize: treatment by conditioned reflexing is of great value, as it always has been, whether under that name or as hypnotic suggestion; its technique is well worth further investigation and its methods of improvement. But it should be regarded as a subsidiary form of psychotherapy and not as a substitute for analysis: it has its limitations.

To take an analogy: if a person has a mild appendicitis, he may be cured by 'conservative' methods, such as fomentations and anti-biotics; but as long as the appendix is there he is always liable to a recurrence. Sometimes it goes beyond that, in which case the surgeon is called in to remove the appendix, a more severe form of treatment, but more radical, for it means that the patient will never suffer again from appendicitis. It is not surprising that some surgeons consider that it is best even in mild cases to get rid of this source of danger once and for all.

Those who treat the neurosis 'conservatively' by suggestion and conditioning may often be successful and sometimes permanently so, for instance when they break a vicious circle, or when the patient has no further use for the symptom. Other cases require 'surgical' treatment in the form of analysis: and it is not surprising that some psychotherapists, being confronted with the worst cases as they usually are, prefer to go straight to the analysis to remove the source of the trouble.

PART V
MINOR PROPHETS
AND UNORTHODOX SYNTHESIS

D

CHAPTER XV

MINOR PROPHETS

We must now consider several authors each of which emphasized a particular aspect of psychotherapy, thereby making their distinctive though minor contributions to the subject. They are not dealt with here in chronological order—most were indeed after Freud—but they are in logical order in that they represent preanalytic approaches and methods.

TREATMENT BY REST: WEIR MITCHELL (1875)

The patient was put to bed and everything done for him—he was washed, cared for, over-fed and even evacuated by nurses with douches and massage, in fact, treated in every respect like an infant. He was hardly spoken to by the nurses but received a daily visit and talk from Weir Mitchell, who alone had real contact with his patient: all others were as far as possible excluded. The treatment, it was said, was by Dr Diet and Dr Quiet. We class it as psychotherapy, for though the system was apparently mainly physical, it is generally agreed that the success of the Weir Mitchell treatment was Weir Mitchell himself—a kindly Quaker.

Weir Mitchell had many imitators and the 'rest cure' became very popular before the First World War. Many physicians took it up, including Déjerine in France and T. A. Ross, the first Superintendent of the Cassel Hospital in Kent. Both of these gave it up; for if any physician thinks he can permanently cure neuroses by these methods alone, he is missing out the most important ingredient of the treatment, namely, Weir Mitchell.

How then did Weir Mitchell cure by these means, apart from his personality? If we assume that these patients were suffering as most neurotic patients are, from insecurity from early childhood and are therefore craving for it through their symptoms, Weir Mitchell by first returning them back to childhood and then giving them the kindness, understanding and sympathy they lacked, was able to cure them. Once reassured they could go forward in life.

The risk of such treatment is that the patient having achieved the escape from life, and the loving care for which he craves, would be tempted to remain there and not grow up! In fact such treatment might encourage them to be chronic invalids. This indeed was pointed out by the great neurologist Gowers in 1888. How far this is true I do not know.

There is, however, a class of patient for whom rest cure is most valuable, and these are the patients suffering from actual fatigue of body or of the emotions—a condition rarely met with except in war time. There were soldiers, as at Dunkirk, who were suffering from long marches, bombardments, days and nights without sleep till they broke down under the strain. Some of them became temporarily psychotic with 'exhaustion psychosis'. In fact, they suffered complete depletion of energy, from both physical and emotional exhaustion. Complete rest under drugs or deep hypnosis and good food, restored them to health and vigour without further psychotherapy. It is questionable, however, if we can call these conditions neuroses. Being of physiological origin they are better regarded as mild psychoses.

Hypnosis was far better than drugs to secure this result, for whereas drugs have a detrimental effect on the nervous system there are no such bad effects from hypnosis. Moreover under hypnosis we could put the patient into a far deeper and more restful state of sleep, and for a much longer period. Furthermore the rest under hypnosis could be supplemented by suggestions of peace of mind which allayed the state of anxiety. I have kept such patients in a hypnotic sleep for days at a time, even their meals being eaten while they were hypnotized, and they would wake completely refreshed in mind and body. That is rest cure, but not the Weir Mitchell treatment which restored them to health by making infants of them.

The Weir Mitchell treatment is now very little used.

AN APPEAL TO REASON: DUBOIS

Dubois of Berne is the prototype of those of the present-day, many of them both medical and lay, who treat by persuasion, that is to say, by an appeal to reason. Such treatment is directed towards convincing the patient by reasoning that his symptoms are uncalled for: that his legs are not really paralysed, and that there is nothing organically wrong with his heart; that there is no reason to be afraid of the dark, nor of spiders for in this country they can do you no harm; that there is no need for depression or defeatism—lots of people are worse off! 'All you have to do is to pull yourself together!' If a man suffers from a sense of grievance, we persuade him that it does no good, that he only makes himself unhappy and best let bygones be bygones. If a wife is unnecessarily jealous we persuade her that her husband (as is often the case), has no eye for any other woman but only for her, and there are far worse husbands. She, however, may admit that her jealousy is unreasonable, but protests that she cannot help it.

This indeed is the 'common sense' method of treatment adopted in everyday life by friends of the patient, by moralists, and often by doctors in hospitals who have no time, or perhaps inclination or ability, to go deeper into the basic causes. That is why it is worthy of consideration.

Treatment by persuasion is in contrast with treatment by suggestion; it is an appeal to reason, to an effort of will, whereas suggestion is an appeal to the subconscious mind, to the feelings, effort of will being left in abeyance. It has some success, or people would not go on using it, but only in a limited number of mild cases.

'The object of treatment', says Dubois, 'ought to make the patient master of himself; the means to this end is the education of the will, or more exactly, of the reason.' As a case in point. 'A young man is neurasthenic, irritable, effeminate, weak and cannot walk. We must persuade him that he can control his irritability'. You show him sympathy as a sick man, become his friend and 'show him by well chosen examples from your experience how much there is in moral courage and the continual striving towards the perfection of a moral personality.'

Dubois is all for the will, and all against emotion. Fatigue he says is due to emotionalism. He tells his patient that fatigue is an illusion, that 'he must get rid of his fatigue by suppressing its primary cause, emotionalism'. (That of course is precisely the opposite to Freud's methods the object of which was to release the repressed emotion). The purpose of treatment is to re-establish the morale of the patient by re-education of his will. When the patient says, 'I'll try to eat!' Dubois replies, 'What is the use of that! you must say, 'I'm going to eat!'

So Dubois tells a patient suffering from insomnia 'Don't try to clutch it because it flies further away!' (very good advice) 'but suppress by a sane philosophy the futile preoccupations which possess you.' (The patient says, 'If only I could!').

In this way Dubois sets out to build up the morale of the patient. The psychotherapist, he says, must believe in the 'sweets of persuasion'. He admits (*The Psychic Treatment of Nervous Disorders*, 1909, p. 207) that his treatment is more ethical and moralizing than scientific.

Dubois will have nothing to do with Weir Mitchell's treatment; for it is by exertion, by the exercise of your will that you gain control of your emotions. He is opposed to Janet, who tried to get down to causes by delving into the patient's past. Dubois told his patients to 'pass a sponge over the past and wipe out all the phobias'—just as we tell one another, 'Oh! forget it!'

He is also opposed to treatment by suggestion as used by Janet. The trouble with the hysteric patient, says Dubois, is that he is already too suggestible and his reason is insufficiently developed.

The aim of treatment is to rid him of suggestibility; it is therefore not a good plan to cultivate his suggestibility or credulity. (The two are not the same!) Our reason, he said, should control our feelings and our emotions.

His objection to suggestion treatment is that it appeals to the lower nature of the patient and is a degradation to the physician who uses it. He declared that he blushes when he remembers that he once used suggestion to cure a child of bed-wetting (Shocking! but I do not suppose the mother of the child so cured blushed, unless with joy.) He says, 'The difference between persuasion and suggestion is the difference between a good bit of advice and a practical joke.' (To which it might be replied that some people would prefer a bad joke which cured them, to a good bit of advice that didn't.)

'How', says Dubois, (ibid., p. 336) can M. Janet consent to enter the mind of his patient by this back door' (suggestibility). To which Janet nicely replied: 'I am a person of humble disposition, and in order to make my way into the mind of the sufferer, I would willingly avail myself of the tradesman's entrance!'

Dubois appears to labour under the erroneous idea that in suggestion you are telling a person what is not true; you are playing on his credulity. That is not the case; when we tell a man with a hysterical paralysis that he can walk, we are telling him nothing but the plain truth. The delusion in his belief that he cannot walk, and this morbid auto-suggestion prevents him from walking. No 'good bit of advice' would be of any effect.

As regards those who seek to discover the cause of the neurotic condition (psychoanalysis was in its infancy), he says, 'It is not sufficient to fight the causes ... it is necessary to prevent the recurrence of the attack by making the primary mentality less sensitive.' (The answer of the analyst to this would be that in removing the cause we automatically liberate repressed forces into consciousness which brings them under the control of the will and so enables the patient to re-adjust himself to them and to life. You cannot have a recurrence of appendicitis if your appendix has been removed).

This method of persuasion was extensively used in the First World War at Seale Hayne Hospital for war neuroses. A man has a paralysed hand: he is persuaded that there is nothing organically wrong with it, and he is told to try to use it. He can't do so. But by being urged he gets a slight movement which is pointed out to him. By persistence and after perhaps two or three hours effort, the patient does manage to move his hand—for the principle practised by the doctors was always to cure the condition in one sitting however long it took. Excellent results were claimed.

No doubt many survived since such treatment, though it did not deal with causes, could have the effect of breaking a vicious circle. I had quite a number of their patients later who unfortunately had relapsed.

Persuasion is of value in mild cases. It is everyone's experience that if one is feeling down or despondent, one can sometimes 'pull oneself together'—we can sometimes 'snap out of it'. This is the more effective if we have the backing of friends who encourage us to cheer up. Such treatment boosts our morale; it appeals to our reason, it strengthens our will. This is the ethical approach, and in many cases a most effective one. What would be the use of the will if it could not do just that?

This approach to reason and common sense is also of value in cases of misapprehension, for such may be corrected. The patient whose father died of cancer is greatly relieved to know that the pain in his abdomen is not cancer—and his morbid fear goes. Another is greatly relieved to know that his phobia of going out alone does *not* mean that he is going insane, as he imagines. The physician is bringing reason to bear on the case. Many children, we find in analysis, suffer neuroses as the result of misunderstanding such as when a mother goes to hospital and the child feels she no longer loves him. Such cases require no long analysis. We hear physicians say, 'All this analysis is no use. Why, I cured a patient of his depression in three visits!' We all have such luck! But that does not exclude the need of more drastic treatment in more deep-seated neuroses.

Unfortunately, treatment by an appeal to reason and will is ineffective in severe cases. In the first place, as we now know, the neurosis is due to a dissociated state of mind, forming a complex which is inaccessible to the will. The analyst does not discount the will, but the will is only operative on material of which it is aware.

In the second place, neurotic disorders do not belong to the sphere of the reason but to that of the emotional life which is inaccessible to reason. To try to persuade the patient that his fear, anxieties, depression or jealousy are silly is futile, for the patient knows that as well as the doctor; it is because he knows that they are irrational that he has come to have them put right. He wants to know why he has these foolish ideas and feelings, and why even with the greatest exertion of his will he has not been able to control them. It is that which the analyst tries to discover. To tell the patient that they have no basis in fact is not true for they have a basis in fact, but that fact lies in past forgotten experiences; there is a cause but the cause is unknown, hidden.

When the persuasionist doctor cannot cure his patient he resorts to the excuse, 'Well, of course, if you don't accept what I say!'—

to which the patient replies, 'Doctor I do accept what you say, but I can't do it!' Finally the doctor resorts to the argument 'Nobody can cure you except yourself!', thereby committing two fallacies; first, the patient cannot cure himself; and secondly, others can cure him though not by that method.

The fact is that treatment by persuasion is not in fact merely an appeal to reason. In all such treatment suggestibility and emotion play a most important part in the treatment. It is the trust and confidence this patient has in the doctor which makes him accept the doctor's reasoning. Dubois himself tacitly admits this, for he speaks of the need for sympathy, friendship, enthusiasm, fervour and authoritativeness. None of these are functions of reason all depend on emotion and all are conducive to suggestibility on the part of the patient, which leads him to accept the doctor's reassurances. Recognizing this there is no reason why we should not use it in the ordinary situations of everyday life. People are cured not by Dubois' persuasion but by his persuasiveness.

The fact that reasoning cannot cure the most deep-rooted neuroses does not mean that the general practitioner should not use it, for many cases, especially mild cases and cases in which the cause of the lapse of morale is known, are accessible to such treatment which gives the patient moral support and encouragement, even if it does not radically cure.

The very fact that somebody cares is in itself a great morale booster to the patient. Ferenczi, a Freudian psycho-analyst, has said that the patient is cured by the love of the analyst.

THE IMPORTANCE OF EMOTION: DÉJERINE

As Dubois emphasized the importance of reason, Déjerine emphasized the importance of emotion. He recognized the need to appeal to the reason; but maintained that it was not until you got an emotional reaction that your patient was cured. (It must be realized, however, that he was long after Freud whose work he no doubt knew, but his methods were pre-analytic).

Déjerine started off by treating his patients along orthodox Weir Mitchell lines—methods of rest and isolation—but he gave it up.

He noted that the classical saying *mens sana in corpore sano* (a sound mind in a sound body) is not correct, for there are numerous people who have very sound bodies with unsound minds. Indeed, he stated the reverse that 'if the body is not sound, it is because the morale is unhealthy.' (That is true of psycho-somatic disorders, p. 285.) His views are set out in his book *Psycho-neuroses and Psychotherapy* (1913). 'Physicians', he said, 'know that health of body may be seriously affected by grief and vexation'. Emotional experiences may send a man crazy. The causes of neuroses being emotional, emotion is necessary to cure. The aim of the physician is therefore to uncover the emotional factors which are present in all.

Not only emotional disturbances of the present may cause these conditions, but previous emotional experiences may play an important part in the present-day breakdown. There is often a delayed reaction, so that the earlier experience may have the same effect as a present-day situation. Whereas Dubois maintained that the patient must exert his will to suppress his morbid thoughts and feelings, Déjerine says that 'The essential thing for a neurasthenic is, first of all, "*not to struggle* . . . but rather to forget".' It is a strange fact that cases like alcoholism have been cured when the victim ceased to struggle against it. A present-day religious body has, as a motto, Let Go! Let God!')

This advice is given to a worried individual suffering under an insult, 'Forget all about it'; or this to a girl who has been jilted, 'He is not worth worrying about.'

The advice is valuable as a first-aid measure in minor cases, and minor cases cover a very large proportion of the patients met with by the general practitioner; but as Freud has proved the trouble with most neurotics is that they have forgotten all about the cause, but the problem and complex are still there and are still operative in perpetuating the neurosis. Nevertheless Déjerine says, 'We need to explain to the patient why he felt ill, and how; and how he can be cured'. He agrees with Dubois in that the whole work of psychotherapy ought to be to build up the patient's morale, but this requires an emotional appeal.

An appeal to reason, he says, is not enough or else reading philosophies and moral works would be enough. But the moment the emotional element appears, the personality of the subject is moved and affected by it.

Since the emphasis is on emotion rather than reason, his method of building up the morale depends on the personal relationship of doctor and patient. He says, 'From my point of view, psycho-therapy depends wholly and exclusively upon the beneficial influence of one person on another'. People are not cured by logic. 'They are only cured when they come to believe in you.' (This is pure suggestibility which Déjerine scorns!) In short, psychotherapy can only be effective when the person on whom you are practising has 'confessed his entire life.' The trouble about this is that the patient cannot confess his entire life, for he does not know it. That is the trouble with all treatment by confession.

D*

Priests have been known to say that analysis is not necessary because all that the analyst does can be done in the confessional. Confession is undoubtedly a valuable therapeutic procedure and repentance an effective emotional response, but one can confess only what is conscious; we cannot confess guilt of which we are unaware, yet it is precisely the unconscious guilt which causes the obsessional neuroses.

Déjerine is surely one of the first to apply psychotherapy to children (ibid., p.385). 'Little things who flush or turn pale or who start and tremble at nothing, who are alternately sad and exuberant, who fear new faces, but who cling desperately to those in whom they had confidence . . .—such children will grow up to be lacking in confidence, take only a half-hearted interest in their work, fear reproach, and will not stand any criticism.' According to Déjerine it is their emotionalism which is at fault. 'It is necessary to teach them whenever they feel a wave of emotion to look for the cause of it; and to get hold of themselves by examining it, as it were from an intellectual point of view.'

Since emotion is the important factor in the production of neuroses, to do all we can to avoid emotional upsets would be the surest guarantee against relapse.

THE IMPORTANCE OF SUGGESTIBILITY: BABINSKI

The term hysteria has never been clearly defined. It is Greek for the womb—and signifies a disorder arising from the womb wandering about the body seeking satisfaction—an anticipation of Freud's theory of the sexual origin of these disorders. It was obvious that hysteria was a woman's complaint. It was treated with valerian the filthy smell of which was enough to send any womb quickly back to its place! Indeed 'valerian and assafoetida' was used to treat hysteria until quite recent years, though not for this same purpose.

The fact that numerous men in the First World War suffered from precisely the same disorders put count to that theory and incidentally to the sexual theory in these cases. But the term unfortunately persists—sometimes as equivalent to the neuroses in general, but more commonly of specific forms of neurosis now known as conversion hysteria (paralysis, &c.) and anxiety hysteria. Babinski (a neurologist and discoverer of the plantar reflex known as 'Babinski's sign'), tried to change all that, but without success; for the term hysteria is still used at the present day. He regarded all these conditions as characterized by suggestibility, so he gave them the name pithiatism, i.e., due to suggestion. The name has not caught on probably because suggestion is too simple an explanation of all these conditions.

At one time there was a vogue for what was termed 'medical suggestion'. The doctor asks a patient, 'Have you any pain there?' —the patient answers 'No'; but by the next visit of the doctor the patient has got a pain there as a result of the medical suggestion. With many years experience I cannot recall one neurotic patient in whom this has happened, although there is no reason why it should not. It is more likely to occur in cases of malingering, in which the 'patient' may be glad to pick up the idea from the doctor.

But I have most frequently found that the symptoms have been suggested not by the doctor but by a *previous experience or illness*, the hysteric symptom often being derived from an organic disease, an illustration of which has been given (pp. 52, 306). A child felt left out and wanted sympathy. He then found he got it when he was ill and had a headache. Later when he was particularly craving sympathy the headache automatically occurs; so he gets the sympathy he wants—but quite unconsciously. Suggestion therefore plays an important part in the hysteric symptom. But to say that the symptom is thus suggested or not to say that the illness itself is due to suggestion. Therefore Babinski's name survives by his plantar reflex and not by his incursions into psychology. It is also a warning against any one trying to change names, however absurd the name may be!

DISSOCIATION OF PERSONALITY: MORTON PRINCE

Morton Prince of the United States may be mentioned here for his contribution to the study of dual personalities and fugue states, a subject Janet had also studied extensively. Indeed when Janet went to lecture in the States he looked forward to the visit as he considered the States to be the home of dual personalities from the writings of Morton Prince, whereas he found that Morton Prince was looking forward to Janet's visit for he considered France to be the home of the dual personalities! Morton Prince's description of Sally Beauchamp, who changed her personality, gay at one time, morose at another, the one personality being dissociated and unaware of the other, became a classic. (Compare Janet's case of Marie, p. 52.) So also was the case of Ansel Bourne who disappeared as a parson and was surprised to find himself some years later when he 'came to' serving in a sweet shop hundreds of miles away. Sally was a case of dual personality, Ansel Bourne a fugue state. We have already considered such cases (p. 55).

Morton Prince described a group of neuroses as 'association neuroses', on the grounds that the symptoms arose as the result of association of ideas; for instance when a woman got an attack of asthma whenever she went into a room with flowers—even if the flowers were artificial and devoid of pollen. This would in these days be explained as a conditioned reflex. This concept of symptoms being the result of association is so far quite true and must not be ignored, but it does not account for the whole neurosis. Why does a particular association persist as a symptom whereas thousands of other daily associations pass without trace? It is always because a deeper problem is involved.

Morton Prince's explanation of these cases as due to association classes him as conforming to the static rather than the dynamic school of psychology.

A good example of what Morton Prince called association neurosis was the case mentioned by Freud of an English governess in Austria, who was secretly in love with her employer. She received a message to return to England. She was distraught, but suddenly 'came to' with the smell of burnt pudding which she had neglected; and she thereafter suffered from a hysteric smell of burnt pudding, since this was associated with a distressing experience. Prince would call that an association neurosis. I would regard its persistence as due to its being an unresolved problem (p. 291).

CHAPTER XVI

UNORTHODOX SYSTEMS OF PSYCHOTHERAPY

No account of psychotherapy would be complete without reference to unorthodox methods of treatment. In these we may include those at Lourdes, Christian Science, various forms of Faith Healing, and Spiritual Healing. I take them at this point because their healing is pre-analytic. They are usually dubbed as 'quackery' by the orthodox; but we have much to learn from 'quacks'. I recall the case of a patient who visited a Harley Street specialist who gave him six months to live. Four years after, still alive, he happened to meet the specialist, and reminded him of his case. 'You told me that I had six months to live, and now, four years after, here I am fit and well'. 'Ah!', said the specialist, 'you must have been going to some quack!'

In dealing with unorthodox methods of treatment we need to keep two principles in mind. To ridicule them without investigation shows lack of scientific precision. To say that the cures are impossible is going beyond what we are ever justified in asserting. It is little else than arrogance to declare that they are impossible. What proof have we?

Nor are the unorthodox necessarily charlatans. A charlatan (like the South Sea Islander with his hairs, p. 13) is one who deliberately dupes his victims. The systems I shall describe are all sincere, though we may consider them misguided.

LOURDES

The miraculous cure of pilgrims to Lourdes may be taken as typical of spiritual healing in its broad sense. The majority of cases of healing at Lourdes or other shrines are of neuropaths. Those, however, are carefully excluded by a medical panel and no claim of a 'miracle' is made in these cases. Only cases of organic disease are claimed as such. But I am told that in the last 30 years, only one case of a 'miracle' has been claimed from the British Isles. But even granting that those healed are mainly neuropaths and hysterics, that is not to discredit or ignore them. For as Janet says, 'Nothing is more difficult than to cure a confirmed neuropath and Lourdes would deserve all its reputation and more if it were pre-eminent in the cure of neuropaths alone. These neuropaths had obviously been unable to be cured by their own practitioners, and it is time for the latter to scoff at these cures when they have devised more efficient methods.'

At the same time we must consider those who are not cured at Lourdes—for there are far more failures than cures. Many of these must find it difficult to understand why God has chosen not to heal them. We must not underestimate their disappointment, which must be intense. In these cases, apart from the failure in cure, there is often the long and arduous journey, time spent by themselves and by those who bring them, and the cost of the whole proceeding—so that not only is the patient worse off materially but may be thrown into despair mentally. Keeping these facts in mind one wonders whether the cures are an adequate offset to the failures. The Catholic Church, however, now emphasizes the spiritual help received rather than physical cures as the main feature of the Pilgrimage to Lourdes.

CHRISTIAN SCIENCE

Whatever we may think of Christian Science as a philosophy or as a religion, there is no doubt that, especially in the United States, the movement has had a salutary effect in counteracting the excessive materialism of the day. If in its philosophy it went to an extreme in denying the existence of matter, yet it emphasized the paramount influence of the mind and the power of thought quite apart from the many cures it claimed. It placed spiritual values first: 'Man does not live by bread alone.' At the same time it was a spur to American enterprise for it maintained that there was nothing that man could not achieve by the power of mind over matter.

Christian Science originated with Quimby (1802–1866) in America. He was at first an ordinary magnetist, but like Faria and Braid came to discredit the magnetic fluid. He was convinced of this by accident, for when he found that the wrong medicine given by his assistant cured just as effectively as the prescribed medicine, he turned his attention to discover the reason and found the essential factor to lie in the mind of the patient. So he enunciated the principle that we must appeal to the 'power that lies within us', the power of thought. He went further and held that thinking was potent even against the maladies of the body.

He thus became the precursor of Christian Science, and Mrs Eddy (1821–1910).

Mrs Eddy was his patient and his pupil. She had had a somewhat tempestious early life. She was a spoilt child, she was also an invalid. On both scores she claimed the centre of the stage; she must have attention; she must have her own way. This gave her a great sense of dominance over her fellow men. At the same time her invalidism, which was not confined to childhood, gave her a sympathy with the sufferings of her fellows. The combination of these two qualities, power and sympathy, made her a great pioneer in the alleviation of suffering. But she reached there the hard way, by suffering. In adult life she suffered from two unhappy marriages and with her children, hardship and poverty. She developed a number of hysteric symptoms including convulsions. Even as an adult she had infantile traits such as the desire to be put into a cot and be rocked—what we now call a regression.

When she joined Quimby she at last found the cure (or partial cure) of her symptoms including paralysis. But she also found outlet for the desire to dominate the lives of others, a quality which she had retained as a legacy from her childhood. She was never herself successful as a practitioner but trained others to practise. Indeed she later became jealous of her followers, and was obsessed with the idea that people were doing her harm in practising subversive magnetism. I was in Boston when she was still alive, and was told by Dr McComb of the Emmanuel Movement that she never emerged from her estate outside Boston because she feared the evil magnetic influence of those who had left the movement.

Her doctrine was the supreme dominance of the mind over matter; indeed matter did not exist, and therefore illness was a delusion.

In assessing the contribution she has made to psychotherapy, we may excuse such excesses as the claim of the woman Christian Scientist who treated a horse for indigestion by telling it that it was God's horse, and therefore could not have indigestion, thus curing the horse within an hour (Janet, *Psychological Healing*, p. 92).

I was once at a Christian Science meeting in Edinburgh and the whole service, in a most beautiful church, was on a high spiritual level—until a large and opulent looking lady from the States started to tell how she had been cured of a corn by Christian Science. The anti-climax destroyed the spiritual atmosphere.

As for cures, there is no need to disbelieve that Christian Science can and does cure many hysteric and similar disorders—and it differs in no respect from treatment by suggestion except that the appeal of Divine Power has a more forceful effect. In particular there is no difficulty in believing that it can abolish pain—whether this is done by direct suggestion, or by the belief that as there is no such thing as your material body it cannot be in pain.

When a hypnotist tells a patient that he feels no pain when his arm is pricked, there is no pain. So if we convince him that there is no such thing as matter and therefore he has no indigestion, the discomfort may go—but not necessarily the indigestion. Yet if the indigestion is caused by worry and the hypnotist or spiritual healer gives peace of mind, the indigestion itself may disappear. (See p. 288).

No doubt many cures of neuropathic disorders, and of the pain even of organic conditions, does take place, but I do not know of any authentic evidence that a broken leg can be healed immediately by the belief that it is not broken—unless by a mistake in diagnosis. Nevertheless, if Christian Science can rid its adherents of fear, which it claims to do, and often does, it is a therapeutic agency of the greatest value, for fear is the source of most neurotic diseases and also of psychosomatic conditions like nervous indigestion—but not of a broken leg nor even of a corn.

THE EMMANUEL MOVEMENT

In the early part of this century, at the Emmanuel Episcopal Church in Boston, U.S.A., Dr Worcester and Dr McComb, the clergy, quite frankly used suggestion, particularly for alcoholism and drug addiction. They had the co-operation and advice of the neurologist Coriat. They were most successful in their results. I was privileged to 'sit-in' with Dr McComb whilst he treated patients in the year 1912. Their suggestions were greatly enhanced by the appeal to Divine help for each individual: and on a Wednesday evening they had a service in Church for their patients, past and present, which was most impressive. In the use of suggestion they were quite orthodox, they were 'unorthodox' only in their call for Divine help!

FAITH HEALING AND SPIRITUAL HEALING

There are various movements which claim to cure disease of all kinds, organic as well as functional, which go under the names of Faith healing, Spiritual healing or Spirit healing. The first, Faith healing, places the emphasis on the faith of the patient—'Thy faith hath made thee whole.' Spiritual healing or Divine healing depends more on outside influence such as the power and intervention of God. Others heal by the medium-ship of Spirits such as those of Lister, Pasteur and of Christ. They all agree, however, in that the healing takes place by the instrumentality of the mind rather than by physical means, and therefore come under the category of psycho-therapy, except that their approach is not scientific.

The methods most commonly used by religious bodies in healing is the laying on of hands, unction (anointing with oil), and prayer. In many districts there is co-operation between doctors and clergy on the grounds that man is unity and body and mind must therefore be healed as one. They insist that there are no sicknesses, but only sick persons. Therefore every sick person requires mental or spirit-ual treatment as well as physical. There is no doubt that a calm and confident mind greatly helps in the recovery of a physically sick person; but does a young man who has broken his leg at Rugger and who is quite happy flirting with nurses in hospital require spiritual help for his recovery? Perhaps he does!

The rationale of Spiritual healing in its claim to cure organic diseases like cancer as well as hysteric disorders, is that nothing is beyond the power of God and that therefore God can heal diseases of all kinds. The answer is (to those who believe in God), that God can heal all types of illnesses; the question is whether God does do so by such means. For in producing 'miracles' he would be defying His own laws of nature. In any case why should God cure one person who happens to know of a clergyman who uses prayer and unction, and continue to let suffer one without such advantage?

THE MEDICAL POINT OF VIEW

In recent years there have been two Commissions appointed by Archbishop Lang and Archbishop Fisher to enquire into the subject—on both of which I was privileged to serve. Both commissions consisted of churchmen and doctors. In the second commission, the British Medical Association was asked for its co-operation and a committee was appointed on which I also served.

Numerous cases of Spiritual, Spirit and Faith healing were investigated. The general conclusion by the British Medical Association committee was that *they could find no evidence that any type of disorder could be cured by these means which could not be cured by orthodox medical means* (including of course suggestion as now orthodox).

We said specifically any type of case, for there are individual cases of hysterical disorders which are cured by a faith healer which the general practioner had failed to cure. Further, our dictum did not say dogmatically that there were no such cases, but that in investigating numerous cases we could find no evidence of this.

What then is the medical attitude towards those unorthodox cures? In general, it is that any disorder of a psychogenic disorder, such as the neuroses, may be cured by any of these means: but we cannot find any evidence that organic diseases like cancer, broken legs or leukaemia are so cured. There is this to be said, however, and every medical man would agree, that a quiet, calm or cheerful attitude helps the patients' recovery, and if so, may even turn the scale, say in a case of pneumonia, whereas a depressed patient who has nothing to live for would die. But that does not mean that we can exclude the physical treatment. A woman doctor gave evidence that she had been cured of a skin disease by spiritual healing, but it was found that she was also taking the pills prescribed by the dermatologist!

In all scientific investigation there must be the observation and collection of data followed by a correct interpretation of those facts. Both of these require training, for not everyone can observe facts correctly: and most facts of experience are capable of more than one explanation. The mesmerists observed the facts correctly: indeed they made a most accurate study of the cases. But their explanation of these as due to a magnetic fluid was proved wrong. This is important in our assessment of faith healing at the hands of non-medical practitioners.

In view then of the apparently well-authenticated cases of cure of organic conditions by faith healers, what justification have we for maintaining this sceptical attitude towards these cures?

In the first place, *the cure of a pain does not mean the cure of the disease which causes the pain.* Let us remind ourselves that all pain is a psychic phenomena. It may originate in an organic disease or it may originate in the mind itself. If I hypnotize a person and tell him he has a severe pain in the arm, he has that pain as 'real' as any pain organically caused. If under hypnosis I tell him he has no pain when I open an absess he has none—he does not simply imagine he hasn't—for pain is a phenomena of consciousness which can be abolished by suggestion. If then the Faith Healer or Christian Scientist, backed by the suggestive effect of Divine influence says the patient has no pain, this may have the effect of abolishing the pain.

Take a case of rheumatoid arthritis, a very painful disease due to the inflammation of a joint—a case said to be cured by spirit healing. A woman patient went to a meeting for spirit healing, hobbled up on to the platform on her crutches, where the healer did his habora-cadabora with some manipulation, and she walked off the platform without crutches and without pain. A miracle! In this case the pain was abolished, some would say by the manipulation, for a physiotherapist by manipulation can remove the fluid the pressure of which on a nerve is causing the pain. Others would say the pain was abolished by suggestion. But the inflammation of the joint was not cured: and it would do the joint no good to be walked upon. This was confirmed; for after the meeting, as people left the hall, a medical friend of mine saw this same woman walking away in the street on her crutches, and apparently in as great pain as ever! The 'miracle' in the hall was a disaster outside, made all the worse no doubt by her disappointment. The suggestion of her having 'no pain' had worn off.

A further source of errors is *false diagnosis.* Many of the cases which the spiritual healer 'cures' are said to be 'organic'. Unfortunately that argument makes no impression on those of us who practice psychotherapy and who realize how difficult it is in many cases to make a correct diagnosis as to whether a condition is organic or functional. This is still more liable to happen with the general practitioner who has had little training in diagnosing neurotic disorders. In particular there are many psycho-somatic disorders (physical disorders like nervous indigestion or headaches due to worry—see Chap. XXXII), which are misdiagnosed as organic by those not trained to recognize psychogenic ailments. Any form of mental treatment may be successful in such cases, but it is not a cure of organic disease.

I once 'cured' a young woman of a severe pain in the shoulder by getting her to relax her shoulder blades. She had previously had an injury and with any such injury, one automatically tenses the muscles so as to immobilize the part to avoid pain of movement. The injury was healed months before, but by tensing the muscles, which she continued to do by habit, she got painful cramp in the muscles. By getting her to relax her muscles the pain departed. If a spirtual healer had brought about such relaxation, he would undoubtedly have claimed cure of an organic condition, an injured shoulder, by spiritual means. It was of course no such thing!

Another source of error is that of *remission*, a pit into which many spiritual healers fall. Many illnesses have remissions—periods of illness followed by periods of apparent health. A schizophrenic or manic-depressive may have these remissions when to a casual observer he is 'cured'; but not to the physician who may warn the friends that the patient may and probably will have relapses.

If a spiritual healer gets to work on such a case just before a remission is due, and the patient 'recovers', that is naturally taken as a 'cure' of the condition. The patient will probably relapse later in the ordinary course of the illness, but the spiritual healer may know nothing of this, and his records show a 'miraculous cure'. As a case in point: while our Commissions were sitting a boy was submitted to the B.M.A., Committee as a case of cure of leukaemia by Spirit healing. His doctor had diagnosed leukaemia and the laboratory tests confirmed this. He informed the parents that the boy's condition was incurable and that he would die. The boy went to a healer and 'recovered'—declared to be cured by spirit healing. With the parents' consent we referred the boy back to his doctor who after examination said the boy still had leukaemia and that he would still die of it. His present state of well-being was a remission of the disease such as often happens. As expected, the boy later died. The spirit healer then claimed that the boy had not died of leukaemia but of a broken leg: he also pointed to the fact that at the time of death the boy's blood tests did not give signs of leukaemia.

What the healer, being non-medical, did not appreciate was, first, that in leukaemia the bones get very brittle, and that the boy's broken leg was due to this disease. In the second place, a person can die of the results of leukaemia without there being an active leukaemia at the time of death—just as a person can die of a haemorrhage of the lungs originating in T.B. without having any active Tuberculous organisms in his lungs: the previous active disease had made in-roads in an artery and later it only took a severe cough to rupture the weakened artery.

Another source of error is that a person may suffer from an organic disease such as neuritis; and even when the organic condition is cured, the pain may persist as a neurotic symptom (case on p. 306). The cure of such pain by any form of faith healing is then taken as a cure by an organic disease, where as it is a cure of the neurotic aftermath. No doubt it is a most welcome cure from the patient's point of view, but it cannot be claimed as a cure of an organic disease, for it is that no longer.

Finally there are some organic diseases, sometimes even cancer, which recover spontaneously, without any treatment at all. If these cases coincide with spiritual healing of any kind, the cure is put down to the latter.

PART VI
MODERN SCHOOLS : DYNAMIC PSYCHOLOGY

CHAPTER XVII

THE BASIC INSTINCTS:
WILLIAM McDOUGALL

Most of the schools of psychotherapy already described are 'static' in their outlook. They proceed on the assumption that the mind is 'built up'. Janet, for instance, held that the personality was a 'synthesis' of all the experiences of the day. The hypnotic school set out to fill the mind with suggestions of courage and confidence, of cheerfulness, and of the abolition of pain, instead of fear. The behaviourist school regarded all behaviour as being 'learned'. There is of course a great deal of truth in all these. But as we now see it the mind is not so much 'built up' as a response to life.

The more modern schools are dynamic; they have emphasized the fact that the personality contains innate potentialities, which respond to conditions of the outside world. The infant is not a sheet of paper or wax on which impressions are made, but a going concern from the start.

Freud is dynamic in his theory of the *libido*: Jung is dynamic in his concept of the 'collective unconscious'. Adler is dynamic in his 'urge to power'. Janet was dynamic in so far as he regarded the synthesis of the personality as held together by psychic energy or tension. Even Watson and the behaviourists, who are not dynamic in their approach, and who emphasized the environmental influences which could determine whether a child becomes a professor, a vagrant, or a criminal, had to admit that there must be something in the individual which enabled him to respond to these outside influences, and so admitted fear, aggressiveness and 'sex in the Freudian sense', as innate.

The most systematic exponent of the dynamic view is however William McDougall of Oxford who made a study of the basic instincts in man, their accompanying emotions, their biological origin, their uses in life, and their effect on social behaviour. These findings are incorporated in his valuable book *An introduction to Social Psychology*. It is not that he added a great deal to our knowledge of the causes of psychoneurotic disorders, but in his description of the instincts he presents us with a sound biological background for our study of the psychoneuroses and psychotherapy.

Because of this systematic study we venture to take him out of chronological order, to give his account of these instincts and emotions. We can do this with greater justification because his views owe little or nothing to Freud, although he was a few years after Freud and a contemporary of Jung.

Wm. McDougall was one of a distinguished triumvirate of Cambridge psychologists—the other two being Chas. Myers who was the founder of the Institute of Industrial Psychology; and Rivers whose interests were mainly anthropological—who had a great influence on psychological thought in Cambridge in the post-First World War period. All three were students of Ward of Cambridge who may be considered the father of English psychology.

McDougall was not only a medical man, but a physiologist and an anthropologist, his first-hand study on Borneo and its people standing unique.

McDougall came to Oxford as Wilde Reader in Psychology in 1900 when I attended his first course of lectures and came under his influence as teacher. Later he was my tutor in research work in anthropology and religion and finally as friend and colleague in the treatment of 'shell-shock' cases in the First World War. His work *Abnormal Psychology* sets out his views on this subject and is sound common sense.

He was unfortunate in some ways. He came to Oxford a scientific psychologist, but was not wholly welcome to the philosophers there who regarded psychology as their preserve.

When therefore during the First World War he was invited to Harvard University, he accepted; but by the end of the war the Senior common rooms at Oxford had come round to becoming more tolerant of the 'new psychology' and its scientific approach, mainly on account of their therapeutic success in the treatment of shell-shock people at its gates. (The Vice-Chancellor of that time, Sir David Ross, Philosopher and Master of Oriel College, and other dons, visited the hospital at Littlemore, and several times 'sat in' with me while I treated the patients.) By the end of the war, McDougall regretted that he had promised to go to Harvard, and told me that he would never have accepted had he anticipated the changed attitude at Oxford. Moreover, when he arrived at Harvard, he found America in the throes of behaviourism and his views on the instincts were regarded as anathema.

I mention these misfortunes in his life because it partly accounts for the fact that he has never met with the recognition he deserved. Nevertheless his *Social Psychology* has had far wider influence even amongst those who disagreed with him, than they would admit. Indeed, he once complained to me with a smile that when people quoted his views they would merely say, 'Psychologists say....' Apart from that he was an individualist and such men, often pioneers in their field, rarely get the acclaim that those do whose views are propagated by a composite group of followers, which was the case with both Freud and Jung.

Starting to write a book on social psychology, he found he could get no further until he studied the motivations of individual behaviour and these he found in the human instincts. Thus his book on social psychology took the form of a treatise on the primary instincts and their effect on human life.

McDougall's main contributions to psycho-pathology and psychotherapy were:—

(a) The dynamic approach to human life—far more specifically advocated by him than by Freud, who implied it rather than enunciated it in his libido theory.

(b) His biological approach and description of the primary instincts as shared by animals.

(c) His description of the emotions as accompanying the instincts.

(d) His demonstration of the re-direction of the instincts to higher social uses (which Freud called 'sublimation' but McDougall showed far more clearly how they were re-directed in each case).

(e) His insistence on hormic psychology—the psychology of purpose, the pursuit of ends.

His approach was biological—an approach characteristic of British psychology since it follows the tradition of the great biologists Darwin, Huxley and others. He made a study of animal as well as of human life, and he found in the higher animals the same instincts as are to be found in human beings, which is not surprising, for after all, humans are higher animals.

This biological approach is an eminently sound basis as a starting point for the study of human nature and indeed, I would suggest, of psychology in general, for all man's mental equipment, higher as well as lower, such as memory, imagination, intelligence and reason, serve the function of adaptation to life.

The word 'instinctive' is usually used to denote whatever mental qualities in human nature are innate and inborn, and therefore unlearnt. It implies that we are born with certain potentialities by means of which we respond or react in specific ways to certain stimuli from the environment.

Thus in the broad sense, reflex actions like swallowing are instinctive, whereas conditioned reflexes like avoidance of poisonous berries are not instinctive, but acquired. We hear people say that a person has an instinctive love of orchestral music, or of chess; it is a wrong use of the term.

As I have elsewhere defined them, *instincts are innate potentialities of response*

McDougall's definition of instinct is more detailed:

An instinct is an inherited or innate psycho-physical disposition which determines its subject to perceive, and to pay attention to objects of certain class, to experience an emotional excitement of a particular quality upon perceiving such an object, and to act in regard to it in a particular manner, or at least to experience an impulse to such action. (*Social Psychology* p. 29).

We perceive danger, we experience the emotion of fear with changes within our central nervous system, and we respond by flight.

McDougall gave the name of 'primary instincts' to certain of these instincts which are held in common with the higher animals.

A Freudian writer has made the statement that Freud made nonsense of McDougall's views. I should have thought, considering the sources of their descriptions, it was the other way round. I prefer the views of Ernest Jones, right hand man of Freud, erstwhile President of the International Association of Psycho-analysis and always a fair-minded critic, who gave a truer assessment of the situation. He mentions the fact (*Freud*, Vol. 111, p. 328) that Freud almost never refers to the correspondence between animal instincts and those in men, and rightly calls this a 'curious omission'. The psychoanalysts have never made any serious attempt to define the innate tendencies and propensities; their description, for instance, of 'ego instincts' or the 'nutritive instinct', is quite haphazard (see p. 126).

The primary instincts, as defined by McDougall, are of the same nature as reflexes. Indeed they are often defined as 'complex reflex actions'; for in both are the three phases; stimulus, internal changes in the organism, and response. But the instincts differ in many respects from reflexes.

(a) In the first place native reflexes and even conditioned reflexes are ordinarily devoid of consciousness, whereas the primary instincts like fright, sex, and aggression are not only conscious of what they are doing, but conscious of what they are doing it for, of the end or result of the action. When we run away from a wild animal, or pursue our prey, we are perfectly aware of the object of our behaviour. This consciousness of our behaviour gives us a certain control over our actions, whereas we have little control over our reflexes.

(b) Secondly, the instincts are more generalized than reflex action. The pupil reflex, the swallowing reflex, or the withdrawal of the foot when pricked, are all local reactions, only in a minor degree do they affect the body as a whole. But when a man is afraid, sexually aroused or angry, the whole of his organism is activated. This reaction of the whole organism is provided for partly by the endocrine secretions like the adrenal in the blood stream, which are rapidly spread throughout the whole body, and the auto-nomic nervous system with its ramifications throughout the body, thereby mobilizing the whole body for action. For the sake of distinction then we may speak with profit of the 'responses' of the whole organism as against the localized 'reflexes'.

(c) Thirdly, perhaps the most important distinction between the reflex actions and the primary instincts is that the basic instincts are accompanied by deep and strong emotions, which give driving force to our actions and make them far more effective.

The primary instincts, therefore, and their accompanying emotions are: the instinct of flight and the emotion of fear; the instinct of pugnacity and the emotion of anger; the instinct of reproduction and sexual emotion; the instinct of repulsion and the emotion of disgust; the instinct of curiosity and the emotion of wonder: also the instincts and emotion of subjection, of self-assertion and elation; the gregarious instinct; the instinct of acquisition; and of construction.

These of course do not exhaust all innate human potentialities. There are for instance, as McDougall points out, innate tendencies such as imitation (the transmission of actions), sympathy (of feeling) and suggestibility (of ideas), but these do not conform to the three phases of afferent impulses, central changes, and efferent impulses therefore do not count as primary instincts; nor are they connected with specific emotions.

There are also instinctive patterns of behaviour such as crawling, creeping and walking, the potentialities of which are innate. Some of these, like sucking and crying, are operative at birth; others like walking, talking, and falling in love do not emerge till later, that is to say till the nervous system which regulates these functions come into activity. This is the process of *maturation* which I have fully described in *Childhood and Adolescence* (Penguin p. 29 ff.), I have defined maturation as 'the development of innate patterns in ordered sequence'. This group of innate tendencies is not, however, defined by McDougall, but it was left to the Americans who have made a special study of it. They are all, however, 'instinctive in that they are innate potentialities.

McDougall has been criticized on the grounds that the instincts are regarded as themselves agencies, so that people say 'fear made me run away': 'rage made me do this'. This is a justifiable criticism, but that is not McDougall's view. His definition of the instincts makes it clear that they are responses to stimuli, psycho-physical dispositions which require conditions to arouse them.

It has always been a problem in which experts have differed as to whether the primary instincts, like fear and flight, have a source of energy *per se*, or whether there is a common source of energy throughout the body which all the instincts can draw upon, the instinctive action being merely the expression or manifestation of this common pool of energy.

The general view would favour the latter 'common source' theory. Janet in particular obviously held that view. Yet there are indications that some instincts have an identity of their own, and even individuality; for it is the lactogenic hormone which not only produces milk in the mother, but the milk of human kindness and tenderness, the 'maternal instinct'; it is the stimulation of the gonadotrophic hormone which activates the sexual functions and feelings, the lack of which hormones means the absence of sex desire, and consequently of sex action. Again the supra-renal glands are specifically activated in anger and fear. So we may say that some, at least, of the primary instincts are associated with specific bodily functions and in that sense have a certain individuality. But that may mean nothing more than that these glandular secretions determine the form in which the instinctive common energy manifests itself.

No particular glandular secretion, nor any specific nucleus in the brain is yet discovered associated with the instincts of curiosity or submission; but that may simply be that we have not yet discovered them.

Re-direction of our instinctive drives

McDougall made a most notable contribution to psychotherapy, to mental health and indeed to ethics, when he demonstrated that the primary instincts could be diverted from their original aims and re-directed towards new objects, and into channels more in keeping with social demands.

Freud discovered the same process which he called 'sublimation'; but his idea was very limited, for he referred it only to the sex instinct and was very vague as to how the sex instinct could in fact be sublimated. He also referred it only to people of artistic ability, (p. 144). McDougall described the process of re-direction with much greater precision and showed how in each primary instinct it could affect the whole of our social life.

Sublimation is simply re-direction, and is better understood as such. A good but simple example is that of a sheep dog. In its native wolf-like state it has the propensity in hunting prey to round it up with other wolves and devour it. This natural propensity in certain types of dog is made use of by the farmer who directs this natural propensity to round up flocks of sheep and drive them through the narrow gate into a pen. That of course is re-conditioning, but in as far as a natural instinction propensity is re-directed to higher social uses, it is sublimation.

Sublimation is a process by which the crude instincts are raised to a higher potential: and by 'higher' we mean more in conformity with biological and social aims. (See McDougall, *Energies of Men*, p. 307). Sex, for instance, is sublimated in love. The youth has natural sex desires towards a girl; but then develops respect for her qualities, admiration for her beauty apart from its sex appeal, and for her tenderness and love, all of which makes him drawn to her as a companion and friend. All of these components of love make for greater stability in married life and a better chance for their offspring. Sex has now been raised to a higher potential by being modified by all these other aspects of love: he is 'in love' with her and is prepared to protect her through life.

Fear is transformed into caution; and by developing measures to avoid danger we can venture with courage and daring. Self-assertiveness is transformed by self discipline into achievement: anger into grim determination.

This re-direction solves the vexed problem of repression; for it means that there is no need for repression of our native instincts for they can be re-directed to higher purposes. Man is therefore not under the necessity of being either bad or neurotic—being bad, by giving way to his natural impulses in an anti-social way, or being neurotic, by repressing them: he can re-direct them, thus giving satisfaction to both the demands of society and the needs of individual expression. The secret of mental health is the harmonization of all the potentialities in our nature by their being directed to a common aim and end, This makes for efficiency as well as for peace of mind.

McDougall was one of the pioneers of *hormic psychology*, which deals with ends and aims (hormé = end). Hormic psychology recognizes that man's behaviour is determined not merely by instinctive drives from behind (*vis a tergo*), but by the pursuit of ends and aims before us (*vis a fronte*). This conscious pursuit of aims we call 'purpose'. He defines purposive behaviour as that in which we have a conscious end or aim, and in which this consciousness of the end is the determining factor in our behaviour. So important does he consider this pursuit of conscious ends that he says 'Purposiveness seems to be of the essence of mental activity . . . the fundamental category of psychology'. Reflex action is purposive in the sense that it achieves useful ends; but it is not 'purpose' in the full sense, for it is an unconscious process and the ends are not consciously pursued.

Most of the important decisions in our life are made with an end in view. What are we aiming at? What do we want to achieve? The term 'motive' may be used of the motive force which comes from the primary instincts: but by 'motive' we also mean why, to what end? Having a purpose in life is of vital importance for human life and happiness. Rob a man of his aims in life, of something to live for, and you soon rob him of life itself, for without aims to call forth his energies he falls into stagnation of body as well as of mind, as many men do when they retire. Man needs an outlet for his energies, for that alone is 'living'. This appears to be what Jung meant when he said that most of his middle-aged patients who suffered from neurotic disorders did so because of 'lack of religion': or shall we say, for lack of a purpose in life—for religion is that to which we are 'bound' or devoted (Latin, *religio*). A philosophy of life, a purpose is as necessary to a successful life as a compass to the mariner, to guide him. It is also necessary to mental health.

There is a school of thought opposed to hormic psychology which maintains that the human organism is merely a machine. McDougall countered that by pointing out that a machine itself is a purposive object: a machine is not a mere conglomoration of bits and pieces of metal; it is an ordered combination of parts designed for and serving a purpose, as a sewing machine for sewing; a car for travelling. Man is a machine, if you wish, but like all machines is designed with a purpose.

McDougall's psychology is therefore both dynamic and hormic: it is dynamic in that it emphasizes the drives in human nature: it is hormic in that it recognizes that for peace and harmony of mind as well as for efficiency, it is necessary that these dynamic forces should be diverted from their natural ends and redirected towards the ends and aims of the personality as a whole.

The pursuit of ends is a point emphasized by Jung also, who stresses the point in contrast to Freud. Freud, Jung says, regards human nature only from the point of view of causality (a very necessary proceeding notwithstanding), but Jung regards it from the point of view of finality—of the goal and purpose of life. Freud's philosophy of life tends, therefore, to be pessimistic. Adler also is hormic in holding to the principle of the masculine urge or the urge to power, and in saying that 'neuroses are always due to false ideals'.

Regarding man from this biological and purposive approach we can see how there are four main forms of breakdown.

The first occurs when an individual is confronted with circumstances in life too great for him to cope with—as men did in the war. Too great a demand is made upon his resources.

The second is the opposite: people break down because they have not enough to engage their energies, because they have no aim or purpose in life; they have not enough to bite on. They suffer from stagnation. To make an analogy, the Sea of Galilee is fresh, there are birds upon its waters, fish within its depths; whereas the Dead Sea is dead, with no living thing in or upon its waters. Why? Not because there is no inlet, for both have fresh water pouring into them; but the Sea of Galilee is fresh because it has also an outlet; whereas the Dead Sea is dead because there is no outlet; it is therefore stagnant. Similarly many people's lives stagnate. To keep alive and mentally healthy we need something to live for, something to call forth our energies to be used for the purposes of life.

The third group relates to the wrong direction of the primary instincts and emotion. Self-assertion, instead of being directed to ambition and achievement is wrongly directed to cruelty or quarrelsomeness, which creates not only a conflict with the community in which we live, but with ourselves. The instinct of curiosity may be transformed into prying and gossip. Fear, instead of enabling us to avoid danger or to develop caution so that we are enabled to meet danger with confidence, may fill our whole lives with morbid fears which render us altogether incapable of meeting our responsibilities. Sex can be subject to perversions like sadism or fetishism which defeat the ends of nature. Delinquency and crime are usually the mis-direction of our energies to wrong ends. Perversion is the term used to describe wrong direction.

Finally, the instincts may be repressed, so that not only is the personality deprived of these strong and necessary forces and so handicapped in the pursuit of life, but their instinctive emotions, refused normal outlet in life, emerge in the form of neurosis. But we owe the development of this last group to Freud rather than to McDougall.

The New Morality

I doubt whether McDougall himself realized it, but this concept of the transformation of the basic instincts had a profound effect on ethics as well as on mental health. Whereas previously the instincts were regarded as essentially evil and the result of 'original sin', to be repressed at all costs, the new morality (shall we call it), regarded the instincts as the raw material out of which higher forms of social and spiritual life could be developed. For such re-direction however, restraint is necessary to divert our instincts, but not repression, for if we repress our native instincts we cannot use or direct them. To re-direct them we must give outlet to our primitive impulses which are therefore not repressed: but to re-direct them we need to restrain and discipline them. This concept of the value of the instincts transforms our training of children, which I have dealt with in my *Childhood and Adolescence*. Freedom is necessary if we are to have a full life, but discipline is necessary if we are to direct our impulses to right ends so that we may not only live in harmony with our fellows, but in harmony with ourselves.

McDougall, therefore, held and advocated the 'normal' view of the instincts as being of the greatest value biologically as well as socially, whereas Freud clung to the idea of 'original sin' in the form of incestuous desires which were inevitable if not innate, the forbidden fruit which brought upon man the curse of neurosis.

In view of these contributions of McDougall to human psycho-ology it is not surprising that Professor Flügel, himself a Freudian psycho-analyst, writes that 'McDougall has given us a systematic treatment of conation and affect that, in completeness and thoroughness, is without rival.' (*One Hundred Years of Psychology*, p. 222).

CHAPTER XVIII

PSYCHO-ANALYSIS: FREUD

There can be little doubt that Freud is the outstanding personality in the field of psychotherapy during the past century; and this stands true although we may disagree with him on fundamental issues—as indeed the present writer does. It was Freud who gave the impetus to most modern analytic work; though he too was dependent on previous discoveries.

His main contributions are:

(a) To psychology in general—especially 'psychic determinism', 'repression', and 'the unconscious'.

(b) His discovery of free association as a means of gaining access to the contents of the unconscious and of reviving long since forgotten experiences—a substitute for hypnotism.

(c) His mental mechanisms, such as conflict, repression, projection, displacement and sympton formation.

(d) His structure of the personality. Id, Ego and Super-Ego.

(e) His psychopathology, in particular his discovery that the basic causes of neuroses go back to predisposing experiences in early childhood.

FREUD'S CONTRIBUTION TO PSYCHOLOGY

In the first place he insisted on the principle of psychic determinism—namely that every mental process is causally related with previous mental processes: every mental event like every physical event follows the principle of strict causality. Every slip of the tongue, however trifling; every compulsive act, however stupid; every abnormal fear however irrational, has a cause, and this cause can be discovered. Nothing comes 'out of the blue', unless by that we mean the blue of the unconscious.

This puts psychopathology on a scientific basis: it means that we are justified in looking for a cause for every psychic event, every neurotic fear, every sex aberration, every peculiar trait of character; and if we look far enough we shall find it.

Freud's further contribution to psychology was in his investigation of 'the unconscious'. He was not by any means the first to discover the unconscious. Philosophers had found it necessary to assume unconscious mental processes in order to explain what appeared on the surface of consciousness. But while they assumed that there 'must be' such hidden processes, Freud with his open sesame of free association and dream interpretation walked right into the Aladdin's cave, and opened up to us the often unsavoury contents of the unconscious mind. It was because of this discovery that he was able to say that in the mind there is a cause for everything and set psychopathology on a scientific basis. It was, he said, from the unconscious that neuroses spring.

FREE ASSOCIATION

Freud's first method of the investigation of the deep-seated unconscious motivation of the neuroses was one already employed by Charcot, more systematically by Janet, and by Breuer and others —namely hypnosis. But Freud on his own admission was not skilled in hypnotizing. 'I could not', he said, 'succeed in bringing more than a fraction of my patients into a hypnotic state', (*Two Short Essays*, p. 46).

This lack of skill in hypnotizing is fortunate for us, for it led him to discover the more generally applicable and equally effective method of free association.

Freud was by no means the first to discover free association. The credit of this must be given to Galton who demonstrated that 'whole strata of mental operations that have lapsed out of ordinary consciousness admit of being dragged into light'. The psychologists Cattell and Wundt also experimented in it. But Freud seems to have been the first to extend its use to clinical work as a means of discovering the latent causes of neurotic symptons.

This was in some respects Freud's greatest discovery for, by a process which was accessible to everyone (which hypnosis was not), it opened up the unconscious mind, revealing the causes of neurosis in early childhood and therefore making it possible for anyone to make deductions regarding mental processes.

His discovery came about in this way. When he visited Bernheim in Nancy, the latter demonstrated the well-known fact that a patient deeply hypnotized could not recall on waking what had taken place during the trance. Nevertheless Bernheim told him that if the patient was then pressed to remember, he could be made to recall what had taken place in that dissociated state.

Freud argued that if such a restoration of memory was possible in the dissociated state of deep hypnosis, it should be possible to restore in the same way the forgotten memories in the dissociated state of hysteria, and so to discover the forgotten causes of hysteric pain and anxieties. He tried it and it succeeded: thereby the method of free association came into being.

In the use of free association Freud at first adopted Bernheim's 'pressure' method of trying to remember—an active process. He however found this 'was a laborious procedure and in the end an exhausting one'. He says that it was successful for a few cases, but afterwards it failed, the patient bringing up a lot of irrelevant material (*Two Short Essays*, p. 55).

This failure we can well understand, for as I shall mention later, the effort to remember automatically sets up a corresponding resistance to the emergence of the material, which is just what we want to avoid. Later Freud employed a more passive method in which the patient relaxed and said whatever came into his mind, whether relevant or not.

Freud then devised certain rules for free association. The patient was instructed to relate everything that came into his mind (a) however improbable, that is whether it is true or not, for many memories at first appear to be quite inconceivable and yet later prove to be true; (b) however repugnant, unpleasant or painful—for we must remember that these experiences are repressed because they are unpleasant, and their recall is bound also to be unpleasant to the patient; (c) however irrelevant—because of the principle of psychic determinism namely, that every thought in the mind is causally related with the previous thought, and is therefore relevant.

This method of free association has considerable advantages over the use of hypnosis, the main one being that it can be almost universally applied, whereas even a skilled hypnotist can hypnotize only a proportion of his patients deeply enough to revive buried complexes. Apart from that many patients object to being hypnotized, being under the false impression that there is something 'spooky' about it, an idea encouraged by some hypnotists! (See Chap. XI.)

Free association, however, has not in practice altogether displaced hypnosis, which many physicians still use as the most direct method of reviving infantile memories, in the form of hypno-analysis. Each psychotherapist must choose his method for himself.

Freud then brought forward more positive objections to hypnosis which, however, are not tenable. He objected to hypnosis as a means of investigation on these grounds. First, because he found that under hypnosis patients brought up 'memories' of assault which turned out not to be true but phantasies. This meant the hypnosis was unreliable. In the second place he maintained that hypnosis was a form of sexual 'transference' and therefore blocked the way to the deeper cause of these disorders in the Oedipus Complex (*Introd. Lectures*, p. 373). That objection, of course, depends on a certain theory of hypnosis which others of us do not accept (p. 59) The fact that we can hypnotize a crayfish or a hen does not encourage that idea.

The most cogent reason appears to come from the fact that, like Charcot, another theorist, he was bad at it. That indeed is one of the main difficulties, namely that we cannot hypnotize most patients deeply enough; but for those who can it is the most direct route to the causes of neurosis.

I used hypnosis for the first eight years of my analytic career especially in shell-shocked soldiers in the First World War, but on account of its uncertainty in civilian cases, I resorted to free association as the more certain method, and by its proper use I find little difficulty in reviving memories even to the first year of life. In many cases the patient gets into a state of complete dissociation, not distinguishable from the hypnotic state, living completely in the infantile experience, with all its feelings and emotions, terror-stricken at one moment, depressed or furious at another, as the memories are revived and the experience re-lived.

FREUD'S CONCEPT OF THE PERSONALITY

(i) *Ego instincts and sex instincts*
At first, on purely empirical grounds, Freud divided the personality into the sex instincts and ego instincts. He saw from treatment of patients that the sex instincts were repressed; and if so, they must be repressed by something. By what? So he lumped the repressing forces under the term 'Ego instincts' without defining them much further.

Later he gave point to this classification and opposed the 'pleasure' principles (erotic desires), and the 'reality' principle (the demands of life). These reality demands compel one to repress the infantile erotic instincts of the individual if he is to survive. The ego instincts are now identified with self-preservative instincts, as Freud specifically states. This modification in his views came about largely as a result of the War.

Still later he brought even the Ego instincts under the libido or sex theory, for what after all is self-preservation than self love? Thus even the war neuroses and 'shell shock' came under the libido theory.

(ii) *Conscious, Pre-conscious and Unconscious.*
Looking at the personality from another angle, already we observe that one part of the personality is repressed and so becomes unconscious. What more natural then than to divide the personality into what is conscious and what is repressed or unconscious.

'The division of the mental life into what is conscious and what is unconscious is the fundamental premise on which psycho-analysis is based' (*The Ego and the Id*, p. 9). Consider these aspects of the personality.

The conscious, as used by Freud, has a very limited function being a kind of sense organ and consisting only of what we are aware of at the present moment.

The unconscious is divisible into two parts; one of which consists of past experiences which are recoverable into consciousness at will and at any moment, and another part which is so deeply repressed that it can be recalled only by special methods such as hypnotism, free association or dream interpretation. 'We have' says Freud, 'two kinds of unconscious, that which is latent but capable of being conscious, and that which is repressed and not capable of being conscious in the ordinary way.' (Ibid, p. 12.) The former he calls the pre-conscious, the latter the unconscious; so that the personality is now divided into the conscious, the pre-conscious and the unconscious.

The pre-conscious, so far, is very similar to the 'sub-conscious' of previous psychologists, but Freud disliked the latter term because it simply implied a form of consciousness which was 'sub', not fully conscious; whereas the pre-conscious as he conceived it had more positive functions. It stands as a go-between, linking the unconscious (consisting of infantile sexual wishes) and conscious life; it acts as a censor, its function being to make acceptable to consciousness the crude infantile sexual wishes of the unconscious which are otherwise unacceptable. Some it turns back; which are thus repressed; others are modified. This accounts for instance for the symbolism in dreams; for even in dreams a man may not wish to depict himself having sex relations with his mother: so the pre-conscious transforms her into 'a queen'. The pre-conscious further makes the wishes of the unconscious more presentable by distortion. It transforms a wish to kill to a fear of killing, or to a fear of knives. The pre-conscious therefore is concerned more with reality and with the outside world than is the unconscious.

The unconscious, according to Freud, consists only of infantile sexual wishes: 'It can therefore only wish'. The infantile sexual wishes correspond to the pleasure principle and are incompatible with the reality principle. These infantile desires must, therefore, be either repressed altogether or transformed in such a way as to be compatible with everyday life. This transformation as we have seen, is the work of the pre-conscious; but the wish is still there and appears in dreams, though even then in symbolic form and in disguise.

Therefore the most direct method, according to Freud, of investigating the contents of the unconscious is by means of dreams. Dreams are the 'royal road to the unconscious'. But owing to the fact that they are disguised and symbolic they require interpretation. The task of dream interpretation is to transfer the symbols back to their real meaning which are found to lie in infantile sexual wishes.

The concept of the unconscious, as we have seen, was known to philosophers long before Freud. Kant said, for instance, 'Innumerable are the sensations and perceptions whereof we are not conscious.'

Freud went further than the philosophers. To him the unconscious was not merely something that was not conscious, but something dynamic. He showed us that the unconscious consisted of forces active in everyday life. Moreover he opened this Pandora's Box and released all the evils that were there—and, as in Pandora's Box, hope.

Philosophers object to the concept of the 'unconscious mind,' for they say that mental processes consist only of what is conscious, and therefore to speak of an unconscious conscious is a contradiction in terms.

We may suggest an explanation by an analogy. When we want to put on a gramophone record, we may say 'the music is in that cupboard'. We do not mean the actual music as such; but the potentialities of its revival. So although our experiences of the past are no longer conscious, they are in some way retained and can be reproduced.

(iii) *Id, Ego, Super-Ego*

Freud then advanced another theory as to the structure of the personality, namely that it consists of the Id, which referred to the primitive instincts before they have been modified by experiences in life: the Ego which is the self as built up by the interaction of these instincts with environmental experiences; and the Super-Ego which is the moral self, incorporated by identification, an adoption of the moral standards of others.

The Id is the most primitive part of our nature, unmodified by circumstances. It represents the instinctive passions. It is inherited and in it are stored up vestiges of the existence of countless former egos that have passed away, 'assuring them a resurrection' (*Ego and Id*, p. 52).

According to Nietzsche the Es is the impersonal part of ourselves—under its influence we not so much live as 'are lived'. It was Groddeck who introduced the idea of Id or Es into clinical psychology and held a view very similar to Nietzsche, but he told me he had given up using the term since Freud had stolen it and used it in a different sense. (Groddeck was an odd fellow! His methods were very unorthodox. He told me he treated a man with a duodenal ulcer by kneeling on his stomach. I asked what happened to the patient? 'Oh! he died', said he!).

The Ego is 'merely the part of the Id that is modified by the influence of the perceptual system'. 'It is essentially the representative of the external world or reality.' Hence the term 'ego instincts'. 'It represents what we call reason and sanity in contrast to the Id which contains the passions' (*Ego and Id*, p. 29). It stands for self-preservation, protecting a person against his own dangerous wishes of the unconscious as well as from the danger of objective life.

The Super-Ego is derived in the first place by identification with the father in the case of a boy, who wishes to take the father's place with the mother. So he takes over the father's characteristics, even his moral structures. This makes him repress his own forbidden desires particularly his incestuous desires towards his mother, for fear of castration. That forms the Oepidus Complex.

The Super-Ego thus represents the moral self. 'Whereas the Ego is essentially the representation of the external world of reality, the Super-Ego stands in relation to it as the representative of the inner world of the Id.' We have now two opposing forces confronting one another in the personality, constituting the endo-psychic conflict: the Ego or natural self and the Super-Ego or moral self. Indeed it may be said that every neurosis resolves itself into the conflict between the Ego and the Super-Ego.

Ego ideal. The terms Ego ideal and Super-Ego were at first used indiscriminately by Freud, but they have come to be distinguished, the former being employed to represent our ordinary conscious moral standards, whereas the Super-Ego is based in the unconscious. Since the Super-Ego, as Freud says, is largely derived from identification with the parent in early childhood, it has its roots in the unconscious. There is therefore not only a conscious conscience due to failure to achieve our conscious moral standards, but an unconscious conscience, which produces an unconscious source of guilt, which emerges in the obsessions.

There is here a serious inconsistency. If the Super-Ego, which is the moral self, has its roots in the unconscious, this contradicts Freud's other statement that the unconscious consists only of infantile sexual desires. There is obviously a conflict in the unconscious between the Super-Ego and the infantile wishes.

The nature of the Super-Ego, derived by identification with the parent, may have disastrous effects on the child's happiness.

If, for instance, the Super-Ego is too severe, then the child is too severe with itself, repressing natural impulses which should be used for the purposes of life. Indeed, in some obsessions the condemnation of the Super-Ego is so vicious that it will not allow the wretched patient a moment's peace. He is hag-ridden by his own conscience and spends his day in self-condemnation, performing compulsive propitiatory acts to avert the imaginary danger. Yet he is quite unaware of that of which he is guilty, or why he should perform these acts. Freud speaks of this as the 'raging Super-Ego.'

Freud regards the Ego as the repository of all anxiety.

'The Ego is a poor creature owing service to three masters and consequently menaced by three separate dangers, from the libido of the Id, from the external world, and from the severity of the Super-Ego. Three kinds of anxiety correspond to these three dangers, since anxiety is an expression of a recoil from danger. The Ego is the true abode of anxiety.'

It appears to me that Freud is here confusing two meanings of the word Ego—the Ego, in the limited sense defined above, as contrasted with the Id and Super-Ego, and Ego in the sense of 'the Self', or personality as a whole. The latter is of course the real abode of fear. Surely the moral Super-Ego can be just as much afraid of the primitive impulses of the Id, and for that matter of the Ego, or natural self, as the Ego has cause to fear the Id. So the Id can fear the punishment of the Super-Ego. Fear is not confined to the Ego in Freud's restricted use of the term. It is the Ego, in the sense of the whole personality, which fears. The important point, however, is that neurotic fear comes from within.

Freud's concept of the personality differs from Janet's and from Jung's: indeed he changed his own concept from time to time as we have seen. That does not mean that any one of them is right and the others wrong: for any classification is made to serve a purpose. Trees are classified quite differently according to whether you are a timber merchant, in which case a distinction of hard-woods or soft woods is important; or a landscape gardener in which the distinction between deciduous trees and evergreens is important; or a botanist whose concern is with genus and species. Each classification of the personality may, therefore, be correct for its own purpose.

CHAPTER XIX

FREUD'S MENTAL MECHANISMS

One of Freud's outstanding achievements was his description of mental mechanisms, which revealed to us how the mind works.

It is not that these were not known before; conflict in the form of moral conflict is one of the principle themes of ethics. Over-compensation was clearly described in Shakespeare's—'The lady doth protest too much, me thinks.' Repression is contained in the often repeated advice, 'Oh! forget it!'

But Freud gave to these mechanisms greater precision and definition.

REPRESSION

Of all these mental mechanisms undoubtedly repression is the most important. Freud himself regards it as so; for he says 'The doctrine of repression is the foundation stone on which the whole structure of psycho-analysis rests' (*Col. Works*, Vol. I, p. 267).

When he started to investigate the origin of a neurosis, he found that the patient was able to tell him a certain amount about the circumstances of the onset, but there came the point beyond which he could go no further—he could remember no more, although there was obviously more to be told. This was not mere forgetting of things that did not matter, for it was often the most crucial points which evaded return into memory. In brief, Freud found that there was a positive resistance to the recovery of such material. 'One noticed a resistance making itself evident in opposition to the work of analysis and inducing a failure to recall memories in order to frustrate it.' (*Coll. works*, Vol. I, p. 267).

It is indeed this internal active resistance to the recall of memories which is the main stumbling block in analysis, which even the conscious will and effort of the patient is helpless to overcome, and it is this which makes necessary special methods for recovering the memories, such as hypnosis, free association, and dream interpretation.

He then realized that what was causing the resistance to the recall of these experiences was the fact that they had been actively repressed. 'The same forces,' he says, 'which in the form of resistance were now offering opposition to the forgotten material being made conscious, must formerly have brought about the forgetting and must have pushed the pathogenic experiences in question out of consciousness. I gave the name "repression" to this hypothetical process' (*Two Essays*, p. 48). We have here something very different from ordinary passive forgetting:

Reason for repression. When Freud first discovered that incestuous desires were at the root of neurotic symptoms, he at the same time recognized that it was not these alone but their repression which brought about the neurotic state. What is it then that represses these desires? In the first place he said that it was fear of castration; the boy desiring incestuous relations with his mother feared the revenge of his father who was his rival. (This fear is a very natural one amongst Jewish boys, in that they suffer 'castration' in the form of circumcision at the hands of the Rabbi—a father figure). Freud says that with the girl it is the fear that she has already been castrated.

Later Freud said impulses and wishes were repressed because they were incompatible with the rest of the personality. It was not so much a fear of castration as defence against the instinctive drives of the Id. 'All these experiences', he says, 'had involved the emergence of a wishful impulse which was in sharp contrast to the patient's other wishes and which proved incompatible with the ethical and aesthetic standard of his personality.'

But there is another more formidable reason for the repression of infantile sex desires. An infant would love, like Ulysses's followers, to remain in the land of the Lotus Eaters—in the state of sensuous lethargy; but there are the demands of life to be faced, so that these sensuous pleasures must be abandoned. So Ulysses called his followers out of this state of sensuous bliss for there was work to be done, voyages to be made, hardships to be endured in the land of reality. Sexual pleasures are thus repressed by the demands of reality: repression is the result of the conflict between the 'pleasure principle' and the 'reality principle'.

Freud gives an instance of repression: a girl was in love with her brother-in-law. Her sister, the wife, died, and at the death bed the thought came to the girl, 'Now he is free to marry me!' This loathsome thought was immediately repressed and she forgot the whole experience. Here was a true repression, and resistance to its recall. It was repressed and in consequence she suffered from a neurosis.

Characteristics of repression. But we must be clear as to Freud's use of the term repression, for he uses it in a technical sense and this has given rise to a good deal of confusion and misunderstanding. The girl just mentioned illustrates all the following points.

(a) In the first place, as already indicated, repression is an active process: the forgetting associated with it is not a passive passing out of the mind of what is insignificant; it is a pushing out of the mind of what is most significant, but unpleasant and incompatible. Far from being insignificant we repress and forget some of the most important and emotionally charged experiences of our lives. We repress them because they are reprehensible, and we are careful to keep them repressed. It takes quite a lot of energy to keep them repressed and the effort to do so often results in neurosis.

(b) Nevertheless 'repression', as Freud uses it, is always an unconscious process. So completely do we repress the experience that we are not aware that we are repressing the wish or the experience, and what we repress also becomes unconscious, and dissociated. So it was with the girl whose sister died: she was later quite unaware of having had this loathsome thought.

If therefore a patient says he knows quite well what is the cause of his neurosis, we may with certainty say that that is not the whole cause; for if he were aware of the real cause he would be able to deal with it. That indeed is the function of analysis—to make him aware of what he is repressing and so adjust himself to it. The girl mentioned must needs be brought to face this fact that she had this undesirable wish.

It is obvious that repression, as an unconscious process, is quite different from processes like restraint—say of our impulses of anger. Restraint and self-control are conscious processes and acts of will. It is true that true repression may start off with a temporary phase of conscious suppression; probably the girl patient mentioned must have been momentarily horrified at the thought of taking advantage of her sister's death before deliberately pushing it out of her mind, so that the whole experience was completely repressed and forgotten. In many other cases, the repression is immediate and automatic; the conscious plays no part in it as it does in restraint and self-control.

Again, to discard is not to repress. The girl in question might have acknowledged the fact that she had such thoughts and decided not to be so beastly: in that way she discards the thought and deliberately rejects it. That is a commonplace and conscious process by which we deal with our undesirable impulses.

(c) The third and very important characteristic of repression is that repression is always by oneself. A mother may scold a child for playing with his faeces or for masturbation. In popular language that is 'repressing' the child; but that is not so in the Freudian sense, for it is neither unconscious nor by the child itself. Such a child may be defiant against the mother and do it when the mother is not looking. But if the child takes over and adopts the mother's attitude towards itself, it turns on itself, saying to itself. 'You nasty dirty little thing!'; or in an even more self-righteous attitude may make its dolls do the forbidden thing by projection—and then scolds the dolls for their filthiness, completely unaware that she is the filthy person. The moral attitude the child adopts from her mother constitutes her Super-Ego, which perpetuates the repression.

THE EFFECTS OF REPRESSION

Dissociation. The immediate effect of repression is dissociation—one part of the mind being split off from the rest. Freud adopted the idea of dissociation from Janet; but he favours the use of the word 'repression' rather than dissociation. It seems to me, however, that the two terms must be clearly distinguished. Repression is the means whereby the dissociation takes place; dissociation is the result. It is dissociation, however, the splitting off of an experience, which is the crucial factor in the development of a neurosis, as Janet always insisted. It is because of dissociation that the repressed experiences are forgotten; it is because of dissociation that the impulses contained in the complexes are beyond the control of the will.

Janet and Freud also had different views as to the cause of the dissociation. Janet's view, as we have seen, was that the dissociation in hysteria was due to psychic weakness which rendered the patients 'incapable of holding together the multiplicity of mental processes into a unity.' Freud's view, was that the dissociation was due to repression, an active and intentional although unconscious pushing away of unpleasant or unacceptable material out of the mind, so that they became split off.

Both are correct, on different occasions a severe shock such as a car accident or even a severe illness can result in a splitting off of some part of consciousness (retrograde amnesia); a repugnant thought also can lead to repression and hence to dissociation.

If I may be permitted a personal reference, I have experienced both. After a severe illness I went too soon on a tiring journey to the sea-side, and that night woke having completely forgotten where I was, why I was there, that I had been ill, and the name of my doctor. I have no doubt that dissociation was due to the lowering of my energy from fatigue. It was only after a night's sleep that my memory returned. In the other case, at the birth of my eldest son my wife was seriously ill and I had to go off to give the first of a series of lecturers at a provincial university. After the lecture I was handed a telegram and when I read it my doctor friend asked if it was news of my wife. I replied 'No! It has nothing to do with it!' Only an hour or so afterwards I took the telegram out of my pocket and read it again. 'A boy, both doing well!' I was so dreading bad news of the mother and of the child, that my mind quite unconsciously refused to take in the message of the telegram, lest it should be bad as I expected, even though the news proved to be good. Experience of that kind convinces one of the reality of repression and dissociation in the Freudian sense, but it is not to deny dissociation of the Janet type as in the first instance. It also demonstrates that the repression is an automatic and unconscious process, and by oneself.

THE COMPLEX

These elements of the mind which have been repressed and dissociated have been given the name of 'complex'. What then, is a complex? There is nothing mysterious about it. A 'complex' is simply an experience which, because of its incompatibility with the rest of the personality, is repressed and becomes dissociated from the rest of the mind. To use Freud's definition, a 'complex is a group of interdependent ideational elements charged with affect' (*Two Short Essays*, p. 58).

An important feature of a complex is therefore that since it is dissociated, we are quite unaware of its existence. Another consequence of a complex being dissociated is that it is no longer under the control of the will. 'The unconscious', says Freud, 'stands wholly outside the conscious will.' A third feature is that these complexes, being emotionally charged, are still active, and (like a naughty boy cast out of school who can do more damage outside by throwing stones, than when in school) are more out of control than when in consciousness. An obsessional compulsion to wash the hands is far more out of control than a boy's conscious annoyance at having to wash his hands! Since these dissociated contents are no longer under the control of the will, it is obvious that the old idea that we can cure our phobias and obsessions by effort of will, and by 'pulling ourselves together' is completely erroneous. To be told to do so only adds to the distress of the patient suffering from these disorders. To pull oneself together is precisely what the patient cannot do—for as Bernard Hart says, he does not know what to pull together!

These complexes then give rise to other mechanisms or forms of abnormal behaviour common to everyday life.

It is because of repression that we *over-compensate* for what we need to hide; it is because of repression of undesirable qualities in ourselves that we pin them on others by *projection*; it is because we repress such qualities in ourselves that we find excuses for our behaviour in *rationalization*. In particular it is because of repression that natural tendencies become perverted into *abnormal character traits*, and because of repression that they are turned into *neurotic symptoms*.

Over-compensation. As a result of our repressing something in ourselves which is distasteful to us, we try to hide it by going to the opposite extreme in our behaviour, and we do this in order to dissociate ourselves from it. We hide it not only from others but from ourselves. So the basically sensuous person adopts an ascetic attitude completely oblivious of his basic sensuousness, the aggressive person is ingratiating, the sexually timid or deficient person poses as being a bit of a lad. People compensate for their feeling of inferiority by being excessively hearty. Who of us when confronted with a person who is too ingratiating, to smarmy, does not immediately react with the feeling 'What is he up to?' They protest to much! Religiosity (not religion as such) is the result of a basic sense of guilt.

Yet the person who is over-compensating may be quite unaware of being so, because he is quite unaware of these propensities in himself for which he is over-compensating. The little girl with the dolls really set out to be very clean and pure.

But like the lark who flutters over the nest they reveal the very thing they would hide. Others suspect these extremes of behaviour; the 'uncoguid', as the Scots call them, are not admired for their excessive piety!

Rationalization. When we repress some characteristic in ourselves because of its unpleasantness, it may nevertheless insist on showing its face in our ordinary behaviour, and in that case needs explanation. Finding it impossible to prevent altogether these characteristics showing themselves, our only option is to put the best face on it. We do this by 'rationalization' which means ascribing to our behaviour motives more plausible than the real ones—in ordinary language 'making excuses'.

A mother had always been at loggerheads with her son. In adult life her son would never receive a gift from her: he said in refusing, 'Oh, No! You are too generous! I couldn't take it from you!' His real reason: 'I'm not going to be beholden to *you!*'

Projection. We go a step further when we are so blind to our own faults that we ascribe them to others whom we condemn for what is unconsciously in ourselves. It is a general principle that we hate most in others what is in ourselves. The girl said that it was her dolls who were so filthy.

I once mentioned this principle to a lady who replied 'that cannot be true, because I simply hate snobs!' After a moment's pause she said, 'You don't think I am a snob, do you?' I replied, 'I don't know, I hardly know you!' With that she went, but on her return visit the first thing she said was, 'You were quite right,

I am a snob!' She had been quite unaware of it in herself and had indignantly rejected the idea: so she had projected it on to others. As she hated and repressed it in herself, so she hated it in others. We can see how misunderstandings and false judgements can arise in our estimates of others, when we charge them with our own faults—but faults which we are unaware of in ourselves.

A modification of such projection is commonly exemplified in a patient who, in describing his actions, will say, 'You would say it is my conceit,' or 'You would say it serves me right,' when you are thinking no such thing. It is he who is accusing himself of conceit and who thinks it serves him right! But he dislikes self-condemnation, so projects the accusation on to you.

Such projections, like over-compensation, are usually over-done. A child may be brought up to be honest and so to love honesty in herself by identification with his honest parents. That is normal. Such a person does not get worked up about it. But take the man who says emphatically, 'There is one thing above all others that I can't stand, and that is dishonesty!' Such a man might have suffered from some grievous act of dishonesty against himself and so becomes over-sensitive to it. On the other hand he may have himself been dishonest and repressed it so that, hating it (unconsciously) in himself, he is always on the alert for it in others and may see it where it does not exist. Moreover, projecting his own dishonesty on to others, he must exaggerate his hate to hide the fact that it is in himself.

Introjection is the opposite of projection: it is taking another's personality into oneself. Some people suffer every now and then from hearing 'voices' saying, 'You silly fool', 'you conceited ass' or even, 'you are a murderer!' In some cases such people are insane, but in many cases these voices come from complexes. (The insane think the voices are real, objective: the neurotic patient knows they are not, but he is harassed by them). These condemning voices originally came from the mother or other persons, and they were incorporated so that the child condemned itself for these things. That is introjection. But it is a very unpleasant experience always to be condemning oneself; so the child in turn projects them, in which case they appear to come from without—so that the patient feels that people passing in the street are saying 'What a wicked woman!' The condemnation started from without, becomes a condemnation of herself, but because she rejects the condemnation, she projects it on to others, so that it once more seems to come from without.

Identification. Projection and introjection are both forms of a broader principle of identification; but in identification there is a more complete taking over, not of one characteristic only, but of the whole personality, to such an extent that for the time being one is that personality. The boy who hero-worships in imagination, so completely takes over the qualities of adventure or chivalry, or it may be of brutality, from his hero, that he feels himself to be that hero. It is from such identification that we develop our moral standards.

Freud's explanation of identification is that the boy identifies himself with his father, whose place he wishes to take in order to possess the mother, towards whom he has incestuous desires. That in itself creates a conflict, because the child is attempting to identify himself with the father who is at the same time his rival and who threatens him. That theory is too limited a view. Identification is a phase of ordinary life serving very important biological functions. It is a phase of maturation observed in most children about the age of three or four. When the boy plays, 'I'm the baker man!' 'I'm the postman!' or the girl says, 'I'm Mummy doing the washing up', this is in response to a biological urge of the greatest service in adaptation to life. There is nothing sexual about a boy's identification with the postman, even as a father substitute. It is a natural propensity of value for living. For by taking over the activities and attitudes of the adult the child is learning those skills which will enable him to meet the demands of life. For the moment, therefore, the child is not imitating the baker or driver; he *is* the baker and driver! Indeed, for the moment he is more the person with whom he is identified than he is himself. Identification is therefore the basis of sympathy, fellow-feeling for others, and therefore of value for social life. (See my *Childhood and Adolescence*, Pengiun, p. 125). It is also largely the source of altruism. We sympathize with others, and do things for them because we 'put ourselves in their place'. But that is going beyond Freud. I have dealt with that concept in *Psychology and Morals* (p. 114).

Displacement. Feelings and emotions which are aroused by one object, are commonly transferred to other subjects, usually of a similar nature. This Freud calls 'the displacement of affect'.

A story is told of the businessman whose wife burnt the bacon for breakfast. He did not want to have a row with his wife so he bottled up his resentment, but at his office he let it off on his chief clerk whom he told off for some trifling error. The clerk could not answer back because he did not want to lose his job, so he kept quiet with the boss, but let it off on the office boy who was too scared to reply. But in the evening the office boy had a row with his girl friend, who was so upset that she gave notice to her employer, who was the wife who had that morning burnt the bacon. A series of displacements of affect.

In each case there was the suppression of emotion towards one person and its displacement on to some other person. In analysis we often meet with cases of this sort. A man has a mother complex, he marries a wife and is supremely happy. But later when she has children and becomes a 'mother', it is found that he lets off on to her all the repressed feelings of resentment that he had felt towards his mother, and which have little or no relation to his wife at all. Meanwhile the suffering wife cannot understand what has come over him, nor can he!

Neurotic symptoms are commonly of this type. A man has a suffocation at birth, a terrifying experience which he represses. But though the original cause is forgotten, the emotion of fear survives and he transfers his fear on to travelling in underground trains, upon which his fear is now displaced. Sex impulses frustrated from their natural expression are displaced on to abnormal objects like fetichisms or persons, as in homosexuality.

A man says that he blushes because of a fear that he will blush, and so it appears. Analyze it out and we find that the blushing was originally due to some humiliating experience. He repressed the whole experience and so displaces the feelings of humiliation on to the blushing itself as though it is the cause of his distress and humiliation. It relieves him of having to face up to the original humiliation; which however, he does in analysis and is thereby cured.

The need to cleanse the soul of an unconscious guilt is displaced on to the need to wash the hands fifty times a day. The fear of an explosion of one's repressed forbidden desires transfers itself on to a fear of a gas explosion, so that the patient is compelled to see that the gas fire is turned off over and over again, even to getting out of bed at midnight to do so. I have found in analysis that all sexual fetichisms such as corsets or shoes are breast substitutes (*Psychology and Mental Health*, pp. 337–376). The breast is forbidden in infancy, but its substitute is not, so the pleasure is transferred to the substitute.

Transference. A specific form of displacement is that of transference, which Freud again uses in a technical sense, and which he reserves for the situation in analysis in which emotions and feelings which belonged to the parents in infantile life are transferred and felt towards the analyst. For the time being the patient may really think that such feelings belong to the analyst. It may be a love transference in which sex feelings are transferred from parents to analyst, so that the patient considers the analyst the most wonderful person in the world (a belief which the very young analyst is apt not to dispute!). That is a 'positive' transference. Or there may be a 'negative' transference in which the patient transfers feelings of hate or anger or contempt towards the analyst, whom he accuses of being cruel, telling lies, being cynical, lacking sympathy, or of hating the patient himself—all of which are found to be reproductions of the repressed feelings he had towards his parents. Sometimes the patient realizes that the accusations are absurd; at other times he really believes them to be true of the analyst, which greatly complicates the treatment.

Transference is defined as the displacement of affect or feeling towards a person (namely the analyst) to whom it does not properly belong. Freud says, 'The patient directs a degree of affection (mingled often enough with hostility), which is based on no real relation between them and which can only be traced back to old phantasies of the patient which have become memories.' (*Two Short Essays*, p. 85–6.)

Freud came about this discovery in this way. One woman patient suddenly flung her arms round his neck. Instead of simply giving expression to the German equivalent of 'Tut! Tut!', he asked himself why she did so. He was apparantly too modest to assume that she had fallen in love with him, but concluded that she was transferring to him feelings and emotions which belonged to her father in childhood.

Transference, according to Freud, appears in every neurotic who comes under treatment. It is inevitable, he says, in every analysis, 'in its crude sexual or affectionate or hostile form' (*Coll. Works*, Vol. I, p. 293).

But Freud knew from long personal experience how to make use of adversity and how to turn an evil into good. He realized that this transference of emotions to the analyst was an effective way of releasing the repressed emotions relating to the parents. He therefore found that by encouraging the patient to release these repressed emotions to the analyst, he opened the gateway to the patient realizing that these feelings did not really belong to the analyst, but were basically related to his parents in childhood, and so the complex could be resolved.

Thus psychoanalysis was defined as 'overcoming the resistance by means of the transference'. This became a regular procedure. Indeed Ernest Jones states that resistance and transference are 'the essential features of psychoanalytic theory and practice'.

Nevertheless treatment by transference is fraught with difficulties, even on Freud's showing.

In the first place as Freud said, transference is itself a neurosis, a displacement of affect projected on to the analyst, which then needs to be resolved. This is by no means easy: for the transferences may get fixed on to the analyst and refuse to be referred back. Furthermore, it obstructs treatment. If it is a negative tranference of hate, the patient loses confidence in the analyst, will refuse to co-operate and spends his time abusing the analyst, or wallowing in self-pity. But it is little better if it is a positive transference, for if the patient 'loves' the analyst and wants his love, she will be reluctant to reveal unpleasant characteristics about herself.

There is a further complication. Freud said that the reason why the patient transfers his feelings of love or hate to the analyst, is to avoid facing up to the fact that he has incestuous desires towards his mother and to the corresponding hate towards his father. Thus transference is a method the patient adopts *to avoid going back to unpleasant early experiences*, by transferring the feelings to the doctor (See Freud's *Dynamics of the Transference*, *Collected papers*, Vol. 2, p. 312).

On the face of it, therefore, it would not look as if the transferences were a very good method of overcoming the resistances, for it is itself a form of resistence. Such resistance is well illustrated in a patient of mine who said to me, 'Every time you try to make me go back to that horrible experience in childhood, I bring it back to the present and want to attack you.' It is obvious therefore that transference side-tracks the issue. Transference is also not without its dangers. For when the patients transference becomes fixed on to the analyst and refuses to budge, the patient is left uncured.

In view of all these complications it is strange that the psychoanalysts still employ this cumbersome and round-about method instead of going directly to the source of the disorder—a method which Freud originally used and which I have consistently used as Direct Reductive analysis. (Chap. **XXVII**). Treatment by means of the transference was worth trying, but in fact both complicates and prolongs analysis.

Regression. When the libido cannot find outlet it tends to regress. Regression is a return to infantile life. According to Freud the sexual libido may meet with such rebuffs that it turns back to the pleasures of infantile sexuality (*Two Essays*, p. 81 and 85–86). I would prefer to say 'to the security of infantile life'.

One such case of mine was that of an Australian soldier who found the war too much for him and so regressed to being a child between one or two years of age, babbling without speaking, taking slops for food and being cared for quite happily. Another was a businessman, an air raid warden who returned to the age of thirteen, an age free from all responsibility. The tea planter with the fugue state was another case, (p. 56). They all found refuge in regression to childhood.

I have at the moment a patient of twenty-six who intellectually is up to standard, and in fact teaches small children; but emotionally her behaviour is that of a child of three or four; she speaks to people, and so they speak to her, as a small child. She was perfectly normal until she met with two terrifying experiences: an air raid (at the age of 6) in which she was shut up in a cupboard under the stair, followed by measles and then by whooping cough so severe that she was unconscious and was expected to die: it left her chest sunk in. Life was too much for her; she regressed and remained emotionally in childhood.

None of these cases had anything to do with sex: they all had to do with insecurity and a fear of life which they found too much for them. An infant's clinging to the mother is for security as well as for pleasure, but the former is the deeper biological urge.

Endo-psychic conflict. This is one of the most important discoveries of Freud. Every neurosis is the result of endo-psychic conflict. What does that mean? A child is constantly subjected to conflict with the outside world, with its environment, including the parents. But the conflict becomes internal when the child, either through identification or fear or both, takes over the parents' moral attitudes into itself. At that moment there is set up a duality in the child's personality: there is the Ego or natural self: opposed to this is the Super-Ego, or moral self, super-imposed on to the natural self and often repressing it. The conflict is no longer between the self and the environment, but between the self and the self. This is the essential conflict in every neurosis. It is the house that is divided against itself that cannot stand.

That is clear in the case of the girl who found pleasure in the death of her sister (p. 132), since it gave her the chance to marry her brother-in-law. Her moral self came into play and condemned her for having such desires. A duality was formed in her personality— the natural Ego and the condemning Super-Ego, it was an endo-psychic conflict.

Compromise. Every neurotic symptom is a compromise between the forbidden impulse and the repressing forces. The young man who refused the gift from his mother satisfied his own wish to have nothing to do with her, but at the same time his dutifulness as a loving son in being so considerate for his mother's welfare. The girl playing dirty games with dolls satisfies her shocked moral sense in rebuking them, but in playing these dirty games (for it was she not the dolls) she unconsciously gratified those desires in herself. In every case of neurosis the compromise is between two conflicting forces both of which are repressed.

SYMPTON FORMATION

Neurotic symptons according to Freud, are the emergence of repressed libidinous or aggressive wishes in distorted form. Although libidinous desires of childhood are repressed they are emotionally charged and therefore still active—'the repressed wishful impulses continue to exist in the unconscious' (*Two Essays*, p. 52). They await an opportunity to express themselves, and emerge when they are aroused and provoked by outward conditions, or when the repression begins to weaken.

The way in which this conflict can produce neurotic symptoms is illustrated by Freud as follows. A girl has incestuous desires towards her father. She therefore identifies herself with her mother. At the same time she wants to rid herself of her mother and to possess the father. But these wishes fill her with a sense of guilt. Her mother then develops a cough whereupon the girl develops a cough. This is partly identification, but it is also expressive of her guilt, a self-punishment for her forbidden desires. It is as though her Super-Ego says, 'You wanted to be your mother! Very well you shall—and suffer the pain she suffers.'

Alternatively, her sense of guilt for her incestuous desires towards her father may make her over-solicitous towards the mother, over-anxious about her mother's health, which is part guilt, but part wish that the mother should be ill.

Wish fulfilment. The hysteric pain may also be a means of gratifying a masochistic pleasure (the sexual pleasure in having pain inflicted on one). 'We see', says Freud, 'that human beings fall ill when, as a result of external obstacles or of internal lack of adaptation, their satisfaction of their neurotic needs in reality is frustrated. We see that they take flight into illness in order that, by its help, they may find a satisfaction to take the place of what has been frustrated. (*Two Short Essays*, p. 80). 'The symptom', says Freud, 'is fundamentally a wish fulfilment—it is moreover an *erotic* wish fulfilment' (*Introductory Lectures*, p. 252).

In other cases the moral Super-Ego plays the dominant role in the symptom. This takes place particularly in the propitiatory obsessions, in which the patient is compelled to wash his hands, see that the gas is turned off, that the front door is locked and to perform other rituals fifty times a day. This is to propitiate for his sins—although he has no idea what those sins are. The repressed libidinous desires may also emerge as obsessional anxieties, and every time the forbidden impulse begins to emerge the patient is thrown into a state of fear. Obsessional anxiety is the fear of the consequence of our forbidden desires. The purpose of the symptom serves both purposes. It is 'either a sexual gratification or a defence against it. In hysteria it is mainly the former; to obsessions mainly the latter.'

When Freud says that the symptom is always wished, that is not to be taken to mean that the patient wishes to have a headache, or to be paralyzed, or to be persistently going to see if the front door is locked or to tidy his desk. It would be more accurate to say that the symptom represents a wish, for it may be a wish in disguised form, or even a punishment for having the wish. But there is always a wish behind every symptom.

The simplest case is that of the soldier who develops a hysterical paralysis: this satisfies his fear by getting out of the battle, but saves his face by telling himself that of course he cannot be expected to fight when he is paralyzed. The paralysis solves his immediate problem but at the expense of being paralyzed. That is the significance of a neurotic symptom.

The wish is always unconscious and repressed. It is useless to tell a patient that her headache is self-punishment for guilt; she will reply: 'What have I to feel guilty about?' Or she may put this feeling of guilt on to something quite irrelevant. In one case a man who belonged to the religious sect of the Brethren came to me because of the distress that he sometimes played tennis with unbelievers, which was to them a sin. His real sin was that he was having an affair with a girl. This ruse is adopted because it is less distressing than the real cause of guilt. Besides that, if he faced up to the true motive of the guilty, he would have to abandon his sin. It is no use using either persuasion, suggestion or conditioned reflexes to cure this guilt of playing tennis with unbelievers, or trying to persuade him that after all that is not so terrible a sin, for that is not really the point of issue at all. The real cause of guilt we have to discover in analysis, and then, only then, can we resolve the problem.

Sublimation, according to Freud, is the transference of repressed sexual feelings to higher social uses. In some cases the unfulfilled sexual instincts can be directed towards creative and especially artistic activities. (*Two Essays*, p. 81, 82). He says, 'If a person who is at loggerheads with reality possesses an *artistic gift* . . . he can transfer his phantasies into artistic creations instead of into symptoms and by this roundabout path regain his contact with reality.' (*Ibid*. p. 81 and 85, 86). 'The energy of the infantile wishful impulses is not cut off but remains ready for use. By this means such patients avoid neuroses.' That is true, but it is a poor look-out for those who are without the artistic gift! McDougall's concept of the re-direction of the basic instincts is far more comprehensive and of greater practical value (p. 116).

Freud's description of mental mechanisms I have found most valuable in the understanding of patients and of people in general. His discovery of free association I have used more consistently than the Freudians themselves and have found it of the greatest value in the investigation and treatment of patients. Unfortunately I cannot say the same of the psychopathology and theory of the libido as the cause of all neuroses. Not only are these views too speculative, but by the strict use of his method of free association I do not find his theories as to the origin of neuroses confirmed, and have in fact come to very different conclusions as to the basic causes of neuroses, views which I shall describe later under the term 'Direct reductive analysis.'

CHAPTER XX

FREUD'S PSYCHOPATHOLOGY

(i) *Historical*

Freud was a neurologist in Vienna and did some research work of value in that department of science. But his attention was turned to the more human aspect of the study of man. So he went to Paris to study under Charcot, another neurologist, who was doing experimental work with hypnosis in 1885. Under Charcot, Pierre Janet also worked, but was doing far more radical work in the exploration of the origins of neurotic disorders than Charcot himself.

It was from Charcot's experiments that Freud was convinced of the psychogenetic nature of hysterical disorders and went back to Vienna 'agog with these revelations'.

When Freud returned to Vienna, he found that Breuer had been working with hypnosis on similar lines. The original case, which started off psychoanalysis, was that of Anne O. treated by Breuer. 'On one occasion', says Jones, 'she related the details of her first experience of a particular symptom and to Breuer's great astonishment this resulted in its complete disappearance'. Breuer referred to it as 'the talking cure'. (Jones' *Life of Freud*, Vol. 1, p. 222–4).

Later he cured a girl of hysteria which took the form of rigid paralysis, loss of sensation, and disturbance of vision, by putting the girl into a state of mild hypnosis and procuring a revival of the circumstances which caused the neurosis. He then gave the process the name of 'abreaction' (*Studies on Hysteria*, 1895). This led to a most important discovery; which in principle was that when the patient revived and re-lived the original experience, she was cured of her symptoms.

Freud at that time gave Breuer credit for originating psycho-analysis. 'It is a merit to have brought psycho-analysis into being: that merit is not mine. I had no share in its earliest beginnings.' (*Col. Wks.*, Vol. 1, p. 269). Later, however, he changed his methods and his theories so radically that he assumed the entire responsibility for originating psycho-analysis.

We may at this point digress for a moment to refer to a controversy which has arisen as to the relation between Janet and Freud. Janet claims that Breuer and Freud took over many of his ideas and gave them different names. 'They spoke of psycho-analysis where I spoke of psychological analysis'—and so on. (*Psychological Healing*, p. 600.)

Ernest Jones on the other hand is at great pains to show that Freud was in no way indebted to Janet, and indeed states that Janet had not yet come from Le Havre to Paris when Freud was there (Jones, *Freud*, p. 211, 255). And Freud in a private letter to E. A.

Bennet (published in the *B.M.J.* of Jan. 2, 1965) disclaims that he knew Janet when he joined Charcot in 1885–6: 'I never heard his (Janet's) name mentioned and have neither seen him nor spoken to him since'. Unfortunately Freud seems to have forgotten what he had previously stated in public in America. He then paid tribute to Janet in the following words. 'It was his (Charcot's) pupil Pierre Janet who first accepted a deeper approach to the peculiar psychical processes present in hysteria, and we followed his example when we took the splitting of the mind and dissociation of the personality as the centre of our position.' (*Two Short Essays on Psychoanalysis*, p. 44.) That certainly seems to give priority to Janet. As for publication; Janet published his first cases, including that of Marie, mentioned on page 52 in 1889; whereas Breuer and Freud's *Studies in Hysteria* did not appear till 1893–5. Freud (*Introductory Lectures*, p. 218) admits this: 'It is true that Janet independently reached the same result; indeed priority in publication must be granted to the French investigator.' Freud's statement that Janet was the first to make the 'deeper approach' to the processes in hysteria, and Janet's priority in publication should decide that controversy. For him to say that he had never heard of Janet was obviously a lapse of memory, to which Freud was subject on several occasions, as Jones has shown.

It looks as if both Breuer and Janet came to their conclusions independently, since hypnotism was very much the vogue at the time and even the mesmerists had discovered that forgotten memories were spontaneously produced in the mesmeric state, though they did not realize that it was the revival of these memories which cured the patient.

Indeed the cures that the mesmerists obtained probably often resulted from the 'hysterical crisis' with outbursts of emotion, which was precisely what Breuer and Freud discovered and called 'abreaction'. Unfortunately for them they put the cures down to the 'mesmeric' fluid and were just out of luck that they did not hit on the right explanation that in these cases the cure came about by the release of repressed emotion.

There can be little doubt that these experiments of Breuer and Janet with hypnosis opened up a prospect of cure for the neurotic patient which was never before possible—and radical cure at that, surpassing treatment by suggestion, which dealt mainly with symptoms and not with causes. Freud developed these discoveries of Breuer and has received most of the credit. (One of his small grandsons who stayed with me in the country stated that: 'Someday I am going to be a great jockey and make the name of Freud famous!')

Freud's theories advanced in definite phases.

(ii) *The Traumatic Theory*

This release of pent-up emotion was a sort of purging of the soul to which was given the name of 'catharsis'. Flügel points out that Aristotle also taught that tragedy produces a healthful purging by intense arousal of the emotions of pity and pleasure. The old-time working man got his catharsis by letting off his bottled-up anger, amorous feelings and pathos by getting drunk on Friday night.

These conclusions as to the abolition of hysteric symptoms were described by Breuer and Freud in their *Studies in Hysteria*, a book in which they discovered the mechanism of conflict and repression. It is still very well worth reading.

The conclusions they drew from the treatment of their patients may be summarized as follows:

(a) Hysteric symptoms—paralysis, anaesthesia, fits, &c., are traceable to traumatic events, shocks of some kind.

(b) In such cases it is not the physical injury that is of consequence, but the emotional shock of the experience, the psychic trauma—a view that Charcot had previously insisted upon.

(c) In every case these emotional experiences became repressed, bottled up with 'strangulated affect'.

(d) Conflict. The reason why they were bottled up was that they were 'incompatible with the rest of the personality—either because they were painful, or because they were opposed to moral demands. 'It is an indispensible condition for the acquisition of hysteria that there should arise a relation of incompatibility between the Ego and some of its approaching presentations'.

(e) The result of this conflict is that 'the Ego thrusts out the incompatible element, and crowds it into the unconscious', in fact represses it. The *motive* for the repression then is the *defence of the ego* against its incompatible elements.

(f) The result of this repression is that the experience is split off, dissociated from the rest of the mind and becomes forgotten.

(g) The splitting of consciousness in such cases is thus a desired and intentional one.

Forgetting, therefore, according to Freud, is an active process—we forget because we wish to forget, because we *don't want to remember*.

(h) But though this exclusion from consciousness is an intentional process it is not necessarily a conscious process. Repression as we have seen (p. 133), is an unconscious process and the material that is repressed remains unconscious.

(h) The symptoms spring from the repressed emotional experiences. The emotion denied normal outlet because of resistance emerges into consciousness in a substitute form.

(i) The mental state is turned into a physical symptom. If a patient suffers from self-pity, and this self-pity is repressed, it may emerge as a pain in the back. This is the process of 'conversion' and Freud calls such conditions 'conversion hysteria'. Anxiety if repressed may emerge as nervous indigestion or headache. These he called 'Anxiety equivalents', the bodily manifestations of anxiety. They now go under the name of 'Psychosomatic disorders' (p. 285).

(j) 'The hysteric', Freud says in a most pungent statement, 'suffers from reminiscences'. The repressed experience refuses to be silenced; when, therefore, it appears in consciousness, it revives part of the original experience. The symptom is often in fact a revival of part of the original trauma. A claustrophobia may be a reproduction of the suffocation at birth.

(k) It would however be a mistake to think that the neurosis is derived from one experience only. The symptom, Freud said, was always 'over-determined'; many factors go to its development. In particular, what many people regarded as the cause may only be the 'precipitating cause'; there are always factors relating to early childhood which were the 'pre-disposing causes'.

(l) Every hysterical symptom is the expression of a repressed wish; not that the patient wishes to have a hysterical pain in the back, but this pain represents a wish, perhaps a self punishment for a forbidden wish, or in the obsessions, an attempt to propitiate for a forbidden wish.

(m) Therapeutic results. 'The hysteric symptoms immediately disappeared without returning if we succeeded in awakening the memories of the causal process with its accompanying affect'. That occurred in the case of Anna O. to Breuer's surprise.

(n) But the revival of the original experience must be accompanied by an emotional 'affective' response, 'Affectless memories are almost utterly useless'. That answers the criticism often made: 'How does knowing the cause cure?' Freud's answer is that it does not: there has to be a revival of the original emotional reaction; the experience must be re-lived with hallucinatory vividness.

This need for an emotional response, so strongly urged by Freud, is in contrast to those who practice persuasion, with its appeal to the reason only; and also to those who rely upon the interpretive method of explaining to the patient what is the cause of the trouble. I have had patients who have had a psycho-analysis and been persuaded that they had an incestuous desire towards the mother—and say, 'So what! I've still got my headache.' The repressed emotion has to be felt if it is to be released.

(o) The revived experience must also be 'talked out'—that is to say it must be re-associated with the rest of the mind and a re-adjustment effected. In this way the dissociation is resolved.

(p) A picture which does not disappear requires further consideration; a thought which cannot be abolished must be followed further. A recrudescence never occurs if it has been properly adjusted.

It is of course possible for a symptom to disappear without our getting to the cause (as for instance by hypnotic suggestion); on the other hand if any of the symptom remains, it always means that we have not yet discovered the full cause, or all the causes, and the case requires further investigation. A patient is not cured as long as he has symptoms. (See p. 232.)

All this was the original 'traumatic' theory of hysteria as described by Breuer and Freud. In their *Studies on Hysteria* were laid down the basic principle both of the causation and cure of hysterical symptoms. All these points are sound common sense. Not so his further theories.

(iii) *Sexual traumata*

Freud then discovered that the traumatic experiences which gave rise to hysteric symptoms were always of a sexual nature. 'The cause of the life-long hysterical neurosis lies in the sexual experiences of early childhood.' Again, 'In all the cases that I have analyzed, it was the sexual life that has furnished a painful affect of precisely the same character as the one attached to the obsession.' Thus 'Hysteria is an expression of a special behaviour of the sexual functions of the individual.' 'Traumatic hysterias reduce themselves to *sexual traumata of childhood*.' 'In a normal sexual life, no neurosis is possible.'

These sexual seductions usually took place at the hands of parents, servants, governesses, and older brothers and sisters. (Freud himself regarded his father as having sexually assaulted him, but later abandoned the idea.) Moreover, the effective assaults were always in early childhood before puberty. If a later assault appears to have caused the symptom, it was because it aroused an earlier experience. 'The repression of the memory of a painful sex experience of maturer years can take place only in persons in whom these experiences can bring into activity the memory remnants of infantile trauma.'

Breuer could not agree with Freud's sexual theory: therefore they parted. That left Freud free to pursue his libido theory further.

So far all is straightforward, though somewhat dogmatic. But it is what Freud found in his patients.

It is therefore somewhat startling to find Freud completely abandoning this theory and de-bunking these supposed 'memories' of sex assaults as mainly phantasies. How he discovered that these memories were not true is not quite clear, but the decisive factor seems to have come from his own self-analysis; also he could not believe that his own father seduced him. (Jones, *Freud*, p. 266).

Why, then, did the patients bring up these 'memories' of sex assaults if they were not true? He says, 'I have since learned to explain away many a seductive fancy as an attempt at defence against their own sexual activities—that is to say they accuse others in order to excuse themselves, for instance for their own masturbation or other erotic practices.

A further problem presents itself: we naturally ask, 'If these images of sex assaults were not true but phantasies, how could the recovery of such fictitious 'memories' produce such good results, on his own showing?' As far as I know that question remains unanswered. How can pure imaginations cure?

This discovery, however, of the fictitious nature of the sex assaults gave rise to two striking changes in Freud's teaching, one theoretical, one practical.

(iv) *Infantilism of sexuality*

If these stories of sex assaults were fictitious, why do they appear at all? If they are not facts, it must have been that the patients wished them to be true.

Freud, therefore, abandoned the theory of sexual traumata and substituted the theory of infantilism of sexuality, namely the fact that the small child is capable of sexual practices and sexual wishes. The traumatic theory gives place to the wish theory.

He then discovered that these wishes were of a specific nature, namely incestuous desires towards the opposite parent. However, he points out, it was not these wishes alone which caused the trouble, but their repression, by fear of castration.

This led to the formation of a complex, the Oedipus Complex, which now became the basic factor, the 'nuclear complex', in the production of neurotic disorders. Ernest Jones regards Freud's theory of infantile sexuality together with his dream psychology as Freud's two highest achievements (Jones, *Freud*, p. 267).

(v) *Oedipus Complex*

The name comes from Sophocles story of Oedipus who unknowingly killed his father, King Laus, and married his mother not knowing she was his mother. The unconscious element in this procedure is important, pointing to the fact that the incestuous desires are unconscious.

The corresponding complex in the girl came to be called the Electra complex, a bad term which Freud disliked. A far better term would have been 'Antigone complex', for Oedipus's daughter devotedly accompanied her father in exile and through all his sufferings.

The girl has incestuous desires towards the father and hates the mother; but in this case the fear is that she has been castrated by way of punishment, since she lacks the genital organs of the brother.

It must be borne in mind that when Freud used the word incest he used it in the full sense of the word—as the desire of the child for sexual intercourse with the parent; in one place he uses the term 'sexual intercourse' in referring to this desire.

But the question which so often puzzled many of us for so many years was, first, how did Freud come by this theory of the incestuous origin of neurotic disorders? From what evidence did he draw his conclusions?

It cannot have been from the revival and recollection of his patient's experiences, for he had already debunked such memories as mainly phantasies. If the recollections of infantile sexual assaults, (which, being objective experiences, can often be confirmed or otherwise), are fictitious, what reliance can we place on the recollection of infantile incestuous wishes which being subjective, are far less open to verification?

There are some who maintained that Freud's incestuous theory can be upheld on the grounds that it has proved to be a most valuable hypothesis. The use of hypothesis is indeed a justifiable procedure employed in many sciences. But having adopted the hypothesis, the scientist sets about confirming it, or otherwise, by objective verification. That is just what the psycho-analysts as a body have not done, as far as I know.

Bowlby, however, himself a Freudian child psychologist, has made a valuable objective study of child psychology but came to conclusions very different from the Freudian School, as contained in his book with Margery Fry, *Child Care and the Growth of Love* (Penguin).

Did Freud arrive at his theories by intuition, a stroke of genius? Many scientific discoveries are made in this way. For many things are true which are not yet scientifically proved; and Freud's views may be amongst them. But Ernest Jones makes it clear that Freud's discoveries were definitely not a flash of intuition, but by 'slow hard work' (Jones, *Freud*, p. 243). What then was this 'hard work?' It was his own self-analysis.

The true answer as to how Freud came by these views has now been revealed by the discovery of Freud's letters to his friend Fliess, to whom he unburdened his mind and soul. Jones regarded such a revelation as 'extraordinary in the highest degree'. How these letters which Freud wished destroyed (he destroyed Fliess's letter to him), came to be preserved is almost miraculous, the whole intriguing story of which is given in Ernest Jones's *Freud*, Chapter 13.

From these letters it is clear that Freud derived his incest-uous theory mainly from his analysis of the cause of his own neurosis.

He himself had two specific neurotic symptoms, fainting attacks, and fear of travelling (separation anxiety). These appear to relate back to the birth of his brother of whom he was jealous and whose death he wished, and who did die, giving Freud a sense of guilt (Jones, *Freud*, p.14). This accounted for the fainting attacks. His dread of being separated from his mother owing to the arrival of his brother gave him his separation anxiety and fear of travelling.

Freud had fainting attacks on several occasions. One was when at a conference at Munich he had to chide Jung for publishing articles on psycho-analysis without mentioning Freud (ibid., p. 317). Another occasion was when Fliess was breaking off from him. Thirdly, I am told, was when Freud was travelling to America with Jung, and someone at a dinner proposing a toast to Jung stated that in his opinion Jung would supersede Freud. Freud fainted and was 'carried out in the strong arms of Jung'! It is easy to see how in each of these cases there was the same threat to his security as there was from the birth of his brother.

As a result of his self-analysis he thus discovered his symptoms related to his incestuous desires towards his mother. He also recognized that he had, as a parent, incestuous desires towards his own eldest daughter. It was an act of great courage for him to admit these things. He went further: 'He discovered in himself the passion for his own mother and jealousy of his father; he felt sure that this was a general human characteristic' (ibid., Vol. I, p. 326).

That of course was a natural assumption. What is true of one may be true of the lot. Having made this momentous discovery regarding the cause of his own neurosis, it would be more than human if he did not look for confirmation of his theory in his patients. But it is nothing more than an assumption; for what is true of one is by no means necessarily true of the rest.

Freud then proceeded to apply this assumption in treatment; for he then read this explanation into the psychology of his patients, ascribing their neurosis to the same cause as he found in himself. Indeed Fliess, his most intimate friend, accuses him of that very thing—that 'he read his own thoughts into his patients, (ibid., Vol. I, p. 314). This evidence of Jones and Fliess may be taken as absolutely authoritative since they were Freud's two closest profes-sional friends and knew him if anybody did.

It is said that Freud confirmed his theory from his patients. That is not difficult if you first read your interpretation into the patient! Is it surprising to find that Freud himself could not find his theory substantiated in some of the cases, and he was honest enough to say so, although he naively says that he found this 'uncanny'!

So why go for evidence beyond Freud himself, for we have direct evidence from his own letters. He says, 'I find it uncanny when I can't understand someone in terms of myself.' This clearly reveals his method, namely projecting his psychology into his patients, and interpreting their behaviour in terms of his own experience and analysis.

Having discovered, as he thought, the seat of the neuroses to lie in the incestuous desires towards the parent of the opposite sex, it is not surprising that he should apply this to the treatment of his patients, and interpret their symptoms and dreams in terms of that theory. That is what we may call *the interpretive method*, as against the direct reductive method. The interpretive method is well illustrated in this instance: a woman patient dreamt that 'her father walked towards her'. This dream was interpreted to her by the psycho-analyst as a desire for her father to seduce her. It may be and will be if that is the only reason for a father coming towards a daughter. But this is open to some doubt. Such a patient, especially under the influence of a positive transference, is quite ready to accept such an interpretation, whether true or not. Such suggestibility under transference invalidates this interpretive method.

Freud recognizes the difficulty and danger. He says, 'There is no difficulty in making him (the patient) a disciple of any particular theory and thus making it possible for him to share a mistaken belief' (ibid. p. 378); but, he says, it is impossible to put into the patient's mind a sexual experience. But what of those sex traumata he originally discovered, and then found to be false?

To adopt such a theory, interpret the symptom and the dream in terms of that theory and then to claim that the interpretation confirms the theory, is of course to argue in a circle.

It is one thing to adopt a proposition as an hypothesis and then proceed to get objective verification of that proposition; and quite another thing to start off with a theory, read it into the patient's mind, proceed to explain the patient's symptoms and dreams in terms of that theory and then take that to be proof of the theory!

Freud here commits the 'psychologist's fallacy', which is to ascribe to a person's or animal's behaviour our own interpretation of that behaviour. We commit the psychologist's fallacy when we catch a dog slinking away with a stolen bone and say, 'It knows it has done wrong!' Probably it knows no such thing, for that is to ascribe a moral sense to the dog: it is projecting on to the dog what we ourselves should feel if we were placed in such circumstances. So with so many of the interpretations given by psychoanalysts to their patient's symptoms; they are reading their own interpretations into the mind of the patient, which is what Freud did on his own showing and felt it 'uncanny' when he could not find it there. This interpretive method is everywhere evident in psycho-analytic writings. In the case of 'little Hans' whose father, a devoted follower of Freud, analyzed him, Jones mentions that his 'special knowledge' enables him to interpret the remarks made by his five-year-old son. Melanie Klein, who for some years dominated the English psycho-analytic school remarks, 'The analyst has just given an interpretation which brought the patient relief' (*Envy and Gratitude*). Again, she says 'the interpretation should have been given earlier.' 'Sometimes interpretation made no headway. Still more this helpful interpretation may soon become the object of distinctive criticism.' These quotations leave no doubt (a) that interpretations are given to the patient; (b) that sometimes as in the case of Freud and Irma the patient cannot accept the interpretation given. That may be because of resistance; equally it may be because the interpretation is wrong. In either case the refusal to accept the interpretation, even though it may be the true one, is liable to set up the greater resistance, and the patient is the more careful not to let that come up again. Like seeing a joke, the patient must see it for himself for it to be of any value. (See my *Dreams and Nightmares*, Chap. 7.)

(vi) *Symbolic interpretation*
This method of interpreting symptoms and dreams according to a preconceived theory, unreliable in itself, is still more fallacious when the interpretation is of a symbolic nature; for by symbolic interpretation you can 'prove' anything: symbols can be made to represent now one thing, now another. Take a dream symbol such as a snake, which to Freud is a sexual phallic symbol; to Jung, as so often in mythology, it may stand for wisdom; to Adler it is expressive of power; to a child brought up in the Indian jungle it may be an actual experience or a symbol of fear and insecurity. Each may all be right at times, for a patient is capable of using such a symbol to express any of these ideas; and of course if you always interpret such symbols as relating to sex, you will be convinced of the truth of your interpretations. A child plays with the bumping of trains. Melanie Klein interprets this as sexual intercourse between the parents; to Adler it would probably be an expression of power, to make a big bang, which all children like to do.

F

Indeed, Adler has no difficulty in maintaining that sex itself is a manifestation of the need for power, for even the masochist uses her masochism as a means of gratifying her own ends—'she stoops to conquer'.

Without much difficulty one could 'prove' that the basic cause of all neurosis is curiosity; for sex could be explained as the curiosity to have new experiences; indeed it is curiosity to experience what it is like that leads many girls to have such an affair. In one wide investigation a large proportion of such girls gave this as the reason.

G. K. Chesterton has reduced this method to an absurdity in his parody that the basic need of every child is for beer. His 'proof' goes something like this. The use of the word 'Pop' for the father refers of course to the pop of the cork, the father being the supplier of the beer. 'Ma! Ma!' are the tones of satisfaction after drinking beer and a call for more. The child's pleasure in gurgling is a wish to 'gargle' with beer, and the pleasure in making bubbles with its mouth represents the wish to be a 'frothblower'. The child-like pleasure in playing hopping games refers, unconsciously of course, to the hops of which beer is made. Nothing could be more convincing—once you start with the theory! Nor is it any more absurd that the Freudian theory in the First World War that the reason why people feared Zeppelins was because the Zeppelin was a phallic symbol. It may be in an individual case; to universalize it is to commit a fallacy.

All of these interpretations may be right in any particular case. Freud may be right in his interpretation of a sword as sex; Adler may be right in his interpretation of it as power, but in neither case can it be arbitrarily assumed that it always means this in any particular patient; still less can such interpretation be taken as any sort of proof of the theory.

The only adequate way of discovering the true meaning of the symbol is to discover by free association what it means to the patient, what the patient intends to convey by the symbol. Then you find that to one patient the sword means a penis; to another it means power; to another it may mean spiritual striving and endeavour—the 'sword of the spirit!'

Indeed, it is strange that Freud himself, with one of these inconsistencies which beset most men of genius, disapproved of this interpretive method, for he criticized himself for falling into this very error. In reviewing the case of Irma in his *Interpretation of Dreams* he states: 'At that time I had the opinion, *later recognized to be incorrect*, (my italics) that my task was limited to informing patients of the hidden meaning of their symptoms'—a mistake not altogether unknown amongst psycho-analysts at the present time, as in the case of the girl dreaming of her father coming towards her. Again, against the interpretive method he says, 'At one time we thought all that we need to do would be to identify the unconscious matter and then tell the patient what it was. However we know already that that was a short-sighted mistake.' (ibid., p. 364)

It is not surprising that some of Freud's devoted followers, Jung, Adler and Fliess as well as his original colleague Breuer failed to follow him in ascribing the neurosis essentially to incestuous desires, for they found these neither in themselves, nor, what is more important, in their patients, as the basic problem. They cannot all have been so prejudiced!

There are, however, those of his followers who, in the face of such obvious objections, still maintain that although there may be no scientific proof of the theory of the incestuous origin of neurotic disorders, they yet believe in it and intend to stand by it. That is a perfectly justifiable procedure, and there is no reason to quarrel with it; but it makes of psycho-analysis a religion and no longer a science, for it is the essence of a religion that it is based on belief or conviction, and not on scientific proof. It is also characteristic of religion that no argument will alter that belief; and that those who do not conform to their creed are heretical.

Freud, however, somewhat magnaminously makes the following concession: 'Any kind of investigation, no matter what its direction, which recognizes these facts and takes them as its starting point of its work may call itself psycho-analysis, though it arrives at results other than my own.' (*Col. Works*, Vol. I, p. 298). I doubt if the British School of psycho-analysis would accept this for admission into the Psycho-analytic Society.

(vii) *The libido theory*

The sexual urge Freud calls 'libido'; 'Libido stands in the same relation to the sex instinct as hunger does to the nutritional instincts: libido is sexual hunger.' (*Introductory Lectures*, p. 263). Again Freud says, 'Libido is the force by means of which the sexual instinct, as with hunger the nutritional instinct, achieves expression.'

The libido, according to Freud, is derived from various erotogenic zones of the body—the mouth, the anus, the phallus—which then become organized under the genital zone. The mouth for instance he describes as an 'oral sex organ' (Jones, *Freud*, Vol. 1, p. 321).

'The turning point in the child's development is the subordination of all the sexual components under the primacy of the genital zone.' (*Introductory Lectures*, p. 276.)

It is obvious that Freud uses sex in a much wider sense than usual; but he justifies this. For he finds that sex perversions are due to the persistence of infantile activities into adult life, such as the child's interest in the anus (sodomy); its exhibition of its sex organs (exhibitionism); the sexual pleasure in genital stimulation (masturbation). These activities all later appear as sex perversions, so they must be termed sexual.

Libido and character traits. Freud ascribes a number of character traits to the various erotic ones.

Freud attributes collecting and hoarding to anal-erotic activities. A child holding in its faeces finds that this gives it sensuous and sexual pleasure. That encourages the child to persist in that activity, and in some cases produces chronic constipation. But we must not confuse the expression of a tendency with the propensity itself. These anal erotic pleasures may be transferred to pleasure in collecting and holding on to things, but that is not to say that collecting as such is derived from anal erotic activity. That again is to argue in a circle, which is a logical fallacy.

The propensity to collect and to hoard and store things is an innate instinctive disposition serving self-preservation, in man as in animals. I find it hard to believe that the squirrels who store nuts in my loft are actuated by anal-erotic tendencies! The holding in the faeces may encourage that activity, but it did not create it.

So with obstinacy which Freud regards as an anal-erotic trait. The holding in of faeces is only one form by means of which a child's obstinacy is expressed. Obstinacy is of far wider connotation than this particular expression of it. You can bring a child to the pot but you can't make him defecate! It is therefore, one of the few things by which a child can defy you successfully. But there is no reason to call an impulse by the name of one of the forms of its expression. Aggressiveness, as Freud later admitted, is a primary instinct; it can express itself in kicking. Are we then to call kicking a pedal-erotic character trait, because the activity of that organ, the foot, gives great pleasure?

To take another illustration: there is his theory that the child's propensity to play with and manipulate plasticine or clay is associated with the desire to play with faeces; it is 'anal erotic'. That substitution indeed often takes place. But Freud, as so often, does not go back far enough to the biological significance of these forms of behaviour. Why should a child want to play with its faeces? If we try to find out from the patient himself, by free association, we find that it goes back to a desire to manipulate the breast. There is no biological reason why a child should want to play with faeces. In fact many animals know better and avoid them, for they are noxious. The revulsion against excretions is inherent, for good reason, for they are usually foul. But there *is* a biological reason why the infant should want to manipulate the breast, namely to squeeze out the milk. You can observe this any day if you watch an infant sucking, with its hand on its mother's breast, making squeezing and massaging movements. You can see the same thing with lambs with their little paws. The whole activity serves biological functions of self-preservation: the fact that it produces sensuous pleasure does not make it sexual: the pleasure according to a provision of nature serves only to enhance the biological activity.

Libido and the neuroses. I have earlier (p. 143), described the mental mechanisms of hysteric and obsessional symptoms. We must now ask how do these symptoms fit in with the libido theory.

In his early work Freud made the most important statement that 'the hysteric suffers from reminiscences.' In other words symptoms are a revival of part of an earlier experience whether it be paralysis, propitiatory act, depression, or fear.

Later on, as the libido theory developed, distinctive symptoms were related to the erotogenic zones: depression to the oral phase, obsessions to the anal-erotic phase, and conversion hysteria to the genital phase.

Conversion hysteria derives from the genital phases of sexual development, which is the phase when the Oedipus complex towards the opposite parent is dominant. It takes place when the libido, being repressed, takes a physical form, such as a paralysis or a hysteric pain. The pain may be a form of self-punishment for forbidden incestuous desires. The paralized arm or leg, says Freud, 'replace the genital organ . . . behave as a substitute for the genital organ . . . 'a sexual significance must be ascribed to these bodily organs'. (*Introductory Lectures* p. 259).

Anxiety hysteria, like the phobias, is the fear of our forbidden sexual desires. 'Those patients who suffer from agoraphobia . . . are now classified as anxiety hysteria' (ibid., p. 229).

Obsessions, according to Freud, are connected with anal-sadistic activities; they are associated with obstinacy and the so-called 'obsessional drive'. The propitiatory obsessions and rituals, like hand-washing, are a means of avoiding the consequences of our forbidden sexual desires, when they become too pressing. They come, Freud says, from the 'undue strength of one group of sexual tendencies with perverted aim', namely the sadistic group (ibid., p. 260).

Melancholia is derived from the oral or mouth stage which is cannibalistic and destructive. (It is true that primary depression often goes back to early infancy, the breast-sucking age, but it may be due to other causes than oral-erotic activities, such as chronic illness, and deprivation of protective love.)

Neurasthenia is a form of weakness resulting from a too great expenditure of sexual libido, as in excessive masturbation or other forms of sex indulgence.

Anxiety neuroses. In anxiety neuroses, by way of contrast to neurasthenia, there is more libido produced than is spent. It occurs, for instance, when the sexual libido is strongly aroused but frustrated, as with a young wife whose husband proves to be impotent or practises *coitus interruptus* which leaves her unsatisfied.

Both neurasthenia and anxiety neurosis (as distinct from anxiety hysteria) are not psychogenic but the result of physiological exhaustion in one case and physiological tension in the other.

Sexual perversions. The infant experiences various erotic gratifications which, if they persist in adult life, constitute the perversion. For instance, anal erotic pleasure leads to sodomy.

Freud's view of the sex perversions is that they are the mere persistence of infantile perverse activities. 'Perverted sexuality is nothing else but infantile sexuality'. (*Introductory Lectures*, p. 261). That seems to imply that whilst there is a repression in hysteria and the obsessions there is apparently none in the sex perversions. Homosexuality for instance comes merely from a fixation on the mother (Jones, *Freud*, Vol. 17, p. 322). 'Thus the paths of the perversion branches sharply from that of the neurosis', in that they are merely infantile sexual activities, persisting on account of fixation.

It is, however, difficult to see what makes them persist instead of developing into adult forms as they do in any other individual. To say because they are 'fixated' does not answer the question for it only throws us back to why they are fixated.

My experience in analysing numerous cases of sex perversion back to their origin by free association agrees with Freud that perverted sex is infantile sexuality, but, widely differs from his view in that they are the mere persistence of infantile sex activities. I have analyzed out dozens of cases of sex perversion into their actual origin in childhood, and in every case have found that the arrest of development and the fixation is invariably due to a definite repression of the infantile sex activity, often resulting from a punishment, threats or subsequent nightmares. It is because of this repression that the sexual infantile sexuality is arrested in development and so fixated, and for that reason later emerges in that infantile form as a perversion. Instances of this we shall give later (p. 319). When by analysis we discover and remove that repression, the sexuality develops as it would have developed if it had never been repressed and the perversion is cured.

Treatment and cure. Since according to Freud it is the repression of libidinous desires which produce the neurotic symptoms, the obvious cure is to detach the incestuous desires from the parent and release these desires into consciousness. Thus the Oedipus complex is resolved. The release of repressed affect or emotion Freud regarded as essential to cure.

Freud says, 'In order to dissolve the symptom it is necessary to go back to the point at which they originated, to review the conflict from which they proceeded—and to guide it towards a new solution'. (*Introductory Lectures*, p. 380).

The technique to effect this? Sexual and aggressive impulses are repressed because they are incompatible with the rest of the personality. There is therefore resistance to their recall: that is why special methods are required to bring them to the surface of consciousness. The aim of analysis is to overcome these resistances.

This is done partly by reviving the original experiences which caused the repression; also by means of the transferrence, by which the repressed emotions are released towards the analyst, and from him to the original parents; and partly by dream interpretation.

As to how to get rid of the transference once it is attached to the analyst? Freud says, 'the transference is then overcome by showing the patient that his feelings do not originate in the current situation and do not really concern the person of the physician, but that he is reproducing something that has happened to him long ago. In this way we require him to transform his repetition into recollection.' (Ibid., p. 326.)

Again, 'By seeking out the repression . . . discovering the resistances, indicating the repressed, it is actually possible . . . to overcome the resistances, to break down the repression and to change something unconscious into something conscious.' (Ibid., p. 365.) Bringing the material into consciousness brings it under the control of the will, and resolves the problem.

The most effective method of releasing the repressed material however, is by the interpretation of dreams.

CHAPTER XXI

FREUD'S THEORY OF DREAMS

Freud's main method of treatment is by the interpretation of dreams. Although we may not agree with Freud as to his interpretation of dreams, credit is certainly due to him for putting the interpretation of dreams on a scientific footing.

Freud's approach to dreams was scientific in that he showed that they were subject to specific laws such as condensation, distortion and wish fulfilment. I have given an account with illustrations of his views in my *Dreams and Nightmares* (Penguin, Chap. 2) but those who wish for a full account must go to Freud's *The Interpretation of Dreams*. We must however give a brief account here since they are closely concerned with treatment.

Content of dreams. Dreams, said Freud, are the language of the unconscious. Since the unconscious consists only of infantile sexual wishes, dreams consist entirely of infantile sexual wishes. That is the 'wish fulfilment' theory of dreams.

The function of dreams is that by giving halucinatory expression to our sexual wishes, they allow us to sleep.

Value in diagnosis. Dreams come from the unconscious, that is to say from infantile wishes which have been repressed. But so do neuroses. By means of dreams therefore we may discover what are the causes of the neurosis. For dreams are more explicit than symptoms in giving expression to the wish.

Symbolism. But such wishes are incompatible with conscious life, the pleasure principle is inconsistent with the needs of reality, and there is therefore strong resistence to their emergence even in sleep. Therefore, if the wishes of the unconscious are to find expression, they must take more presentable forms, that is to say, disguised and symbolic forms.

Dream work. That transformation is what Freud called the 'dream work', and it is the function of the pre-conscious to bring about the symbolization. Thus the father, rival for the mother's affections, whom the son desires to kill, is represented by a king. By this means the wish is expressed but in a way that fools the censor.

Cause and effect is an abstract idea; so, Freud says, the only way the dreams can express cause and effect is by antecedent and consequent, putting one event before another. A person dreams of sexual pleasure followed by a dream of terrifying disaster. That means that because of the sex pleasure these disasters follow as a result.

The dream, the child and primitive man, are all incapable of abstract thought: they all argue, *Post ho ergo propter hoc*; that because one thing happens after another, it must have been caused by it. That is the way the unconscious mind comes to its conclusions. Indeed, in adult arguments we often use the phrase 'It follows that . . .' meaning cause and effect.

Pictorial dreams. Most people's dreams are in the form of pictures because most people are visualizers, whereas occasionally we find people dreaming by hearing words like: 'That is not the way to do it'—and only free association will discover what it is that they must not do in that way.

Most dreams are in black and white, and to dream in colour is comparatively rare. That is because the cells in the retina of the eye appreciating colour are separate from those of black and white, and are much later developed. Many animals have only the 'rod' cells of black and white vision and have no 'cone' cells for colour.

Terrifying dreams. It is often objected to Freud's theory that many dreams, far from being wish fulfilments are full of anxiety and fear, especially nightmares. Freud answers by saying that such anxiety in dreams occurs when the repressed wishes of the unconscious are pressing too strongly to break through into consciousness. The Ego is terrified of the primitive wishes of the Id. If the wish had not been there, there would be no fear: it is of a forbidden wish that the dreamer is terrified.

Another objection is that many of our dreams are often of things that have happened during the day and have nothing to do with sex. Freud answers by saying that there are two aspects of the dream— the manifest content which may be some occurrence of the day, and the latent content which contains the deeper meaning of the dream. Maurice Nicoll in his book on *The Psychology of Dreams*, likens the dream to a cartoon—the form of which may be derived by the cartoonist from something he has seen during the day, shall we say a stranded ship on the shore; but that is obviously not the whole meaning of the cartoon. He takes this picture to illustrate the fact that the country, if it pursues its present policy, will be stranded.

Dream interpretation goes in reverse from 'dream work'.

It transfers the dream material from its symbolic expression back to the forbidden sexual wishes the unconscious is trying to express. That is what is done in analytic treatment.

F*

'An interpretation of dreams is in fact the royal road to know-ledge of the unconscious'. (*Interpretation of Dreams*, p. 60.) 'If you want to be a psycho-analyst', Freud says, 'study your dreams.'

Since dreams are the language of the unconscious, and the unconscious consists only of infantile sexual wishes, Freud has no hesitation in his interpretation of symbols. If a person dreams of anything long, especially if penetrating like a sword, a stick, a snake, or a knife, that represents the male penis: if of anything which contains things, for example a room, a bag, a building, that is interpreted as the uterus.

Provided you have the key (itself a phallic symbol!) to the symbolic interpretation of dreams, as Freud considered he had, and hold that certain symbols always represent certain sexual wishes, dream interpretation is quite a simple matter. If he dreams of a lake, this represents the uterine waters and a desire to return to the womb. If a woman dreams of her arm being severed, it refers to castration, for her lack of external genital organs convinces her she had been castrated. But underlying that horror is a wish to have a penis like her brother.

If you dream of a lizard it is obviously a phallic symbol and its entering a hole in the ground is sexual intercourse. The girl already mentioned who dreamt of her father coming towards her was told it meant she had a desire for him to seduce her. The simplicity of interpretation explains its popularity. By the time you have done this often enough, it all fits in so nicely that you come to believe it. For an interesting feature of the human mind is that if we understand something, we take it to be true. So we say, 'I understand that!' meaning we accept it.

The trouble is that symbols are capable of various interpretations for after all a symbol is only an object made use of to express an idea, and the same object may be used to express various ideas (p. 155). So a lake in your dream may stand for the uterine waters (Freud); or it may stand for the Collective Unconscious (Jung); or it may stand for the lake in which a patient of mine had tried to drown herself. Jung might say that by trying to drown her-self, she was symbolizing her desire to go down into the collective unconscious; and Freud might say it was a desire to go back to the womb! It's a wonderful world, the world of symbols.

One can only determine what any symbol means to the patient by getting his or her free association—to one of my women patients her handbag stood for the uterus, to another it meant security, for it contained her valuables and she could not do without it, while to another it meant being 'self-contained'.

Differ as we may from Freud, it was certainly he who opened out the world of dreams to us, and gave us the means to study them scientifically and to find in them a logical meaning, instead of their being merely the kaleidoscope of bizarre images which to most people they seem to be. He has brought order out of chaos although we may consider it the wrong order. It is not surprising then that many people regard his *Interpretation of Dreams* as his greatest work.

CRITIQUE OF FREUD

For over fifty years I have used the method of analysis originally pursued by Janet, Freud and others before them; the method of tracing back the symptom by hypnosis and free association to its origin and basic cause. The results obtained in this way do not altogether tally with Freud's later theories as the cause of neurosis, which, as we have seen, were derived from his own self-analysis. Some modifications are called for. Indeed the Freudians themselves have had deviations, such as those of Melanie Klein, and Karen Horney, so that there are various schools of Freudian psychoanalysis. I have already had reason to criticize some of Freud's views such as his explanation of character traits being based on infantile erotic activities and his interpretive method which appears to be unreliable. There are other serious defects in his theories.

(i) *The sensuous and the sexual*
As we have seen Freud uses the term sexual in a much wider sense than most people, and justifies himself on the grounds that infantile erotic tendencies appear later as sex perversion. For instance he regards the sucking activities of infancy as 'sexual'. In doing so he confuses the sexual with the sensuous. They must be clearly distinguished: for all sensuous pleasure is not sexual.

There are many physiological activities in infancy, such as sucking, urination, defecation, kicking the limbs, exposing the body to air, all of which are associated with sensuous pleasure. All these physiological functions are egoistic and self-preservative and primarily quite independent of the reproductive functions which serve race preservation. The primary function of sucking for instance is nutritive and the fact that it is pleasurable does not make it sexual.

The biological function of this sensuous pleasure is obviously to enhance these activities and to encourage them since they are necessary to life.

It is true that these sensuous pleasures later come to be transferred to the sexual activities of adult life and are normally used to enhance the functions of reproduction. Kissing for instance, was originally a sucking tendency, but later is transferred to love-making to enhance the sexual pleasure. These are the 'wooing' tendencies. But it also still retains its function as an expression of affection—as in a mother with her sick child.

It is true also that under certain conditions these infantile sensuous activities may persist to the exclusion of normal sex functions, in which case they constitute the perversion. The child's natural tendency to call attention to itself for reasons of self preservation may develop into sexual exhibitionism. But that is not to say that the original activities were sexual. Nor are we justified in confusing a natural function with its perverted use.

(ii) *Sex and love*

As Freud confuses the sensuous with the sexual so he confuses sex with love. He says, 'We call by that name (libido or sexual hunger) the energy of those instincts which have to do with all that may be comprised under the word love.' In other words sex and love are synonymous. Again in his *Introductory Lectures* (p. 277) he says, 'We speak of love when we lay the accent on the mental side of *the sexual impulses.*'

Under sex, therefore, he includes such qualities as admiration and respect which he calls 'aim-restricted', that is to say, sexual tendencies robbed of the sexual aim or end.

This is a confusion: sex is a basic instinct whose natural and biological end is reproduction. Love is what psychologists call a sentiment' (Shand), namely a group of emotional tendencies centred round an object, person or idea. Love is a many splendoured thing. The constituents of the sentiment of love are tenderness (which is dominant in mother love), aggressiveness (as in patriotism), submissiveness (as in obedience to a loved parent, or service to a cause), and respect, admiration, devotion and sexual love. Love is not simply one aspect of sex, as Freud implies: sex is one aspect of love.

The form taken by the sentiment of love depends on the particular component of love. In the films, sex is the dominant motive; but love means something very different to the mother of a family, and again different for a saint. That is why some have found love so difficult to define, since being a sentiment it can mean so many things. In one or two places Freud seems to have misgivings as to whether sex and love are synonymous, as when he says, that sex is more characteristic of the boy and love of the girl; but he does not pursue the matter as far as I am aware. In reductive analysis, we find that the child differentiates them clearly enough. A child sexually stimulated by an unscrupulous nurse when it is frightened and wanting security, gets furiously angry at the nurse at being deprived of what it really wants, which is protective love. Indeed, the fundamental distinction between sex and protective love is supported by the fact that they are associated with different hormone secretions of the body, sex being derived from the gonadotrophic (sex producing) hormone of the pituitary gland, whereas tenderness is associated with the lactogenic hormone, producing not only milk but the milk of human kindness.

This distinction is important in the treatment of the neuroses. Love is protective as well as sexual, and the protective side of love is of far greater importance in the production of a neurosis than the sexual aspect. (Chap. XXXIV).

(iii) *The Oedipus complex*

According to Freud this is the basic fact in neurosis, the 'nuclear complex'; it consists of the incestuous desires of a child towards the opposite parent. 'The first object choice in mankind is regularly an incestuous one.'

It is of course conceivable that there is an innate sexual attraction for the opposite sex even in childhood. The infantile attraction, if it exists, may be determined by the most primitive sense of smell. But that is quite speculative and at present there is no evidence of it either way.

In analysis by free association, I have not found that the Oedipus complex is the basic cause of the neuroses: nor have I found it to be either innate or inevitable. Nor is the attraction by any means always to the opposite parent. In earliest infancy, both boy and girl are usually attached to the mother; and this attachment is not sensuous only but protective. In fact, in recovering early memories we often find that the boy may be put off the mother and get at cross purposes with her in breast feeding and then turns to the father for security and love. To say that this attachment to his father is in order to possess the mother is quite the reverse of the fact: he often turns to his father because he dislikes his mother.

Freud (*Introd. Lectures*, p. 279) rightly says that by direct observation of children 'It is easy to see that the little man wants his mother all to himself and finds his father in the way.' But direct observation shows that the little girl also wants her mother all to herself and sometimes resents the intrusion of the father. Freud goes on to say that 'observation is rendered puzzling by the circumstances that the son on other occasions at this period will display great affection for the father.' Why not? Is it so extraordinary that the boy should like his father? It is puzzling only to those who start off with the Oedipus theory that the boy regards his father as his rival for the sexual possession of the mother. To others there is no reason why he should not love his father, and curiously enough many boys do.

The attachment of the child to the opposite parent is, as a matter of common observation, not to be denied, but it arises in another way. Most mothers are more attached to their sons: and fathers, less commonly, to their daughters. The result is that the child naturally responds more to the parent who shows it most attention and affection. The sexual selection is primarily on the part of the parent not of the child. Freud himself was his mother's favourite and so he would naturally respond to her caresses the more, and resent the father's interference.

Freud mentions the possibility of this in his *Introductory Lectures*, (p. 280) he says, 'The father in an unmistakable manner prefers his little daughter, and the mother her son', but he adds; 'Even this does not seriously impugn the spontaneous nature of the infantile Oedipus complex.' It does—very seriously! We find it to be the basis of the child's attraction to the parent.

Nor is this attachment necessarily sexual; most commonly it is simply a fondness or affection for the parent who loves the child the more.

But it *may* take a sexual form. This happens if the parent in his or her fondness for the child, intentionally or not, arouses the child's sexual feelings; for instance in the father's fondling and cosseting his little daughter, and giving her 'rides' on his knee or foot; the mother by romping with the little boy in her bed in the morning, and herself being sexually aroused by such play; or when the mother deliberately sexually stimulates the boy, with the excuse that he is 'too young to understand'. But all these are artifacts produced by circumstances and are neither innate nor inevitable, as the Oedipus complex is said to be.

In breast feeding, too, both boy and girl are often sexually stimulated even to the extent of an erection and an orgasm. This is particularly noticeable in the boy because of the external configuration of his genitals, by contact with the mother's body. For that same reason the boy's sexuality is more likely to be repressed than the girl's. The mother, observing the boy's erection is shocked and may push him away, all the more so if, as often happens, his orgasm arouses her sex feelings, which makes her ashamed. The same, however, happens to the girl sexually stimulated by either father or mother, who thereupon begins to masturbate, which also may lead to rebuke and repression. For these reasons the Oedipus complex is probably more common in the boy than the Electra complex in the girl. But Freud deals very little with the girl. He drags her into the picture, but his speculations about her are even less convincing than in the case of the boy. It is not surprising that some women psycho-analysts, like Melanie Klein, have jibbed at such treatment of their sex!

In Freud's description of the Oedipus complex he makes great play of the boy's jealousy of his rival, the father, a jealousy which the boy represses, according to Freud, because of a fear of castration. This jealousy of the father we find sometimes to occur, such as when the father has been away at the war or on business and the little boy has had his mother all to himself. The child naturally bitterly resents the intrusion of this interloper claiming possession of the mother, who, unfaithful woman, actually welcomes this stranger in her bed and turns the boy out. More often we find that this rivalry arises from the jealousy of the father for the son. This occurs particularly when the father is emotionally immature (for many fathers have a mother fixation). When the mother becomes absorbed with her little son, the father, who up till now has received all the mother's affection and admiration, has to stand aside and see the mother doting on the child. He does not like it. He does not show his jealousy outwardly—indeed he is probably unaware of it—but he is apt to take it out of the son on the grounds that 'You are spoiling that child'—which is probably true. He is strict with the boy and calls this 'discipline,' whereas it is really getting his own back. The mother similarly jealous of the father's affection for his daughter, and takes it out of her by dressing her in plain clothes or unattractive hair-style, or by constant fault finding. These attitudes may be observed in ordinary life if you have eyes to perceive.

Such a child sensing the hostility of the jealous parent and not knowing why, is filled with anxiety and insecurity; also with a bewildered sense of wrong—'What have I done wrong—that my father, or my mother, does not love me.' which makes the child cling the more to the other, the devoted parent.

This jealousy of the father for his son is not on account of sexual deprivation for that is not denied to the father when the mother dotes on the son, but a deprivation of affection. Man is a territorial bird, and like the robin resents the intrusion of other mates in his domain. This territorialism is partly for sexual reasons, no doubt, but not primarily so, for the female robin is also territorial in winter time when there is no question of mating. It is primarily a matter of food supply, a question of self-preservation and security. So with the immature father who is jealous of his son: he should have grown out of it.

Our version of the Oedipus complex is indeed in conformity with the original Greek myth as told by Sophocles, in which it was the father, Laius, King of Thebes, who was in the first place jealous of his son and took steps to have him destroyed. We are on the side of Sophocles, whose version we find truer to life than Freud's. It was in fact a Laius complex which was the root of the trouble.

As regards the Electra complex it is true that Electra took part in the murder of her mother, Clytemnestra, because of her mother's unfaithfulness to her father Agamemnon; but it was at the instigation of Orestes, her brother. That does not look like a mother fixation or Oedipus complex, on the part of Orestes!

Indeed, when you look at the original story, the Oedipus complex is basically one of insecurity, not primarily of sex. As an infant, Oedipus was abandoned by his parents and slung up by his foot (Oedipus = swollen foot) on a tree to die at the instigation of his father. It was the basic insecurity derived from this experience which dogged him all his life and led to his neurosis. It is no wonder if unconsciously he sought to revenge himself on his father for the wrong he had done him, and sought his mother for security. The fact of his having sex relations with his mother is symbolic of a need for her protective love.

There are, in fact, two types of mother complex, one sexual the other protective. Certainly the sexual involvement of the child with the parent in the ways mentioned is often a cause of arrest of development and consequently of a neurosis. But equally excessive *dependence* upon the mother for other than sexual reasons, such as illness, suffocation and terror from outside sources, gives the child the sense of insecurity and so arrests the child's development. This produces neurosis owing to a fear of life. We find that most neuroses are due to insecurity not to sex. It was this sense of security of which Oedipus was deprived in infancy. It is that insecurity which produced his neurosis. This is borne out by the parallel story of Perseus, whose jealous grandfather cast him and his mother out to sea in a barrel, where one could assume they had ample opportunity for incest. But Perseus developed no complex. Far from developing a neurosis he later became a hero, rescued Andromeda and married the girl. Why the difference? Because whilst Oedipus, strung upside down on the tree and deserted by everyone, was filled with fear and insecurity, Perseus though cast out to sea still had the love and comfort of his mother, and therefore developed a sense of confidence to face life. They were wise people these Greek writers! They had a true insight into human nature and it is not for us to distort the story to fit any theory.

Far more common than the jealousy between parent and child is the jealousy of an older child for a younger who now usurps the place in his mother's affection, or a girl for the petted boy. This happened in Freud's case, for his neurosis started with his jealousy of his brother. When the older child wants to regain his mother's affection, it is told 'run away. Can't you see I'm busy?' which is precisely what the older child does see and does object to. This feeling of being unloved and unwanted is a prolific cause of neuroses.

The Freudian insistence on the incestuous Oedipus complex arouses my sympathy for the boy of nine who with his father and mother was returning from one of the classical tours of Greece. The parents entered into a long and tedious discussion of the Oedipus complex, till the boy could stand it no longer and left saying, 'I can understand Oedipus wanting to kill his father, but I can't understand him wanting to marry his mother'—and walked out. As Max Beerbhom said, 'They are a peculiar family, these Oedipuses!'

CHAPTER XXII

ANALYTICAL PSYCHOLOGY: CARL JUNG

(i) *Historical*

Carl Gustav Jung is often spoken of as a pupil of Freud. That is only partially true. It is true that he visited Vienna to work with Freud and Freud visited Jung in Zurich; but he had previously established himself as a psychiatrist. His work on schizophrenia, and the word association tests, were completely independent, and he had come by his basic theories before he knew Freud. His attention had already been arrested by strange phenomena observed in his mental hospital patients, and this led to his most distinctive contribution to psychology, namely that of the collective unconscious. When he found that Freud also was working on the unconscious he made contact with him.

Freud on the other hand at first welcomed Jung because of the latter's eminence, for he had a very poor opinion of his colleagues in Vienna (Jones, *Freud*, Vol. 2, p. 484). Jung also thought little of them: so did Ernest Jones (E. A. Bennet, *C. G. Jung*, p. 384).

Alder once told me (with what truth I don't know!) that Freud would come round to his rooms of an evening for a chat because he was so bored with his own colleagues! Freud also welcomed Jung as a non-Jew, because psycho-analysis was becoming too much identified with Jews and Freud felt it would suffer by becoming a 'Jewish national affair' (Jones, *Freud*, Vol. 2, p. 53). In fact it was known in Berlin as 'Jewish psychology.'

In point of fact, there may be some reason for this racial predeliction, for those of the Jewish race would be more prone to accept Freud's theory of the castration complex as being the basic cause of repression, because of their own experiences of the trauma of ceremonial circumcision in infancy at the hands of a Rabbi.

Freud's immediate followers on the other hand resented Jung partly out of jealousy of his being Freud's favourite, but also because they assumed him to be anti-Jewish. That reputation clung to him although in fact some of his closest and eminent colleagues were Jews. (Bennet, ibid., p. 37–38.) Ultimately Freud was as disappointed in Jung's independence of mind and judgment, as Jung was disillusioned about Freud.

His work with Freud led only in the end to disillusion since he could not accept Freud's limited concept of the unconscious; nor could he accept Freud's incestuous theory as to the origin of the neurosis. Indeed Jung suggested to Freud that the latter's cases on which he built up his theory of sexual traumata were in fact invented by the patients to please Freud—just as Charcot's patients under hypnosis continued to produce the many hysterical symptoms which were expected of them, and which Charcot took to be genuine results of hypnotism as such (p. 41). Freud himself, as we have seen, later admitted the fiction of these sex assaults.

Jung pays many just and handsome tributes to Freud (see Bennet's *C. G. Jung*, p. 30). Yet he adds in *Analytical Psychology*, 'Unfortunately Freud was led to an over-valuation of sexuality and this has brought upon him the justifiable reproach of pan-sexualism. Nevertheless', he adds, 'all these things are the merest trifle compared with the psychological principles whose discovery is Freud's greatest merit.' (*Collected Works*, Vol. 3, p. 4).

Prior to his attachment to Freud, Jung had attended Janet's lectures in Paris in 1902 for six months. He says he adopted from Janet the idea of 'dissociation', but disagreed with the latter who held that dissociation and neurosis were caused by a lowering of psychic energy. He did this on the ground that a 'complex' functioned with considerable strength and vigour, which was incompatible with a lowering of tension (Bennet, ibid, p. 26). Janet might however reply that it was the weakening of the controlling forces of the personality, due to lowering of tension which allowed the complex to emerge with such force, just as a person may be more bad-tempered when he is tired.

I mention the historical background of these pioneers in psychotherapy since it is of some interest in understanding their views. Important also are their previous trainings. Janet and McDougall were psychologists and the latter also an anthropologist of note: Freud was a neurologist; and Jung a psychiatrist. Janet based his theories on hundreds of well-authenticated cases: Freud based his original theory on only eleven cases. McDougall made a systematic study of the instincts in man, and corrected them by reference to the instincts in animals. Freud entirely ignored the animals as well he might when it came to the Oedipus complex.

All were medical men, but the influence of such backgrounds can be seen in their theories. Jung's theory of the archetypes, for instance, was in the first place derived from his observations of his psychotic patients. I have often wondered if he would have derived the same theories from neurotic patients alone, whose disorders unlike the psychotics, appear to derive more from personal experiences than from archetypal material. Bizarre archetypal material is more commonly observed in psychotics, which were Jung's first objects of study.

But the two men, Freud and Jung, were of very different types and it was not at all surprising that they gradually diverged. Jung was a man of very independent thought, while insisting that his theories were only hypotheses, whereas Freud also a man of independent thought, was dogmatic and resentful of criticism.

Jung once told me that this was the final point on which he and Freud split. Freud had maintained that the unconscious consisted only of infantile sexual wishes; that there was therefore no conflict and therefore no sense of guilt in the unconscious. Jung argued with him that there was such a conflict and therefore that a person could have guilt in the unconscious. Freud then declared that this attitude of Jung was merely 'the adolescent rebellion of the son against the father'. As Jung said, a scientific argument cannot be carried on under such conditions and he broke away.

In point of fact later psycho-analytical theory tends to support Jung when it maintained that the Super-Ego, or moral self, had its roots in the unconscious. If the Super-Ego or moral self has its roots in the unconscious there must be a conflict in the unconscious, and the unconscious does not consist only of sexual wishes.

The difference in theory finally produced the break between the two geniuses in 1912.

(ii) *Discovery of the Collective Unconscious*
Jung, as we have said, was a psychiatrist and started his professional life working in a mental institution. In that institution his attention was drawn to the fact that in the delusions and hallucinations of his patients there emerged bizarre images and strange ideas which could not have come out of the patient's personal experiences. He concluded therefore that they must have come from some deeper source of an archaic nature in the human psyche. This was confirmed by the discovery that these images were not confined to individuals, but that the same patterns appeared constantly in myths from all parts of the world, from different races and different cultures. Not only so, but he found that the same sort of material appeared in the dreams of varied people of various races; and in the spontaneous drawings of patients—all pointing to a common source.

He therefore felt justified in assuming that this strange and bizarre material, common to all mankind must be of ancestral origin, as much inherited as our bodily organism which also we have in common with all our fellow men. In our bodies we have vestiges of our animal ancestry in gills (the Eustachian tube), in tails (with which some children are born), and with a now useless appendix. In the same way we inherit vestiges of *mental ancestral traits* which confront us in the bizarre material which emerges in dreams. 'Inasmuch as the new-born child is presented with a ready-made highly developed brain which owes its differentiation to the accretion of untold centuries of ancestral life, the unconscious psyche consists of inherited instincts, functions, and forms that are peculiar to the ancestral psyche.'

This part of the psyche he therefore called the Collective unconscious. He was encouraged in his concept of the Collective unconscious by a dream of his own. In this dream he wandered in his home until he came down to a Roman-like cellar, and beneath that, covered up, a cave or tomb with prehistoric bones and skulls. This he took to refer to deeper layers of the unconscious in his archaic inheritance.

(iii) *Jung's concept of the personality*
Jung therefore classified the psyche into the conscious; the personal unconscious; and the collective unconscious—as distinct from Freud's conscious, pre-conscious, and unconscious—their contents being quite different from Freud's three classes.

(a) *The conscious* we derived not so much from the experiences of the day, but largely from the upsurging of material from the collective unconscious.

Conscious and unconscious. Most of us would regard our conscious life as derived through our senses from objective experiences. To Jung, it is the other way round: conscious life itself is determined by and derived from the unconscious. His concept of consciousness is entirely opposed to the commonly accepted views of philosophers like Locke, who held that the mind at birth was like a sheet of wax on which impressions were made through the organs of sound and sight, the personality being 'built up' from such experiences from without. Bennet has pointed out that Jung held the opposite views that all consciousness is inspired from the unconscious, whose forms and images are constantly pressing to come into consciousness, often in the form of dreams and visions. They are a part of our daily experience but come up from within. 'The collective unconscious is the basis and condition of all consciousness.' (*Collected Works*, 16, p. 34.)

(b) *The personal unconscious.* This consists of experiences of the individual during his personal life which have been forgotten and become unconscious. This corresponds to some extent with Freud's unconscious, which consists of repressed material, although Jung would certainly not agree that it consisted entirely of infantile sexual wishes. It is made up essentially of contents which have at some time been conscious, but which have disappeared from consciousness through having been forgotten or repressed. As it consists of personal experiences he called it the personal unconscious. He gives considerable importance to the personal experiences of early life; indeed, he says that a man's

individuality depends very largely on his infantile metier, especially his relations with his parents.

But even in saying this, he places the emphasis on the collective
unconscious and does not accord to these personal experiences
the importance which others of us do who regard them as the
determining factor in the formation of a neurosis. This of course
is natural since the collective unconscious is his own discovery
and he is naturally out to stress its full implications in the life of the
individual. In this he differs from Freud who traced the neuroses
back to personal experiences, namely the sexual attachment to the
opposite parent and the repression of these incestuous wishes.

It is clear then that whilst for Freud there was only one unconscious, consisting of repressed infantile sexual wishes, Jung divides
the unconscious into the two distinct parts containing entirely different material, one consisting of personal experiences and the other
of archaic and primordial material, which belongs, not to the
individual, but to the common heritage of the race. It is the
non-personal aspect of our psyche, very similar to Neitzsche's
concept of the Id or Es (p. 128).

(c) *The Collective unconscious.* This is Jung's particular contribution to psychotherapy: it went far deeper than anything Freud
described. The collective unconscious consists of ancestral traits,
of racial experiences handed down through countless generations
in the constitution of the individual. As contrasted with the personal
unconscious 'the contents of the collective unconscious have
never been in consciousness and therefore have never been
individually acquired but owe their existence exclusively to
heredity' (*Collected Works*, Vol. 9, p. 92). Therefore, they cannot
be said to be repressed, although they are suppressed, being
denied expression in consciousness.

The contents of the personal unconscious, he called complexes;
the contents of the collective unconscious he called archetypes.
'Archetypes are to the collective unconscious what complexes are
to the personal unconscious.' In analysis we are confronted with
both complexes and archetypes.

Thus, 'The concept of the collective unconscious psyche is a
functional system consisting of pre-existing forms of a universal
non-personal character which does not develop individually but is
inherited.' (Jung, *The Concept of the Collective Unconscious*, p. 44,
46). 'Everything is in the mind when a child is born.' This implies
that 'man will behave much as his ancestors behaved right back to
Methuselah.'

Again, 'So far', he says 'as the collective unconscious contents
are concerned, we are dealing with archaic, or I would say primi-

tive types. That is to say with a universal image that has existed since remotest times.' (*Collected Works*, Vol.9, p.934). The collective unconscious is 'the repository of all the ancestral experiences of the race.'

Indeed, Jung goes so far as to say that 'These images contain not only every beautiful and great thought and feeling of humanity, but also every deed of shame and devilry of which human beings have ever been capable.' (*Analytical Psychology*, p.414). As distinct from McDougall's archaic instincts which are biologically normal Jung's collective unconscious contains much that is essentially evil.

Jung, however, is careful to stress that it is not the ideas themselves which are inherited, but only their potentialities. 'This collective inheritance is by no means made up of inherited ideas as such but rather of the possibilities of such ideas,' (*Two Essays*, p.139)—just, might we suggest, as a tape recorder is not music but the potentialities of music.

(d) Jung gives various terms to this aspect of the human psyche: he calls it the 'collective unconscious', the 'racial unconscious', the 'autonomous', the 'impersonal' and the 'objective' unconscious. Each of these terms serves a purpose since each refers to different aspects of its functions. 'Collective' means that it is a quality of the psyche possessed by all, because it is inherited, as is our bodily structure. 'Racial' means that it is developed in the human race as this develops. 'Autonomous' points to the fact that it acts on its own, beyond the control of a conscious will; 'impersonal' because it is by way of contrast to the 'personal' unconscious which consists of personal experiences during life. Jung himself prefers the term collective unconscious.

(e) *The Unconscious as the source of life.* The collective unconscious is therefore more than a repository of racial experiences. It is the source of all our energies, the matrix of life itself. From it the conscious life derives all its strength and material. It is 'the eternal creative mother of consciousness'.

'It is the permanent and creative feature in man, the never-failing source of all art and of all productivity.' (*Contributions to Analytical Psychology*, p. 305.) To tap the collective unconscious is the very essence of life. To integrate all these forces into the personality is the task of man, and his mental health depends upon it. 'The collective unconscious is the mighty spiritual inheritance of human development, re-born in every individual constitution.'

(f) *Integration.* The conscious and the unconscious therefore have separate functions in life. The function of the conscious is that of adaptation to external life. The collective unconscious, is the source and well-spring of our lives and supplies the material for all conscious striving. Thus the conscious is perpetually drawing upon the resources of the unconscious and assimilating it into itself, controlling and directing it for adaptation to life. That is integration. By integrating the resources of the unconscious into itself the personality is developed and in this way reaches his fulfilment.

(g) *Individuation.* An ideal life is one in which the conscious is able to integrate into itself all that is emerging from the unconscious so that a balance of harmony is attained and fullness of life. That is the process of individuation 'in which a patient becomes what he really *is*'. (*Collected Works*, Vol. 16, p.10.)

(h) *The moral task.* This process of individuation is a task requiring the highest moral endeavour. 'Whoever is incapable of moral resolution, of this loyalty to himself, will never be relieved of his neurosis; on the other hand whoever is capable of it will certainly find the way to fulfil himself—it is the moral factor which is decisive for health or illness.' 'It is a highly moral task of immense educational value.' (*Collected Works*, Vol. 7, p. 288.)

(iv) *The Libido.*
The unconscious manifests itself as libido. Jung's concept of the libido is very different from that of Freud. By 'libido' Freud meant sexual hunger; for Jung libido is psychic energy, which is equivalent to the intensity with which psychic contents are charged. (*Collected Works*, Vol. 7, p. 52.)

'We term libido that energy which manifests itself by vital processes which are subjectively perceived as aspiration, longing and striving' (ibid., p. 39). 'It is libido which pulses through all the forms of the psychic system.—It is the foundation and regulation of all psychic existence.' Thus Jung's libido is akin to Janet's psychic energy; to the Hormé of Aristotle and to the *élan vital* of Bergson, though it differs in some respects from each of them.

Just as we speak of physical energy in the material world, so we speak of psychic energy in the psychological world. 'All psychological phenomena can be considered as manifestations of energy . . . which is subjectively conceived as desire. I call it libido, *using the world in the original meaning of the term*, (my italics) which is by no means merely sexual' (*Papers on Analytical Psychology*, p. 237).

The source of libido is also differently conceived. According to

Freud the libido is derived from the erotogenic zones of the body, such as the mouth, the anus, the phallus and the breasts. These then become concentrated in the genital zone. To Jung the process is the other way round: the libido starts off as undifferentiated energy: (*Collected Works*, Vol. 7, p. 85). It then becomes differentiated into the various forms, developing first into hunger (in the infant), through the various instincts, and ultimately sex. (*Analytical Psychology*, p. 231.) Freud starts from the many to the one: Jung starts with the one which is then differentiated out into the many functions. 'The early idea of the sexual components must be given up and its place taken by *libido which is capable of manifold applications.*'

(v) *The destiny of the libido*
Libido may be progressive, or it may be regressive. Its function is to enable us to face up to the demands of life. 'The libido is directive: it enables the psyche to be adjusted to the demands of life—that is progress. On the other hand if the psyche meets with difficulties which demand more than it can cope with, it fails to progress and regresses back to an earlier mode of life. That is why a neurotic revives infantile forms of reaction (*Collected Papers*, p. 230–232).

Jung gives an interesting analogy of the way in which a neurosis is formed, taken from mountain climbing in his native Switzerland. Several persons are confronted with a high and difficult mountain. One person admits it is difficult but strives with sacrifice and suffering till he succeeds in overcoming his difficulties. He is the man of achievement, of strong will, of healthy character, a well-integrated personality. Another sees the difficulties, accepts his limitations and finds an easier mountain. He also lives happily, though of less achievement. (Most of us probably belong to this category!) A third is ambitious, but seeing the difficulty bluffs himself that the mountain is inaccessible and physically unattainable. By this means he saves his self-esteem and can still brag of his courage. Another retreats into a world of fantasy, dreaming of climbing inaccessible mountains, substituting introversion for extroversion, phantasy for reality. Finally there is the man who develops a neurotic disability, which excuses him from trying to scale the mountain. 'If only' he had not this pain in the back; what might he achieve. Neurosis is an attempt at adaptation which has failed.

(vi) *How does the Neurosis arise?*
(a) As long as the conscious can manage to integrate the material emerging from the unconscious, the individual is healthy and

well-balanced: indeed he is a person of great achievement because he is drawing upon this source of power. The process of individuation and integration are running smoothly. But there are times when the material coming up from the collective unconscious is such that it cannot be integrated into the conscious, nor rendered adaptable to the circumstances of everyday life.

This creates a conflict between the emerging material from the unconscious, and the conscious which cannot make use of it nor adjust to it.

(b) *Dissociation*. This further results in dissociation in the personality. Dissociation has now gained still another meaning. To Janet it was due to a falling apart of the personality due to the lowering of vitality; to Freud it was due to active repression: to Jung it is split between the conscious and the unconscious, between the progressive and the regressive parts of the personality.

One form of this conflict is observed in the conflict between two phases of development as in adolescence, when a new phase of development is trying to emerge in the ordinary course of maturation, but is prevented by an earlier phase which clings to childhood with its security, and refuses to give way. The youth must perforce grow up; but something in him clings to childhood. In such cases there is an arrest of development. 'The libido lingers, but time does not stand still; and the development of the individual is always proceeding apace. The physical maturation increases the contrast. The more the libido is in arrears, the more severe is the conflict.' The result is that there is conflict in the personality, a split between these two incompatibles—consciousness, and the unconscious material which it cannot integrate into itself.

In minor cases that failure of integration results in a *neurosis*: in more severe cases the material from the collective unconscious is so overpowering that it overwhelms consciousness. In this case the patient suffers from a *psychosis* (insanity), in which the individual is completely possessed by the bizarre ideas and strange phantasies which have emerged.

A neurosis then is a failure in adaptation—not so much to objective life, although this is a precipitating factor, but to the forces emerging from the unconscious.

(c) *Regression*. When the libido fails to find outlet in normal activity and progress, it tends to regress into childhood. For, whenever the libido, in the process of adaptation, meets with an obstacle an accumulation takes place. Normally this should give rise to increased effort to overcome the obstacle, but if the obstacle seems insurmountable, 'the stored-up libido undergoes a regression and returns to a former and more primitive way of adaptation.' (*Collected Papers*, Vol. 16, p. 231). So a neurosis is produced, taking the form of some infantile form of behaviour.

Regression then is the return to an infantile mode of reaction: every neurotic behaves like a child. 'Regression', says Jung, 'is a movement away from the responsibilities of life back towards that condition of security which the infant experiences in its mother's arms.' The regression is purposive. It is the utilization of a symptom to escape from life. But childhood experiences, says Jung, are only the apparent causes, not the real causes of the neurosis.

Herein is another difference between Freud and Jung. Freud regards the neurosis as being due to a fixation in childhood (the sexual fixation of a boy to his mother followed by repression), so that the personality fails to develop. Jung regards the neurosis as due to *regression*, a retreat back to childhood for security when the patient meets with difficulties too great for him.

(vii) *Present-day conflict*

This regression to the past however is not the real cause of the conflict. The cause of the neurosis lies not in the past, but in the present, in the inability to integrate material from the collective unconscious. 'Therefore', says Jung, 'I no longer find the cause of the neurosis in the past but in the present' (ibid., p. 222). 'I ask what is the necessary task which the patient will not accept?' 'The pathogenic conflict exists only in the present moment; only in the present are the effective causes, and only here are the possibilities of recovering them.' The essential question then is 'What is the responsibility that the patient is refusing to face?'

The precipitation of the breakdown occurs at the moment when a new psychological adjustment, a new adaptation is demanded (ibid., p. 229).

The *symptom*, as we have observed, takes the form of an earlier mode of reaction as a means of avoiding the difficulty.

This difference in theory has obviously a marked influence on the method of treatment. If the basic trouble is a fixation of libido in early childhood, as Freud says, our obvious task is to revert back to that and unravel that complex and so release the libido. This is the reductive method. If, on the other hand, we regard with Jung the cause of the neurosis as the inability to cope with the present emergence of material from the collective unconscious, then our task is in the present, to resolve the present day problem.

In *treatment* therefore while Jung devotes his attention to the present day problem of the material which is trying to emerge from the collective unconscious and which is mainly manifest in dreams, the reductive analyst considers that it is more effective to discover and deal with these infantile experiences which are holding up the personality and arresting its development. When he does so, he finds the key to the neurosis, and at the same time releases the emotions which were then held up. Consequently, these potentialities automatically develop as they would have developed if they had not been arrested. When Jung says that it is often first necessary to analyze out the complexes of the personal unconscious (that is to say experiences in early childhood) which hold up the material from the collective unconscious, he is a reductive analyst! The reductive analysts (not only the Freudians) maintain that this as a rule is all that is necessary, and that this removal of the basic cause in childhood we usually find sufficient for cure. For when these emotions are liberated they no longer form a complex, the symptom is abolished and the personality is free. This method is described later under the term 'direct reductive analysis' and many instances are given in the last chapter.

(viii) *Present-day analysis and reductive analysis*
Obviously, as Jung claims, the patient's problem is a present-day problem and it is his present distress which brings him for treatment. But the crucial question at issue is whether the *sources* of the problem lie in present-day difficulties or in the past; and whether therefore treatment should be directed towards the present-day situation or whether the analyst should delve in the past.

At this point, therefore, we may step aside to consider the differences of approach between these two methods for they are fundamental. By reductive analysis I mean all those systems of psychotherapy whose methods are to go into the past to discover the causes of the neurosis in childhood experiences, as against those schools which deal with the neurosis only as a present-day problem.

We recall that the behaviourist school with their re-conditioning (p. 87) deal with the problem only as a present-day issue, but their approach is quite different from that of Jung. They deal with behaviour only, whereas Jung deals with dynamic forces which fail to be integrated into the conscious personality. The hypnotist also deals only with the present-day symptom.

I personally favour the reductive method as more radical, though far from agreeing with Freud as to what the infantile causes are. There is of course a present-day problem, but we maintain that *there would not have been the present-day problem were it not for the predisposing causes in childhood,* and therefore it is these we must primarily deal with.

Both approaches are justified and both produce good results. To put it crudely, a Jungian might argue; 'If a house is on fire one needs to deal with that fire and not start to enquire as to its origin.' To which the reductive analyst may reply, 'If there is a bad smell of a dead rat, you do not deal with the situation by deodorants, but by discovering the dead rat, whereupon the smell disappears automatically, for you cannot have the smell without the rat!'—all of which means that you cannot prove anything by analogy.

The difference of point of view between the 'present-day' approach and the 'reductive' method may be illustrated by the treatment of a case of claustrophobia. If a person has claustrophobia, this may be taken, and quite correctly, to mean that his personality is shut in and confined, not daring to express itself, afraid to venture. The physical shut-in-ness at theatres is symbolic of the shut-in-ness of his personality as a whole, obviously a present-day problem. This is reflected in his dreams, which depict him shut in a narrow tunnel with the sense of appalling dread. The analyst points this out to him, and encourages him to be bolder, to express himself the more, to take risks and he will find everything is all right. No doubt this may meet with considerable success. The constriction of his personality is a present-day problem which has to be tackled as it exists at present. The reductive analyst goes about it in a different way, 'What is it', he asks, 'originally caused the claustrophobia?' What originally shut in the personality? Ultimately he traces it back to a suffocation at birth, a most terrifying experience; and the patient revives the *feeling* of passing through the long dark tunnel which is the vaginal track at birth. He re-lives the experience so vividly that he has no doubt as to this being the origin. How does this infantile experience relate to his present-day problem? Simply in this way: the child who has such an experience starts off with a fear of life in general; and it is this fear which cramps his personality; so that he suffers from claustrophobia, the fear of being shut in by his fears.

Jung would say that the patient goes back to childhood to *borrow* his symptom from his infantile experience. The reductive analysis says that this infantile experience is the *cause* of the later shut-in-ness of the personality.

You may relieve the situation in the present by encouraging the patient to be more bold and confident. You may also trace the fear back to the infantile experience and get rid of the fears which are holding him down. As he revives this experience he realizes it is exactly the same fear as he now has in his terror in a cinema or railway carriage. Moreover when he revives this infantile experience with all its emotion, he experiences a great sense of relief and the symptoms may entirely disappear—many instances of which are given in Chapter XXXVIII. He is now full of confidence and can venture into life. No more shut in, he is free!

(ix) *Pre-disposing factors*

It may be asked, 'Why is it that some people are capable of integrating what is emerging from this unconscious while other fail to do so and become neurotic?' Jung's answer is 'constitutional sensitivity'. (*Collected Works*, Vol. 7, p. 57.) 'A certain innate sensitiveness leads to special reactions to infantile events, which are not without their own influence in the development of the patient's conception of life.' 'This sensitivity causes difficulties even to the infant at the mother's breast in the form of unnecessary irritation and resistances.' Congenital sensitivity is the cause of the resistance against adaptation.

There is no doubt that sensitivity is indeed a characteristic feature in most neurotic patients, for they feel the rebuffs of life more than others. Rarely do we find the man of the 'bull-dog breed' coming into the consulting room, and when he does it is usually about his sensitive wife, not himself; or his children whom his lack of sensitivity and understanding has turned into rebels or worse.

Yet I cannot believe that sensitivity is enough to cover the whole predisposing cause. Not all sensitive children become neurotic although they may be more liable to neurotic breakdown. It depends on circumstances; for if the sensitive child is brought up with security and confidence, it does not break down. Whilst, therefore, we accept constitutional sensitivity as an important factor in the production of a neurosis, it is after all environmental conditions which decide whether or not the sensitive child falls victim to neurosis.

Jung to a certain extent agrees with this, for a further predisposition according to Jung's teaching, lies in childhood experiences, 'a neurosis is partly due to infantile predisposition' (*Collected Papers*, p. 230) .This, he says, is partly due to the 'characteristic relations of the child to the parent', such as the anxiety of the parent, too great fondness of the parent, or if the parents are neglectful or cruel. It is these experiences which the reductive analyst regards as the more important, and devotes himself to getting rid of them.

With all this it is a little difficult to understand how Jung can say that '*only* in the present are the causes of the neuroses', for these predisposing factors clearly indicate that these infantile experiences are causative factors in the production of the neurosis. If he had left out the 'only' in each case and said the 'essential' factors, it would be more understandable and acceptable, for obviously we are dealing with a present-day problem.

(x) *Aims in Treatment*

Since neurosis, as we have seen, is caused by the inability of the conscious mind to incorporate and integrate material emerging from the unconscious, the aim of treatment is obviously to help the patient to release these oncoming potentialities, to make the integration possible. The function of the analyst, we may say, is to act as a mid-wife to facilitate the birth of these potentialities. 'Coming to terms with the contents of the collective unconscious in general: that is *the* great task of the integration process (*Collected Works*, Vol. 9, Part I, p. 31). 'The libido is always there, though inaccessible to the patient. It is the task of psycho-analysts to search for that hidden place where the libido dwells.... That hidden place is the unconscious.'

The ultimate purpose of analysis is to make the patient whole, and that means the totality of the individual, conscious and unconscious.

This urge to wholeness or completeness was a concept to which I drew attention in a chapter in my *Psychology and Morals* in 1920, entitled 'The Urge to Completeness,' showing how it is to be found in every organism; so that if an animal is wounded or a plant damaged the resources of the organism are directed towards healing the wound and making the individual whole again.

This is what Jung calls integration of the personality. Man cannot be whole until his unconscious is integrated into his conscious personality. How is this release to be effected?

JUNG'S METHODS OF TREATMENT

First on the negative side: Jung discards both suggestion treatment and also the use of Freud's free association.

(a) *Suggestion treatment.* 'The principles of analytical therapy', he says, 'are so entirely different from those of therapeutic suggestion that they are not comparable, they are absolutely opposed. Methods of treatment based on suggestion are deceptive make-shifts: they are incompatible with the principles of analytical therapy and should be avoided if at all possible' (*Collected Works*, Vol. 16, p. 147), but he admits that 'Suggestion happens of its own accord without the doctor being able to prevent it or taking the slightest trouble to produce it'. (Ibid., p. 173.) 'Suggestion', he says, 'depends on putting something into the patient whereas analysis is releasing something from within the patient'. (He overlooks the fact that suggestion may be used to release those very potentialities, and to remove the obstacles to their expression). (See p. 56.)

He says that 'Suggestion is a kind of magic that works in the dark, (ibid., p. 146). This, as we have seen in the Chapter on

Hypnosis (Chap. XI), is an old-fashioned view of suggestion and hypnotism, for suggestion is a common experience of every-day life and is of the greatest value in biological adjustment and survival. It is also almost invariably found in the transference relation between doctor and patient, of which Jung approves.

(b) *Free association*. Jung also discards the use of Free Association which was the method devised by Freud. 'Free association will get us nowhere . . . it will bring out all the complexes (that is, buried experiences of our personal uneasiness), but hardly ever the meaning of a dream (or its archetypal significances)' (ibid., p.149–150). This objection of Jung is difficult to understand, for he himself says that we need in analysis to deal first with the experiences and complexes of the personal unconscious since these stand in the way of the emergence of material for the collective unconscious. Surely if that is what we want to achieve, it can best be done by free association, which as he says 'brings out all the complexes'.

He objects also to going into the past by free association, for that is to encourage the patient to wallow in those past experiences instead of facing the real present-day issue. Freud on the other hand tells us that the patient resists going into the past because of its unpleasantness. Which is right? As usual both may be. For some patients love to wallow in self-pity which was an infantile experience, yet may show the greatest resistance to reviving the distressing experiences which gave rise to the self-pity. It is a fact that the patient constantly reverts back both in his dreams and in his neurotic symptoms, to those experiences, which are by no means always pleasant. We may say this is because he wants to wallow in them. But in reality it is because they are problems which call for solution.

Again, Jung says also that in free association to childhood the individual likes to put the blame on others for his neurosis. In our view it is the childhood situation (not necessarily the parent who may have known no better), which is responsible for his condition, and the sooner he discovers the real cause of his distortions, the sooner he will find the solution to his symptoms, which thereupon disappear.

Coming now to Jung's more positive methods of treatment:

(c) *The dialectic method*. Jung has no fixed technique in treating his patients as Freud has. He makes use of what he calls 'the dialectic method', which means talking to his patients as 'man to man', helping him to interpret his dreams both as regards his everyday problems and by means of analogies from the myths.

'This treatment is in the form of a discussion between two persons, in the manner of Socrates; question and answer, in which the analyst reveals himself as does the patient to the analyst!' 'The physician also must step out of his anonymity and give an account of himself exactly as he demands of his patient.' (*Collected Works*, Vol. 16, pp. 3ff, 116.)

In this dialectic method he makes no use of relaxation on the couch to release the emerging material from the unconscious. This is a matter of some surprise since phantasies, and presumably material from the collective unconscious, emerge much more readily when we are relaxed, just as they emerge more readily in dreams in the relaxed state of sleep. Perhaps he would reply that they are emerging readily enough already.

(d) *Active imagination.* This is a method which a patient can carry out for himself, in which free rein is given to the imagination allowing any phantasy from the unconscious to come into consciousness, without reason nor restraint. This is a valuable method, but not without its dangers, as Jung says, for the release of unconscious material may be too much for the conscious to control, let alone to integrate. 'To identify ourselves with the primitive impulses would mean living out our bestial impulses without restraint.' He says, 'In this process of releasing the contents of the unconscious the accepted standards of the patient may be swept away; therefore this dissolution of the accepted standards of the patient has to be approached with caution.' 'It is important', he says, 'that the conscious attitude should not be overthrown but must integrate the unconscious attitude into itself.'

Indeed, 'the analytic process in general, which means hacking through layer upon layer to the inner core, is an arduous process not without its dangers, for the unconscious being released may take possession of the conscious and a worse condition result.' It is necessary therefore that throughout analysis the conscious should retain its integrity and its ethical standards; otherwise there is no one or nothing to do the integrating. That is of course particularly liable to happen if the patient is constitutionally psychotic.

(e) *Amplification.* Instead of free association Jung uses the method he calls 'amplification' (Bennet, *C. G. Jung*, p.135). In Freud's free association, conscious control is eliminated as far as possible so that the associations are influenced and determined by the unconscious. In amplification the contents of the neurosis are worked out in a fully conscious state by discussion between the patient and the analyst.

G

(f) *Automatic drawings*. A further method is that of automatic drawing which represents the problem in the same way as dreams do. For in both cases creative and purposeful forces arise for the unconscious. They help us therefore not only to discover what is the problem, but to see how they may be integrated. A patient of mine drew an automatic picture of a ghost-like figure of a woman in a fluttering night dress, but had no idea what it meant. It might easily have been interpreted as representing the archetypal mother. In fact it was found to relate to her hysterical mother in an air-raid when the patient was two years of age. (See page 346.) I personally find that these automatic drawings, like dreams, are often reproductions in part of actual earlier experiences not of archetypes.

(g) *Word association*. A more technical method is that of word association tests, as devised by Jung. This method of giving a word to the patient and getting him to respond with the first word which comes to his mind sounds simple enough, but in all kinds of ways it indicates, without the patient knowing what he is revealing, complexes from which he suffers and experiences he is hiding.

If the word you give arouses a latent complex, the patient's emotion is aroused. This is indicated in the reply and in the mode of the reply: thus you know that you have touched on a complex which needs further investigation. These complex indicators, as they are called, produce embarrassment and that is indicated in various ways. They are: a long silence before answering (since emotion checks thought); replying with an unusual word (i.e., if you give 'book' and the patient replies 'South Africa' there must be some unusual association); the repetition of the similar word (the patient given 'book' replied 'book' as though playing for time); an inability to reply at all; or simply by 'don't know' a refusal to co-operate. The list of words may be given twice over and the answers in each case compared. Differences in the response indicate that a complex has been touched and thereby reveal the complex.

This word association method is not in fact used very much in ordinary psychological treatment, but is of great value for the discovery of the facts in cases of suspected crime or delinquency. It is of particular value with the unco-operative patient. A young delinquent may tell you nothing about the event, but he may be willing to tell you the first word that comes to his mind, because that, he thinks, will not give him away. When I last entertained Jung, he was using this method to find out the culprit in an embezzlement in a Swiss bank, and was discovering that the culprit was other than the previously suspected person. The tests may reveal a patient's guilt, but it may also reveal his innocence, as in the case of a boy expelled from public school for writing indecent letters, whom I found to be innocent by this method, so that the boy was taken back to school. The diagnosis was confirmed when the real culprit afterwards confessed. (Reported in my *Psychology and Mental Health*, p. 407.)

(h) *Relation of patient to analyst; transference.* Jung laid great stress on the transference of the patient's feelings towards the analyst; but his idea was very different from Freud's. Freud's views, we may remember, represent the transference of the patient's incestuous or hostile feelings from the parent to the analyst 'to whom they do not properly belong'. Jung, looking as usual to the positive and more purposive side of things regards the transference as 'an effort of the patient to establish a psychological rapport with the doctor: only if this fails will it revert to a sexual form'. The transference must be understood by physician and patient alike or else 'violent resistances make their appearance' (*Collected Papers*, p. 407). Jung therefore says, 'We do not work with the transference to the doctor (in the Freudian sense), but in spite of it.' He sees in the transference the libido (by no means merely sexual), trying to emerge from the collective unconscious: in that sense it must therefore be encouraged. 'If the transference to the physician takes place and is accepted, a natural channel has thus been found which makes a discharge of the energy possible and provides a course that is relatively free from conflict. There then takes place a dissolution of the transference, whereby the libido is freed from the unconscious, and released also from its attachment to the physician.

Analysis therefore assumes the form of an 'interplay of two personalities.' But what if the analyst himself has distortions in his own personality (and what analyst has not in spite of himself being analysed?) This interaction between two personalities is bound to affect the patient adversely. This is no imaginary danger, as I know from experience. For the analyst 'to step out of his anonymity and reveal himself' sounds very frank and honest, but suppose the revelation is of something abnormal in himself? Will it not affect a patient especially now that a transference has been set up between them in which, as so often, the patient identifies himself with the analyst? The distortion in the analyst's personality is bound to affect the patient's personality, whether by acceptance or by revolt against it. For instance, the question whether the analyst is religious or irreligious (a sceptic patient said to a religious analyst, 'You don't accept that nonsense do you?'); whether the analyst has a residue of rebellion against authority; whether he is over-sensitive to criticism or whether he is an extrovert dealing with an introvert patient—all these may be sensed by the patient whose personality is thereby adversely affected.

Apart from any distortion in the analyst's personality, what may be perfectly right for the analyst and his temperament may be entirely wrong for the patient's temperament. If a patient has a positive transference to such an analyst, he will be imposing on himself a line of life not really applicable to his own personality.

No doubt the Jungians have ways of combating these dangers: it is not easy to see what they are. In the last case the difficulty is partly met since the analyst's object is to bring out the patient's own personality as revealed for instance in dreams. But a patient with strong transference to the analyst may prefer to be the analyst rather than himself!

(i) *The analyst as catalyst.* The alternate method, I prefer, is that the analyst should be a catalyst (a chemical substance whose presence brings about chemical changes in other bodies without itself being changed). By this method the analyst keeps himself detached: his object is to keep the patient confronted with his neurosis alone. That seems to me the quickest and most direct way to cure—leaving the analyst only as the catalytic agent. This is done in direct reductive analysis (see p. 221), whereby the patient and the analyst concentrate on the original cause of the neurotic symptom, the relation of the patient to the analyst being merely one of confidence which enables the patient to pursue the analysis. (See p. 240.)

CHAPTER XXIII

JUNG'S DREAM INTERPRETATION

Jung's main method of revealing and of releasing the contents of the collective unconscious and integrating them into the personality is by the interpretation of dreams.

The collective unconscious is, according to Jung, the repository of all the potentialities of life, the creative mother, the spring, the source of life. When the conscious is incapable of integrating this material emerging from the unconscious, neurosis occurs.

It is the function of analytic treatment, therefore, to discover and to help to release this material so that it may be integrated into the personality and the neurosis dispelled.

How do we become aware of what the material is that is trying to emerge, and how are we to help its release? The answer is by dreams. Dreams are the language of the unconscious. They 'are the revelation of the collective unconscious. The emergence of such material into consciousness during sleep therefore affords us the easiest access to the contents of the unconscious. Dreams are a direct expression of unconscious activities.' (*Collected Works*, Vol. 16, p.140.)

His interpretation of dreams differs very radically from Freud's wish fulfilment theory. It is far more positive and more purposive. In brief, dreams represent not what we wish, but what we *need* for life.

This is Jung's compensatory theory of dreams—namely that the dream material shows in what we are deficient in our conscious lives, and is trying therefore to compensate for these deficiencies, to make perfect our imperfect lives.

It is easy to see, therefore, how the popular view arose that 'Dreams go by opposites'. The timid man dreams of fighting; the arrogant man is humiliated; the pious hermit has his nights filled with struggles against lascivious houris; and the pompous man finds himself in his dreams the object of ridicule. In reverse you can tell people's characters by their dreams.

Such dreams are not in fact mere wish fulfilments; they are correctives. A woman patient of mine who is too punctilious about her appearance before others (her *persona*), dreams of being married in her working clothes, and takes the whole thing as a joke; especially as there was not even a bridegroom. It was great fun. This dream was not primarily concerned with marriage as such, but with appearances. A dream like this, on the face of it, tells us diagnostically about the person herself, namely that in ordinary life she has too marked a *persona*, (the mask that she wears before others), that she is too conventional. Compensatorially the dream is encouraging her not to be so formal, not so conventional, to be more casual, not to take things so seriously. Moreover, by showing her to herself acting in that unconventional way it encourages her to be so, and indeed gives her some practice in it: and she finds it effective. It tells her how much more fun she would get out of life if she were more spontaneous and less conventional. Call that wish-fulfilment if you wish, but it is the wish or urge to fulfil her whole personality, nor is it sexual.

This compensatory theory throws a very different light on dream interpretation, the differences of which we may illustrate by a very common dream: namely, of the patient walking down the main street of the town without clothes on. Almost invariably the dreamer is quite unconcerned, or if he feels slightly embarrassed he notices that no one else is taking any particular notice of him: they too are quite unconcerned.

The Freudian interpretation would be that it is an exhibitionist tendency, a wish fulfilment to be sexually exposed. Jung would admit that this may be true, interpreting the dream reductively, but that does not exhaust the meaning of the dream. The physical nudity in the dream is symbolic of the patient's personality. Applying the principles of compensation, it tells us that such a person in ordinary life is too secretive, too shut in; and prognostically he needs to be more frank, less secretive, less self-conscious, more open in his relationship with others. The dream is purposive in that it shows his personality exposed to the world in a state of nudity and nothing happens, nobody is shocked, and he may be surprised to find that he also is not shocked, there is nothing to it. It is obvious that even without any dream interpretation, the dreamer, by the very fact of living through that experience is accustoming himself to play that role of open-mindedness.

I find that these two interpretations are not incompatible. For if we analyse it out reductively we find that one arises out of the other. The secretiveness originated in an actual sexual exhibitionist experience in childhood which was severely rebuked, so that the child was filled with shame at any form of self display, and retreated into herself with a self-consciousness which has persisted even though the cause of it has long since disappeared. Freud would be right in saying that the dream pointed to a wish for exhibitionism (in childhood) as a causal factor in the symptom; Jung would be right in regarding the reserve as a present-day problem, for which the exhibitionism in the dream is a compensation. The theories are therefore not incompatible for the early sexual exhibitionism with the subsequent humiliation was the cause of the present-day secretiveness. In treatment we may deal with present-day secretiveness; in reductive analysis with the causes. When the sexual exhibitionism of childhood is discovered and the emotions released, the present-day feelings of shame and self-consciousness attendant upon that experience are resolved and the resultant shyness and secretiveness vanish.

But to show the complexity of dream interpretation; the meaning of the dream may have the very opposite interpretation. The patient might be one who, far from being secretive, in everyday life is trying to get attention by self display: In that case the dream may be concerned with correcting that attitude: It may be saying, 'You don't need to think that everyone wants to look at you', the emphasis being not on the nakedness, but on the fact that nobody was taking notice. It says, 'Even in such an extreme illustration as walking down the street naked, nobody is bothered about you! You are not as important as all that'. Which is the right interpretation can only be derived from what we know of the patient's personality and by free association.

In brief, the Freudian interpretation of a dream is causative, and deals with the wish: the Jungian interpretation is purposive, a guide to life. I shall later (p. 243) advance the theory that the dream has a still deeper biological meaning than even compensation, namely that the biological function of every dream is an attempt to solve the unsolved problems of life. (chap. XXIX).

It is probably this purposive aspect of Jung's psychology which inspired Freud's implied sneer against Jung. 'C. G. Jung at a time when this investigator (Jung) was a mere psycho-analyst and did not yet aspire to be a prophet....' After all was not Freud himself playing the 'prophet' when he wrote *The Future of an Illusion*, in which he tried to de-bunk religion?

To give an illustration of this purposive aspect of the dream and the need to know something of the patient, let us look at another simple dream. A woman patient of mine, in later life, having retired from a very successful business and professional life has a dream that she removes her brassiere and covers her head with it. That is all. In Freudian terms it might represent a breast eroticism. That is an arbitrary interpretation which might or might not be true. Her history was that her mother died when the patient was an infant: she was brought up by a severe spinster aunt who regarded her as a nuisance, and gave her no love or affection. She was sent to school in shabby dresses: and being unaccustomed to any other children was quarrelsome and thoroughly unpopular with children and teachers alike. But she then found herself top of the class: so now at last she had a place in the sun, So she abandoned all desire for affection, and put all her energy into her brains and became a very succesful business woman—the only woman in fact in her particular profession—deliberately starving herself of love. Passing middle life her success began to wear thin and the love craving to make itself felt, but as it had to be repressed, it emerged as depression, for which she came for treatment. Then came the dream. In association she said, 'I realize my brassiere covering by breasts represents covering my love and affection: and my head obviously meant my intellectual side on which I concentrated.' What then was the dream telling her? It made her uncover her breasts, which she took to mean release of her love. The brassiere was then used to cover up her head, that is, toning down her intellectual side. In the dream she was made to do the opposite of what she was compelled to do in childhood. It was encouraging her to be less concentrated on her intellect and to give more play to affection, more outlet for her love in social life. The dream did more; in putting her brassiere on her head, she was combining love and intellect. Ultimately she took up antiquarian pursuits, which had always interested her, but for which she previously had no time. This occupied her intellect, but was also a labour of love, and brought her socially in contact with others. The analysis, helped by the dream, was making her whole, her intellect and affection were now harmonized in the same pursuit. The dream solved her problem!

One could interpret that dream as a mere wish fulfilment, the exposure of her breast; but in that case what are we to make of covering her head? The last part of any dream is the most important since that is what the dream is working up to (see p. 261). It may be termed 'compensatory' in that it gives expression to her love side which had always been starved. But her dream was even more than that. I would regard it as problem solving, since it solved the problem of the conflict between her emotional and her intellectual life, which had been split apart in childhood. The analysis produced a harmonization between the two, and she was cured of her depression. Which was caused by the lack of love.

Dreams as diagnostic. In the first place then, dreams tell us what is actually taking place in the psyche. Thus in analysis, 'Dreams, particularly dreams which appear at the very outset of the treatment, often bring to light the essential analytical facts in the most unmistakable way.' 'They show the inner truth and reality of the patient as he really is . . . not as I conjecture it to be, and not as he would like it to be, *but as he is.* . . . I take dreams as valuable facts' (*Psychotherapy*, p.143). Thus 'the manifest dream contains the *whole* meaning of the dream' (ibid., p.149).

Dreams as prognostic. But dreams have a more positive and

creative function than merely telling us what is taking place in the psyche. In as much as the unconscious is the source of all creative energy, the matrix of our lives, dreams tell us what we need for life. Therefore 'The aim of dream analysis is to uncover and realize those hitherto unconscious contents which are considered to be of importance to the treatment of a neurosis' (*Col. wks.*, Vol. 10, p.139) Freud says dreams are mere wish fulfilments to enable us to sleep: Jung, that they contain the creative material we need for our lives.

Therefore, 'If a person holds the view that the unconscious plays a decisive part in the aetiology of neuroses, he will attribute a high practical importance to dreams as a *direct expression of the unconscious* (ibid., Vol. 10, p.139). 'The avowed aim of dream analysis is to uncover and realize those hitherto unconscious contents which are considered to be of importance to the treatment of a neurosis.'

Symbolic Representation in Dreams. Jung's concept of symbolism is somewhat different from Freud's. With Freud the purpose of symbolism was to disguise the forbidden unconscious wishes, so as to make them conformable to consciousness. We kill the king instead of killing the father; we make use of an urn when we mean a womb. Jung's concept of symbolism seems to be that the collective unconscious being archaic and primitive, it is incapable of abstract thought, and that it has to resort to concrete symbols in its attempt to express itself. The symbol is an indication of what is emerging from the unconscious.

So the unconscious mind makes use of pictorial language, images, imagination, phantasies, visions and bizarre situations, all of which are symbolic representations of what it is trying to express. The German word for symbol is 'Sinnbild', i.e., 'Sinn' a meaning, and 'Bild' a picture— a meaningful picture. The value of a symbol therefore is that it gives expression to something which cannot otherwise be expressed—just as music conveys to us what cannot be expressed in words. 'It is these symbols that we must study if we are to interpret a dream.'

Sometimes psychological entities may be represented by animals or people. Thus rage may be represented in the form of a furious monster: sex as a vampire which sucks our blood and saps our vitality: the idea of growth is symbolized as a tree: the collective unconscious itself may be represented by a mother, or by a lake, or a cave containing hidden treasure. It must not be thought therefore that these persons and situations are the real objects about which the dream is concerned: they are representative of deeper processes within ourselves. The 'dream work' (as Freud would call it) consists in turning the primitive thoughts or feelings into their relevant

G*

symbols; dream interpretation consists of reversing the process and discovering the psychological realities which they represent.

Some of these symbols are so appropriate that we find them over and over again in myths, such as the 'tree' of life, the idea of re-birth (the phoenix), or the lake for the unconscious. So images like that of the snake, the fish, the sphinx or helpful animals all represent and symbolize functions taking place in the collective unconscious. They are projections of these unconscious processes. They may however be personal as well as collective symbols (*Psychological Types*, p. 605).

In other cases we pick on persons to represent what we are trying to express: thus cynicism may be represented by a cynical person of our acquaintence; self-pity, or sympathy may be projected on to and be represented by, self-pitying or sympathetic persons. Our neurotic self, may be represented by a neurotic person whom we may or may not know. Thus the dream, as Maurice Nicholl in *Dream Psychology* has shown, is a drama in which the *dramatis personae* represent certain ideas or emotions, and their relationships to one another, *King Lear* and *Hamlet* are not stories about persons: they represent basic human experiences in disaster, in-gratitude and indecision. So, if a woman appears in a dream, she may stand for a woman we know, concerning whom we have some problem; or symbolically she may stand for vanity, (our vanity, that is), or she may represent in a man the *anima* or feminine part of his nature; or she may stand for a mother complex, or finally, for the archetypal 'mother' in the unconscious.

Thus Jung rejects the idea of fixed symbols in dream interpreta-tion—that is to say that a certain symbol represents a certain fact—such as Freud's interpretation of anything long representing the penis. Indeed he maintains that when sex itself comes in a dream it may signify sex, but sex may be symbolic of something deeper in the unconscious. 'To assume standard symbols ... would be a contradiction of Jung's conception of the nature and structure of the psyche.' (*Jacobi*, p.74). So the snake in mythology is not merely a phallic symbol although it may be; it is the symbol also of wis-dom, or craftiness, as it often is in dreams. It may also stand for healing, as with Moses in the wilderness, and as such perpetuated in the emblem of Aesculapius and in the badge of the R.A.M.C.

Jung says that primitive people would never have dreamed of confusing the phallus, a ritualistic symbol, with the penis. The Phallus is the creative mana, the power of healing, of fertility, of the extraordinarily potent. (*Principle of Psychotherapy*, p.137.) If I remember rightly, the Australian aboriginal men of the Arunta tribe have a ceremony in which they make a hole in the ground, gather round and throw spears into this hole—obviously a sexual symbol, but just as obviously this does not refer to sex as such, for why should they thus represent symbolically something concerning which they have no inhibitions whatever? In this ceremony sex itself is used as a symbol of fertility, which is the essential and true meaning of the ceremony. These fertility rites refer to fertility of the soil—a far more pressing and anxious matter than sex to the aboriginal. Since the primitive mind produces effects of imitation (sticking pins into a clay image of a man to injure him), so they produce fertility by imitating it by the sexual ceremony. That is why the ritual is directed to the soil, to make it fertile.

How then in any particular case can it be decided which interpretation to follow: what for instance 'the woman' in one dream stands for? First, by 'amplification', and discussion with the patient as to what the symbol signifies to him. Secondly, the dream must be evaluated according to the meaning in the context. Thirdly, by reference to the myths of the race.

Myths. Myths of the race represent the same material of the unconscious as dreams in the individual. We therefore resort to myths to tell us what certain symbols stand for. (Freud also resorted to myths but the one he was most concerned with was the Oedipus myth, (the sexual attachment of a boy to his mother), which is certainly an important one but not the only one).

Jung thus finds a solution to this problem of interpretation in myths. 'We are able in dreams to experience, as if they were real, the myths and legends that are real when waking'. Therefore by a study of the myths and their meaning we shall be able to interpret the dream material. A knowledge of the myths of man is, therefore, a necessary equipment for the interpretation of dreams for the analytical psychologist. 'The collective unconscious can only be fully interpreted by resort to myths and legends—for the unconscious is expressed in these terms. We must therefore scan the earth to discover the myths of all nations, to interpret as we might interpret ancient hieroglyphics, what it is the dream is trying to tell us and what is the meaning of its symbolic figures. The myth of the hero grappling with the monster represents a man's struggle with the instincts and monsters of his unconscious life. So with St. George and the Dragon. St. Paul expresses the same idea when he says, 'We fight not against flesh and blood, but against principalities and powers and world rulers of darkness in heavenly places.'

Although Jung discards the idea of fixed symbols he does at times appear to break his own rule—though I do not think it would bother him to be told so—for he declares, for instance, that 'the sea always signifies a collecting place, that is the collective unconscious'. This, however, does not invalidate his general principle. Cut out the always and substitute usually and the dictum holds.

Causality and finality. It is obvious from these illustrations that, according to Jung, dreams have a purposive aspect; they deal with what the personality is striving to be, and with any luck is going to be; for they deal with the creative sources of power within us striving for expression.

This indeed illustrates a marked difference between Jung's whole attitude towards life and that of Freud. Jung expresses their difference in this way: Freud looks upon life from the point of view of *causality;* Jung regards life from the point of view of *finality*, what it is leading us to, what is its meaning and purpose (*Col. Papers*, Vol. 16, p. 278). 'Causality' Jung says, 'is only one principle and psychology cannot by its very nature be exhausted by causal explanation alone, for the psyche is also purposive.' (*Analytical Psychology*, Edit. 1917, pp. x–xii). 'The creative element in our psyche and its manifestations can neither be demonstrated or explained causally.' Again, 'The concept of finality is indispensable since no explanation of nature that is purely mechanistic suffices.' (*Col. Works*, Vol. 16, p. 278.) Indeed as regards the mechanistic, we may remind ourselves, as McDougall pointed out (p.120), that even a machine is not 'merely mechanical'; it is a purposive instrument. The causative principle may be sufficient for pure science, but not for an understanding of man who is purposive in his aims. From the purely scientific angle Freud is right; for all science is based on cause and effect and we cannot truly understand any phenomena without knowing its cause, nor can we adequately cure any disorders without understanding its origin. But from the point of view of the pursuit of life, Jung's concept of finality is necessary. We are not merely pushed forward in life by our impulses, we are drawn forward in pursuit of our ends and aims. It is purpose which gives incentive, zest and inspiration to life; and calls forth our greatest endeavour.

Jung, like McDougall, is essentially 'hormic' in his psychology (p. 119). They are both also dynamic, but both realize that the dynamic forces of life must be directed towards right ends. This purposive element in life is missing in Freud's teaching which therefore tends to be pessimistic. It is this purposeful aspect which compels Jung to accept the spiritual meaning of life. He recognizes, of course, the importance of the sex instinct (Freud) and of power instinct (Adler), but he is insistent upon the spiritual and religious needs of man which he regards as also inborn in the psyche. 'The spiritual appears in the psyche as a drive or pure passion. It is not a derivation of another drive (presumably he refers to sex) but a principle *sui generis.*' (*Contribution to Analytical Psychology*, p. 66.) 'About a third of all cases,' he says, 'suffer from no clinical demonstrable neurosis whatever but from the meaninglessness and purposelessness of their life.' (*Modern Man*, p. 71). It is this positive and purposive element in Jung's teaching which makes him more acceptable to the clergy and religious people than Freud, because he 'believes in religion,' whereas Freud regards religion as an 'illusion'. But Jung's idea of religion is very different from the orthodox view. That is evident from his book on Job in which, as I understand it, he interprets the atonement as the atonement of God to man for having played Job such a dirty trick as to submit him to all kinds of suffering for the sake of proving Job's loyalty to Himself. (I suspect that in this diatribe against God, Jung is having a whack at his own very authoritative Lutheran father!)

It should, therefore, be pointed out that when he says that the essential factor in the breakdown of those over middle age is lack of 'religion', we can take him to mean a lack of purpose, of a philosophy of life.

Both Freud's and Jung's aim in analysis is a liberation, but Freud's is a liberation of the motive forces of sex and aggression which have been repressed in childhood, whereas Jung's is a liberation of the potentialities of the collective unconscious which the patient has been so far unable to integrate into his personality. If Freud neglects too much the purposive element in life, I think Jung, perhaps as a reaction to Freud, does not pay sufficient regard to the importance of actual experiences in early childhood which stifle the instinctual forces within us and so cause the neuroses.

Pioneers in any field naturally emphasize and often exaggerate the importance of their discoveries to the detriment of the discoveries of others. Those of us who are on-lookers should be able to appreciate the importance of all these contributions.

To summarize: Jung has revealed many new factors of the human personality, and has launched many new ideas on to the sea of human culture, which are of great interest and value. His main contributions to psychotherapy are (a) the discovery of the collective unconscious, and of the archaic in man; (b) the importance and effect of the collective unconscious on consciousness in every day life; (c) its value as the source of all creative energy; (d) its effect in causing neurotic disorders when it cannot be integrated into the personality; (e) his emphasis on present-day conflicts as the precipitating cause of neurotic disorders; (f) the purposive nature of human life and endeavour in general, and of dreams in particular; (g) finally, the spiritual nature of man.

CHAPTER XXIV

JUNG'S PERSONALITY TYPES

The specific symptom from which a patient suffers, whether hysteria, obsession or a sexual perversion, depends largely upon early experiences, by the process of regression: the patient 'borrows' a symptom from the past. But it also depends largely on the constitutional make-up or type of the patient—and in the first place whether he is an extrovert or an introvert. This determines his specific response to life.

The terms 'extroversion' and 'introversion', invented by Jung, have entered into everyday language: the extrovert being considered the person whose interests are directed to the outside objective world, (roughly speaking the typical builder or the geologist), while the introvert's interest is in the inside subjective world, it may be the philosopher or the poet.

'Introversion,' says Jung, 'is the withdrawal of libido from outside objects to the inner psychic world.' Extroversion is turning towards the outside world, and regarding the subjective as insignificant. The man with the extroverted attitude 'loses himself primarily in social relationships'; the other, the introvert, has no interest in social relationships, regarding them as terrifying (*Collected Works*, Vol. 16, p.117).

Jacobi, whose book *The Psychology of C. G. Jung* is approved by Jung says, 'The extrovert thinks, feels and acts in relation to the *object*: he associates himself predominantly with what lies outside him. With the introvert, the *subject* is the starting point and the object is accorded at most a secondary indirect value.'

The types have been described before under different names. They largely correspond to what Wm. James called the 'tough' type and the 'tender' type; and to what others called the 'motor' type and the 'sensory' type. Indeed, they correspond very largely to the 'schizoid' and the 'cycloid' types of Kretschmer, the schizoid being introverted, the cycloid extroverted.

Both extroversion and introversion are normal attitudes. In the West we normally regard the extrovert as the more healthy type and the introvert as less healthy, whereas in the 'mystic East' the reverse is usually the case, the mystic being given an honoured place in communal life. Both are normal but both may go wrong. Jung says (*Collected Works*, Vol. 16, p. 33), 'Both extroversion and introversion are good ways of living; so long as they co-operate reasonably well. It is a dominating one-sidedness that leads to disaster.' The two attitudes are, nevertheless, opposed and compensatory. If the conscious attitude is extroverted, the unconscious is introverted, undifferentiated and under-developed.

But there seems to be some dubiety as to the exact meaning of the terms—possibly because of a change in Jung's own concept, for Bennet, who knew the mind of Jung as well as anybody else, being a personal friend as well as a colleague, gives more subtle definitions of these terms. He states that the introvert can be intensely interested in the objects of the outside world, but he is interested in them *only in so far as they affect him*. The extrovert on the other hand is mainly interested in objects as such, and hardly recognizes that he has a subjective side to his nature. (Bennet, *C. G. Jung*, p. 69.) Thus introversion and extroversion can be distinguished in terms of motives. The introvert is concerned with the fact that he is moved or terrified by some situation; the extrovert does not realize that he is moved and attributes everything to the object— which he sees as 'wonderful' or 'terrifying.'

A difficulty here arises. How are we to judge as to whether a person is extrovert or introvert? Some persons or children are of a constitutionally extroverted type and then, because of some happening such as a humiliation, become introverted and self-conscious, concerned with their own feelings and how things affect them. To which type would you say the child belonged? Jung recognizes this difficulty but makes it clear (*Collected Works*, Vol. 16, p. 415) that he regards these types as referring to the constitutional or inborn type and not due to reaction to the environment in childhood. Bennet also makes it clear that either extroversion or introversion is the constitutional attitude in which the patient is naturally inclined to act. Yet he says, 'When introversion or extroversion is habitual, natural, one speaks of an introverted or an extroverted type. (Bennet, *C. G. Jung*, p. 70).

That does not seem to me to overcome the difficulty, for a person does not necessarily 'habitually' act according to his constitution: for if a person is overcompensating, his 'habitual' attitude and behaviour are of this over-compensating type and does not represent his basic constitutional type. The person who is constitutionally extroverted may on account of circumstances become shy and self-conscious, and this is now his 'habitual' mode of behaviour—but it is not his constitutional type. On the other hand a person who constitutionally is somewhat shy and reserved may for that very reason try to cover up his reserve by a 'habitual' hail-fellow-well-met attitude to social life. It makes it very difficult without a lot of investigation to discover what the constitutional type of any particular person really is.

That these types were not as clear-cut in practice as they were defined, is illustrated in the fact that Jung regarded McDougall (so the latter told me) as a typical introvert: whereas Baynes—at that time Jung's right-hand man, regarded him as an extrovert.

However, as Bennet (ibid., p. 69) says, 'Whether or not extrovert or introvert exist in reality is not for Jung the essence of the matter . . . he finds his typology gives some understanding of the psychology of the individual.' And after all that is all that matters. The terms simply indicate 'the direction of psychic energy in the average person' (ibid., p. 70). That is true; the distinction is very useful as long as we remember that people are not always what they seem on the surface! Otherwise we may make serious mistakes in assessing their characters.

Jung further classified aspects of the personality into four categories, each of which can be either extroverted or introverted. These were the *thinking type*, the *feeling type*, the *intuition type* and the *sensation type*—so that, for instance, we have an extrovert thinking type, and the intuitive type may be either extroverted or introverted—eight personality types in all. They may be represented in a diagram

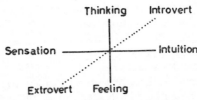

These types are in some sense opposed to one another, the thinking type being the opposite of the feeling type and the sensation type the opposite of the intuitive type. If one of these types is dominant and well-developed in any particular individual, the opposite type is under-developed, undifferentiated and crude. So if sensation is dominant, intuition is insufficiently developed; if feeling is dominant, thinking is undifferentiated and crude.

It is through these functions of thinking, feeling, sensation and intuition that we are conscious of the outside world, respond to it and adopt an attitude towards it. When a situation is presented to us we think about it, or we may simply have sensations relating to it, or we may 'value' it by our feeling (for some reason Jung connects feeling with value), or we may make intuitive judgments regarding it. Thus people's reactions to an event like an accident in the street may be entirely different according to their types and how they approach it; so that they might well be describing quite different events. In a court of Law they will give entirely different versions of what happened. The introvert will be concentrated on how it affects him; the extrovert will be concerned as to the actual facts: the thinking type may be considering how the accident happened; the intuitive type may have a hunch as to how such accidents can be avoided. The feeling type may, if extroverted, be concerned with what it means in suffering to those in the accident, or maybe is concerned with his own distress, so that all he can say is 'how awful it all was!'; while the sensation type is simply thrilled by the whole thing.

To describe these types rather more specifically: the thinking type is one which is mainly ruled by reflective thinking so that every important action proceeds from intellectually considered motives (*Psychological Types*, p. 434). If this thinking type is concerned with objective data he is a thinking extrovert. If his approach is subjective, how it affects him, he is a thinking introvert. For the latter, views and opinions are more important than facts. He does not derive the idea from the facts, although he may think he does, but selects only those facts which conform to his views.

I remember a discussion in about the year 1920 in which William Brown, the Oxford medical psychologist, brought forward a number of clinical data from the war to prove a point. Wildon Carr, the philosopher, then rose and said: 'I'm bored stiff with facts!' Both were undoubtedly thinking types but one was a thinking extrovert, the other a thinking introvert.

The *extroverted feeling* type is opposite to the extroverted *thinker*. He is affected by tradition or good form or desire to accommodate. Such people conform to fashions, they support social and philanthropic enterprises; they flock to church, cinemas and concerts, wherever people congregate, without thinking why. This type, Jung says, is more common among women. A woman chooses her husband without being informed of his character but is simply guided by her love feeling. 'I love him and that is all that matters,' is a common saying of girls contemplating an indiscreet marriage. 'Stop and think of the consequences,' says her thinking extrovert father!—while the mother, a feeling introvert, is absorbed with the distress it causes her—'It gave me a terrible shock.'

The *introverted feeling* types—also mostly women, are of the 'still waters run deep' type. They are somewhat unapproachable, difficult to understand and withdrawn. They are cold and indifferent on the surface but have great depth of feeling and may surprise everyone by great acts of heroism.

The *intuitive type* is the one who has hunches, who can see round corners, who has premonitions but does not know where they come from. In this, as in the other types, the function may be either introverted or extroverted according to whether the data of the intuition is coming from the inside or outside world.

The *sensation type* is the one whose response is mainly not in thinking nor feeling but in the senses. The main concern of these people is the effect of events upon their sensations, how it affects them. They tend to be 'thrilled' by this or that, they are always looking for a new sensation. They may be looking for their satisfaction in the outside world or in themselves—the one is the extroverted sensation, the other the introverted sensation type. When such a man has 'sensed' something, everything essential has been said and done. 'No other human type can equal the extroverted sensation type in realism. His source of objective facts is extraordinarily developed.' His life is an accumulation of actual experiences. He may be sensual or gross: or he may differentiate his sensations to a new higher pitch of aesthetic purity.'

I should think one could gauge a man's type pretty well by the type of holiday he chooses—climbing mountains; a quiet cottage reading; dashing all over the continent in a car; or quietly fishing in a Highland lock.

In a perfect human being all these aspects of the personality should be cultivated—the thinking type, for instance, should set about cultivating his capacity to feel—but that is more than most of us can hope to do.

Psychological types and neurosis. As already noted, the opposite to the dominant or superior type is undeveloped, crude, indifferentiated: and therefore tends to emerge in crude form as a symptom. The clash between the undeveloped inferior function which is always craving for expression and the dominant superior function, is apt to produce a neurosis and the neurotic symptom is mainly an expression of the repressed undifferentiated function.

According to the personality type, so the specific form of neurosis. Thus the introverted thinking type—that is to say the person who thinks, but whose thinking relates to the effect on himself, has a struggle to preserve his individuality. The result is exhaustion and neurasthenia. The introverted sensation type represses his intuition (which is the opposite to the sensation) and so suffers from compulsion neurosis.

I shall not illustrate further: for though I regard these types as of useful descriptive value, I cannot see how these neuroses logically follow. Jung's description leaves one with the impression that he tends to force the symptoms to fit the various categories, describing what he conceives the symptoms ought to be in the different types rather than what they are found to be—a characteristic, as Jung says, of the thinking introvert. But I do not press my criticism for one is liable to be critical of what one doesn't understand, and as I was told by Jung that I am of the intuitive type, I cannot be expected to understand the thinking type.

If we are apt to criticize Jung's views as I have in some cases done, Jung would have no objection to such criticism. For he was insistent that these ideas of his are merely hypothesis, to be accepted or corrected by future knowledge. He was not dogmatic nor intolerant of criticism but was ready to listen to the opinions of any one in any group discussion. He claims, however, that what he describes is what he sees in human nature, when he looks into his own and his patients' lives.

As to the scientific proof of his theories he had a long discussion with Bennet, published in the latter's book: *C. G. Jung*. His attitude seems to be that the truth of any conception is that of its applicability. If it 'applies,' if it is found to work, that is evidence enough. What is called scientific proof is no more acceptable and indeed is often proved to be wrong. This theory is reminiscent of the pragmatism of Wm. James, with which Jung was no doubt acquainted, which teaches briefly that we tend to believe as true what works in practice.

CHAPTER XXV

THE ARCHETYPES

I leave to the end a consideration of the archetypes, because they are of dubious origin. We have met them in the consideration of dreams. Their definition is by no means clear.

The presence of the archaic in human life is accepted by biologists and psychologists alike. As already stated, there are archaic residues in our bodies, like the gills of aquatic life which persist in the Eustachian tube between the mouth and the ear, enabling us to hear; the appendix, once provided digestive juices for herbiverous animals, but now not only useless but dangerous.

The concept of the archaic in mental life should not be difficult to accept. We possess a mental inheritance in our instincts which are innate and inborn potentialities which are called forth into action by environmental stimuli; such as fear and flight in a situation of danger, anger when we are frustrated.

There are also mental qualities like intelligence, imagination, intuition and wisdom all of which are archaic and inherited.

Jung's concept of the archetypes differs from all of these in that they are images—they are 'primordial archetypal images'.

The idea of the archetypes was derived from Plato who said that everything on earth had its ideal form in heaven—a table for instance. This ideal form stands in a different category from all the forms on earth, just as, if I may take a flippant example, the Paris model stands unique as distinct from all the copies of it.

It was St Augustine, however, who first used the word archetype.

Jung's archetypes are of that nature, ideal images or patterns of thought, but he would say that they came not from heaven but from our collective unconscious.

The Archetypes and instincts. The archetypes are akin to the instincts in that they are both innate. They are both impersonal, both universal and both necessary to life. But whilst the instincts are dynamic forces, drives or urges, the archetypes are primordial *images*, they are 'thought feelings', pictures by which the instincts present themselves in consciousness. They are 'psychological processes transformed into pictures' (Jacobi *The Psychology of C. G. Jung*, p. 44). They are inherited potentialities of imagination or ways of thinking.' Bennet makes the contrast that 'whereas instincts are inborn manners of *acting*, the archetypes are inborn manners of *comprehension*.'

There is another important distinction: the instincts are mainly aroused from stimuli from the outside world, such as flight in a situation of danger, whereas archetypes are conceived by Jung as emerging from the collective unconscious, irrespective of circumstances. They affect consciousness from within and indeed are the source of conscious thinking. They do not spring from conscious experiences (that is the personal unconscious), but on the contrary they affect and determine consciousness. Jung's idea of the archetypes are, therefore, not urges but innate images.

Archetypes and Complexes. A contrast must also be drawn between archetypes and complexes. Complexes arise from personal experiences that have been repressed and forgotten; archetypes come from racial experiences which are impersonal and have never yet been experienced personally. 'Whereas the personal unconscious consists for the most part of complexes, the contents of the collective unconscious is made up essentially of archetypes' (*Collected Works*, Vol. 9, Part 1, p. 42). 'Archetypes are to the collective unconscious what complexes are to the personal unconscious.' The archetypes, we may say, are the forms taken by the material emerging from the collective unconscious.

To get a clearer view of what Jung calls the archetypes let us briefly review one or two of them.

The *hero* struggling with the monster, St George and the dragon, Jonah and the whale which swallows him up, represent man's eternal struggle with the mighty forces in the unconscious, which threaten to swallow him up. This is an eternal struggle common to all men; it is therefore archetypal. But the only way in which this abstract idea can be envisaged is by a hero archetype.

Persona. Everyone is aware that we have two aspects of our personality: there is the one we present to the outside world, the aim of which is to be acceptable to our community. This is not our 'real self': it is the 'persona' or mask we wear before our fellows. It represents not what we really are but what we appear to be. (*Two Essays*, p.165.) It is a compromise between the individual and the society in which he lives. It is also the attitude through which connection is maintained with the outside world. (Bennet, *C. G. Jung*, p.139.) 'The persona is a function necessitated by adaptation to the external world' (*Jung, Psychological Types*, p. 541). It nevertheless has its value. 'A well-fitting and functioning *persona* is an essential condition of psychic health,' since it facilitates our individual adaptation to society (Jacob ibid., p. 21). But of course it may constitute a conflict between the thing that we are and the thing that we pose as being.

The persona may thus become a danger. When it is over-developed by too rigid an identification with the demands of society, it stifles one's real individuality. 'Behind such a mask the individual shrivels and becomes empty.' To many people an office or a title is an incentive to achievement: but in other cases the 'prestige symbols' may be adopted as a façade to compensate for a poor creature inside. Reliance is placed on that conventional pose to the detriment of the real individual which never gets a chance and shrinks more and more. The clothes that 'makyth man' may end by suffocating him. We all know people whose conventionality does not give their real selves a chance to develop. They are uninteresting because they are never themselves, for only when a person is being himself is he really interesting, and everyone who is himself is interesting. Analysis often consists in unmasking a personality. Jung calls the persona an archetype.

Anima. Behind this mask or persona there lies the soul-image, in Jung's term the anima. The function of the persona and anima are different. 'The persona is a meditating function between the Ego and the outside world; but the soul image, the anima, is the corresponding mediating function between the Ego and their inner world.' (Jacobi, ibid, p.108). Furthermore the nature or character of the anima is opposite to that of the persona. 'If the persona is intellectual the soul image is quite certainly sentimental.' This is in accordance with Jung's principles of the 'play of opposites' or 'compensation'. Jung speaks of 'anima' in the man, and 'animus' in the woman: the anima is the female part of the man; the animus is the male part in the woman. 'Every man carries the Eve in himself and every woman carries the man in herself.' This applies physiologically as well as psychologically: the male has miniature breasts and a diminutive uterus, whereas the woman has the male counterpart in the clitoris, an anatomical enlargement of which is often associated with a masculine type of woman. But there are all grades in between, some men being excessively male, of the Herculean type, whereas other men are of the feminine or Hermes type, more gentle. The woman who by nature and psychological make-up is more masculine, is the 'virago' of Italy, now a term of opprobrium, but at one time a term of commendation and prestige. So with the term 'Amazon' which means 'lack of breast', which she is said to have cut off to wield her weapon more effectively—a masculine rôle. Women athletes in the Olympics have to be physically examined to make sure they are not of this masculine type since one of them changed and became a man.

In a man the anima may be variously represented in dreams as a timid maid, a pure virgin, a goddess, a beggar woman or a whore, according to the nature of the anima in the man's unconscious. The animus in a woman's dreams may appear as a strong masculine figure, as the hero, the prince charming, Valentino or the latest film star. The soul image being suppressed and unrecognized has to be projected on to these outward symbols; but they give us a clue in treatment as to the specific nature of the patient's anima or animus, that is to say how far it is abnormal.

For a completely integrated personality the development of both these sides of our nature is necessary. A man may be greatly assisted in life by his intuition, a feminine quality, and a woman by her practical capabilities.

All this, therefore, has practical applications. A man's attitude to his anima, to the female part of himself, of which he is unaware, is often projected on to his wife in objective life, against whom he may feel resentment, animosity or fear, according to what is his attitude towards his own anima. It may also account for his moodiness which is the worse side of a woman's character.

Again, we need to be conversant with our anima in our life, for not only does it require expression in our lives, but as intuition it is a fairly safe guide in life and its voice should be heard and be given recognition. In my '*Dreams and Nightmares*' (Penguin p. 85–87), I have given an illustration of the anima appearing in the form of a female. In this dream a man (like Prometheus) is stealing fire for himself and meets with a negro (representing his primitive self), whom he is about to slay: then a female form (anima or intuition) appears saying, 'Don't kill him, but send him to a reformatory'—in other words 'Don't try to destroy your primitive self, but develop it and make full use of it'—a truly 'purposive' dream.

The shadow. Behind and beyond even the anima in the collective unconscious, is the shadowy self, dark and mysterious, which we only vaguely percieve but of which we get strange glimpses in our dreams. This Jung calls the 'Shadow'. It may also appear in dreams as 'the dark brother' or 'the stranger'. The conscious personality may be incapable of coping with it and it is therefore regarded in dreams as dangerous (Jacobi ibid., p.102). It is the Mr Hyde as opposed to the more civilized Dr Jekyll: it is the Caliban, projected as a primaeval monster. Children are particularly frightened of it for such shadowy dreams are very vivid. They are the bogies of the child's imagination.

The wise old man. There is deep within our human nature a propensity not only to observe and record facts, but to discover the meaning of things, to find out the significance of events. It is the spiritual principle in our lives. Jung strongly emphasizes the spiritual nature of man, and man's need to fulfil his spiritual longings. This, Jung says, is an archetype, a racial characteristic, which is projected in our dreams as a 'wise old man', or as a prophet or a magician who can work wonders, the Magi or wise men of the East, or simply as a leader. In women it appears as the great mother, the goddess, the sylph, the princess.

Readers of Kon Tiki will recall that the author in his researches on Easter Island, found that every man had his Aku-Aku, a guardian spirit who directs his life and actions and sees to it that he makes right decisions in life. This is the projection, the image of his intuition. These functions represent the guiding principles of our lives, the wider vision by which our lives find their fulfilment, giving us 'a great sense of exaltation'. If on the other hand he identifies himself too much with them, he suffers from megalomania in which he himself becomes, in his imagination, the god.

The mother archetype. In ordinary life every child in its helplessness has a need of protection and security, and depends for everything in life, food, warmth, comfort and life itself, upon its mother. Jung claims that behind the actual mother lies the collective unconscious which is the matrix, the mother of all life, supplying us with all the needs of our psychic life. This is the archetypal mother. It represents all that is creative in human life as well as all that is protective. Indeed the collective unconscious is the mother, the source from which all consciousness springs. He goes further and claims that the idea we have of our personal mother may be derived from the archetypal mother which is pre-existent. Therefore Jung says, 'I attribute to the *personal* mother only a limited aetiological significance.' 'All the influences which the pedagogue describes as being exerted on the children does not come from the mother herself but rather from the archetype projected on to her, which gives her a mythological background and invests her with authority.' This perhaps explains why it is that Jung appears to attach comparatively little significance to the actual early experience of a child and its treatment by the mother, in the production of neurotic disorders. It is the archetypal mother who is projected on to the actual mother and takes on various forms and qualities which are now wrongly attributed to the real mother. She is sometimes goddess, sometimes the fairy mother, sometimes a witch and sometimes the 'terrible mother', like Siva the Indian god.

In the treatment of the patient therefore, Jung says that what the patient attributes to his personal mother may really be a projection on to her of the archetypal mother within his unconscious, and must therefore be referred back to this.

Critique of the archetypes. I am myself very dubious about the archetypes as Jung regards them. If he is maintaining that besides the instincts which are powerful drives, there are also innate patterns of thought which appear as images and that these patterns or ways of thinking may well be called archetypes, as distinct from the potentialities we call the instincts, there is little to which we can take exception. For the instincts certainly do not exhaust all that is innate in our mental functioning. Intelligence, intuition, imagination, suggestibility and other mental functions are equally innate, inherited and universal; they also may be said to be creative—imagination for instance. When these functions are operative in dreams, they are naturally represented in visual or pictorial forms, such as a female form standing for one's intuition, giving guidance to men.

For there is in human nature a strong tendency, especially in children and in dreams, where the primitive mind is operative, to objectify, project and personalize our mental functions; for only by doing so can we grasp and express abstract ideas. So with our instincts which are so strong and overpowering that in our dreams we objectify them so that our rage appears as an overwhelming monster and our sex passions as vampires as sucking our blood. In our fight to control these passions we depict ourselves as 'the hero' like St George.

So with our other qualities, such as our intelligence and intuition. When the child experiences these in himself they are so abstract that he pictures them as persons. So Nausicaa's intuition telling her not to be so hoydenish, but to care more for her appearance, appeared in her dream as the goddess Athene (Homer). So our intellectual powers may be depicted—objectified and personalized—as a brainy university don. What then more natural when we wish to depict our wisdom than that we should do so in the form of a 'wise old man'.

These qualities in human nature are innate and inherited, and therefore are both archaic and universal. We can, if we like, become poetic and call all such inherited qualities of the human mind 'archetypes', though we should understand that these *archetypes are nothing more than the projections, objectifications and personalizations of mental processes.*

There are other experiences, however, which are not innate or archaic, but personal experiences which we also project in the same way. Chief among these is the 'archetype' of the 'terrible mother', an angry woman with staring eyes which often appears in dreams. Analyze such a dream reductively and you find that it relates to the real mother, for what mother at some time does not get irritated and angry, with staring eyes, which terrifies the child;

for the mother who is usually so kind and gentle suddenly turns into a wolf! The child dreams of the terrible mother because the mother is terrible. As for its near-universality, such an image may appear in dreams and mythology all over the world because such an infant's experience of the mother is well-nigh universal.

The so-called archetypes therefore have a simple explanation, and I see no reason for making them mysterious.

Jacobi (ibid, p. 44) says, 'The Aristotelian would say "The archetypes are conceptions derived from experiences of the real father or mother". The Platonist would say; "father and mother have sprung from the archetypes, for these are the primordial images".' I would put myself strongly on the side of Aristotle, and hold the belief that neurotic disorders spring from actual experiences of early childhood.

CHAPTER XXVI

INDIVIDUAL PSYCHOLOGY: ADLER

Adler's is the psychology without tears. It is easy to understand; it is easy to apply, and it is applicable to many cases.

Adler was the discoverer of the inferiority complex—a most popular complex; for, as we have pointed out, when people say that they have an inferiority complex it signifies that they are really much finer fellows than they think they are—a back-handed compliment. But largely true, for none of us lives up to his whole potential.

The Adlerian system underwent two phases. The first was characterized by 'organ inferiority.' The second phase by 'lack of co-operation.'

First phase—organ inferiority. He said a person starts off with an 'organ inferiority', that is to say some physical defect, which makes him feel inferior—it may be because he is small of stature; or that he is lame, or ugly, or red-haired or that he stammers. Because of this inferiority he must compensate, and he does so by aiming at some great achievement in other ways—he must be a great success in business, a great musician, a great scholar, a great explorer. But to achieve this end he *over*-compensates and he sets before himself ideals and aims which in fact are beyond him. These are 'fictitious goals.' Then he finds he cannot reach them. But to admit failure would mean that he would sink back into his dreadful state of inferiority. What then is he to do? He develops an illness of some sort—for then he can say, 'If it were not for this illness what could I not have achieved!' There is no doubt that many cases of neurosis follow this pattern.

In contrast to Freud, therefore, who emphasizes sex, Adler emphasizes power; but in contrast to both Freud and Jung, Adler makes no call upon any 'unconscious' to explain the phenomena; it is all plane sailing. His views were set forth in his book *The Neurotic Constitution.*

'*Somatic (bodily) inferiority*', he says, 'is a compelling force in the development of the psyche, it lowers self-esteem and produces uncertainty; hence arises the 'urge for power'.

The causes of somatic inferiority are such conditions as small stature, glandular defects producing the 'weed'; poor show at games; left-handedness (more so previously than now); effeminacy; menstrual disorders, the climacteric. Included also are lack of sex knowledge, and failure at examinations. Adler himself was small of stature, and had a great sense of power, which he achieved with a world-wide reputation.

213

Such defects, producing the sense of inferiority may severely shake the courage, the self-esteem and the confidence of the child. The result is the development of fictitious goals. 'It is the feeling of uncertainty which forces the neurotic to a stronger attachment to fictitious dogmas and ideals.' This result is 'splitting of the personality,' in seeking to do justice both to the real and to the imaginary world. Thus Adler provides us with a still further theory of dissociation, differing from those of Janet, Freud and Jung (pp. 51, 134, 180).

The symptoms he develops are first of all to get attention: it is to heighten Ego consciousness. It represents 'the will to seem'. He quotes Goethe's letter to Lavater; 'This longing to elevate as high as possible the apex of the pyramid of my existence outweighs all else and is scarcely a moment absent from my thought.' What a series of superlatives! 'One may assume without fear of contradiction,' says Adler, 'that a neurotic wishes to have everything'; or as another writer has said 'he claims all rights and no responsibilities'. He quotes the case of a man in a crowd of thousands of people at a religious congress in Budapest who threw himself on the ground crying, 'I am the chief of sinners!' He had, says Adler, to be 'chief of something.'

The symptom, as we have seen, is a method of excusing the patient for his failure in reaching his fictitious goal, and at the same time maintaining his fiction of power: 'If only I had not this pain, this paralysis, this stammer, what could I not achieve.' The symptoms also save him from making decisions, for to make decisions is to court possible failure. 'In fainting, in paralysis, in hysteric pain and functional disturbances, he seeks to attract attention or to avoid decisions which are feared.'

Adler's attitude to sex is interesting; sex also is a craving for power. 'Sexual precocity and falling in love are forms of expression for heightened tendency to captivate.' Sadism represents the desire to play the wild man in order to overcome the feeling of inferiority.

But what of masochism, the desire to be sexually over-mastered? That does not bother Adler; it is a way of achieving power: 'She stoops to conquer'. 'The final object is the same, the domination over others which is felt as a masochistic triumph.'

How does a sense of guilt conform with this 'power psychology'? It arises when the urge to power is excessive and threatens to lower Ego consciousness by its failure. If a man feels guilty about trifling things, it only calls attention to his holiness, to the magnificence of his ideals. If he depreciates his success it is only to emphasize what he is really capable of doing—like the golfer who said, 'I've played golf for forty years and have never been on my game yet!'

Crime is obviously an expression of power. The fear of committing crimes is because we shrink from them since they threaten Ego consciousness if we fail; but we nevertheless feel ourselves capable of great crimes.

Second phase. Then Adler went to lecture in the United States and came back with 'uplift'. His theory now was that the neuroses were due to lack of co-operation. His theme was 'the pampered child'. I asked him how this theory was consistent with that of 'organ inferiority'. He replied that it is the pampered child who wants his own way, who must have power.

I put to him also on more than one occasion, the fact that many neuroses originated not because the child was pampered but because it was neglected—instancing a case I had at the time, of an adolescent delinquent whose mother died at his birth and who thereafter suffered from neglect. Adler's reply was that a 'pampered child is not necessarily a child who is pampered.' Make of that what you will. What I make of it is that by 'pampered' he means wants pampering, which is a very different thing. Wanting to be pampered may come from being pampered too much (though most children get tired of that), or from being deprived of the love and affection the child needs, which makes him want it the more. There is much truth in Adler's theory and it applies to some. Many people suffer from having physical defects, feel inferior, and compensate by a desire to achieve. But I think it requires revision.

What is the origin of the inferiority complex? Adler says it is a physical inferiority. If we investigated an 'inferiority' complex back to its source in our patients, we come to a very different conclusion. We find that by far the most common cause of a feeling of inferiority is the feeling of being unwanted. The child does not feel inferior because he has an 'organ inferiority.' It is the other way round. The child who feels unwanted—perhaps because he is in fact unwanted, say because of the arrival of another baby, or because the mother dotes on the boy and she has a girl—naturally asks, 'Why am I not loved like other children?' He looks round for a cause, and says 'It must be because the baby has curly hair and mine is straight; or because the baby is pretty and I am not.' The girl looking round for a reason why her brother is so loved by the mother and she is apparently not, assumes, 'It must be because he has a penis and I have not'—this being the only perceivable difference to account for it. In other words the organ inferiority is not the cause of the inferiority complex, it is the object on to which the inferiority is placed; it is the explanation the child gives itself as to why it is apparently unloved and unwanted. The girl who is fully loved does not get a 'penis envy', and there are many people with 'inferiority of organs'— left-handed, red-haired, ugly features, small stature, who because they have the reassurance of love, go forth in the world with no sense of inferiority at all but in full confidence and happiness. An insignificant man, physically speaking, was head of an Oxford College. Someone coming in to a meeting when he was speaking, turned to his neighbour and said 'Who is that inspired mouse?' There was no inferiority complex there in spite of his defect of physique.

I may here mention an incident which throws light on Adler's views, and justifies my re-interpretation of those views. Adler used to tell the story of a small boy out shopping with his mother when news was brought to her that the older brother had been run over and killed. The mother, he said, laughed loudly. The little boy was shocked at her callousness, and it affected his whole life. Adler told me privately, (though not in confidence), that this was himself as a small boy. What shocked the lad was his mother's lack of love.

The mother's laughter was obviously hysterical because the news was too much to bear. It showed not her callousness, but her concern at the tragedy; but the little boy was not to know that. One can well understand Adler becoming disillusioned about love from his mother's apparent callousness, and developing a power psychology as a compensation, which undoubtedly he had. Whether as a result or not I do not know, but he had a psychosomatic symptom. On a number of occasions I entertained him to dinner before a lecture and he could eat little because of pain in his 'sto-mach!'

He achieved greatness, and made a great contribution in pointing to what is often a real cause of neurotic symptoms, namely the inferiority complex. This is an important cause of neurosis, especially if we accept the reconstruction I have suggested of the cause of inferiority. For most patients lack confidence and, in that sense, have an inferiority complex. To instil confidence in a neurotic patient is half the cure. It may be done by suggestion.

Adler therefore said that all neuroses were due to false ideals, to fictitious goals; and they are fictitious because their one purpose is to compensate for the feeling of organ inferiority. These fictitious goals are quite different from normal ideals and aims which are in fact necessary to mental health. Normal ideals and aims are adopted voluntarily, because we like them, and we joyfully pursue them with real hope of attainment. Normal ideals and aims are an incentive; they unify the personality and direct all its potentialities: fictitious goals try to compensate for inferiority, and split the personality which is thereafter in constant conflict with itself.

Take as an instance the Kaiser Wilhelm. He was born with a paralyzed arm: in addition he also suffered because he knew that Englishmen never considered him quite a gentleman (unloved)

He therefore must show his worth, so he set out to be the War Lord, the conqueror of Europe—just to show them! He failed to achieve his fictitious goal and ended his days chopping down trees instead of nations.

A recent illustration is that of the obscure artist Han Von Meegeren who was a poor down-trodden weed, thin, with sunken chest, bullied by his father, despised by his fellow-students and with his work ignored by the art critics and dealers. He took his revenge on authority by faking Vermeers, which fooled all the authorities and fetched fabulous prices. Only by his own confession was he discovered, because he preferred a sentence of a year for forgery rather than a life imprisonment for collaborating with the enemy by exporting valuable antique works of art!

Sandow, at one time considered to be the strongest man in the world, was a premature baby and was not expected to live. Dwarfs (a condition due to the deficiency of pituitary gland) often manage to get into the limelight by exploiting their defects and becoming comic clowns.

These people who have to overcompensate for feelings of inferiority often succeed and do great things in life, as long as they do not attempt too much, as long as their goal is not too extravagant and fantastic. But it must sometimes be a great strain, and it is not surprising that they sometimes break down under the strain. I had one patient who had worked his way up from the bottom, and who now had 1,700 men under him, who came for treatment because he felt he had been a failure.

Adler's method of treatment (to judge by one or two of my patients who consulted him), was to encourage them to get rid of the feeling of inferiority, to give them confidence in themselves, to persuade them that they were really fine fellows. One can see how encouraging and helpful such advice would be. At the same time they must get rid of fictitious goals and develop healthy ones to pursue, if the cure is to last.

Adler, like Jung and McDougall, emphasizes the forward-looking aspect of life, as distinct from Freud who is preoccupied with the past and says little about the integration of life. Indeed Adler's whole psychology depends on the pursuit of goals, fictitious or otherwise. 'Every psychic phenomena can be grasped and understood only if regarded as a preparation of some goal.'

Adler's theory is true, but not universally true of all neurotics. There are persons, fine specimens of humanity, with no discernible physical defects of any kind, who suffer from anxiety states of various kinds.

As I see it, Freud, Jung and Adler each present us with one facet of truth. Each has an important contribution to make; and no doubt each has deficiencies since no man is omniscient. The greatest fault indeed is to regard one's discoveries as the whole truth, and the views of others as nonsense.

PART VII
DIRECT REDUCTIVE ANALYSIS

CHAPTER XXVII

DIRECT REDUCTIVE ANALYSIS: ITS AIMS

The method which I call direct reductive analysis follows in principle the procedure originally employed by Janet, Freud and others.

This method, which I have employed for over fifty years consists in taking the symptom, tracing it back by hypnosis or more usually by free association to its basic cause, discovering the experiences which originally gave rise to it, releasing the emotions there repressed, bringing them into consciousness under control of the will, and resolving the problem in the light of reason and common sense. So the personality is made whole, and the symptoms disappear.

It is a sound scientific procedure, followed in ordinary medical practice. If a patient complains, say of a pain in the chest, we take the symptom, enquire as to the nature of the pain, whether stabbing, only in deep breathing, or an ache, discover how it originated, and then make a differential diagnosis as to whether it is pleurisy, pneumonia, tuberculosis, coronary thrombosis, or an injury. Finally by treating the cause, we not only get rid of the symptom, but restore the patient to health.

So in direct reductive analysis we start off with the symptom, be it phobia, anxiety, depression, a sex perversion like homosexuality, or an obsessional act like hand-washing; or it may be a delinquency like stealing, or a character trait like bad temper, jealousy or morbid suspicion. We then trace that symptom back by free association to unearth the experiences which gave rise to it and so deal with the disorder of personality which resulted from them. Just as we use a microscope to discover the unseen cause of a physical infection, so we use free association to discover the unconscious and forgotten cause of a neurotic symptom.

The earliest recorded use of this method was probably that of Déspine. In the years 1837–9 Charles Déspine had a patient, a girl suffering from paralysis of the legs. This originated in a slight fall, but 'under circumstances arousing a good deal of emotion.' This experience was completely forgotten and dissociated from consciousness. Déspine 'magnetized' (hypnotized) her, whereupon she went into a hysterical crisis, reproducing the fall. In this hypnotized state she became completely normal; but when she was wakened, she reverted to her symptoms. (This was obviously because the experience was still dissociated from her waking state). Finally 'a complete cure was effected through a sort of fusion of the waking state with the state of crisis'—the dissociation was resolved. It may be noted here that the explanation of the cure was not that of catharsis as Freud later maintained, for the patient let off plenty of emotion during the 'crisis' under hypnosis, but by the 'fusion' or readjustment of the dissociated and unconscious experience into consciousness. This case is described in Janet's *Psychological Healing* (p.789). It took place 125 years ago, over forty years before Breuer's first case in 1890–92, and fifty years before Freud started hypnotic treatment.

This, as far as I know, was the first recorded case to be treated by this method. But recently I was amazed to find that the same method is regularly employed for the treatment of ills amongst the Negritos, a primitive pigmy tribe of the Philippines, as described by Kilton Stewart in his book, *Dwarfs and Dream Giants*. The author, a psychologist, wished to make certain psychological tests of these primitives, and in order to gain their confidence, set out to alleviate their physical illnesses, especially their skin diseases. But the treatment itself was painful, so he hypnotized his patient to alleviate the pain. To his surprise his patient went into a hysterical crisis, and visualized (without prompting) a quarrel between his parents in his childhood. The author, somewhat alarmed, was about to bring him out of this hysterical state, but was prevented from doing so by the other natives, who were quite unperturbed. They were insistent that the patient should go right through with it. It then transpired that this 'abreaction' method was a normal way they employed of treating illness; and those who had gone through it, some of them a number of times, became 'Healers', both men and women, and applied the method to others for the cure of their headaches and other ills.

A striking feature of this cure was that the patient had to bring back from the 'cave' (the unconscious) in which he was confronted by a spirit (the complex), a song and dance of some kind. It was the need to do this which led the natives to restrain the author from bringing the patient out of the trance, for without it he could not be cured. Why this was essential they did not reveal, but I take it to mean that by doing so he brought the dissociated state back into consciousness, a process which in the first instance was omitted in Déspines case, who was not cured until the 'fusion with consciousness' took place.

The Mesmerists as a whole, who kept very strict records, had noted that people in a somnambulic state revived memories of which they were quite unaware in their waking life, but made nothing of it therapeutically, for they were not concerned with psychological causes but only with the mesmeric fluid.

Pierre Janet in 1889 published a number of cases in *Automatisme psychologique* such as that of Marie mentioned on page 52.

These are typical cases of what I call Direct reductive analysis, and of the cure of neurotic disorders by tracking down the symptoms to discover the causes. It is noteworthy that the causes were found to lie in actual experiences of earlier years. It is a common-sense method.

In this method we may use either hypnosis to recover the cause, or free association. For some years I used hypnosis, but later adopted 'free association', as I found it possible to recover even infantile experiences just as completely by this method, and more reliably than by hypnosis, for one cannot be sure of hypnotizing a patient deeply enough.

By this method we start off with the symptom for it is the symptom of which the patient complains, and it is of the symptom he wants to be cured. He is therefore prepared to give his full co-operation. He may be quite interested to know that he had incestuous desires towards his mother in childhood, but he is more interested in the cure of his headaches or to get rid of his depression.

There is a further reason for taking the symptom as our starting point. The symptom is the epitome of the original experience, the precipitate of the original problem which caused the neurosis. Indeed, it is very often a reproduction of part of that experience. So the terror of claustrophobia may be a reproduction of the original terror of suffocation at birth: the pain in the thigh in another case was a reproduction of an experience the child had when she was seized by the hip and beaten by her father. In other cases, however, the symptoms may be symbolic—a knife representing either a repressed desire to kill, or a phallic symbol from repressed sex. But even in symbolic cases the symptom carries us back to actual experiences which gave rise to the impulse to kill, such as from jealousy of a rival child. The symptom is the royal road to discover the basic cause of the neurosis.

It is not that our aim is merely to abolish the symptom. A physical pain can be abolished by morphia; a hysteria pain can be abolished by hypnotic suggestion, but in neither case is that a cure.

On the other hand, as long as the symptom, or any part of it remains, it is a sure sign that the person is not cured. It is not much use a woman patient discovering that she had a sexual fixation for her father, as she may have had, if she still has her depression, for this means that the whole cause has not been discovered or revealed. As we have seen (p.153) Freud himself discovered his incestuous desires towards his mother but he still suffered from his fainting attacks (p.153). A partially cured person is one in whom the whole cause has not been discovered, very commonly because we do not go deeply enough, or far enough back. Instances of this are given in Chapter XXXVIII. When this basic cause of the disorder is discovered and dealt with, the symptom is usually automatically eradicated and the personality restored to health.

I call this procedure Direct reductive analysis; 'direct' because it goes straight to the root cause without resorting to the roundabout method of the transference; 'reductive' because it reduces the disorder back to the basic cause in childhood as well as dealing with precipitating causes; 'analysis', for this term, as used in psychotherapy, refers not merely to the discovery of the known precipitatory causes, but more particularly to the discovery of the unconscious causes of these disorders.

This indeed is nature's method of cure, especially observed in traumatic cases like shell-shock or car accidents. There are many instances where some experience suddenly recalls to the patient the whole horrifying experience which precipitated the neurosis, and his headache, paralysis, and loss of memory are automatically cured. Spontaneous cure of hysterical blindness or recovery of speech are common instances of this, as reported in the press. It is nature's method; we follow it in reductive analysis.

Indeed, this mental process closely follows the same principle as the physical. If we get a bit of thorn under the skin, the first endeavour of the body is to expel it with the pus. If it is unable to do that it surrounds it with scar tissue to separate it from the rest of the body, to isolate the infection. The latter is equivalent to repression and dissociation in the mental sphere. In this state the patient may remain apparently quite well for years, and the trouble may be said to have cured itself; just as some say that patients get rid of the neurosis without treatment. This process however is not completely satisfactory, for the foreign body, like the dissociated complex, may still cause pain and later, it may be many years later, the wound may flare up, until the thorn is brought to the surface and expelled. Thus the wound is completely healed. That is the same with buried complexes. There are many untoward experiences which a child may appear to adjust itself to quite satisfactorily, like getting over a horrifying experience of separation, in which a spontaneous 'cure' takes place. But years later circumstances may be such that the original experience is revived and appears as the symptom. That indeed is the most common mechanism of a neurotic disorder—the revival of repressed emotions—involving both predisposing as well as precipitating causes.

The function of analysis, like that of surgery, is, when nature has failed to expel the noxious material, to delve down to the root cause of the trouble and get rid of it, so that the patient never suffers from it again. The cure is permanent, provided you discover the root cause, just as if you remove an appendix you can never suffer from appendicitis again. The analyst is more a surgeon, while the psychotherapist who treats by suggestion is more a physician.

Let us give an illustration of this method with the discovery of the cause of the neurosis. A strongly built man of thirty-four (whom we shall call Case 1), a sixfooter, has a nervous breakdown in which he suffered from both agoraphobia and claustrophobia—a very common combination. He was terrified of going out of the house without his mother, having an absurd panic that he would 'pass out'. Subsidiary symptoms were a complete distrust of women in general, so that he never married. He also suffered from a sense of unreality, deep depression and a horror of 'sizzling noises' like the running of a bath tap. As for the claustrophobia— he could not bear to stay put in a dentist's or even a hairdresser's chair. He also could not bear anyone to touch his chest or shoulder, and he had a dread of being hurt. At school he funked all rough games and was consequently regarded as a 'sissy.'

In direct reductive analysis we applied free association to discover the forgotten origin of his symptoms. We asked him to visualize the first time he ever had these symptoms, and to tell us whatever came to his mind. It revealed the following.

The *precipitating* circumstances were that at the age of twenty-six during a visit to the dentist where he had gas, he made a big fuss and was scolded by the dentist for 'behaving like a nine-year-old child'. About the same time he was having difficulty with a love affair in which he was ultimately jilted by the girl.

These are common enough experiences, and were obviously not enough in themselves to produce a breakdown; there must be deeper causes. This is confirmed by the nature of his symptoms which were on the face of it a reversal to infantile behaviour— clinging to his mother, literally, for security, behaving like a child.

Turning, by free association, to the *predisposing* causes, we find the separation anxiety was traced to a tonsil operation, at the age of three, and most of his symptoms were found to be a reproduction of that experience. His mother took him to hospital, handed him over to strange creatures in white gowns and masks, and in spite of his yells, deserted him. He was seized struggling, held down and suffocated (the anaesthetic) by these strangers, and passed out; and when he came to, instead of his throat being better, as his mother promised it would be, it was far more painful. Is it surprising that he could no longer trust his mother, nor any woman thereafter; and yet when he returned home, he must cling to her as the only security he had in a world of terrors. He then visualized an earlier experience in analysis; as an infant in the first year of life, terrified of 'things that bump in the night', he cried out for his mother. She came, stopped a short time, then said, 'Now you are all right'—

when he was not all right at all. Again he could not rely on his mother; he had to rely on himself. But he could not rely on himself because he was a weak and helpless infant; so he had to face life without security and without confidence either in himself or in others. A Freudian would interpret this clinging to his mother as an incest wish. He clung to his mother, not for incest, but for security, but even she is unreliable. In reviving these experiences he vividly re-lived and felt the terror, the loneliness, the insecurity of these early experiences: he also realized that the present-day phobias were an exact reproduction of these earlier experiences; they were identical. At no point in his analysis did he reveal incestuous desires towards his mother. But how right Freud was when he said, 'The hysteric suffers from reminiscences'—for these symptoms, like so many, were revivals of actual infantile experiences.

This case explained his symptoms. The dentist's anaesthetic revived the horror of the anaesthetic at the tonsil operation, in each case with the horror of 'passing out'. He hated being held in a dentist's or barber's chair because he had to 'stay put', a revival of when he was held down screaming in the operation, when he did pass out. His horror of being touched on the chest or shoulder also recalled his being held down by the chest and shoulders at the operation. He could not stand any sizzling noise because it recalled the sizzling noise of the anaesthetic gas. All these experiences explained his claustrophobia. As for the separation anxiety or agoraphobia: this dread originated in his being handed over by his mother at the hospital and 'deserted' by her. It was recalled later by the girl's jilting him, and this revived the infantile sense of desertion, so that he lost all confidence in women, because his mother 'let him down', as did the girl. By the revelation of these causes, he was cured of his symptoms. He realized that while his panic was natural in the circumstances of the operation, it no longer applied.

This case is typical of the method of direct reductive analysis and of its results. There was no transference; and no interpretation was required: the facts spoke for themselves.

Furthermore, this procedure of direct reductive analysis presumes no theory; nor does it start with any pre-suppositions, except that a neurosis has a cause, and that it is the business of the psychotherapist to discover and deal with that cause. It takes each case individually and discovers in each case what originates that person's neurosis.

In reductive analysis we accept what we find. If it discovers in a patient sexual desires towards the opposite parent, as Freud discovered in himself, well and good, they are accepted. We often find that a man's attachment to his mother goes back to sexual experiences in childhood. But equally and more often we find this attachment related back to insecurity in early childhood, which has nothing to do with sex. If we find, like Jung, archaic material emerging in the course of treatment, we accept that. But we also find that what appears to be archetypal often relates to early experiences, and that what appears to the patient in dreams as a terrible archetypal monster is none other than an angry mother. Certainly too we find with Adler that many people have an inferiority complex due to ugliness or physical defects of various kinds, and this gives rise to insecurity and an overwhelming craving for power; under which they break down. But we find that the inferiority complex dates back much more to the feeling of being unwanted and unloved.

The method therefore does not assume—nor deny—any theory whether Oedipal or archetypal; it is applicable to people of all social status whether aspidistral or orchidaceous. Facts speak for themselves and require little interpretation.

This method of direct reductive analysis is in conformity with Freud's original method but in direct contrast to Freud's later interpretative methods. (See p. 154).

So much for differences in method: now for the differences in theory. I could not follow Freud in his later excursions in theory any more than in his change in practice. His incestuous theories appeared to be far too speculative, nor at that time was it at all clear how he had come by them. Only occasionally did incestuous desires appear in our patients as the cause of the neurosis. Now that it is clear from his letters (p. 153) that he derived his theory from his own self-analysis, his theories are hardly more acceptable.

Why, then, if direct reductive analysis is so sound a method of treatment, did Freud abandon it, since on his own showing (*Studies in Hysteria*) it was highly successful in curing the patients? Partly because he found that many of these 'memories' of sex assaults turned out to be fictitious, but mainly because he now thought from his own analysis that he had the key to all neurotic disorders, namely incestuous desires, which enabled him to interpret to the patient the causes of his symptoms. He looked for the same cause in his patients as he had found in himself (p. 153). Another subsidiary reason, which must not be ignored, is that he was bad at hypnotizing (p. 124) and also found free association boring. It does indeed demand a great deal of patience, for it is essential that the causes should come from the patient himself, and it is such a temptation to tell the patient what is wrong with him. But he has to discover it for himself.

There is, however, I suggest, another reason why Freud abandoned his original method which had proved so successful. That is, that Freud was essentially a pioneer, an explorer. Any explorer in mountainous country may leave behind a more fertile valley in the urge to go on to further heights. Indeed he and his followers may remain in those higher regions, although in point of fact the valley they have left may be much more fertile of practical results. So Freud in his exploration of the human mind. He tried out various concepts of the personality (p.126), he tried out various theories such as the traumatic and the 'wish' theories, and he tried out various methods such as free association and transference.

He recognized in himself the role of pioneer when he says, 'We cannot do without people who have the courage to think these things before they are in a position to demonstrate them.' (Jones, in his Freud, p. 247.) Jung has done the same with his pioneer exploration of the archetypes. But Jung always admitted that his views are hypothetical, requiring further confirmation. Both Jung and Freud were more than clinicians: they both applied their theories to religion, to social problems, to biology, to anthropology, child psychology and philosophy. These discoveries and speculations are of the greatest interest—that is not contested— but whether they are clinically more effective in curing the neurotic patient is another matter.

With Freud's conclusions that the 'memories' of infantile sex assaults are largely fictitious I would fully agree, but for a very different reason—namely that rarely do my patients produce such assaults and when they do, there is no reason to doubt their veracity. Why should this be so? The difference may be due to a difference between the Viennese and the British mentality; or it may be that Freud inadvertently suggested to his patient this explanation of 'sex assault'. It would be naive to suggest that sexual assaults of the kind he mentioned never take place; nor does Freud say so. He says he explained 'many' a seduction fantasy. Indeed, I have met with three cases of mothers who in analysis have confessed to having deliberately sexually stimulated their little boys in the absence of their husbands as in war time, excusing themselves on the grounds that the child is 'too young to understand.' True but it is not too young to feel, and thereby to get a morbid attachment to the mother. This may produce an arrest of sexual development which may culminate in either sexual impotence because of the fixation to the mother, or sex perversion if these sexual activities are later repressed. One of these sons, whom the mother admitted to have seduced, I met later as a young man. He was shy, shut in, reserved—but whether from schizophrenia or from the mother's seduction I had no means of judging, for it was the mother not the son who was my patient. As most of my patients never mention sex assaults anyway, fictitious or otherwise, I discounted Freud's objections to this method.

In my opinion and experience, Freud discarded his original methods too rashly and on insufficient grounds. Because the 'memories' of infantile sex assaults proved to be largely fallacies, that does not mean that all such memories are to be regarded as unreliable. Indeed, I have dealt in Chapter XXXVIII with the proof of the reliability of such memories, with many illustrations.

For these reasons I have stuck to free association and have found it a most reliable method of getting to the actual facts and experiences in childhood causing the neurosis, and effective in cure.

War shock cures. But I have no doubt that my main reason for retaining Janet's and Freud's original method was a practical one. For in the First World War I had several hundreds of war shock cases to treat individually both in the Navy and later in the Army, to which I was transferred, and, together with many others, applied the 'abreactive' technique as a method of treatment, usually under hypnosis. This method consisted of reviving and re-living the traumatic experiences of being blown up or buried 'with hallucinatory vividness'. The results of such treatment were so immediate as to leave no doubt as to the relation of treatment and cure, and so dramatic as to leave no doubt as to the efficiency of such treatment. A man for instance who had been paralysed for two years was cured of his paralysis in a few minutes when he revived, under hypnosis, the experience of being blown up and buried. Indeed not a few patients were cured by the spontaneous recovery of such experiences in their dreams.

As to the permanency of the cure, I made a follow up of the first hundred cases at the Ashurst hospital at Oxford, published in the *Medical Annual*, 1921. These cases were of the most severe kind, almost all of whom had undergone experiences such as being blown up or buried; they could be taken as 100 per cent unfit. Some of them had had their symptoms for years. The questions put to them in this follow-up were made as objective as possible. (One of the difficulties of getting statistical evidence of cures in psychotherapy is that we cannot rely altogether upon the verdict of the patient, for he may say he is better to please the doctor, or to avoid returning for treatment; or say he is worse to get more pension.) A year after discharge 90 per cent were back working at their old job, with an average of seven hours a day. The average pensions they were receiving were a nominal 25 per cent but that was for all complaints, physical as well as psychological. Only 10 had had to return for hospital treatment, and of these two had definitely been diagnosed as of a psychotic type.

It is often suggested that these patients would have got better anyway. Possibly; but the fact remains that many of them had been ill with paralysis or anxiety states for two or three years without improvement, whereas they were cured in a few weeks with abreactive analytic treatment. Again it was often said, during the war, that these 'shell-shock' patients would automatically get better as soon as the war was over. As against that, I took particular note of my sixty patients in the ward when the Armistice was declared, and I could detect no differences at all either in the patients' general attitude and demeanour, nor in their symptoms. On the other hand, the patients got better immediately on the recovery of the experience of being blown up or buried whether this took place during the war or after. In 93 per cent of these patients the radical improvement took place while the war was still on.

These results were by no means unique, nor were they confined to my experience. William Brown of Oxford and others used these methods with great effect. Indeed it is a significant fact that in the Freudian publication *War Neurosis*, although the libido theory was maintained (fear of shells and self preservation being interpreted as self-love), when it came to treatment, the only effective method advocated in that book was the revival of the original traumatic experience by abreaction.

Since such methods were so effective in the war cases, I could see no reason why they should not with equal effect be applied to civilian cases, which I have done for over fifty years.

It is true there are differences between these traumatic 'shell-shock' cases and civilian cases, most of which are non-traumatic. In the First World War everyone was emphasizing that there was no difference between war neuroses and ordinary civilian neuroses, and for that reason the term 'shell-shock' came into disfavour. This, however, was a point with which I could not entirely agree. In my experience the actual physiological shock was an important factor in the development of the neurosis, for it rendered the patient still less capable of coping with the traumatic situation. The same applies to civilian traumatic cases, such as car and cycle accidents; for a man partly 'concussed' cannot deal with his emotional stress. As we have seen, dissociation of consciousness may be produced either by physiological shock (as Janet maintained), or by repression (as Freud has shown us). The former plays an important part in traumatic cases, in which also there is repression, whereas in non-traumatic cases repression is by far the more important factor.

The other distinction is that in ordinary civilian non-traumatic cases the causes are usually far more complicated, for there are so many predisposing and contributory factors, whereas the traumatic cases usually relate to one devastating experience. Civilian cases, therefore, take much longer, so that it is open to the objector to say that the patient would have got better anyway. Nevertheless the rapid cure of these 'shell-shock' patients demonstrates the principle that Freud originally enunciated, that the revival of the original experience leads to immediate cure.

In view of these arguments there seemed to be no reason for abandoning a method which had proved so successful.

There are, however, certain popular objections to analysis in general. One is, 'What is the good of raking up the past?' 'Why not let sleeping dogs lie?' The trouble is that sleeping dogs won't lie! Something more radical needs to be done to allay these complexes when once aroused. The other objection is, 'How can knowing the cause cure?' Knowing the cause does not cure as we shall see (p. 238) though usually necessary to radical cure. In a neurosis emotions have been repressed; only by their release can the symptoms be radically cured and only by their release can they be directed towards the use and purpose of the personality as a whole.

We come to the question then, How does analysis and getting down to the cause cure? But first of all what do we mean by cure?

Cure. By 'cure,' as we have seen, we certainly do not mean merely the abolition of the symptom; for that can be done by hypnotic suggestion or in some cases by tranquillizers, without touching the cause. That is not a cure any more then we can cure a cancer by morphia: for as long as the cause is left untouched the patient is not cured. If by such means we get rid of the symptom, it often emerges again, either in its original form, or in a substitute form (p. 45). A hysteric pain got rid of by hypnotic suggestion may appear as an anxiety state; an anxiety state as an obsession; an obsession gives place to depression. Indeed that substitute of one symptom by another often occurs in the course of analysis: it is like peeling an onion, as one layer is skinned off another comes to the surface. If the subconscious mind cannot get what it wants by a hysteric paralysis it will try a phobia: if you rid yourself of a propitiatory obsession due to guilt, there emerges the anxiety from the consequences from which the hand-washing was intended to save you. You do not cure a disorder of the personality by curing the symptom, for the symptom is only the manifestation in consciousness of the basic disorder of personality.

In analysis the primary symptom for which the patient comes often disappears quite early in treatment, but we do not stop there. The symptom is the best guide to the origin of the disorder, but we are not content till we discover and treat the personality disorder which gave rise to the symptom. The symptom is merely the rash from the measles: we do not cure the measles by treating the rash with soothing ointments. The function of the symptom is like that of physical pain, indicating that there is something wrong, but to get rid of the pain is not necessarily to get rid of the disease. On the other hand, as we have seen, if any of the symptom remains it is a sure sign that the patient is *not* completely cured, nor the personality completely restored to mental health.

Our aim in analytic treatment is to restore the patient to mental health which means that all the functions and potentialities of the personality should no longer be repressed to produce neurotic disorders, but should be liberated for the use and purpose of the personality as a whole.

The person, some of whose emotions are repressed suffers from what Janet calls the feeling of incompleteness (p. 50). By liberating these emotions he is restored to health and happiness.

We pass then to the practical question, How is this done?

CHAPTER XXVIII

TECHNIQUE OF DIRECT
REDUCTIVE ANALYSIS

The first step in the process of cure is the discovery of the original experiences which caused the neurosis. As they are always repressed and resist recall, it is necessary to use specific methods such as hypnosis, dream interpretation and particularly free association. We start with the symptom, tracing it back to its source; for the symptom, as we have said, is the royal road to the hidden complex. Dreams also are used for they are an expression in consciousness of unconscious problems, and are often a revival of the original experiences which produced the neurosis.

(a) First it is necessary to get from the patient a history of the circumstances of the onset of the breakdown, as far as he knows it. A history, however, can never be a complete account, for the real cause in neurotic disorders is always dissociated and forgotten.

(b) Even more necessary is it to get from the patient a very precise and detailed description of the nature of the symptom, for since the symptom is usually an epitome of the disorder, and indeed is often a reproduction of the original experience, it acts as a useful guide and stimulus in reviving the original experience. Moreover, each and every detail of the symptom must be fully explained before the patient can be said to be cured. A good illustration of this is given on page 352 (which may profitably be read now), of a man with a masochistic fetishism in which there was an exact correspondence between the present-day symptoms and the original experience. In our Case 1 (p. 225) there were a number of trifling symptoms like the sizzling noise and being touched on the chest which had to be explained, and which were explained in the tonsil operation.

I have adopted Freud's rules for free association, namely that the patient, starting with the symptom or dream, should say whatever comes into his mind, however painful, however improbable and however irrelevant (p. 125). In recent years I have always kept strictly to free association throughout analysis and find this sufficient to reveal the true causes of the neurosis without resort either to hypnosis or to interpretation of symptoms.

The injunction which I find it most necessary to impress on patients is that of 'however improbable', 'however untrue'. What we want, of course, is the truth as to childhood experiences and it is natural that the patient will question whether what comes to his mind was true or not. But that is precisely what the patient must avoid, for trying to remember is fatal to remembering. It is like trying to catch a pigeon, the harder you try the further it flies. In free association we must not try to remember, but starting off with the symptoms we tell the patient to visualize or picture when it first started—saying what comes into the mind whether it is true or not. The association must be free of every conscious control even that of trying to remember. Many failures in analysis are due to neglect of this principle.

It may be objected that what comes up is entirely imaginary and not the real cause. Indeed, Freud found that to be the case with the imagined sex assaults. All 'revivals' are not necessarily true; but there is yet some reason why that particular idea comes to mind: even an untrue vision is relevant.

The whole value of free association is that it is not free, but is subject to the law of psychic determinism and to the laws of association. It is free in that it is free from conscious control: no feelings of propriety, no sense of shame, of embarrassment or of disgust, must stand in the way of the patient freely revealing whatever comes to his mind. But if he excludes such resistance and says, whatever comes to the mind, the laws of association get to work and will ultimately bring to the surface of consciousness the memories of these experiences even in earliest childhood.

The instruction to say anything that comes into the mind sounds very simple, but it is not so simple in practice because of natural resistance and it needs years of experience. The whole skill in analysis depends on the skill with which we are able to get the patient associating freely; given that, and there is no experience which should be beyond the reach of revival, even of birth experiences.

But on what do we freely associate? Usually the symptom itself; and when first the patient had it. Or we may start with a dream and let the patient free associate on that. Other analysts prefer the association to be entirely free of any specific object, symptom, dream or other starting point, and simply tell the patient to carry on saying whatever comes to mind—on the principle presumably that if you give him rope enough he will hang himself; for the complex being dynamically charged is bound to come up sooner or later.

In my experience this does not work because the patient will inevitably skirt round the unpleasant memories instead of facing and tackling them, and bring up, as Freud himself found, 'a lot of irrelevant material'. The analyst needs, time and again, to keep the patient to a painful experience—say a sexual episode in which the patient had a bad sense of shame and guilt, or a childhood experience associated with a deep sense of fear or disgust.

In using free association to discover the original cause, it is sometimes the emotion which emerges first: the patient reports 'I begin to feel angry (or miserable) though I don't know why!' 'Something makes me feel self pity'. He suddenly bursts out crying, but remarks 'It's silly! I've nothing to cry about'. Tracing that feeling back, the whole experience which gave rise to the emotion is revived. In one dramatic case of a patient suffering from claustrophobia, the first time he lay on the couch, he went into a spasm, contracting his whole body in pain with his arms above his head, which turned out to be a reproduction of being born.

In other cases it is the picture or imagination which comes first. 'I picture myself in the garden of our first house, about the age of three', and carrying on with that association he finds that there is some distressing emotional experience connected with this of which he was quite unaware when he started. At first the picture may seem irrelevant; but it almost invariably leads to a complex.

The Precipitating Cause. Having discovered the precise nature of the symptom we trace it back first to its precipitating cause, where it started as a symptom, it may be last year or it may be years ago. An elucidation of the circumstances of the precipitating cause will often reveal the nature of the problem involved. In our Case 1 it was a visit to the dentist and being jilted by the girl, producing in him both the sense of desertion and the horror of suffocation. But that of course does not account fully for a phobia that lasted for years: they were merely the precipitating circumstances. We must then go earlier to the predisposing cause which was the tonsil operation at the age of three.

The precipitory cause is often taken to be the whole cause. Indeed the analysis of that alone often given the patient great relief.

In virtually all neuroses, however, there are both precipitating and predisposing causes, which vary in importance, for either may predominate.

In traumatic cases, (car accidents and shell-shock), the precipitating factor may be the more important, and the breakdown may occur in people who previously passed for normal. In such cases, as we found in the war, it is usually enough to recover the forgotten experiences (for some of it is always forgotten), by abreaction, for the patient to be restored to health.

A young man after a motor cycling accident suffered from throbbing noises which were naturally put down to physiological disturbances of the middle ear. In analysis the whole memory of the accident previously forgotten was recovered. While lying 'concussed' he could hear the throbbing noise of the engine which was still racing. This was reproduced in his symptom. The cause of the trouble lay in the dissociated complex, not in the middle ear. When the dissociation was brought into consciousness, the symptom disappeared, without further analysis.

We find, however, even in traumatic cases like shell-shock or car accidents, that these precipitating causes would not have produced a neurosis—unless the patient was already predisposed by earlier experiences, which may be of a similar nature or of general insecurity.

The prevailing view is that such traumatic cases are due to concussion, the theory being that there is a complete disruption of the molecules of the brain with the result that all consciousness is obliterated. That is the physical explanation. Unfortunately against that view it can be proved that in these cases consciousness is not obliterated for the memory of the whole experience can be recovered. In brief the recovery of such memories indicates that the loss of consciousness in so-called concussion is due to psychological repression, not to physical causes. I had dozens of these cases in the First World War and took a particular interest in them. It was possible in every case, except one in which there was a fracture of the skull (contusion), to recover the entire memory, in every detail, of the traumatic experience, with the consequent cure of the patient. (See my *Psychology and Mental Health*, p.182.)

This is worth mentioning for there are numerous people going about the country who have had accidents resulting in headaches and other pains and disabilities which are put down to 'concussion' and left uncured, whereas they could be cured by recovering the whole memory of the experience with all the emotions. This is not a difficult task and requires no long term analysis. It can be done under drugs like evipan, pentothal and lysergic acid (L.S.D.), but more completely and satisfactorily by hypnosis or free association, expecially as in the latter cases the repressed material can be more completely adjusted to the conscious mind by suggestion.

In most non-traumatic cases the precipitating experiences are not the entire cause nor is their analysis as a rule sufficient to produce a cure. For such experiences are often very trifling—as in Case 1—a visit to the dentist or a jilting by a girl does not precipitate a neurosis in most people. The significance of these experiences is that they have aroused a hornets' nest of early childhood complexes, whose emotions are now added to the emotions of the present situation: so that the present-day emotions are exaggerated far beyond the demands of the present day. In our Case 1 it aroused all the emotions attending on the tonsil operation and his desertion by his mother with the arousal of the infantile fear, which the jilting by the girl alone would never do.

In his adult agoraphobia therefore he behaves like a little child unable to go out without his mother. It is this exaggeration of emotion, which is seen by the patient himself not to be justified by present circumstances, that brings him for treatment.

The analysis of the precipitating cause gives one a clue as to the nature of the fear and that leads to the predisposing causes. This often takes place spontaneously. When our patient was reviving the anaesthetic at the dentist's, the revival carried him spontaneously to the earlier experience of a similar nature. 'Now', he says, 'a picture comes back to me of my being taken to hospital. I expect this relates to a tonsil operation which I am told I had at the age of three'. Here we do not ask him to try to remember, but to feel himself back there and try to re-live it. This he does in free association without prompting or suggestion from the analyst as to what probably happened, for this only interferes with the patient's own free flow of association. Thus he revives the 'desertion' of his mother, and the horror of the anaesthetics in which he 'passed out'.

That was indeed quite sufficient to produce in a child a persisting fear of life, and fear of being hurt, which he always suffered from, even before this phobia was precipitated. He realizes the link up between the two experiences; that the symptom from which he now suffers is precisely of the same nature, indeed was derived from, these infantile experiences.

As a rule it is not one specific experience that causes the neurosis but many contributory causes. Do we then need to analyze out all the experiences which are contributory causes of the neurosis? Fortunately not. For we find that there are certain experiences which we may call 'nuclear incidents', which are turning points in the child's development: for instance when from being amenable he becomes defiant; from being defiant he becomes docile; from being sexual he becomes ascetic; from being spontaneous he becomes prudish or over-conscientious, or as in Case 1 from being confident he becomes timid. These nuclear incidents give us a clue to the problem: for they tell us what is repressed, why it is repressed, and in favour of what attitude it was repressed: in brief it explains the whole problem.

In this process of reductive analysis there are certain other points of technique that are necessary to cure, and need emphasis.

(a) It is necessary that the emotion contained in the complex, and repressed in the original experience, should be released. I fully agree with Freud on this point. 'Affectless memories are almost entirely useless!' Freud later effected this by way of the transference, letting off the emotion of love or hate towards the analyst. The release of emotion is much more effectively done by re-living the actual original experience with all its emotions.

This method avoids the complications of the transference; for the patient lets off his love, his hate, his fear, his contempt, towards those to whom it properly belongs. He feels the actual rage, the self-pity or the depression. Sometimes he may suddenly burst out, 'I feel like strangling you', which is negative transference. In such a case we immediately take the emotion back to the experience in childhood we are analyzing, and almost invariably find that it belongs to some person in the incident we are analyzing.

This answers the objection already referred to, which so many have brought against analysis; 'How does knowing cure?' It does not. Knowing the cause is an essential element in cure; but it cures only when there is an emotional response, for that alone releases the emotion. For the patient to know that he had a difficult birth, that he had incestuous desires towards his mother, that he had an inferiority complex, that he tried to murder the baby, all those facts are very interesting, but then he says 'So what! What about my fear of leaving home?' Sometimes, it is true, the knowledge may automatically awaken the emotion associated with it and gets an emotional response. Usually it is necessary to arouse the emotion by the patient's re-living the original experience.

(b) In this process it is also necessary that the *whole* of the emotion should be released. Otherwise the bit of the emotion which is left repressed perpetuates the symptom—just a bit of shrapnel left behind keeps the wound open. Therefore we may need to return to the same material over and over again and keep the patient to it, till the whole of the emotion is released. The patient objects that 'we have had all that before. I am bored stiff with it and I am sure you must be'. That of course is resistance which indicates there is more to come out. He must be kept to it. The whole of the emotion is far more effectively released by re-living the original experience than by the vicarious release of emotion in the transference.

(c) It is also most necessary that *all the emotions* involved should be discovered and released—for a complex is a complex of conflicting emotions, centered round the object, all of which must be released.

A boy beaten by his father unjustly, re-living the experience, first experiences great dread of his father. But when he has got the fear fully off his chest he then feels the anger which was also originally there but repressed by the fear. He then falls into a state of self-pity and sheds tears; finally he experiences the sex feelings produced by the beating. As long as one emotion is left repressed the complex is not fully resolved and the patient not completely cured.

A man suffers from blushing. He says that what makes him blush is simply his fear that he is going to blush. But what made him blush in the first place? Did the hen or the egg come first? His blushing started when in childhood he exposed himself sexually to get attention and was badly reproved in public by his mother. The humiliating experience was so painful that it was repressed; it was too shameful to remember. So he attached the shame to the blushing which in fact was the result of his shame, not, as he says, the cause. This revelation of the cause of the blushing gives him a great sense of relief. But the blushing while less marked does not entirely disappear; and until it does it means that we have not eradicated the whole or all of the causes. Pursuing the analysis of the original experience we find that the morbid blushing consists not only of the blush of shame, but the flush of anger. This is a common combination, for when a child is humiliated he feels shame and also furious anger at being humiliated. Only by the elucidation of all the causes, and the release of all the emotions was he cured radically of his blushing.

(d) It is further necessary *to attach the present-day morbid emotion to its original object*. Emotions because they are repressed are usually dissociated and attach themselves to other objects. Thus a fear of desertion by the mother now becomes a fear of travelling by train: suffocation at birth is attached to any close space like a cinema or crowd of people.

An essential stage in the analysis is therefore that the fear, anger, suspicion, depression, defeatism, guilt or perverted sex feelings should be referred back to the original experience, and not only intellectually, but emotionally felt towards the object or person to whom they properly belong. It was when the throbbing noise in the man's ears was related to and felt towards the racing of the motorbicycle that the patient was rid of it. (p. 235).

(e) Being now attached to their rightful objects these emotions are de-tached from the present day objects or persons to whom they have been morbidly attached, so that the symptom disappears. If Lady Macbeth could have been made to accept that her feelings of contamination were due to her guilt in her soul for the murders, she would no longer have had to persist in the silly action of washing her hands, which was the substitute on to which the need for cleansing was put.

The homosexual, realizing that his fear of women related to a justifiable fear of his mother, or in another case, of a nurse who seduced him, detaches his fear from women of the present day and (in both cases) was cured of his homosexuality.

(f) Re-direction and re-orientation. What happens then to the emotions thus detached and liberated? These emotions no longer chained to their unconscious complexes are now released and can now develop as they would have developed if they have never been suppressed. Anger and hate turn to confidence and strength of will: infantile sex feelings are developed into adult love and consideration for others; and fear, no longer called for, is abolished as no longer applicable. These potentialities which were arrested in their development by this repression, are now used for life and the purposes of the personality. The individual is restored to health.

(g) *Transference*. What of the transference in direct reductive analysis? Passing references have been made to this important subject, but we may summarize them. In by far the majority of cases, if we keep strictly by free association to the original experience, transference in the Freudian meaning of the term (p. 39) does not occur—the patient's mind is too preoccupied with the past events. Throughout the analysis of this Case 1, and indeed the large majority of cases treated by direct reductive analysis, there was no transference to the analyst, in the Freudian sense.

To this, the answer of the psycho-analyst is that the transference is inevitable, it is bound to occur anyway.

That depends on what we mean by the term. If we use it in a wide sense of an emotional relationship between doctor and patient which is the way some psycho-analysts use it, the statement is true. But that is not Freud's use of the term, and after all he invented it in this connection. He says quite definitely that it is the transference of feelings and emotions to whom it does not properly belong: it is itself a morbid condition, a neurosis and a means of evading the issue (p. 141).

This use of the term therefore must be clearly distinguished from the confidence which the patient has in the analyst. This also is an emotional relationship but a healthy one: far from being a morbid condition; it is of the greatest value in treatment—just as the confidence that the patient has in the surgeon who operates on him is a help to recovery in giving him a quiet mind. Such an emotional attitude does properly belong to the analyst. It makes the patient co-operative and ready to reveal everything freely in free association. That is why we get far better results from patients who come as a recommendation from previous patients we have cured, than from those who come reluctantly, sent by a doctor.

On the other hand there are serious objections to treatment by means of the transference, which is the Freudian method. It is a round-about and complicated method to transfer the emotions first to the analyst and then from the analyst back to the parents. Moreover in some cases the transference gets fixed on to the analyst with the result that the patient is hung up in mid-air and not cured. Apart from that, the treatment by transference is very time-consuming so that the analysis is prolonged.

Freud says that transference is the displacement of affect to a person 'to whom it does not properly belong', namely the analyst. Then why not take these feelings straight back to the persons to whom they do properly belong?—to the parents or situations in childhood. This we do in *direct* reductive analysis.

There are other objections to transference which Freud himself points out. Freud says that patients resort to the transference to avoid facing up to the real issue, namely their sex desires towards their parents (p. 141). Why then pamper the patient by encouraging the transference? Why not insist on the patient going straight back, and keeping back, to the real cause of the neurosis, whether or not that lies in incestuous desires towards the parent or in some quite different cause.

Again, Freud insisted on the importance of re-living all the emotions, for 'affectless memories are almost useless'. It is true that emotion can be released towards the analyst in the transference and then transferred back to the parents; but that is far more effectively done by going back and reliving the actual original experience in all its emotional vividness, thereby releasing all their repressed emotions, as is done in direct reductive analysis.

That does not mean that transference never occurs in the method of direct analysis. Transitory transferences not uncommonly occur. A patient recovering some experience of childhood will say; 'You don't seem to be very sympathetic towards me'. 'I feel I want you to hold my hand'. 'I feel afraid of you for some reason.' How do we deal with these? These feelings almost invariably relate to the incident we are at the moment analyzing. So when a transitory transference of this sort occurs, we immediately take it back to the situation in childhood, and we find there the reason for the emotion. We say, 'Take it back to what you were analyzing', and we then find that the 'lack of interest' arose from the similar feelings regarding the mother: that the impulse to strangle comes a desire to do so to the loathsome baby: that the fear of the analyst was fear of the father who gave him or her a beating.

In view of these objections and dangers involved in the use of transference it is difficult to understand why the Freudians still stick to a method which is so cumbersome and has so many pitfalls, instead of the simpler method of going directly back by free association to the original causes of the neurosis.

It may be that like Freud they find free association too boring for it requires a great deal of patience and perseverance to get these things out of the patient and it is far easier, though less effective, to give the patient interpretations of his symptoms and dreams. It also requires a good deal of experience and skill, just as is required to become a good surgeon. Any doctor can do an operation to remove the appendix: some are more skilful than others!

To summarize: by direct reductive analysis we go, by means of the symptom and by dreams, to recover the actual experiences, both precipitating and predisposing, which gave rise to the neurosis. By this means we avoid the complication of the transference. Further, by reliving the original experiences we release the repressed emotion far more effectively than by the vicarious method of the transference. Finally by relating the morbid emotions back to their actual causes, we detach them from the present-day symptoms to which they have been attached. By discovering what was the basic problem we are able to deal with it in a way we could not do at the time in early childhood. This is the final process of re-adjustment and emotional re-habilitation. The emotions being no longer repressed, no longer cause symptoms, and being released into consciousness are brought under the control of the will and directed to the uses and purpose of the personality as a whole. The patient not only loses his symptom but he is restored to health.

CHAPTER XXIX

DREAMS: THE BIOLOGICAL THEORY

Dreams are the activity of the mind during sleep. In direct reductive analysis we use dreams as well as symptoms as guides to the underlying causes of neurosis.

Even in primitive society, dreams had their significance, for primitive man took dreams for reality: so that if a savage dreamt that the next tribe was prepared to attack his tribe, he told his chiefs and they prepared to meet the attack. Nor was he necessarily far wrong, for he may have had the intuition that such was the case from slight indications, and intuition comes from the same sphere of the mind as dreams. The Greeks, too, put great store on their dreams.

A Red Indian accused a missionary of stealing his pumpkin because he had seen him doing it in his dream. The fact that the missionary was 200 miles away on the night, and that the pumpkin was still in the Indian's garden made no difference. He had seen him doing it with his own eyes.

The idea that dreams are the result of a heavy supper is confused. A heavy supper with its disorders of circulation in the brain may instigate a dream into consciousness; it cannot determine what we dream. A pork pie can account for the fact that we dream, but it cannot account for the fact that we dream of being lost in a desert, or of being chased, or of making love. What then is the significance of dreams?

When we are asleep the higher functions of the cortex of the brain are in abeyance; whereupon (a) the more primitive modes of mental functioning came into operation; (b) problems pushed aside during the day and relegated to the unconscious, come up for attention.

The biological function of dreams is, by repeating the left-over problems of the day, to work towards a solution. This is a theory I have propounded in my *Dreams and Nightmares* (Penguin). This theory gives to dreams a far greater biological significance than Freud's view that the function of the dream is simply to give expression to the wish so as to enable us to sleep. It is nearer to Jung's compensatory view but even more explicit.

It is because the patient could not solve the problem in the day by a process of reasoning that it recurs at night, when the subconscious mind takes over and attempts to solve the problem by the more primitive processes and often succeeds when reason fails.

The primitive mind, which is normally operative in the animal and the child, is capable of working out problems of living just as the reasoning mind does, but by different methods. It does so by methods of the association of ideas, analogy, similarities, conditioned reflexes, intuition and by trial and error (p. 66). When the higher functions of reason are in abeyance, as they are in sleep and in hypnosis, or absent, as they are in the small child, in the drunken man and the animal, then the functions of the subcortical subconscious mind come into operation, and take over the problems of life. Animals and children using these more primitive methods are thus quite capable of working out the ordinary problems of life without any resort to reason, which is not yet developed.

Perseveration. Dreams work out the problems of life by virtue of what psychologists call 'perseveration', defined as 'the tendency of the mind to revert back to an unfinished train of thought', including of course, unresolved problems. Whenever we have a problem to face, the mind tends of itself automatically to go on working at it persistently until it solves it. Only if it fails to do so does the mind repress it.

The simplest form of perseveration is that of ordinary worry. We have some difficulty to which we cannot find an answer: so we say 'Oh! forget it.' But will it let us? By no means. In spite of our efforts the problem keeps bobbing up at most inappropriate moments, and to our great annoyance: it will not let us alone. This recurrence is, of course, most likely to happen when our minds are relaxed and not otherwise engaged—as in sleep.

We have thus in the mind two separate principles working against one another—the principle of repression trying to evade the issue and forget about it; and the principle of perseveration, insisting on our attending to it. Repression says 'Oh! forget all about it.' Perseveration says 'Oh no you don't!'.

Curiously enough, both these principles are of biological significance. The tendency to repression is of practical value in spite of what the psychologists say, for if we cannot solve a problem it is no use wasting time and energy on it in face of the more immediate practical demands of life; it is no use bashing our heads against a wall which refuses to yield; so best forget it! On the other hand, it would never do for us to avoid every difficulty, to shirk every responsibility by pushing it aside. To be efficient we must face up to our problems in life. The individual who is in the habit of side tracking every difficult issue is not likely to make headway in the struggle for existence. To face our difficulties is the way of progress. Therefore there is instilled into us the propensity which will not let us shirk the difficulties of life and which forces them unwillingly upon us till we have solved them. Put in more scientific language, it is those animals, including man, which have developed this propensity to perseveration for the working out of difficult problems, which best survive. Perseveration is a biological necessity.

But what is a biological necessity often turns out to be a psychological disaster, for if we cannot solve the problem it comes to harass us perpetually: it becomes an obsession. Far from assisting us in our lives, it incapacitates us. This is the state of the constant worrier. He worries about the future, he worries about the past; he worries about his health, and he worries because he worries. He is the centre of a cyclone tossed about by winds from every direction.

This conflict between repression and perseveration leads to two striking results: neurotic symptoms and dreams. Thus if we have a feeling of guilt which we find most unpleasant, we repress it and forget it. But perseveration will not let is do so and insists on our facing up to the problem. A compromise has to be attempted which takes the form of hand-washing, which is a false attempt to solve the problem by giving ourselves the feeling that we are pure and guiltless. But perseveration is not bluffed by this self-deception, so that when we are asleep, the problem emerges, taking the form of a dream, shall we say of being tried in a court of law for a crime and the horror of being found guilty.

Thus even when we give up trying to solve the problem, our subconscious mind refuses to give up and takes over the problem to try to solve it. Both symptoms and dreams are the products of perseveration.

Whenever then, during the day we are confronted with a difficulty we first set about overcoming it, solving the problem by the process of reason and will. Secondly, if we cannot solve it we push it aside and repress it, for we must get on with the business of life. But thirdly, at night when the conscious will is in abeyance the problem is relegated to the subconscious mind and recurs, night after night, as dreams.

Dreams and symptoms. Just as in disorders of the body the function of pain is to call our attention to the fact that there is something wrong with the body, which needs attention, so the distress of the neurotic disability calls attention to the fact that there is something wrong with the personality and points to where it went wrong. But whereas the symptom gives up the struggle and resorts to a neurosis as a means of escape, the dream refuses to do so. By the repetition of the problem over and over again, perhaps in the same, perhaps in different forms, the dream works towards a solution.

Use of dreams in analysis. Both dreams and symptoms therefore are useful in pointing to the source of the trouble whether it be the objective repetitive dreams of the soldier being blown up, or dreams of loneliness and isolation reproducing an experience in infancy; or subjective dreams of overwhelming monsters which represent passions which we have failed to control. If the problem is of a more abstract nature, since the primitive subconscious mind is incapable of dealing with abstract ideas, the problem must take symbolic form, such as the dream of wandering about a large empty house which symbolizes the patient's feeling of being lost in life and unable to find his way about.

Dreams have the advantage over symptoms in that they are far more explicit than symptoms and often offer a positive solution.

But in so far as dreams are symbolic, they are capable of various interpretations. It is therefore preferable in the first place to take the symptom since it takes us back more directly to the actual origin of the trouble. (See p. 223.)

The wise psychotherapist therefore uses both dreams and symptoms as a means of discovering what is the latent problem, and secondly what solution, if any, the dream has to suggest.

Let us take a simple instance of the problem-solving function of dreams. You are out sailing, running before the wind. Suddenly there is a change of wind and you gybe. The boom swings over and nearly knocks your child overboard. But fortunately nothing happens and you dismiss it from your mind. 'He did not go over, so why worry'! You ignore it not only because it is unpleasant to contemplate what might have happened, but because it reflects on your poor seamanship. Your mind, however, refuses to allow you to push it aside; at night the incident recurs in a dream—and what do you dream? The first night you dream that the swinging boom does carry him overboard and you wake up in terror. The dream does not let you get away with it, and impresses upon you the danger of the situation and your bad seamanship, of what might have happened. Night after night you may dream of the same incident: but it changes, and in later dreams you begin to do something about it. It may be that seeing the danger you snatch at your child so that he does not go overboard; or you turn an accidental gybe into an intentional gybe by letting out the sheet more slowly so that it does not carry over with such force; or you are more careful in watching for a gybe and so rectify it before it takes place, by steering off-wind. This kind of succession in dreams, with change of content, was very common with shell-shock patients. They are all attempts to solve the problem, telling you what you might have done.

Again, if you are driving in mountainous country and round a bend meet an oncoming car and nearly go over the precipice. That night you repeat the experience; but this time you are flung over the precipice and wake up with horror. In later dreams you find ways of solving the problem and in that case sleep peacefully. Freud says dreams are to allow you to sleep: they sometimes do, but only if they offer some solution to the problem.

From such simple traumatic dreams of objective situations we may draw conclusions as to the significance of dreams in general.

(a) In the first place, the very fact that you actually experience what might have happened impresses the danger of the situation on you, so that you will be more careful in future. That is a very important function of dreams, to impress on you the problem.

(b) Dreams thus stand in the place of experience, so that if you are subjected to the same experience another time, as you are likely to be if you are a sailor or drive a car, you are far better able to cope with the situation because you have been through the experience not once but a dozen times; you automatically do the right thing. Such dreams are obviously not just wish fulfilments; they stand in the place of experience and, by the process of trial and error, work towards a solution.

(c) Dreams thus serve the same purpose as ideational processes, but by different methods. In other words your dream is doing precisely what you would be doing if after the event you set down and thought out what you should have done. If you had reasoned it out you would probably not have dreamt about it since the problems would be solved. Why did you not do so? Because you do not like to think of so unpleasant a possibility of disaster, nor of your lack of skill, so you cast it out and say, 'Forget it!' When your conscious mind of reason dismisses the problem, it is taken over by the subconscious mind which often solves it, and thus prepares you for future emergencies.

(d) An interesting feature of dreams is that they are often reproductions in part of the actual experiences which cause the problem. The man who has a motor-car accident may dream of flying through the air, or of a bang on the head, or of the racing of the engine. These dreams are most valuable for diagnostic purposes, pointing the way. The nightmares of children are often of this order, being an almost exact reproduction, say of a terrifying female with staring eyes at the foot of the bed, this being an angry mother; or dreams of suffocation or isolation reproducing actual experiences.

(e) On the other hand it is characteristic of most dreams that rarely are they exact reproductions of the experience—sometimes the emotion is far stronger, or the facts are different. People say they dream only of what happened in the day. Study the dream and you rarely find it the same. That is because the dream in attempting to solve the problem, tries various solutions.

Repetition in dreams. This explains also the repetitive nature of dreams, which repeat themselves over and over again in an attempt to find a solution. If it fails to do so in one way, it does so in another; if by one symbol it fails to impress, it attempts to do so by another symbol (p. 257), Pharoah's dream.

The emotions of such dreams are far more exaggerated than the event of the day, for which the dreams spring. This has the effect of impressing the experience on the mind. If it is in fact a near car accident, in your dream you do have a crash, or do go over the cliff with terror. The dog which jumps up on a small child in the street becomes a wild monster in his dreams so that he is terrified of dogs all the next day. A slight from a friend in the day turns into a bad snub in your dream. An angry mother turns into an avenging witch.

Such exaggerations have been taken to prove that these monstrous beings in our dreams are archaic and archetypal, monsters from our racial ancestry, our collective unconscious.

The reason for the exaggeration is far simpler. In conscious waking life our emotions are automatically held in check by the inhibitions of our higher cortical centres: in sleep these inhibitions are removed, so that the emotions emerge with full terrifying force. It is as simple as that.

When analyzing a painful childhood experience I have often asked patients if they dreamt afterwards. Sometimes not: but often they visualize a dream, and that dream is almost always more terrifying than the actual experience of the day. Very commonly it is the dream which compels the repression when the incident itself would not have done so. A sexual orgasm in an infant is sufficiently frightening; but when it returns in the form of an overwhelming monster it is infinitely more terrifying and causes the child to repress its sexuality once and for all. Thus sexuality and anger are often repressed by exaggeration in dreams. The value of this emotional content is obvious. Thinking things out in the cold light of reason may be more accurate in its results. Dreams on the other hand have the advantage in that we actually re-live the experience emotionally, which is far more effective than cold reasoning.

Content of dreams. The material with which dreams are concerned is by no means merely sexual. Since dreams according to our theory relate to unsolved problems, they can relate to any problem, objective or subjective, present-day or relating to the past, conscious as well as unconscious. The one criterion is that the problem is unsolved. It is then shelved but comes into action when our minds are relaxed in sleep. In brief *whatever we worry about we can dream about.*

Many dreams relate to the ordinary problems of everyday life, and people are often right when they say that they dream of what happened in the day. If such dreams are analyzed it is always found that these experiences contain an unresolved problem. They may relate to objective difficulties, to business or domestic problems, or how to deal with a troublesome neighbour. More often they deal with subjective psychological problems arising from a conflict of impulses or desires, or moral problems which assail us. Instances of all of these have already been given. How does this problem-solving theory link up with Freud's theory of wish fulfilment? It is because the frustration of our wishes, sexual and otherwise, constitute some of the most important problems of our lives. But it is not the wish, but the fact that it creates an unsolved problem which causes the distress and also explains why it persists in striving for a solution in our dreams.

A typical and simple instance of such a dream is that of arctic explorers who dream of wonderful meals: of a little boy who dreams of a plum pudding the size of a house (have we not said that dreams exaggerated!); or the unhappy little girl who day-dreams of being adopted by kindly parents (the so-called 'foster parent fantasy'); or the adolescent who dreams of making love which he is denied. More subjectively, the religious hermit who dreams of ravishing females is frustrated not by external circumstances but by his own moral inhibitions. They are all wishes, and they all create problems. If we cannot satisfy our wishes let us at least imagine we do. Even such dreams serve a biological function, for they at least give us respite, an oasis in the all too dreary conflicts of life. It puts before the arctic explorer something to look forward to, even though he wakes up to the drab realities of life. At least he had a good time while it lasted and that oasis refreshes and spurs him on. It is a poor solution but it does something. But most dreams do better than that.

Children's day-dreams are often of this nature: prolonged day dreaming in children indicates that they are none too happy in their everyday life. Taken by parents to be a sign of contentment, it is often the result of disillusion.

Dreams as Diagnostic. To solve a problem we must first discover and state the problem. To see a problem clearly is two-thirds towards solving it. That is what dreams help us to do, they point to the source of the trouble; and sometimes go no further. They may do this by reproducing part of the original experience. Other dreams go further and offer a solution. Thus some dreams are merely diagnostic, others are therapeutic.

A dream often takes the form of part of the original experiences, recalling a certain place where we once had a holiday or of being back at school. We may be sure that there is a problem and an unsolved one relating to these situations; for by the principle of perseveration the mind is saying, 'That is where the problem lies.' This is particularly so in nightmares, which in analysis, are found to revert to actual experiences. They are diagnostic.

The following dream illustrates very clearly the diagnostic value of dreams, and the relation between the symptom and the dream. It relates to a moral problem.

A woman comes for treatment because she has an obsessional phobia that something she might do would cause her son to have T.B. The patient as a child was one of a large family and un-wanted. She found solace, however, with a kindly vicar who interested her in books, and later she became a very good teacher receiving high commendations from her headmaster. At last she had got some appreciation. She then married a man she despised to get away from home, and had a son to whom she was completely devoted. To help to pay for him to go to university (he became a solicitor) she returned to teaching. Unfortunately this resulted in her son complaining that she was 'never at home'—so she got no credit for her 'sacrifice' as she did for her teaching. This aroused a conflict in her mind. She had a simple short dream; it said, 'Your son is standing in your way.' I asked her in what conceivable way might her son be standing in her way, and without a moments hesitation she said 'In my career.'

Note the following points about this dream and the symptoms.

(a) The dream is definitely diagnostic: it points to the actual cause of the trouble. It says 'Look here! You think your fear of something happening to your son is a sign of your great devotion to him. The opposite is the case: your son is standing in your way and you want him out of your way. Your very devotion to him is a hinderance to t he fulfilment of your own life.'

But of course she will not for a moment entertain such a thing as being rid of her son; that was too repugnant to her moral sense: yet that desire was too pressing to be ignored altogether. So a moral conflict is precipitated and a compromise is arrived at: her sub-conscious mind suggested; 'If only by some unlucky chance he caught T.B. that would solve the problem.' But even this thought, let alone the wish, could not be entertained. So the symptom took the form of a fear—a fear that some harm might come to her son. This fear like all obsessional fears (p. 331) is a fear of her forbidden wish.

But note that even the symptom would not allow her to disclaim all responsibility: for it was something she, the mother, might do, not the maid who had T.B., which would cause her son to get the disease. That was what was so horrifying.

To compare then the symptom with the dream: her symptom

showed that there was something drastically wrong with her personality: her dream showed her what was wrong. Unknown to herself it reveals to her quite explicitly and briefly the cause of her symptom—her son was standing in the way of the fulfilment of her life. Her symptom says, 'What a horrible thought that something I should do would give my son T.B.' The dream is far more explicit than the symptom in pointing to the real cause of the neurosis.

The dream thus deals not simply with a wish, unconscious or otherwise, but with a moral issue; the conflict between her devotion to her son, which predominated, and her craving for approval which she got in her career, but which was so sadly lacking in her early life. It was the latter which she had to repress in favour of her son; and it was this which revealed itself in the symptom.

The dream like the symptom *deals with an unsolved problem*, but simply in a diagnostic way pointing to the cause of this trouble without suggesting a definite solution. Nevertheless, pointing to the cause of a problem is the first step towards solving it.

Let us take another dream to illustrate a factual experience involving a moral problem. A patient has a dream of a boat on a river: it caught in some barbed wire and capsized, and the patient was horrified to see a corpse on the bank of the stream, dripping and lifeless. No doubt we could find a symbolic interpretation for such a dream. To Freud the boat is a phallic symbol, the barbed wire perhaps relating to castration. To Jung the boat on the stream might relate to birth, as it often does in mythology (e.g., Moses), and the meaning of the dream relating to rebirth from the collective unconscious.

But in giving it a symbolic representation we may miss the real significance of the dream. When we investigate in free association the origins of the dream, the patient revives a memory long since forgotten of being furiously jealous of her pretty younger sister who not only got all the admiration and attention but who jeered at the patient, and nobody stopped her. At last the patient could stand it no longer so that when (the patient being seven and her sister three) both were in the bath, she pushed her sister under and held her there till she lost consciousness and went limp. Taking fright the patient rushed out, called the nanny who pulled the child out and then ran for the father who gave artificial respiration so that the child lived. The long boat was the bath, and drowning person was her sister who was held down by the patient, symbolized by the barbed wire, and the horror was of seeing her sister's inert dripping body lying on the bath mat. The patient had quite forgotten the whole incident, but remembered it when it was revived. Her symptom was a hatred of her *own* child (displacement).

I

The dream was, of course symbolic; but it was symbolic of an objective fact of experience. It was put into symbolic form because the patient, even in dreams, was unwilling to look at the painful facts, whereas perseveration compelled her to take note of so significant an experience, which affected her whole life, for it produced a sense of guilt which, though unconscious, made her repress all assertiveness and therefore lack confidence to face life. The moral problem in her case was her murderous hatred of her sister which because of its disastrous consequences was repressed. The dream compels her to face up to the problem and overcome the repression, by calling attention to the event which caused it. This dream illustrates certain other characteristics of dreams.

(a) *Symbolism.* The question remains 'Why does the dream use symbols?' It was in this case partly to evade the real issue; for the actual experience was most painful. The perseveration forces up the unsolved problem but repression will not allow it except in symbolic and disguised form.

The more fundamental reason for symbolism is that the dream is the activity of the primitive mind, and the primitive mind, like that of the savage, is incapable of abstract ideas and thinks in terms of concrete symbols.

(b) Dreams relate to actual experiences far more than is generally supposed. They are not all to be interpreted as symbolic, and always to interpret them so is to miss the causal factors of the neurosis in childhood. It is a mistake to rush for a symbolic interpretation when a factual one is called for. Dreams of passing through a long tunnel with great anxiety are regarded by some as symbolic of the personality being shut in and confined. The symptoms of claustrophobia are similarly interpreted as we have seen (p.183). If we analyze the dream reductively we discover two facts; first that the dream reverts to an actual experience of a bad birth; secondly, that this primal fear in infancy is the cause of that child's later lack of confidence, so that his personality is stifled.

This is important therapeutically, for we often find that the discovery and elucidation of the actual experience which caused the problem is enough to get rid of the basic fear and so cure the patient, whereas to deal only with the later symbolic meaning without getting rid of their basic cause only half cures the patient.

(c) *Distress in dreams.* Dreams are distressing simply because they are concerned with distressing problems. These problems are repressed because they are distressing, so obviously they are distressing when they are revived in dreams, whether it be the fact of being blown up, or the thought of getting rid of a son. Yet if the dream has to solve the problem it must revive these distressing experiences in order to make the patient face facts.

Another reason which accentuates the distress is, as we have seen, that all emotions—fear, anger, sex, are greatly exaggerated since they are no longer subject to the inhibitions and control of the conscious mind.

The third reason why dreams are distressing is when they cannot find a solution to the problem, as frequently they can't. In that case there is an accumulation of emotional energy, which, failing to find an outlet, fills us with distress and anxiety. Dreams which suggest a solution are peaceful and quiet.

Freud would have us believe that the function of dreams is merely the gratifying of our forbidden desires, and so, by releasing the tension, allow us to sleep. If that is their function they often woefully fail, for far from letting us sleep they often wake us up: far from gratifying wishes they are often distressing, depressing, and terrifying. Can any one maintain that the soldier who night after night dreams of being blown up, is giving expression to a wish, unless a wish to live. His nights are so filled with horror that he dare not go to sleep. The persistence of such terrifying dreams, reproducing the actual facts, are not a wish fulfilment but an attempt to face and solve the problem—that between his self preservation and his sense of duty. The simple problem is 'What is a chap to do in these circumstances?' Well, what is the answer? His answer is the development of a neurosis, a paralysis shall we say, which enables him to escape from the whole situation, and gets him out of the firing line. But that does not solve the problem, which continues long after the war is over, and constantly recurs in his dream, the problem of fear and courage.

Indeed Freud himself finds these traumatic dreams an exception to his wish fulfilment theory for obviously they do not allow one to sleep. He does not thereupon revise his theory of dreams, but says that in those cases 'the function of dreams is upset.' In other words, if the dreams do not fit in with his theory, so much the worse for dreams! It is obviously not the function of dreams which is upset, but his theory of dreams, for 'the exception proves (i.e., tests) the rule,' and proves in this case that the rule of wish fulfilment as a basic principle is wrong. Dreams have a far more important biological function than mere wish fulfilment or allowing us to sleep. By attempting and often succeeding in solving one's problems they are a definite means of adaptation to life and an aid to survival. That is why I call it the biological theory of dreams.

(d) *Resistance*. Sometimes there is very strong resistance on the part of the patient to look at what the dream is trying to tell us.

This is well illustrated in the following dream. The patient, a professional woman, suffers from depression. She was the eldest child and was spoilt for three years until another baby arrived when she was pushed aside. She became rebellious, disobedient and bloody-minded. Her mother 'didn't know what to do with her.' The patient dreamt 'There was a coffin; and a corpse inside the coffin. A man partly opened it and wanted me to look inside: but I couldn't—it was so horrible. I couldnt bear to look at it.' The man was myself, the analyst, urging her to look inside herself. No doubt such a dream could be interpreted as sexual symbolism. In free association I told her to look at that coffin and tell me whatever came to her mind as to what was inside. 'Nothing at all!' she said, 'All that keeps coming into my mind is that I can't think of anything that I can't bear to look at.'

As she blocked so rigidly in her free association on the dream I said, 'Very well, we'll leave that and go back to what we were analyzing last time.' The result was interesting: in spite of her resistance and my suggestion to leave the subject, the perseveration of her problem of the coffin would not allow her to leave it. She continued: 'I think of my mother and I think that what I can't bear to look at is something to do with her. I seem to be ill in bed and to hear my father and mother talking in the next room. My father says, 'She seems to be dying.' My mother replies, 'It would not altogether be a bad thing if she did.' (At this the patient burst out sobbing.) 'It was a terrible blow! I was depressed and then I was angry. But I realized it was because I was jealous of my sister and hated her and was antagonistic towards my mother. The thought that they did not love me and wanted me to die was awful. Then I thought I might hide any hatred of her from them: in fact I went further and would not admit it to myself. (Patient then became restless on the couch). 'I feel cold and shivery and it has to do with fear'. (Of what?) 'Not the fear of death, but of my parents' hostility and that they were willing for me to die. I blame them for my illness.'

This dream is typical of these dreams which merely point out the origin and source of the problem. The problem she as a child had to face was the intolerable one of being unloved and unwanted, with the loss of protection and security, even in illness. No wonder she was depressed. The coffin was of course her coffin, if her parents left her to die. The abreaction of sobbing was the release of pent-up feelings of self-pity. True the dream was symbolic, but the symbolism related to an actual experience and it was this very experience which was the original cause of her neurosis. Had we interpreted the dream purely symbolically, as relating shall we say, to the death of some peculiarity in herself, or a horror of looking at incestuous guilt or wish for the death of her mother, we should have missed the whole significance of the dream. It was this recovery of the actual experience in childhood which relieved the patient of her depression.

(e) *All dreams are personal.* They relate to personal problems. They often just tell us about ourselves and in doing so are diagnostic. They frequently reveal qualities in ourselves which we did not know existed: they show us up for what we are. One day a man refused a coin to a beggar: there is nothing particularly upsetting about that. Why then does the incident recur in his dream? It may call his attention to his meanness as though to say, 'You might have been more generous.' Or it may be a reminder to him of the time when he needed help and was denied it. In fact the dream was reproving him for his callous nature. The following dream reveals an opposite characteristic and gives opposite moral advice. A man dreams that he and his daughter are seated at a restaurant table at which two other people, strangers, are seated. At the end of the meal the strangers find they have no money to pay for their meal, whereupon the man generously offers to pay for them. But when he comes to open his wallet he found he had only a ten shilling note, not enough to pay for himself and the strangers: he felt foolish. His free associations were that he had recently given considerable sums of money to his daughter, but the thought crossed his mind that he might be running himself short in his retirement—to him an unworthy thought which he immediately dismissed from his mind—saying he had given the money and that's that. But the problem must have been worrying him at the back of his mind, so that when he was asleep, and his will in abeyance, the problem returned. The dream says in effect. 'Look here,' it is all very well being generous but you haven't got enough money to be so lavish in your generosity.' The dream brings him down to earth to take a more realistic view and compels him to face facts. But why should the dream apparently encourage him to be selfish? Free association on the dream made him realize that the reason for his lavishness to his daughter was not generosity at all but vanity and a desire to ingratiate himself—another problem which he had not faced up to.

(f) *Universality.* Why is it that the same type of dream appears in myths and fairy tales all over the world, a fact emphasized by Jung. It has been argued that the universality of such dreams proves their ancestral origin. Not necessarily so; it may mean simply that they are all derived from a very common individual experience in childhood, exaggerated because of the lack of inhibition. As already pointed out, experience of an angry mother with staring eyes are common to childhood all the world over and are well-nigh universal, for what child has not at some time been terrified of an angry mother, who to the child is a great gigantic monster. The child dreams of the mother as a monster because to the child she is monstrous. The law of the 'parsimony of hypothesis' compels us to accept the simpler explanation that such experiences are acquired not inherited: they are well-nigh universal and so appear in myths, fairy stories and dreams all over the world. Apart from which, we find in reductive analysis that such dreams do in fact revert to such childhood experiences.

(g) *Waking from a dream.* We wake up from a dream because the dream has no solution to offer for the problem—as in the coffin dream. For just as we go to sleep to escape the cares of the day, so we wake from sleep to escape the unsolved distressing problems of the night. Such dreams are therefore of the greatest diagnostic value, for they point simply to the problem and offer no solution. This particularly applies to nightmares which I find almost always revert to an infantile experience which the helpless infant of course cannot solve: so it wakes up.

Dreams as Problem-Solving
Dreams not only direct us towards the problem; by repeating the problem over and over again they tend towards a solution. That is their biological function: that is the problem-solving theory of dreams. Instances of this have already been given in passing when illustrating the diagnostic aspect of dreams. A down-trodden man dreams of standing up to his bullying boss, and his boss respects him for it. Such a dream might be interpreted as 'compensatory' to his conscious cringing attitude (Jung). It may also be regarded as wish-fulfilment (Freud); and so far it is. But it is more than both, for he has a problem, and the function of the dream is to solve his problem. It encourages him to rectify this being more assertive, by standing up for himself. It further assures him that if he does so there is nothing to fear; that people will respect him the more. Which is in fact true. The fact that he dreams it is of value quite apart from any interpretation; for the mere fact that he experiences being more assertive in his dream shows him that he has it in him. Having once done it in his dream, he says, 'and why not?', during the day.

The evidence for the problem-solving function of dreams is not far to seek: it is scientifically established. For many scientific problems have been solved in dreams, instances of which are given in Beresford's *The Art of Scientific Investigation*, and some in my *Dreams and Nightmares*. (Chap. 5). A notable instance was the discovery of the Benzene ring which revolutionized organic chemistry. Kekulé was writing a book on chemistry and got stuck on a problem. 'It did not go well. . . . I turned the chair to the fireplace and sank into a half sleep. Wriggling before my eyes came snakes: one of them seized its own tail and that gave me the clue to the Benzene ring.'

Indeed the principle of the computer was discovered by intuition and subconscious inference. William Phillips had tried to advance from the calculating machine consisting of holes in cards to the use of rays of light, but was completely stumped—'the death of a grand idea!' he puts it. Then he writes (*Sunday Times*, Sept. 5, 1965, p.18) 'Half asleep in a deck chair on a transatlantic liner in 1925 I suddenly saw a worked-out binary long multiplication *turn of its own volition*' and this gave rise to the modern computer.

Some scientists, Beresford tells us, when confronted with a problem they cannot solve deliberately put themselves into a relaxed state in hope of a solution—leaving the solution to the subconscious mind. But why go further than our ordinary lives. Who of us has not, when he has a problem on his mind that he cannot solve, or a decision he cannot make, has not said 'Let's sleep on it!'—and in the morning the solution may be as clear as day?

Thus the subconscious mind, by its different methods of free association and analogy, can solve problems which the logical mind of reason fails to do, and that is precisely the function of dreams. Kekulé's solution was obviously by the subcortical process of analogy.

Dreams as intuition. Dreams as we have indicated are of the same nature, serve the same functions and come from the same sphere of the mind as intuition. Indeed, it might be said that dreams are the expression of our intuition. Both dreams and intuition appear to come out of the blue (p. 272), but both in fact are based on data dealt with by the methods of the subconscious mind.

There are numerous classical instances of intuitive judgments emerging in dreams. Reference has already been made to Homer's Odyssey, how the adolescent girl Nausicaa in her hoydenish phase of adolescence, has a dream in which the goddess Athene comes and tells her that this will not do. She must attend more to her appearance, she must tidy herself up, or she will never get a husband. She listens to her dream and passes from this hoydenish phase to the attractive phase of adolescence, falling for Ulysees—'the kind of man I would like to marry.' The goddess Athene was of course her intuition, projected and personalized as a goddess in her dream. But it solved her problem.

Take Pharoah's dream of the seven lean kine coming out of the river and swallowing the seven fat kine, a dream which Joseph interpreted intuitively as meaning seven years of plenty being swallowed up by seven years of famine. Pharoah could not interpret the dream, but he had an intuitive sense that it meant something important, for it worried him a great deal so that he searched the land for a wise man to interpret it. The symbolism was clear: for the corn crop and the cattle depended on the river Nile overflowing its banks and irrigating the land. If it failed to do so there were no crops and the cattle starved. The dream says in effect, 'Don't count too much on your present fortune. You had better save some of it for bad seasons.' The dream was diagnostic; it also clearly points to a solution of the problem. He could have done the same by caution and foresight; but he had probably taken the attitude 'take your fill, blow the consequences.' Hence the necessity of the dream.

We have here an illustration of the same problem appearing in different symbolisms: at first the dream was of cattle: but in case Pharoah could not understand its meaning, his subconscious mind changed this symbolism and made it seven sheaves of corn swallowing up the seven fat sheaves. That was much clearer and much more to the point; for the dream did refer to harvests of corn.

Why is it that dreams and intuition sometimes succeed when reason fails? One reason for this failure of reason is that it can draw conclusions only from verified data, which are very limited in our ordinary experience, whereas intuition is based on associations and feelings, sees things as a whole and takes in the whole of our past experiences, although it is not consciously aware what those experiences are. So we 'feel' that this is the right thing to do, we are 'convinced' that our judgment is right, although we may not have reason for thinking so, because our whole past experience is brought into activity and tells us so.

In other words the subcortical mind operates in precisely the same way as the electronic brain in which we feed certain material concerning a problem into the brain and immediately receive an answer. The answers they give are extraordinarily shrewd.

Yet neither the electronic brain nor the subconscious mind is always right, for the correct answer can be given only if all the factors in the case are brought in and that is not always possible. Thus a computer, set the task of discovering which of the students in a co-educational college should marry, 'married' a man to his sister. So the subconscious mind and intuition may make the wrong judgments if a person's experiences in life are abnormal. We may dislike a person not because he is dislikable but because of our own complexes.

Repetitiveness in dreams. As already explained the problem-solving functions explain the repetitiveness of dreams, on the principle of preservation. Some dreams which recur night after night appear in the same form. They are of particular value for diagnostic purposes, because they are perpetually calling our attention to our problem which requires investigation and solution. This is particularly the case with nightmares—say of a dark figure hovering over the bed; or the common dream of being chased by some monster but being rooted to the spot. Such dreams are usually reproductions of childhood experiences.

Freud, confronted with the dreams of war-shocked soldiers, could not but accept the obvious fact that traumatic dreams were subject to the repetitive process. He does not seem to have realized that the same is true of all dreams; they are all repetitive of unsolved problems, of which the Oedipus complex is only one.

At other times, the dream takes different forms, but is found to deal with the same problem by means of different symbols. Thus if one dream does not convince us, it is as though the subconscious mind says, 'Well, look at it this way," and puts it in another form, by other symbols, so the dream tries by various reproductions to call attention to the same problem. So it was in Pharoah's dream, now of cattle, now of corn, to impress upon him the nature of the problem.

The therapeutic value of dreams

The problem-solving function of dreams calls attention to their therapeutic value. They are a means, and a most valuable means, of coping with the problems of life, both objective and subjective. They tell us not merely what is the basic problem causing our neurosis, a fact which in conscious life we repress and of which we are unaware, but many of them go a step further and suggest how the problem may be solved. They are therefore, rightly interpreted, of the greatest value in analysis in restoring the patient to health and happiness, for they indicate what the patient suggests is the solution of the problem, which may be quite different from what the analyst may think right.

Take a simple every-day dream such as this: A middle-aged woman suffering from depression, defeatism and a complete lack of confidence in herself, has a dream that she is offered a better job in the hospital in which she works. One of the other workers says to her scornfully, 'You will never be able to carry off that job!' She replies 'In my younger days I ran a large office in the city (a fact), and if I did that I could take this job in my stride.' This attitude in the dream is exactly the opposite of her defeatist attitude in every-day life.

Is that merely a wish-fulfilment? I don't think so at all. It is telling her what she is capable of doing; it is solving her immediate

I*

problem by reminding her of her past successes—'You have done it before! You can do it again,' says the dream. This of course is precisely what she might have said to herself in her waking life; but her defeatism and lack of confidence was too great for her to entertain the idea. So her subconscious mind, her intuition, comes to the rescue. It urges her to a restoration of her old self-confidence.

A very pretty problem-solving and therapeutic dream is the following:

A woman of twenty-seven, suffering from regression, cannot leave home and go anywhere without her mother. Reductive analysis reveals that she was too attached to her mother because of childhood illness and fears; and as a child she had always been content to remain under the shelter of her mother's protection. She dreams that 'she and her mother are going to catch a train (representing progress in life). They are holding an umbrella between them (mutual protection). Then a gust of wind blows the umbrella away and she chases it, her mother taking no part in this proceeding. The patient at last retrieves the umbrella. But instead of putting the umbrella up to shelter her from the storm, she lets it down, she has no need of it, as she is now able to stand up to the storm without it, though with some difficulty. Finally she catches the next train and later meets her mother, to continue the journey.' The main theme of the dream and its most striking feature is her initial dependence on her mother (under one umbrella); it reveals the situation as it is, and is therefore diagnostic. It then works towards her being entirely independent of her mother. Not only so, she no longer needs the umbrella. The first part states the problem; the latter part gives the solution.

It tells her, 'If only you let go your hold on your mother you will find you will be perfectly able to stand on your own: you will not only not need your mother, you will be able to do without external support (the umbrella) altogether. You will be independent and self-sufficient; and proceed to the train, to progress in life.' Look at the dream in reverse; suppose a patient was trying to solve that problem of her dependence on her mother, but had to express the solution pictorially, how better could she express it than by such symbolism? Dreams show extraordinary genius, both in transforming a psychological problem into visual and concrete forms, but in working towards a solution.

Take another dream: a homosexual, by means of treatment is brought to realize the causes of his condition in early childhood: and is becoming hetero-sexual. Then he has a dream. There are three persons before him—a man (representing homosexuality), a very feminine woman; and a mannish woman (representing a compromise between homo- and hetero-sexuality). In the dream he ponders which he should fall in love with. He discards immediately the man—he has finished with homosexuality. He ponders for a long time over the middle person: shall he compromise and choose the half-way position to gratify both sides of his nature? (Many homosexuals are of this order, being indifferent as to whether the object of their love is male or female). Ultimately he discards this mannish person and goes off with the very feminine woman. The dream obviously encourages him to the right solution. This case is mentioned on page 323/4.

Since the main function of a dream is that of subconsciously solving our problems, we shall find that in a complete dream, the first part of the dream contains the problem, the latter part works towards a solution. That can be verified by many of the dreams quoted, such as that of the girl and her mother sheltering underneath the same umbrella. That is her problem; her complete dependence on her mother. Then the solution; the storm separates them and she is shown that she is quite capable of looking after herself. So in a series of dreams of this same night, the first dream of the series deals with the problem, that is diagnostic, and the later dreams of the night work towards a solution; they are therapeutic. Both are important in showing the analyst (a) what is the basic trouble, and (b) what the patient's intuition suggests as a solution. Another such dream is given on page 193.

The suggested solution which the dream offers, however, is not necessarily final nor always right, for the dream often has to make tentative suggestions before it arrives at a right solution, but even those suggestions are worth consideration as a step in the right direction. The subconscious mind works by trial and error which is not at all a bad method, but not invariably right in its conclusions.

Progress in dreams. As the analysis proceeds the suggestions change. It is indeed most fascinating to watch the progress of the patient in analysis by the changes in the dream. Take the dream of missing trains, which usually means progress in life. At first we are always missing the train, a dream which shows us to be arrested in development. As analysis proceeds we only just catch it; and finally we catch it with the greatest of ease. We may even picture another person (our arrested self) trying to catch the train and we help him to do so successfully.

So the dreams progress from one problem to another. When we have worked out one problem the patient often has a period when he has no dreams; then when he dreams again it is usually of quite a different problem. Such dreams clearly show the progress the patient is making.

Here is a simple illustration of a change in the problem and of the working out of each problem as it arises.

A woman of thirty-five, unmarried, is being paid court to by a man well-to-do, but somewhat younger. The question is, should she marry at her age and in present circumstances. That is an important present-day problem which she finds difficult to decide. She has a dream, 'She has a car (which, in fact, she has), and she is being persuaded by her friends to sell her car. She is reluctant to do so for her car means a great deal to her. But they keep telling her that if she sells it in America she will get a lot of money for it. So ultimately she does: and when it comes to the payment she finds that she has been given only eight pounds and is very disappointed.' The dream though put in objective terms is not concerned with objective issues, for as she says she has no intention whatever of selling her car. The dream is clearly symbolic. Her association with the car is that it enables her to do a lot of things she could not do otherwise; to play golf, visit her friends in the country, go for picnics and independent holidays—indeed, it greatly enlarges the scope of her activities and gives her much greater freedom to do what she wants in life. The car therefore represents her freedom and a more expansive life.

We can now see the meaning of the dream in terms of her present-day problem. Should she surrender her bachelor freedom and marry: would marriage offer an adequate compensation for the loss of this freedom (her car). Her friends all encourage her to marry. They tell her she will be well off and get many compensations in marriage; so in the dream she yields, and what does she get? A miserable eight pounds. It wasn't worth it. What the dream in other words is telling her is, 'You had better think twice before marriage under these circumstances.' Marriage may look very attractive (America is a rich country), but the dream, in other words her intuition, is telling her that she would be disappointed, that she will get very little out of it: marriage would be a wash-out. This solution of the problem might be very different from that of her friends or the analyst who might have assumed that marriage was the right thing for her.

Having decided to dispense with marriage the question naturally arises, what about at least satisfying her sex instincts apart from marriage. She then has the following dream: she dreams of a waterfall, above which is a long unoccupied toy boat, which was carried along towards the fall and then over the swirling waters. At the foot of the fall it went under a rock and into a deep cave. She was very disappointed that she could not stop it from going into the cave.' Her immediate association was 'This is a Freudian dream!' The long narrow boat was a phallic symbol: the waterfall, her being swept along by her sexual passion. The boat down below went under the rock, which is the pubic bone, and into the vaginal 'cave'. Obviously the dream was a sexual wish fulfilment on lines of a Freudian interpretation. But that was not the whole dream; for the dream ends in disappointment that she could not stop it going into the cave. That disappointment was just as important a part of the dream as being carried away by her passion. No doubt the dream deals with a wish; but far from being a wish-fulfilment, it warns her that to fulfil that wish would be disastrous. If we assume that in a dream cause and effect are represented by before and after, (as Freud says) the dream carries a very different significance. It says in effect 'If you let yourself be carried away by your sex feelings, it will only lead to disappointment!' It is a very pressing present-day moral problem; it is a sexual problem, but has nothing to do with Oedipus. Her intuition provides her with a common-sense solution. It was not simply a wish; it was a warning. To take only the first part of the dream and omit the latter part is to miss the whole point of the dream. The first part of the dream deals with her problem; the latter part of the dream deals with the solution. 'It isn't worth it.' says the dream. 'Sex without love is a disappointment.'

Whenever then we are confronted with a dream, we ask ourselves, first, 'Does this dream relate to some actual experience of the past' —nightmares in infancy for instance, or rejection by the mother— Or is it symbolic of some present-day problem. Further, 'Is the dream diagnostic simply, or is it suggestive of some solution?' Did the patient wake from the dream? if so it was probably purely diagnostic, calling attention to the problem or to the original circumstances which caused the problem.

An exhibitionist dream of walking naked in the street: does it refer primarily to an experience of exhibitionism in childhood which created a problem; or is it symbolic of one's present-day tendency to self-display? Is it merely pointing to the fact that we are sexually exhibitionist (Freud), or is it saying that we ought to be more open and less secretive (Jung)? Only free association and the circumstances of the case can tell us.

A man dreams that his mother is holding him to her breast to feed him, and he rejects it and turns away. Is that what actually happened in childhood and so created a problem, or does it mean that his mother then, as now, is too possessive and that he must break away from her hold over him; or, leaving his mother out of it, does it mean that he himself is too attached to a mother complex from which he needs to break away? We cannot dogmatize. Our only knowledge of the man's problems, and his free association can give us the true interpretation.

The reader may be commenting that he does not have such interesting and clear dreams as those mentioned in this chapter. He may be assured that his dreams are just as interesting and just as important as the foregoing dreams—provided their meaning is revealed. However bizarre, they all have a meaning, and a very significant meaning.

CHAPTER XXX

NATURE'S EQUIPMENT AND ITS
DISORDERS: BIOLOGICAL APPROACH

Having discussed our methods of investigation from symptoms and dreams in direct reductive analysis, we turn to the study of what we find to be the cause of disorders of the mind.

Man's first task is to exist: and nature supplies us with a marvellous equipment by which we maintain existence and cope with the dangers and difficulties of life.

The lower animals like fish are ill-equipped, but they make up for this by the multitude of their offspring. Millions of eggs are produced; only a small proportion survive. Even among humans, in Central Africa half the children die by the age of five.

The higher we go in evolution the more efficient is the equipment provided by nature. So in a rising scale we have reflex action, conditioned reflexes, instincts and emotions, intelligence, intuition, purposive action, reason and intellect.

All these forms of equipment, the highest, like reason, as well as the lowest, like reflexes and instincts, have the one aim in common, namely the survival of the individual and of the race. Functions like memory and intelligence are not merely specimens to be studied by the psychologist in the artificial atmosphere of a laboratory, necessary as that is. They should be regarded as serving an end, namely that of survival, and they cannot be fully understood until they are regarded in that light. We cannot understand any organ, say that of the kidney, without knowing what it is *for*.

Valuable as are these functions they may fail, and give rise to abnormalities of behviour. If we are lacking in any of these, say intelligence, as in the mental deficient, we cannot cope with life and fall victim to circumstances: if they are misdirected they constitute behaviour disorders as in delinquency and crime: if they are repressed we fall victims to neuroses. There is in fact no valuable quality or capacity in human nature which is not subject to disorder.

Let us consider then some of this equipment, for we shall be called upon to deal with the disorders which arise from these.

Physiological. In the first place man is endowed in common with the lower animals and plants, with the gift of life. It is by virtue of life that they can adapt the environment to their own needs, and change their own reactions to the changing environment. Inanimate objects like rocks and iron have no such power, and are incapable of such adaptation. Plants like animals have life, and so can make use of the soil, the air and sunlight to maintain life. Plants differ from animals in that they cannot, like animals and man, move from place to place, when there is a shortage of food or water; so they wither and die, while the animals look for food and water elsewhere, and live.

Man expends energy to fight the battles of life: nature therefore provides him with the extraordinary capacity of extracting new energy from plants and other animals in the form of food, by which he can restore his strength. Any waste products he does not need he has the mechanism to excrete, by the kidneys, the bowels and by sweat.

If by chance he is wounded all the resources of the body are brought to bear on that wound, noxious substances are expelled in the pus, the wound is healed, and he is made whole again. If the body itself is invaded by microbic infection the body produces white blood corpuscles to combat the bacteria, and immunizing bodies to resist further infection. So if once we get smallpox we do not get it again.

Almost all our time and energy are spent in our efforts to maintain physical life. But sometimes these physiological functions fail to fulfil their ends and we fall ill. The loss of blood from a wound may be so severe that we may become weak and die. Sometimes we cannot resist the microbe's invasion and our very existence is threatened: growths in certain parts of the body like cancer may so absorb all the energy of the body that the body dies.

Those failures in physical adaptation are the concern of the physician and surgeon and not of the psychotherapist. But that must not be taken to mean that these disorders can be entirely ignored by the psychotherapist, for body and mind interact, and physical diseases often give rise to mental disorders, such as cerebral syphilis producing delusions of grandeur, jaundice producing a depressed outlook on life, and high blood pressure producing irritability. But these are the concern of the psychiatrist and not of the psychotherapist, for they are treated by physical means.

More serious still are mental deficiency and the psychoses (insanity) which are due to deficiencies in the physiological constitution and largely hereditary.

Reflex action. As we have seen, among the equipment which nature has provided for the adaptation of life in living organisms are reflex actions—blinking to protect the eyes, swallowing to take food, the beating of the heart, the expansion of the lungs, the digestive and secretory functions, sneezing to clear the air passage of noxious germs—all these are innate and inherited reflexes. Many of these operate quite unconsciously.

Valuable as are these native reflexes, left to themselves, they sometimes lead to disaster. Birds follow an innate urge when they migrate; but following that migratory impulse they may be destroyed in a cross-channel storm. The child is naturally attracted to light and warmth and to the health-giving rays of the sun. But when this leads him to put his hand into the flame of a fire, he suffers pain and injury. Reflexes are obviously not enough. Nature cannot be expected to provide reflexes for all possible emergencies; it must think again.

Conditioned reflexes. So nature makes up for these deficiencies by giving us the capacity to acquire new reflexes, in order to cope with contingencies for which there are no innate reflexes. Thus the child once burnt develops a conditioned reflex which makes him automatically avoid the fire; and the child who has been attracted to eat red berries and gets sick, thereafter develops an acquired reflex to avoid all red berries.

Conditioned reflexes are obviously of great biological value. But they too, as we have seen, are open to abuse and disorder. If a child is terrified by a stranger throwing him up into the air—playfully, but not to the child—there is no telling that another stranger will not do the same; so he develops a fear of strangers. That is unfortunate for if one goes through life shy of all strangers he will be greatly handicapped. So with conditioned reflexes such as a fear of water, fear of the dark or terror of being alone or of travelling. Thus what is biologically valuable may be psychologically disastrous.

Numerous behaviour disorders arise in this way. Because a beloved father who was usually kind gave his son a beating, the boy not only feared his father, but thereafter suspected and avoided all forms of kindness. Many people's lives and efficiency have been ruined by such forgotten experiences in early childhood.

The vast number of phobias are of the nature of conditioned reflexes, formed by morbid attattchments usually in childhood. Conditioned reflexes are obviously not enough.

Pain. Nature provides us with a short cut to the formation of conditioned reflexes. As a rule it takes many repetitions to produce a conditioned reflex like teaching a dog to beg. But when consciousness comes into the picture, this speeds the formation of the new reaction and makes it far more effective. One instance of burning or sickness is often enough to avoid the fire or red berries. Pain is of the greatest biological value for survival; it tells us what is wrong. It is therefore constantly used by mothers to check undesirable behaviour, in the form of a smack, when they have not the patience or skill to train the child properly by ordinary conditioning. But pain too may be distorted and many people have hysterical pains when nothing whatever is wrong with their bodies.

The instincts as we have seen are innate responses to life, and specific instincts are aroused in different situations—flight from danger, attacking a foe, and caring for the offspring. They are far more effective than reflex action because they are the responses of the *whole* organism and are accompanied by strong emotions (p.116).

Emotion is the accumulation of energy before discharge (*Psychology and Mental Health*, p. 236). The result of this accumulation is that when the energy is at last released, it discharges itself with far greater force, as with the damming of a mill stream to drive the wheels. The emotion of rage gives us superhuman strength. When chased by a bull an athlete leaped a five-barred gate which he could never reach before or after. Sex passion may lead to violence and murder. I have had a man who under hypnosis was reliving being buried in a trench, when it took four men to hold him down in his terrified strength. The biological significance and value of emotion is that it gives driving force to our actions; it enables us to overcome obstructions which we could never otherwise be able to cope with; it gives power to our lives and strength to our endeavours. All the same, some of the worst disorders arise from our emotions, and those of varying types.

Emotions are therefore very closely related to bodily activities like tension of the muscles, increased heart beat, deeper and more rapid breathing, abolition of digestion as well as increased alertness of mind. All these activities especially of the auto-nomic nervous system are in preparedness for action. When they discharge themselves in action, such as when we manage to escape, the body returns to a state of equilibrium.

(a) *Surplus of emotion.* As civilization advances and security increases, there is less need for the basic instincts. Their emotions like those of sex and aggression are inordinantly strong, as with nature in the raw. The accumulation of the energy then becomes a threat. For we have far more aggressive instincts than we need for our preservation (rarely do we find it necessary to use our fists to attack a foe); nor do we, like the cod, need to produce millions of offspring on the chance that some will survive. The result is that there is within us a great surplus of these emotions; we have a far greater capacity for sex and aggression than we have use for. This fact alone is the cause of many of the disturbances in social life such as crime and rape which results from our incapacity to control and to direct these impulses. One of civilization's greatest problems is what to do with those surplus emotions. So much so that human nature has found it necessary to teach the child to restrain and curb its passions from an early age. Failure to do so produces the delinquent.

(b) *Inhibition.* Nature, however, itself has provided us with the power of inhibition and control even in our physiological constitution; for whereas in the lower part of the brain she has developed these powerful instincts and emotions, in the higher part of the brain, the cortex, she has provided us with the capacity to control our basic impulses and to direct them to the pursuit of our ends. In teaching a child to control its impulses we are merely teaching it to use this power of control and to direct its energies to more useful purposes. Such restraint and self-control are necessary for survival. The man who comes off best in a fight is the man who controls his temper and so directs his blows with greater precision, not the man who hits out wildly. In a situation of danger, say in a burning ship or in a threatened car accident, fear is necessary to escape, but it is the man who keeps his head who avoids disaster, not the man who gets into a panic. The power of inhibition and restraint prevents us from making fools of ourselves by giving way to our sexual passions and getting into all kinds of scrapes. Restraint is not an invention of the puritans but is provided for even in our physiological constitution for efficiency and survival. The very progress of civilization depends on restraint and the re-direction of our native impulses. It is also the condition of the individual's mental health producing harmony and peace of mind. (p. 121).

Yet even this power of inhibition and control may be productive of the most profound disorders; for instead of directing our native instincts and emotions, they may repress them altogether, with the result that we are not only handicapped by the loss (such as the loss of aggressiveness, so that we cannot cope with our responsibilities in life); but these repressed emotions emerge in perverted and distorted forms of neuroses, like obsessions (p. 326).

It is obvious from these considerations that man's problem is not merely to cope with objective difficulties and dangers, but to control his native impulses.

Man's greatest problem in life is with himself. Flying to the moon is child's play compared with the control of human passions.

(c) *Psychosomatic disorders* are due to the frustration of our emotions. For sometimes the situation is such that we cannot discharge our emotions at all: as in the case of the soldier in the trenches under bombardment who cannot give expression to his fear by running away, or the man infuriated with his sneering boss but unable to answer back for fear of losing his job: or the unhappy wife who cannot leave her indifferent husband either for moral considerations or from fear of insecurity. In all such cases the energy, frustrated from outward expression, turns inward and is discharged in disorders such as palpitation of the heart, or headache from congestion in the head. Those are the psychosomatic disorders, the causes of which may be known perfectly well, but cannot be avoided. (p. 285).

A further basic instinct is the herd or gregarious instinct such as we find in the pack of wolves, the herd of bison and the social life of man. This instinct is of immense value for mutual protection from enemies, and for the privileges of the supply of food, the care of the sick in hospital, and the spread of knowledge which increases our ability to cope with life. But this instinct is the source of many behaviour disorders and neuroses. For if we enjoy such privileges we have responsibilities. If we do not want others to steal from us we must not steal from them or run off with their wives or husbands. There is a clash between our instincts. Some people rebel and become delinquent: others willingly obey and become good citizens, while others repress their native impulses in conformity with the demands of society and become neurotic.

The higher qualities in man are no less liable to misuse and distortion.

Intelligence. Nature provides us with means whereby we may use and direct our native instincts and potentialities, and she does this by giving us intelligence. Intelligence enables us to choose the right ends, and to devise the best means to those ends.

To take a revealing illustration. If a man is confronted with a dangerous animal in a field, his natural emotional reaction is to run like hell, under the emotion of fear, which he does with Olympic prowess. But such blind instinct is not necessarily intelligent: for if the danger is from a bull the intelligent thing to do is to climb a tree, because a bull can run faster than he can, but cannot climb a tree. But if the danger is a snake it is useless to climb a tree for the snake can follow him so it is best to run away. His intelligence therefore enables him to modify his actions according to circumstances and in view of his ultimate aim, which is to escape from danger.

Intelligence as such is an innate quality: we are born with a greater or less degree of it. Some, like the 'dull' and the mental deficients, have little of it. Others are endowed with a high degree of it. It is measured by the intelligence quotient. The average child is taken to have an I.Q. of 100. A person with an I.Q. of 170 is particularly gifted: one with an I.Q. of sixty is mentally deficient. Mental deficiency being of a constitutional nature is not the concern of the psychotherapist, but of the psychiatrist and the educationalist.

Intelligence is a great advance on even conditioned reflexes. These reflexes also, as we have seen, enable us to modify our action in accordance with our experience. But there are important differences. For one thing conditioned reflexes are strictly unconsciously produced, whereas intelligence is provided with the blessed gift of consciousness; we see what we are doing and why we are doing it, so that we can modify our actions, according to our conscious aims. Most important is the fact that intelligence is determined by conscious ends and aims—which is what is meant by 'purpose'.

Purpose, as McDougall says, is consciousness of our aims and ends in which the consciousness determines our action. Many people's lives are made unhappy by the choice of wrong purposes in life.

The effectiveness of our intelligence depends on *knowledge*. But intelligence must not be confused with knowledge. A child may be by nature most intelligent, yet if its education has been neglected it may have little knowledge. Intelligence is an innate capacity to profit by experience; knowledge is acquired; although the capacity to acquire knowledge is innate. This is well illustrated in our man in the field: the effective use of his intelligence depended on his memory and the knowledge that a snake can climb a tree and that a bull cannot, but can run faster than he can. He may be a man of high intelligence, but if he is lacking in that knowledge his intelligence has nothing to go upon. On the other hand a yokel may be aware of those facts but may not have the intelligence to apply them to this situation.

A vast amount of disorder occurs in life because of lack of innate intelligence, as with the dull and backward and the mentally deficient: but in most cases the trouble is not because the person is lacking in intelligence but because he does not use it. The young man who gets into debt, embezzles money and then tries to recover his losses by betting on horses may otherwise be quite an intelligent young man but he is not using his intelligence—perhaps because of the panic he has got himself into which obliterates intelligence. The girl who has sexual adventures without consideration of the consequences, but is merely impelled by her passion, is either lacking in intelligence or is not making use of the intelligence she has.

In the use of intelligence we make use of many other innate provisions of nature. *Memory* is one of these, for memory enables us to recall past experiences so that we can profit by them, avoiding past mistakes and encouraging those that suit our aims.

Disorders of memory. There are however people whose lives are ruined by brooding over past memories, past guilt or past grievances. Forgetting is a valuable biological gift saving us from the distresses of the past which might hamper our present efforts. But if what we forget is emotionally charged it may emerge in the form of neurotic symptoms.

Imagination on the other hand enables us to anticipate the probable future results of our actions so that we may modify our actions according to those probabilities without having to go through them as we do with conditioned reflexes with possible disastrous results. Valuable as these are they are prone to disorder.

Imagination of possible disasters in the future is of great value; but a morbid fear of illness, of misfortune, of death may completely rob us of happiness and make life a misery. Many people spend three-quarters of their time and energy in worrying about possible disasters which never happen.

Intuition. Intuition is sub-conscious inference. Whereas reason draws inferences from conscious data, intuition draws its conclusions from sub-conscious or unconscious data. We may not know, for instance, why we like or dislike a person on sight, why we come to certain conclusions, or why we act in this way or that. Indeed these judgments are sometimes unreasonable, but we are convinced that our judgment is right, and commonly it is. (See page 257).

That does not mean that intuitions are not based on definite data: they are. For instance when we take an intuitive (but what many people wrongly call an 'instinctive') dislike to a person, such a judgment is not entirely out of the blue. Children are very intuitive. A child dislikes a visitor at sight. The mother says 'Oh, but he is nice.' The child replies, 'I don't like him.' It does so by intuition without any resort to reason. But that dislike is based on some observations, the way the man smiles with his teeth but not with his eyes (like cinema starlets); or his too great familiarity with the mother when the father is away, a difference of behaviour a child is quite capable of observing. The child does not know that it is upon these observations that he bases his dislike, but the inference is nevertheless based on it. So intuition is the drawing of influences and making judgments upon the basis of experiences which are subconscious or unconsciously observed. 'I do not like thee Dr Fell; the reason why I cannot tell'—but the reason may have been because a doctor did the dirty on him as a child in telling him it would not hurt and then opening an abscess!

I have known of medical diagnoses in difficult cases correctly made by intuition, the experienced physician saying, 'I am sure that is a case of malaria or of congenital syphilis', although the indications are otherwise. He cannot say why he thinks so but he proves to be right. But that does not rule out following up the diagnosis with all the tests which reason has shown us are characteristic of these diseases.

Incidentally, Stekel's analytic methods were based on intuition. I protested to him that you cannot teach doctors to analyze by intuition which was a gift, but he replied that one should do so by going over case after case, and indeed he showed great insight and intuition in two cases I sent him.

Intuition is a more primitive method of drawing conclusions than that of reason. But it is sometimes more accurate than reason in its judgments; for reason can act only on previously proved and established data, whereas, as we have said, intuition draws upon the whole of our past experience, though at the moment we are unaware what that experience was. A very large part of our ordinary life in its decisions and judgments is made up of intuition, and is usually correct. Intuition acts automatically on the same principle as the electronic brain: we feed certain data into it, and from it we automatically get certain answers.

But for that very reason intuition may play us false, for if our past experience on which our intuition is based is abnormal, the judgment based on that intuition will be false if applied to circumstances or people to whom they do not apply. A child frightened by a stranger or tricked by a doctor may develop a strong attitude of suspicion towards people in general and doctors in particular. His judgment is distorted, so he will tell you that he is sure that someone is out to do him down, although he can give no evidence of the fact, and when the person is intending no such thing. This intuitive judgment is wrong because it is based on abnormal experiences.

It is extraordinary the way in which our judgments are affected by experiences long-since forgotten. A woman artist patient wanted to make her living as a portrait painter. But she always made her subjects look severe, which did not make her popular as a painter. Nor could she ever finish a portrait. She had no idea why. It was discovered in free association, that she had a severe nurse, so that in her mind a woman was indelibly associated with severity, and projecting the nurse's image on to the subject of the painting she made her severe. The only finished portraits in her studio were of men. She then discovered that whilst painting the portrait of a woman a vision of her nurse would come up and superimpose itself on her painting so that she could not finish the painting.

False intuitions we call *prejudices*; they may lead us to entirely false conclusions although we may be unaware that we are prejudiced. We may have a prejudice against dictatorial people, so that as soon as a man gets up to speak in a dogmatic manner we take an intuitive dislike to him, and may refuse to accept his opinions although they may happen to be quite correct. That is why it is necessary to check our intuitions by submitting them to reason.

Reason is the capacity to draw conclusions from verified and *established data* according to certain rules of logic. It is an advance in our biological adaptation to life because its conclusions are more stable and reliable than those of intuition. It has its limitations; (a) If the facts or premises are inadequate or wrong, or (b) if our processes of logical reasoning are wrong, our conclusions will be wrong. Far more damage is done in public life by false arguments than is recognized. It was said of de Gaulle that he always did the right thing for the wrong reasons! A senior judge was making the distinction between intuition and reason when he said, 'Give your judgment, it will almost certainly be right; don't give your reasons, they will certainly be wrong'.

Intellect we may take to be capacity to *organize* our knowledge and experiences, in contrast to intelligence which is the capacity to make use of our experience.

Wisdom, the highest function of all, is the capacity to apply all our experiences of life, including all our potentialities, intelligence and reason, to the affairs and conduct of life. But 'Where shall wisdom be found?'

Mental Health. The secret of mental health is to direct these strong impulses to right and useful ends, our aggresive to achievement, our sex to love of wife and family, our fear to devise means of avoiding danger, as in medical services. Such direction of our impulses requires discipline. Discipline rightly considered, is not the repressing of our impulses, but their right direction. This brings harmony and peace to our personality, as well as greater achievement.

This discipline and direction, as we have seen (p.121), solves the problem of delinquent behaviour due to failure to control our impulses; for the energies of the adolescent can be directed to desirable pursuits and useful social activities. It also solves the problem of neurosis. For by giving outlet to our impulses in such ways we avoid repression; and by directing them we avoid crime. Discipline is as necessary to the freedom of the personality, as freedom is necessary to discipline, for no discipline is worth while unless it be self-discipline. This I have dealt with in *Childhood and Adolescence*, on 'Freedom and discipline' (p.109).

To achieve this end, of the co-ordination and direction of all our potentialities, nature provides us with the higher functions of purpose, intelligence, reason and wisdom.

CHAPTER XXXI

BEHAVIOUR DISORDERS

So far we have dealt with the sources of behaviour disorders. We have now to consider their classification. Such disorders are infinite in number: the most common are bad tempers, jealousies, resentment, revenge, sulkiness, sullenness, bitterness, scorn, contempt, suspicion, conceit, arrogance, viciousness; all of them forms of the aggressive impulse. Or timidity, anxiety, despair, laziness, procrastination, indolence, shyness, feelings of inferiority and defeatism, all connected with fear and shrinking from life. There are also abnormalities of sex such as uncontrolled sex passions, sex impotence and numerous sex perversions. These are but a few, for there are many others like prying into others' affairs, gossiping, interfering, inconsiderateness, cynicism, and a perverted sense of humour like sarcasm, which may be as much disturbers of the peace as stealing and violence.

We cannot treat these disorders adequately without knowing their causes; and this is made more difficult by the fact that the same form of behaviour disorder may have quite different causes.

Obviously you cannot treat a man's irritability and bad temper which is due to high blood pressure in the same way and by the same means as you treat the man whose bad temper is simply the result of lack of discipline or self-control. We must therefore distinguish not only different disorders but different *types* of disorder in order to determine whether such a man requires physical treatment punishment or analysis.

So numerous are these disorders and so varied in their causes that it would seem well nigh impossible to classify them. Further study, however, enables us to classify them into four different categories or types of disorder, each of which has a different type of cause, and each therefore calling for different types of treatment.

I have given a full account of these disorders and their treatment in my *Psychology and Mental Health*, chapter III, but a brief account of these types of character traits will not be out of place here, since many of them call for psychotherapeutic treatment.

These are the types:

(a) *Temperamental or constitutional character traits* are those which are due to the physiological constitution, temperament being the influence of the body on the mind.

(b) *Simple traits* are those which are directly produced by environmental conditions, such as that of a boy becoming a delinquent because of bad influences at home or with bad companions.

(c) *Reaction traits* are those which are a reaction to an opposite tendency in ourselves which we repress—such as when we are bombastic to hide a feeling of inferiority.

(d) *Neurotic character traits* are the emergence of the repressed characteristic—such as depression emerging from a repressed complex in childhood, delinquency from repressed resentment, or outbursts of uncontrollable temper from past and forgotten injustices. In the latter two types there is a duality in the personality and dissociation. They are therefore always abnormal.

Let us define these different types of character trait more closely.

Temperamental character traits. Temperament is the mental constitution in so far as it depends on our physiological constitution—as illustrated in the originally described temperaments—the sanguine, the phlegmatic, the choleric and the melancholic, which were conceived as due to the abundance of blood, phlegm, black bile and yellow bile respectively. Though we do not now accept this classification we do consider that physiological conditions and especially the endocrine glands have a marked effect on our behaviour—the thyroidic person being inclined to excitability, the gonadotropic hormones giving rise to sexual feelings. High blood pressure can produce irritability, and changes in the chemistry of the blood can produce depression.

To take a clinical instance: a girl, approaching her first menstruation became hysterical, stole, ran away from home and set fire to a barn. Her periods then came on and she became perfectly normal again. Most husbands are made fully aware of the temperamental changes which can take place in a wife on account of the physiological changes due to menopause.

A man committed a murder, and it was found that he got bouts of violence whenever his blood sugar was low. An enlightened jury exonerated him and he was given adequate medical treatment. The 'acidosis' child is bright and lively at times; but when under the weather, is tired, indolent and lethargic and bed wets. At school he gets the report 'has brains if he would use them'; or 'can do better when he tries', and he is often punished for a physical condition he cannot help. The trouble is that he can't try when he is in that condition. But a course of glucose does wonders and he becomes lively again. But glucose will not cure a child who is bone lazy because his mother had always done everything for him or because he is disillusioned with life. For this is a simple, not a temperamental, trait.

Treatment of these physiological character traits must, of course, be physiological.

Mental deficiency and the psychoses come under this category but the term 'temperament' is used of the milder forms of behaviour disorders, and not of these more serious ones, although they too are constitutional, by which we mean 'due to the bodily make-up', whether hereditarily or otherwise.

Simple character traits are those which are due to the direct influence of the environment and upbringing. Tendencies like assertiveness, vanity, sex and fear are all natural impulses playing an important part in life. If they are exaggerated in childhood, they tend to persist as abnormal character traits throughout life. Thus one child grows up hard-working and industrious and another, lacking self-discipline, becomes sensuous or timid or bad-tempered according to circumstances and the way he is brought up.

In simple character traits there is no repression, no dissociation: they are 'simple' in that sense.

The main sources of these exaggerated traits are (a) if the native impulses themselves have been over-stimulated—so that a child may become abnormally aggressive if he is always frustrated, or excessively sexual if he resorts to this as a solace from the feeling of lack of love, or for a sense of inferiority. (b) They may be developed as the result of imitation or identification, particularly with his parents. I had, for instance, a man who persistently lost his temper with his wife and no-one else—which came from identification with his father who persistently lost his temper with the patient's mother. Thus a boy may be a 'chip off the old block' because he inherits his father's constitution and temperament; or because of his identification with him. Sometimes these elements are mixed, such as when a boy inherits his mother's sensitive temperament, but takes over his father's business-like capabilities by identification. Such conflicts in his personality may produce unhappiness. On the other hand they may combine so that he become an artistic director in an art gallery or in films or stage, as in one such patient of mine.

Treatment. Teaching a child good manners and moral injunctions influences the child, but the acceptance of what is taught is usually dependent on the identification of the child with the parent or teacher through love or admiration. So a child who is selfish and grumbles because of identification with a grumbling father, or ill-tempered by imitating his mother, may entirely break away from such behaviour if he later becomes identified with a sound and healthy club leader. For since simple character traits are free and there being no repression or dissociation, they are free to change; and since these conditions are due to environmental factors the delinquent child is often reformed by removing him from the evil environment to a foster home where new influences and new identifications are brought to bear on him. What he lacks are healthy ideals; so, by being in a new home where he gets affection and at the same time outlet for his energies; or in a youth club where he can identify himself with the leader, he changes his standards of his behaviour and becomes a healthy and happy person.

Punishment is therefore sometimes called for in simple character traits, but these are the only ones of the four types in which it is useful. In the other three it does harm. It would be no use to punish the child who is indolent from lack of blood sugar.

Failing other methods simple abnormal character traits are dealt with by punishment. The child who takes other children's toys, or otherwise makes a nuisance of himself is ostracized by the other children who refuse to allow him to play with them until he conforms. All punishment should be regarded simply as one of the consequences of his action; so that when we have been fined several times for parking in a forbidden area, or driving to the danger of others, we decide to give it up; it is not worth while, and so we conform to social custom. As a magistrate said to a man complaining of his sentence, 'I am not blaming you; I am only fining you.'

It is obvious that such reforms are the task of the social worker, the parson, the probation officer and the parent—not basically of the psychotherapist, who however is often in a position to diagnose and to advise the best form of treatment in any particular case. For the individual finding himself possessed of such undesirable characteristics as impatience, jealousy or suspicion, which make him unhappy and unpopular, but which he finds difficult to control, *suggestion* is of the greatest value in fortifying his will so that he can overcome them. This, as already mentioned, was the work done by Drs Worcester and McComb in Boston (p.106) and could be imitated with profit in the Church to-day.

Normal and abnormal. Some character traits like irritability and despondency we regard as 'abnormal'; others like generosity and consideration we call 'normal'. But why? Under what criterion do we make such judgments? There are two main criteria.

It may be that by normal we mean in conformity with social demands, abnormal when our behaviour goes against the public good. Thus generosity is regarded as normal because others in the community approve of it and benefit by it: violence is otherwise, hurtful to the community. This is the social or moral criterion.

Another criterion is that of mental health, which depends on the *motive* of behaviour. The two are by no means the same. A person's generosity may be approved by the community, who, if his generosity is sufficiently magnificent gives him a knighthood or seat in the House of Lords. But if his generosity is given to ingratiate himself owing to a feeling of guilt that he has made his money by swindling the community, it is—from the point of view of mental health, abnormal. We may remember that when the financier Hooly gave gold communion plate to St. Paul's Cathedral it was suggested that above it at the altar should be inscribed the words 'Hooly! Hooly! Hooly!'

While temperamental and simple character traits may be either normal or abnormal, reaction and psycho-neurotic character traits are always abnormal because they are the result of repression and dissociation.

Reaction character traits are more difficult to understand, yet it is most necessary that they should be understood if we are to avoid bad mistakes in our treatment. Everyone knows that a man who throws his weight about is as likely as not to be suffering from an inferiority complex, and behaves in that way by way of compensation. On the other hand a shy person with a conscious attitude of inferiority may be hiding a repressed conceit—for self-depreciation is often camouflaged conceit. The severely strict moral or religious person may be reacting to strong feelings of sexual indulgence. The person who is always apologizing for himself probably suffers from a repressed sense of superiority. In apologizing he is really saying 'I am not really like that. I'm really a very fine fellow.' We suspect the person who is too ingratiating. Why? because the ingratiation is often to hide hostility; we want to know what he is up to! The child who feels unloved goes to the opposite extreme and becomes aggressive and bloody-minded.

All these are reactions to an opposite tendency in oneself which is repressed. Since they involve a split in the personality they are always abnormal.

A reaction trait is accepted by the individual who adopts them as a counter-blast to other tendencies he represses.

These reaction character traits can often be recognized because they are usually exaggerated; they must go to the opposite extreme to hide what they are repressing. Yet like the lark singing above her nest, they call attention to the very thing they would hide.

It is easy to see how we misunderstand such people, and therefore how wrongly we treat them. The trouble is that we take their overt behaviour as though it is their real selves, and treat these reaction traits as though they were simple character traits; and thereby do more harm than good. We need to treat not their overt behaviour but what lies behind. You do not do any good to the conceited person who is conceited to compensate for his inferior feeling by snubbing him: it makes him worse. On the other hand, a child who is arrogant because his doting mother has made him feel he is a hell of a fellow needs taking down, and his school fellows do it anyway: for this is a 'simple' trait. I had as a patient a weed of a boy of fourteen who constantly stole, in spite of beatings by his father, a sergeant major. But every time he got a belting he went and stole again. So much for those who say that all these youths want is a good hiding. That may be good punishment for the simple character traits: it makes the reaction type worse. Every beating he got made him feel more unloved and so more defiant. I think it would probably be found that the majority of 'recidivists', the delinquents who come over and over again before the Courts or into Borstal, are of this reaction type. They suffer a sense of grievance, from childhood, and the more they are punished the greater their sense of grievance and the more delinquent they become.

These patients are difficult to treat because being truculent they refuse to co-operate. The magistrate scolds them and tells them they are a nuisance to everybody and a disgrace to their family. Their reply is that that is precisely what they intend to be. No remorse with them; they are sullen and uncommunicative.

But these youths are basically unhappy because of the conflict in their souls: deep down they are wanting affection, the lack of which turned them defiant. The only way to tackle them is to win their confidence; to be on their side as it were and deal with their latent unhappiness. Sometimes in such cases it is well not to refer to their delinquency at all.

Analytic treatment to discover the latent cause is the right form of treatment, and providing you can get the patient's confidence, is very rewarding.

Neurotic character traits are the emergence of repressed characteristics: they come from buried complexes and being dissociated are beyond the control of the will. Let us illustrate it by recalling the child first mentioned who, feeling left out and unwanted, became 'difficult' and bloody-minded—a reaction trait. Suppose he is punished so severely that it brings him to heel. From the parent's point of view this 'discipline' is gratifying: the boy has learnt his lesson: he has repressed his aggressiveness. It is, however, by no means obliterated. It is still alive and at some future time circumstances may be such that it is aroused to form uncontrollable bad tempers or stealing; or it may emerge in the form of depression which represents the repressed need of affection. These are psychoneurotic character traits. I remember as a boy, in a walk over the Derbyshire moors with an uncle of very gentle nature, coming across two boys, the larger of whom was bullying the other. To my surprise by uncle gave the bully a most vicious beating across the calves with a heavy stick. It shocked me to see him behave in this way so contrary to his nature. Why did he? Looking back on it I think the cause was this. My uncle had a club foot (in spite of which he used to walk 40 miles in a day) and I conceive he must have been teased and bullied by boys at school and often lost his temper with them. But of course that only made things worse. So he repressed his temper and became docile. The sight of this bullying on the moors would arouse up his old fury and out it came in this outrageous and uncontrollable outburst.

The only adequate treatment for neurotic character traits is analysis, the object of which is to discover the cause and to release the buried emotion such as this aggressiveness, so that instead of this emerging as a symptom, it may be released and directed towards the uses of the personality.

Neurotic character traits differ from neuroses proper like hysterical paralysis or obsessions. Both are the emergence of repressed material, but whereas in what we call neurotic character traits the repressed material comes up as itself—such as temper, defiance, indolence, depression, shyness, or self-pity, the neurotic symptom like paralysis or phobias is more complicated for it is a compromise between the repressing and the suppressing forces. In a neurosis the repressed temper does not emerge as such but as a psychosomatic headache, the shyness as blushing, the self-pity as a hysteric pain. In a phobia of hurting, the fear is as much part of the symptom as the impulse to hurt: it is a compromise.

It is obvious from these considerations that in any case of behaviour disorder it is necessary to investigate the case very thoroughly to discover what type of disorder we are dealing with before we can treat the case properly. Diagnosis is the first essential.

We may illustrate the four different types by reference to stealing, the most common form of delinquency in adolescence.

Stealing may be due to a constitutional lack of moral sense as in the feeble-minded, or in a girl at the time of a distressing period —a temperamental character trait. She feels a physiological *need* of something and so steals. Or it may be a simple character trait in a youth who has been set an example of dishonesty by his parents or gets into bad company. It may be a reaction character trait due to the feeling of deprivation of love to which the youth reacts by defiance and anti-social behaviour. When discovered he is defiant and may deny the stealing although it is perfectly obvious. Punishing him as we have seen does no good but only makes him more defiant, adding to his grievance. But we may find that the boy at school who steals is not the rebel but the well-behaved, hard-working model pupil, who to everyone's surprise and even to his own, is found to have been stealing money from other boys' lockers, money that he does not want or need. This is pathological stealing. (The word klepto-maniac is best reserved for constitutional and psychotic cases.)

It is a compulsion, completely alien to his character, and he is full of remorse when discovered, that he has brought shame upon himself and his parents. Obviously his is quite a different case from the others. Punishing him is not going to do him any good although he would welcome it for his sins; nor is physical treatment for what is in no sense a physical disorder. The only adequate treatment for this is analysis into the cause of his stealing which will be found to lie in some buried complex of resentment of early childhood. This releases the latent aggressiveness which can then be directed to better uses.

The different types of stealing may to some extent be recognized by the attitude of mind of the four types. The boy or girl who steals for physiological reasons is completely bewildered as to what all the fuss is about: he has no sense of having done wrong. The one who steals as a simple character trait simply feels it is a bit of bad luck being discovered, and hopes the punishment will not be too severe: he intends to be more careful next time. The reaction type when discovered is defiant and unco-operative; he knows he has done wrong and is proud of it. The psychoneurotic type is full of remorse, does not understand why he should have done it, and is all too willing to co-operate.

I have taken stealing as a typical example, but almost any abnormal character may be of one or another type—indolence, jealousy, shyness, defeatism, impatience and irritability—any of these may be physiological, simple, reaction or psychoneurotic, and the type of treatment must depend on the type of cause.

Shyness for instance may be evidence of schizophrenia, a constitutional disorder (temperamental) or it may be because as a child the patient was always made to feel inferior or snubbed; (simple). It may be a reaction to a basic feeling of superiority as in false modesty (reaction); or it may be a resurgence of a childhood feeling of inferiority which has been so far successfully repressed (neurotic).

Types of treatment. It is obvious that each type of disorder

K

requires a different type of treatment—whether it be stealing, shyness, arrogance, cynicism or jealousy. We hear people say: 'What they need is more strict discipline!' Some of them do: but it makes others worse. Or they say: 'They only need to pull themselves together. When I feel depressed, I snap out of it'. We all do in ordinary depression; but if the depression comes from a buried source, it is useless. We cannot pull ourselves together because we don't know what to pull together. Others are heard to say: 'They need more kindness and sympathy.' Sometimes lack of sympathy and understanding has been the cause of their delinquency, but that does not mean that giving them sympathy will necessarily cure them, now that they have developed this anti-social attitude. Try it on some 'reaction' deliquents and they will laugh in your face and scoff at your efforts. There are still some, though a diminishing number who put all delinquency down to bad housing or poverty. Yet we have far more delinquency and violence in the welfare state of full employment than in times of want: and most cases of stealing I have had to deal with come from rich homes.

Those with such bees buzzing in their bonnets will be right in a few cases, but wrong in all the others; and the trouble about wrong treatment is not merely that it fails to cure, but that it does definite harm and often makes the patient worse. Before we treat we must know the *type* of disorder we are treating, before we set about it. Diagnosis should always be the first phase of treatment.

CHAPTER XXXII

PSYCHOSOMATIC DISORDERS AND THEIR TREATMENT

We are all too well aware of the fact that a person can get a nervous headache from worry; and nervous indigestion from too suppressed anger. A girl's periods may stop from physical causes; from malnutrition, or because she is pregnant. But they may also stop, not because she is malnourished or pregnant, but because she is *afraid* she is getting an illegitimate baby.

Psychosomatic disorders, of which these are instances, are disorders of a physical nature which however have a psychological origin. I have always thought that they should be called 'neuroses' in contrast to 'psycho-neuroses' like hysteria, in as much as they are actual disturbances of the nervous system. But those who tamper with established words do so at their peril, as Babinski found when he tried to substitute 'pithiatism' instead of the absurd word 'hysteria'.

The emotions as we have seen are due to an accumulation of energy in the body before being discharged in action: they are preparedness for action (p. 268). They are therefore very closely associated with bodily changes such as action of the heart, lungs and digestion.

Whenever in life we are confronted with a critical situation, say that of danger, the whole body is mobilized to meet the danger. Sugar is poured out into the blood stream to give us energy, the muscles become tense ready for action, the heart beats faster to supply the body with more blood, the lungs breathe more rapidly to refresh the blood, the digestion ceases so as to make all the blood available for action. The eyes stare so as to get a clearer vision, the hair stands on end which makes us look larger than life and so frightens the foe, and the senses are alert to catch every sight and sound, all functions of the autonomic system.

These changes are all summarized up in the word emotion, which normally results in action appropriate to the occasion, whether that be of flight or of fight.

When the energy is discharged in action the energy is transferred from the autonomic to the central nervous system, and the organism gradually settles down and returns to a state of equilibrium.

But supposing we cannot act; suppose escape is impossible, as when we are cooped up in a trench in a bombardment, or suppose we are prevented from fighting back, then all the accumulated energy which cannot discharge itself in effective action is dammed back into the organism itself and discharges itself in exaggerated activity of these bodily functions—the heart beats violently and irregularly, missing beats; the breathing becomes suffocating, the muscles of the arms and legs become tense to the degree of paralysis, so that we may be 'paralysed by fear', our digestion goes wrong, we suffer from regurgitation ('getting the wind up'), our excretions may become beyond our control; the blood pumped to the head to refresh the brain for action is congested so that we suffer from pressure headaches. Thus the swain frustrated in love goes off his food; a child made angry before a meal, or made to eat food he does not want, cannot digest it and gets sick, whereupon his mother, frustrated by the child, retires to her bedroom with a 'nervous' headache. Chronic palpitations of the heart may be due to weakness of heart muscle; but it may also be due to chronic fear and anxiety. Many cases of chronic palpitations and other disordered activities of the heart were reported in the war, and D.A.H. (disordered action of the heart) was a common and popular diagnosis.

The damming up of the waters in a mill stream gives extra power to the mill: if held up altogether the waters overflow and cause flood damage both to the machinery of the mill and to all the land around. So it is with the energies of the body.

These disorders can occur with any of the emotions: indigestion and peptic ulcers can be produced as much by suppressed rage as by frustrated fear. If sex is unduly aroused and then frustrated it can give rise to palpitations, or to going off one's food.

Furthermore, it matters little what is the nature of the frustration; whether because of external circumstances which prevent our escape, or because our moral inhibitions prevent us from running away as in battle, or shirking our duty to our family.

These psychosomatic disorders must not be confused with hysterical conditions. Both conditions are physical in their manifestations, and both are psychogenetic, due to emotional and mental causes. But in other respects they are totally different.

(a) In the first place the psychosomatic conditions are an actual physical disorder, not an imagined one like a hysteric pain in the back. Frustrated emotion, whether fear, anger, or love, causes actual cessation of the gastric juices which stop flowing, with the result that we get a real indigestion from lack of digestive juices. That is quite different from the case of the man who has no actual indigestion but unconsciously assumes one for the purpose of getting sympathy or escaping responsibility. So with the nervous headache: when an emotion is aroused, say that of anger, blood rushes to the head; but if there is no discharge in action there is an accumulation of blood in the head, producing actual congestion and consequent pressure which constitutes the headache. It is a real headache due to pressure of blood, not an imagined one.

It is significant that the headache in this case follows the blood sinuses in the skull so that it takes the form of a *casque* or helmet headache round the head; or of pressure in the nape of the neck (the most common amongst soldiers in the war); or a stab at the top of the head. All these are due to actual pressures and are real physical disorders, though they are emotionally caused.

(b) There are also differences in the actual symptoms themselves. The psychosomatic disorders being concerned with preparing the body for action are mainly disorders of the *autonomic* nervous system, that part of the nervous system (like the action of the heart), which are beyond the control of the will, but which are subject to emotional stress; whereas conversion hysteria is of the *central* nervous system, like paralysis of the limbs or disorders of the senses like blindness.

(c) A further distinction is that whereas conversion hysteria like a paralysis of the legs or pain in the back is purposive, though unconsciously so, to get attention or sympathy, a psychosomatic disorder may simply be the direct result of the emotional strain: there is no necessary purpose to it at all; it is simply the *result* of the emotions being repressed and discharging themselves in this way. It should be mentioned however, that a psychosomatic symptom may come to be used purposively; as in the case of the swain who goes off his food with frustrated love and then appeals to his lady love on account of his sorry state. This he may do either consciously or unconsciously. It is then a hysteric condition.

How then are we to deal with these disorders? Remembering that these psychosomatic conditions are due to a greater production of emotional energy than discharge, there are obviously two lines of approach: either (i) to release the pent-up emotion in speech or action, so that it no longer discharges itself within the body; or (ii) we may remove the source of the worry so that the excess of production is cut off. Both are in fact practised in everyday life and both are effective.

(i) As for *letting off the emotions* we say, 'Have a good cry,' which is often more effective than all the doctor's tranquillizers, 'Tell me all about it. Get it all off your chest. I wouldn't stand for that. Go and tell him off,' we say to another. These are popular examples of that form of therapy, and very effective they are. 'I gave him a good talking to and told him what I thought of him and felt much better.' 'It is a great relief just being able to tell you all about it,' says another. To let off the bottled up emotion in words is often enough. Confession often gets rid of guilt.

(ii) The other approach is to cut off the excessive *production* of energy. To a person who insists on getting his own back and taking revenge when he can't do it without damaging his family we say,

'It's no use bashing your head against a brick wall.' We say to a chronic worrier, 'It will be all the same in a hundred years time.' 'Worrying won't help matters.' 'There are other fish in the sea,' we say to the jilted girl. 'The man who can behave like that is not worth bothering about: you should be glad you have found him out in time.' The business man is encouraged to cut his losses, 'After all what is money compared with your health?' It was a great comfort to some of us during the war to decide we will be killed anyway, so why bother. By such means we cut off the supply of emotion so that it no longer discharges itself in physiological disorders. When Winston Churchill was asked whether he found it difficult to sleep in the thick of the war, he replied 'Difficult? Oh, no; I just put my head to the pillow and said, "Damn everbody," and went off.'

It is however sometimes difficult for the patient to apply these measures, for the conditions may be chronic. It is very difficult for the man in a factory to stand the constant sneers of his foreman when his livelihood depends on his job.

The wife may be unable to leave the callous husband on account of the uncertainty of making a living; equally she may be prevented because of her marriage vows, because of the children or because she thinks it wrong. In the latter cases she may put the worry entirely out of her mind and cease to worry, making the best of it. But the situation may be such that it is difficult to shake it off, in which the frustrated emotion and the headache persist. When the patient finds these measures too difficult, *direct suggestion* to a patient in a relaxed state often proves most effective: indeed the mere relaxation is often enough. If a patient is too timid to face some difficulty we may by suggestion give him confidence and boldness to act so that he goes straight out to tackle the problem with excellent result. Or under suggestion treatment we may follow the former method and get the patient to 'let off steam' in a way he would not permit himself to do in his fully waking state.

Such *suggestion treatment* is fully within the competence of the general practioner who is interested and has a mind to it. But has he the time? Only if he is interested will he make time. Also of the parson who gives peace of mind and so can cure many ills of this sort. But his efforts should be directed towards rectifying the psychological disturbance and giving peace of mind, not in the first place in curing the headache, which however will result.

It is necessary to stress that many psychosomatic disorders may arise from present-day worries of which we are quite aware. In that sense they are not, strictly speaking psychoneuroses, which are characterized by dissociation. A wife may be well aware that her headaches are due to her husband's indifferent treatment of her. A husband with a sexually frigid wife may realize that his headaches or palpitations are due to sexual frustration, but cannot do anything about it. In other cases there is partial consciousness. Many a person gets a skin rash from irritability; he knows he is irritated, but he may not connect the irritation with marked effects on the skin. It is such patients that account for a large proportion of those who constantly haunt the doctor's surgery. It is not correct to tell them 'there is nothing wrong with them', for it has been said, 'If a man thinks he is ill when he is not ill, then he must be very ill indeed.'

Some psychosomatic disorders, however, may have their causes in deep-seated and unconscious complexes going back to experience in early childhood, which have left a sense of fear, of guilt or of jealousy which are once more aroused. These cases are of the nature of true neuroses due to dissociation and therefore require analytic treatment to reveal their causes.

CHAPTER XXXIII

WHAT IS A NEUROSIS?

The Characteristics of a Neurosis

In the first place all neuroses are psychogenic; that is to say they originate in mental and emotional causes: and this applies whether the symptom is of a mental type like a phobia, or of a physical type like hysterical paralysis.

They are sometimes called 'functional nervous disorders' because they are disorders of function as against disease like pleurisy or spastic paralysis which are due to organic causes (somatogenic).

It is also this psychological origin which distinguishes the neuroses from the psychoses (insanity), and from mental deficiency, both of which are mainly constitutional in origin and often hereditary, so that we need to enquire into the family history.

The neurosis originates in actual personal experiences in life, and there is nothing hereditary in the disorder unless we include sensitivity, for the person who is constitutionally sensitive is more likely to feel the rebuffs of life and breakdown than the thick-skinned man of the bull-dog breed (p.184). In these cases, therefore, the personal history is more important than the family history.

That does not preclude the fact that there are many mixed cases. We found in the wars for instance that many men of an unstable constitution broke down with a psychosis owing to the stress of conditions who would not have broken down otherwise. Sometimes by treating and getting rid of the psychological complexes, one could render the patient capable of standing up to his constitutional instability. The fact that a breakdown is due to a composite of the constitutional and environmental conditions make it all the more necessary to make a 'differential diagnosis' as to how large a proportion there is of each and treat these accordingly.

What is it that convinces us that there are disorders, even physical ones, of psychological origin? On the following grounds:

Firstly, that they are found to *originate* in emotional disturbances and shocks where there is no injury to the body at all; they are psychic shocks.

Secondly, that in each case *no organic cause* can be found. It is true that this may simply mean that we have not yet discovered the organic cause. (The 'migrains' of the Victorian age were considered to be 'vapours' and hysterical: we now treat migraine more seriously as a physical disorder.) But the fact remains that often the most robust of people in the best of health suffer from neurotic disorders—like my patient suffering from a terror of travelling by train who played cricket for his country and rugby football for his town. His phobia was found to relate to childhood experiences and was thus cured. So a person may be hysterically blind or deaf with no detectable organic defect in eye or ear. 'Eyes have they but they see not. Ears have they but they hear not.'

Thirdly, these disorders can be *produced experimentally* by mental means. If you hypnotize a man as Charcot did (p. 42) you can make him paralyzed, so that when he wakes he cannot move his arm or his leg however much he tries by effort or will. Moreover, this artificial paralysis has exactly the same features as a hysterical paralysis. The only difference is that in this case you have produced it by suggestion, whereas in the hysterical case he has produced it by his own auto-suggestion, although he is quite unaware of the fact.

Finally, you can *cure* these disorders by mental means alone; which you certainly could not do if it were an organic disease. Under hypnosis you can get a man with a hysteric paralysis to walk; and you can wake him up while walking, to his great surprise. This breaks the vicious circle and shakes his belief that he cannot walk.

Every neurosis originates in an unsolved problem
Because it cannot be solved it is repressed, because it is repressed it is dissociated to form a complex: being dissociated it is no longer under the control of the mind and will; but being still active it emerges in the form of a symptom. That is the essence of a neurosis. Let us explain.

Whenever we are faced with a problem in life whether it be of some danger or threat to our life, a material problem of overcoming some difficulty, or a social problem of how to deal with difficult people, or a moral problem involving our conscience, our first impulse is to find means to tackle that problem, and solve it; and for the most part we do by perseveration.

Repression. But if we cannot solve our problem it causes distress of mind; so our next impulse is to say, 'Oh, forget it', and we may succeed in doing so. That, however, does not solve the problem and the result is we suffer from restlessness, worry and anxiety, not necessarily knowing why we feel so. Many people spend their lives in that state of tension. The problem recurs in dreams.

The results of repression
(a) *Dissociation.* The result of repression of a problem we cannot solve is that the whole experience is dissociated, split off from the rest of the mind, to form a 'complex'. Repression is the process by which the problem is pushed aside; dissociation is the result. The

K*

essential feature of a neurosis, as distinct from most character traits is that of dissociation.

Not all abnormalities of behaviour are neuroses: not every burglar or liar is a neurotic for these may be simple character traits (p. 278) in which there is no dissociation; they may have derived these characteristics from a father or mother by imitation. On the other hand I have had a patient who was a businessman whose lying was compulsive and neurotic, due to a buried complex.

Dissociation occurs at two phases. The first occurs when the whole experience is repressed because we cannot solve it; the second is when part of the repressed material is split off from the complex to appear in consciousness to form the symptom. A symptom is a bit of the experience.

(b) *Unconsciousness*. When the experience is repressed and dissociated it is lost to consciousness. The woman with neurotic headaches denies stoutly that she is sorry for herself, and declares quite correctly that when she has a headache, far from seeking sympathy, she goes to her room so as not to bother others. In war the men who broke down were not the funks, but were usually the men of responsibility who denied that they were afraid. In my ward of sixty shell-shock patients there about half were N.C.O.'s. The self-pity in the one case and the fear in the other are quite unconscious. The man who has a phobia for travelling is quite unaware of why he has fears; to him, as to everyone else, the phobia is stupid.

So the patient who suffers from a sense of guilt may have no idea why he feels guilty, indeed he will tell you that he has nothing to feel guilty about. Yet he has to go on doing propitiatory acts like handwashing for a guilt of which he consciously feels quite innocent. He may even continue to perform these acts without any feeling of guilt.

This fact makes it virtually impossible for anyone to cure his own neurosis, for he is unaware of what his problem is. Indeed he is unaware that he has any problem except that of his neurotic symptoms of which he complains. 'It is my hand-washing, my blushing, my headache, that is my problem,' he says, and so it is in consciousness, but of course the real problem lies deeper.

(c) It follows from this dissociation that the repressed material is *beyond the control of the will*, which is characteristic of all neurotic symptoms. We have taken the analogy of the schoolboy, who, because he is naughty, is sent out of school, can do more damage by throwing stones, because he is no longer under control, as he is in class; so the dissociated complex thrust out of consciousness perpetually returns to harass us and we can do nothing about it.

That explains why it is that it is useless to tell a person to exert his will to cure his paralysis, or to tell someone suffering from neurotic depression to snap out of it. They reply they only wish they could. Since the patient cannot control his emotions of fear he then thinks he is going mad which adds to his worry. But he is not, for insanity is mainly constitutional, a phobia is psychologically caused.

(d) A further result of repression and dissociation is that there is formed a duality in the personality, the repressed part or complex on the one hand the repressing forces on the other. This means that there is now a conflict within the personality itself, so that henceforth the objective problem is transformed into a subjective problem. It is no longer a person's struggle against circumstances as it was originally in infancy; it is a struggle against himself, against the forbidden forces trying to emerge into consciousness. It is the house that is divided against itself which cannot stand. That is Freud's theory of the endo-psychic conflict which is of great importance.

(e) *The complex.* The dissociated element forms a complex. What then is a complex? There is nothing particularly mysterious about it: it is simply an experience which, because of its painfulness owing to our inability to cope with it, becomes repressed and so dissociated. It is only mysterious in that, now that it is dissociated we don't know what it is nor of what it consists. So a person may go through life with no confidence in himself, though he has no idea why, for in fact he may be quite competent.

What happens, then, to the repressed complex?
(a) In many cases the problem works itself out automatically for we all have painful experiences and unresolved problems, from birth onwards; but providing later conditions are encouraging, we realize that life is not as bad as we thought it was. Thus many symptoms we had as children tend to pass and no longer worry us. So we can say, 'I used to have a fear of water (or loneliness, of the dark, or people), but that has quite gone.' Thus many symptoms cure themselves as we grow older and get more confidence; bits may remain but we can manage to cope with them. No doubt they affect our efficiency, but they are not worth bothering about, not having been analyzed.
(b) In general the repressed complexes emerge in these main forms.
(i) In dreams.
(ii) In neurotic behaviour disorders.
(iii) In neurotic symptoms.

These are all means whereby the unresolved problem tries to force itself into consciousness by perseveration; but also the means whereby the problem attempts to solve itself.

(i) *Dreams.* Our dreams, as we have seen, always deal with the problems of life which we have failed to solve. We push these problems aside in the day; but when the higher functions of inhibition are removed, as they are in sleep, these problems return into consciousness. They take their chance, and like the persistent child you have pushed aside when you are too busy, return and say, 'Now you can attend to me!' In sleep you turn to escape from the problems of the day only to be confronted with the problems of the night.

(ii) *Neurotic behaviour disorders* like jealousy, suspicion, sulkiness, sensuousness, lack of confidence, defeatism, depression or bad tempers, are all residues of unsolved problems, as we have seen (Chapter XXXI).

(iii) *The neurotic symptom.* Since the complex is emotionally charged, it refuses to lie low and may emerge in the form of a neurotic symptom.

We often find that the complex may be latent for many years and then becomes re-activated by some similar experience. Thus suffocation in infancy may be re-awakened by being shut-up in an underground train. Once they are aroused, like a sleeping tiger they are not so easily shut down again. An infantile desertion long since forgotten was aroused in an Officer when he was lost in the desert and he thereafter suffered from agoraphobia.

The symptom may be variously regarded:

(a) The symptom may be regarded simply as a safety valve, a means of discharging repressed emotion. It is a welcome relief of tension. For the accumulation of emotion in the personality can be very distressing. As it is not permitted to discharge itself in relation to the original object or person, because of the repression, it does so in some substitute form such as a psychosomatic symptom or attaches itself to some innocuous object like a fear of pillar boxes or a sexual fetichism for shoes. The object is usually connected in some way with the original experience.

(b) The symptom may be regarded as a part of the original experience, which it often is; it may be the sense of isolation or a pain in the thigh, experienced in childhood.

(c) The symptom may thus be regarded as a pointer to the original cause of the trouble, just as a pain in the body, and in analysis we must make use of it as a signpost to discover the cause and origin of the neurosis.

(d) The symptom is, furthermore, an attempt to solve the problem even if it is merely as in the first case to relieve the tension by letting off steam. But it may be more specific. If it is a problem of insecurity, the patient develops a phobia about being alone which is a call for help, or a hysteric pain which is a mute appeal for sympathy; or paralysis which is an attempt to escape from responsibility. If the problem is one of guilt which the patient cannot solve on account of his stubbornness in refusing to abandon his forbidden desires, then he tries to solve the problem by overconscientiousness or obsessional propitiations to avert the consequences of the forbidden desires. If the patient can do nothing else, he obliterates the whole problem from his mind and suffers from blindness, deafness or anaesthesia, which is a sham obliteration—he will not look at it; he will not feel anything; he will not listen when the voice of conscience troubles him. Finally, he may go further and obliterate his whole past life by suffering from a 'loss of memory'—a fugue state. These, however, are very unsatisfactory ways of trying to solve the problem, for they solve the problem only at the expense of having an illness or pain.

The choice of symptom is, therefore, largely determined by the *purpose it serves*. If a person cannot adjust a moral problem in his life, at any rate he can get the resemblance of rectitude, by putting his knife, fork and spoon exactly straight as he sits down to table: or by being over-conscientious.

The purposeful nature of the symptom is made clear if we look at it in reverse. If a telephone girl loathes her job but has to stick to it there would be no purpose served if she developed a paralyzed foot, for that could not prevent her from her work: so she suffers from telephone girl's deafness.

My theory that all the neuroses originate in *unsolved problems* differs from those of the other Schools of psychotherapy, but in fact it is the common element in all, though not specifically stated.

According to Janet the problem arose from the inability of the personality to cope with life on account of the lowering of psychological energy. It is a serious problem and many cases are due to this cause: people in a low state of health are more likely to break down than others.

To Freud the essential problem is that of sex, and particularly of incestuous desire towards the opposite parent, which is the 'nuclear complex'. But also the problem of aggression. The boy wishing to possess the mother sexually fears his rival, his father, and the threat of castration. That is surely problem enough. How is he to solve that problem? He cannot do so and falls victim to neurosis.

According to Jung the basic problem is the emergence of material from the collective unconscious which cannot be integrated into consciousness. The inability to solve that problem also results in neurosis.

To Adler the basic problem lies in the feeling of 'organ inferiority' for which the patient has to compensate by an excessive craving for power. Failing to reach this fictitious goal the patient develops a neurosis as an excuse for his failure.

All these theories are at one, first in finding the cause of a neurosis in an unsolved problem; and secondly, in regarding the neurotic symptom as the result of an inability to solve that problem.

Let us be clear on this point: it is here maintained not merely that there is a problem in every neurosis; it is maintained that it is because we cannot solve the problem that we repress it; and it is *on account of the insolubility of the problem that the breakdown occurs.*

To take clinical illustrations: Janet's case (p. 52) of the girl with blindness in one eye and anaesthesia on one side. She loathed being in bed with the girl with impetigo, but had to go on sleeping with her. There was a problem she could not face. The only way to 'solve' the problem was by developing a psychic blindness, so that she could not see the loathsome sight; and an anaesthesia, so that she could not feel the contact with the diseased skin.

It is also well illustrated in Freud's case (p. 132) of the girl who felt pleasure at the thought of her sister's death since it meant a possible marriage to her brother-in-law. The very thought of this wish horrified her as it was incompatible with her moral sense and with her affection for her sister. There was no solution to that problem, because obviously she still harboured the forbidden desire; so she develops a neurosis, a self-punishment for guilt. The problem of the war-shocked soldier between fear and duty was equally unsolved.

Summary. A neurosis is a futile attempt to solve an unsolvable problem a failure in adaptation. The purpose of reductive analysis is to go back and discover what the problem originally was, and enable the patient to resolve the problem which he could not do in childhood. The repressed emotions are thus released, the neurosis disappears and the patient is made whole.

CHAPTER XXXIV

THE BASIC CAUSE OF NEUROTIC DISORDERS

Neurotic disorders, as we have seen, are the result of unresolved problems. If I may repeat: when we cannot resolve a problem we repress it; when it is repressed it is dissociated from ordinary consciousness to form a complex. Nevertheless since it is emotionally charged it appears to consciousness in three forms; as behaviour disorder, as neurotic symptoms, and in dreams, all of which are attempts to solve the problem.

What then are the basic problems which give rise to these disorders? That is a main point on which the various schools differ—Freud emphasizing sex problems: Jung the problems arising from the collective unconscious and Adler those arising from the frustrated urge to power.

For over fifty years I have used the method of free association to discover the causes of the neuroses, and have been forced to conclusions somewhat different from each of these schools.

The basic cause of neuroses lies in the sense of insecurity.

But since the child's security depends upon the protective love and care of the mother, this is normally experienced in the child as a feeling of deprivation of love. There is no lack of evidence in support of this theory.

(i) *Biological evidence.* Self-preservation is the first law of life. Failure to cope with the difficulties of life leads, on the physical side to illness and death; on the psychological side to nervous breakdown.

The human being is of all creatures the most prone to neurotic disorders. The reason for this is that of all creatures, the human infant is the most helpless. Indeed it is a strange fact that the higher we go in evolution, the more helpless is the offspring. The lizard, the fly and the tadpole are capable of fending for themselves immediately on birth by virtue of having fixed reflexes, which make them capable of meeting all the ordinary circumstances of life. At the same time, if they meet with extra-ordinary conditions such as sudden changes in temperature or lack of food, they die, as we say, like flies.

The human infant is far more helpless, because at birth he has comparatively fewer fixed reflexes. This lack of fixed reflexes is of some value, because it gives him greater variability of response, making it possible, by more adequate conditioned reflexes and by the use of intelligence, to vary his response to suit the circumstances, instead of being bound down by fixed reflexes. But the comparative lack of fixed reflexes means that in infancy he is entirely helpless and therefore dependent for his life and sustenance on the care and protection of his mother. She in turn is provided by nature with a maternal instinct to compensate for her child's helplessness. If, therefore, this tenderness and protective love is lacking the human infant is far worse off than the insect and that is why the human infant is prone to develop neurotic disorders, whereas, as far as we know, the tadpole does not suffer nervous breakdowns, nor the sea-squirt from propitiatory obsessions, in spite of its unpleasant behaviour.

This maternal tenderness is associated with the lactogenic hormone which produces not only milk, but the milk of human kindness. Women have this in greater or less degree, so that some women are far more 'motherly' than others. This tender love, be it observed, is quite different from sexual love, although they both give sensuous pleasure, for they originate in entirely different hormones: the one from the lactogenic hormone, the other from the gonadotropic hormone. Each may be experienced quite independently of the other, and each functions quite distinctly from the other. Freud made the great mistake of identifying the two, in saying that by sex is meant all that can be included under the word love. (p. 166).

Love is protective as well as sexual, and the protective aspect of love is far more important in the development of a neurosis than the sexual. A 'mother complex' may be a sexual complex: but it may equally relate to a clinging to the mother for protection and security. It is the lack of this security which is the primary cause of neurotic disorders; agoraphobia, claustrophobia, hysteric pains and paralysis, obsessional guilt and even sex perversions.

(ii) In an atmosphere of security and protective love the child develops confidence to face life. He first has confidence in his mother and thus develops confidence in himself. Secondly, in that atmosphere of security he is free to develop and exercise his native potentialities, free to experiment in life, to try things out, to play, and so to learn the skills which will enable him later to cope with the difficulties of life. With security he has freedom. Thirdly, being given love he develops love for others, the capacity to co-operate with them, with consideration of others, and in family life he gives love to wife and children. It encourages social life. Fourthly, the child who is given love identifies himself with his parents, takes over from them, by identification, stable ideals and standards of behaviour which will be a guide through life.

On the other hand, the child who is deprived of security and protective love will approach life with timidity, with lack of confidence in himself, devoid of that boldness which would enable him to meet the difficulties of life. He dare not venture far for fear of harm, he clings to infantile dependence: he cannot develop the skills which would enable him to adapt himself to life. He cannot afford to love others, for he needs all the love for himself. So he becomes self-centred, selfish, auto-erotic, anxious about himself, preoccupied with his own needs—in brief he becomes a neurotic.

This does not mean that these early reactions necessarily develop into such neuroses: many children have such experiences and get over them providing that they are otherwise reassured of love. But they are the proto-types of neurotic reactions, and turn into neurotic symptoms if conditions are untoward.

(iii) These reactions may be observed in any nursery of children. A typical picture we observe is that of a child feeling left out, perhaps because of the arrival of another baby, and feeling his security threatened. Realizing it is no longer any use to ask for his mother's attention he represses his desire but it emerges in another form: he says, 'I've got a pain in my back: I don't feel well.' This is a hysterical symptom in embryo. Another child in infancy feeling deserted and unprotected gets into a state of dread. This is the prototype of an anxiety state, and the same symptoms are revived later. Another child in his misery resorts to masturbation as a solace, and for this is severely threatened or punished, developing a bad sense of guilt. This may emerge later in the necessity to perform obsessional rituals such as hand-washing as a propitiation for guilt.

In other such cases, however, the repression of the sex feelings means the arrest of sex development, so that the child later suffers from sex impotence, sex frigidity or sex perversions.

(iv) In analysis we find that this confirmed. These disorders are traceable back to such reactions to the deprivation of love.

Fear and anxiety are the most common elements in the neuroses. It is obvious in hysterical anxieties in the phobias like claustrophobia and in obsessional fears. It is also latent in conversion hysteria since the patient resorts to an illness in order to get sympathy and to escape from responsibility. Moreover, fear of consequences is the chief repressing force, compelling a child to repress his forbidden sex and aggressive impulses.

(v) This theory is in keeping with what Freud teaches us: for he insists that it is not the incestuous desires as such which cause a neurosis, but the repression of them. And what represses these incestuous feelings? It is the fear of castration. It is fear then which is the essential element in the production of a neurosis. For what more terrifying to a child than the dread of castration, especially amongst Jewish boys who undergo circumcision so early.

It might be held that the fear of castration is the fear of losing the libidinous pleasure. I have analyzed many cases of the trauma of 'castration', in the operation of circumcision, but in every case but one the fear was one of sheer terror at the *injury*, and the one exception had been reading Freud. One Jewish young man used to scream the place down every night, experiencing nightmares which reproduced his circumcision. Again this points to fear and insecurity as being the basic problem in the neuroses, not sex.

(vi) This thesis of the deprivation of love is further illustrated by Freud's own case (Jones' life of Freud). The basic cause of his fainting attacks and his fear of travelling, described on page 153, originated in the birth of his brother with the deprivation of his mother. This deprivation may be regarded as sexual or as protective. Freud interpreted it as a deprivation of sexual pleasure from his mother whose favourite he was, and this for him may have been the important factor, hence the Oedipus theory. But it may equally be regarded as a deprivation of his security from the loss of his mother's protective love. The latter view is supported by the fact that the natural reaction to the deprivation of sex pleasure would be anger; while the reaction to the loss of security is fear: and fear was Freud's main symptom as manifest in his phobias. Both, however, seem to have been present in his case, for it was the thought of murdering his brother and the horror of it which remained with him all his life. Freud recognized the one, the loss of sex, but not the loss of security. His later fainting attacks came on in situations of an exactly similar nature when his position was threatened by Jung and Fliess, as with his brother in childhood (p.153).

It is usually stated that Freud was cured by making the discovery of his incestuous relations to his mother, which therefore confirms his theory. That was not the case. It is a striking fact, deserving of comment, that in spite of Freud's discovery of his incestuous desires towards his mother and his hatred of his baby brother, this does not seem to have cured his neurosis, or only incompletely; for he continued to have fainting attacks and a fear of travelling later in life. Obviously the whole cause of his neurosis was not discovered. Freud himself said that if you discover the whole of the cause of a neurosis, the symptom disappears 'never to return'. His symptom did return. Obviously the whole cause of his neurosis was not yet discovered, or else why was he not cured?

Might one hazard the suggestion that the reason for this lack of cure was that, while he recognized the sexual element in his neurosis, he did not recognize the deeper sense of insecurity which the apparent loss of his mother must have produced. In other words, that it was his mother's protective love that he missed when his brother usurped his place, even more than the sexual pleasure. That sense of insecurity, therefore, followed him all his life and precipitated the symptom of fainting whenever his security was threatened, as by Fleiss and Jung. The fear of travelling too was obviously a case of insecurity, a separation anxiety related to his loss of his mother's protection.

Reductive analysis into the actual causes of the neurotic symptoms confirms this origin of the neuroses; indeed it was such analysis which compelled us to that conclusion, of that later.

All these facts and arguments, therefore, support the view that the basic cause of neurotic illness is insecurity.

(vii) The main confirmation of this theory however comes from the experience and facts derived from analysis itself, from which our theory was obtained; for this factor of insecurity is found in every case, whether by way of primary dreads in infancy, or fear of consequencies as the *repressing* force of the sex or aggression.

What then are the actual conditions we find in infancy which give rise to these neurotic reactions?

They arise from two general sources.

(a) First of all from situations of objective danger from illness, desertion, loneliness, suffocation, or fear of the loss of the mother's love. These we may call primary fear.

(b) The second source of fear arises from (i) threats from the mother such as punishment for the child's naughtiness, or castration for its sex activities, such fear and threats having the effect of repressing these natural propensities. This creates a subjective problem, a conflict between fear and desire: (ii) the natural consequences of the child's own action, such as terrifying nightmares resulting from sexual orgasms as a result of masturbation. Indeed fear itself may be so devastating and overwhelming that the child is terrified of his own fear, which has to be repressed and may emerge later as a neurotic fear of fear.

All and any of these fears may appear in the symptom from which the patient suffers.

In treatment I find it just as necessary to analyze out the objective fears of infancy which originally gave rise to the unresolved problem, as to analyze the subjective problem as it presents itself at the present day. Very often when we discover the basic cause of his fear in infancy, which appears in his symptom, the whole neurosis automatically disappears, for the patient realizes that there is no need to be straining himself. He is now more relaxed, he can work with far less strain, and his work is more efficient than when he was tense and strained.

CHAPTER XXXV

TYPES OF NEUROSIS: HYSTERIA

Hysterical conditions are characterized by dependence: obsessional conditions by self-will and aggression. Sex perversions by sensuousness and sexuality. All are psychogenic: all are the result of unresolved problems: and also are fundamentally caused by insecurity.

There are three main types of hysteria: (a) Hysterics, (b) Conversion hysteria such as hysterical paralysis or blindness. (c) Anxiety hysteria and phobias, like agoraphobia.

HYSTERICS

The condition popularly known as hysterics is an outburst of uncontrollable emotion, usually after a period of suppression. The patient confronted with a situation he can't bear and arousing emotions too great for him, goes off the deep end, throws his hand in, and helplessly gives way to uncontrolled emotions. Instead of the emotions being directed in purposive action, which is their normal function, they are released in purposeless movements.

In a girls' boarding school one girl got a letter from her boy friend breaking it off and she went into a state of hysterics, weeping, laughing, whereupon all the other girls in the school followed suit. Identifying themselves with their love-stricken school-fellow they went into a state of hysterics. All their inhibitions, school rules and all, went by the board, so that their basic emotions made a field day of it and the Head had to call in a psychiatrist.

The most recent case is the hysterics in the performances of the Beatles and others. What happens in these cases is that by their rhythmic music, also by the rhythmic voices and movements of their bodies, and by the sentimental songs, their low-brow hair do, suggesting their simian ancestry, and their very name (for beetles are a low form of life), they abolish all thinking, all inhibition, so that the minds of the girls in the audience sink down to a lower plane of uncontrolled feelings and emotions which take complete possession of them, as hysteria. They scream and shout like a gaggle of monkey's in the African forest. They say it does them good.

Curiously enough the emotion expressed is sometimes the opposite of what is appropriate to the occasion. When news was brought to Adler's mother that her boy had been run over and killed she burst out laughing—hysterical laughter (p. 216). In this case it was because she could not bear the thought, so she repressed her natural grief—'It can't be true!'; but her emotion had to come out in some way, and so it did so by the opposite,—laughter.

'You must be joking. Ha! ha!' On the other hand when a mother, tense with anxiety at hospital when her child is operated upon hears that the operation is successful, she bursts out crying. In this case, during the period of suspense, she was obsessed with thoughts of possible disaster, but she had to keep this down, for while there is life there is hope. When news of success came, all this suppressed grief that she had been bottling up came out and exploded. In that case the hysterics represented what had been suppressed.

In many such cases the hysterics takes the form of weeping alternating with laughter. One can see why from the last case: for in the period of suspense feelings both of possible joy and of possible grief are bottled up. When the suspense was over both emerged at once or alternating: the mother weeps and laughs at the same time. What people call 'tears of joy' are due to the same cause: they are a release of suppressed feelings.

CONVERSION HYSTERIA

This is the name given to those disorders like paralyses, blindness, pain in the back, for which there is no physical cause but which are of psychological origin—pyscho-genetic.

Conversion hysteria differs from hysterics in several important respects. Firstly, hysterics is the explosion of emotion, whereas conversion hysteria is the result of repressed emotion. Secondly, the explosion in hysterics is purposeless and gets you nowhere, whereas the hysteric pain or paralysis is to get sympathy or to escape responsibility. Thirdly, all the conditions in hysterics may be perfectly conscious as in the illustrations given, whereas in conversion hysteria the patient has no idea why his arm is paralyzed. Finally, conversion hysteria is so called because an emotional problem is transformed into a physical symptom.

Let us look at these conditions because they show most clearly the mechanism of a neurosis, the motive lying behind them, and the way in which they try to solve the underlying problem.

The clearest instance of all is that of a war neurosis, so called 'shell-shock'.

Take a simple case of a man with hysterical paralysis of the legs, of whom I had scores to treat in the First World War. A man is in a trench under bombardment. A shell bursts nearby and he is buried up to the waist. When he is dug out he is found to be paralyzed from the waist downwards.

Hysteria is psycho-genetic. It is naturally assumed that this is on account of injury to the spine. On examination, however, it is found that there is nothing whatever wrong with the spine, nor indeed with the nervous system serving the legs.

This can be proved in two ways. First, by his reflexes: for to take an analogy, if you turn on the electric switch at the door and the electric light goes on you know there is nothing wrong with the current nor with the circuit; so if you tap the knee and the leg jerks normally, it shows that the nervous system is intact.

Secondly, to confirm this you hypnotize him, and in his hypnotic state you can make him walk with his 'paralyzed' legs, and you can wake him up walking. Obviously there is nothing wrong with his nervous system.

If the symptom is an anaesthesia, say loss of sensation in the forearm, you can test it by Janet's 'Yes or No' tests (p. 51), when the patient told to say 'Yes' when you touch his arm says 'No' each time you touch him in the anaesthetic area.

Amnesia. Another characteristic of conversion hysteria is that the experience which precipitates it, or some part of it, is always forgotten because it is dissociated.

The patient can't tell you a thing. He remembers the bombardment, and the next he knows is waking up in hospital. Nor is this loss of memory due to concussion, if by that we mean that the molecules of the brain have been so damaged or disturbed that it has been put out of action—just as a television set might be by a knock. For though he cannot remember what happened, he can be made to remember, under hypnosis or by free association, the whole of the experience in every detail. Moreover, he can be made to re-live it with all its terrifying fears. Obviously the experience has not been obliterated by physical damage; it has only been forgotten by psychological repression.

Repression. The reason for this forgetting, as Freud has shown us, is because the experience has been actively repressed on account of its painfulness, and his inability to cope with the problem. It then forms a dissociated complex.

Dreams. Though repressed, the complex is still active: for the problem is not yet solved, and according to the principle of perseveration it continually surges into consciousness. This happens especially in sleep, when the will is in abeyance, as dreams. Our patient has dreams of a terrifying nature, which are usually a reproduction of part of the horrifying experience. The patient wakes up in horror, not daring to go to sleep again.

The Symptom, too, is usually part of the original problem—in this case the paralysis of the legs. The hysteric patient as Freud said, suffers from reminiscences.

A youth on a destroyer saw the enemy torpedo coming straight for his ship. He was horrified, and wanted to shut his eyes at it, but he could not do that because in his horror he had to look. So he developed a psychic blindness, and remained blind for about two years until the cause was discovered under hypnosis, and he was cured. See also case of cycle accident on p. 235.

The *purpose of the symptom* was an attempt to solve that problem. It satisfied his fear with the desire to get out of the war; it also satisfied his sense of duty, for he had stuck it bravely until he got blind or paralyzed. This solved his problem but at the expense of an illness.

Illness is also the simplest way of escaping from responsibility.

In conversion hysteria the symptom takes a physical form, the form of an illness whether paralysis, blindness or pain in the back. Why is this? Illness is the royal road to sympathy. If the child feels left out and unloved he will resort to illness as a means to get the affection he needs. The hysteric does not want sympathy because he is ill; he is ill because he wants sympathy. One patient, suffering from headaches, reviving an experience in childhood when he was getting attention from a mother otherwise unsympathetic, recalls, 'Then she says to me, "That is fine. You are getting better now" and I thought "What a horrible idea." '

Pre-disposing causes. Why it is that one man gets a hysterical paralysis and another submitted to the same conditions, say being blown up, soon recovers? For an answer to this we need to go to predisposing factors.

There are two predisposing factors which must be given consideration; one is the *constitutional* factor, namely the *temperament* of the individual, for the sensitive or highly strung person feels the rebuffs of life far more than the tough type. But that is not the only factor; for there were many men of a highly sensitive nature who went through the wars with their minds unscathed. The other, is the patient's *disposition* as determined by his earlier upbringing, and whether he has developed a strong well-organized personality with self-discipline and self-confidence. It is the latter predisposing factor such as we find in virtually all conditions.

War cases are very simple and most clearly illustrate the basic causes and mechanism of such conditions. Civilian cases, however, follow exactly the same principles, though they are more complicated.

Take a civilian case of quite a different kind: I had a patient who could not swallow except in tiny pellets: in an unguarded moment I asked him to stay to lunch and it took us two hours. What was the cause? He had been offered a big promotion: he was flattered and anxious to take it; but he suffered from lack of confidence: he doubted that he was up to it and feared he would fail. That was his problem. His difficulty in swallowing was symbolic of this conflict. It said in effect, 'I can't swallow it: I can't take on this job in one gulp. I can take it only in small doses.' The symptom, however, got him out of taking the job and risking failure. He consciously wanted to take the job, and would not admit that he was incapable of taking on the job: but he felt a lack of confidence and the symptoms relieved him of the responsibility. His symptom declared, 'I would like to take the job, but don't you see I am ill, and can't take it.' The lack of confidence was a life-long symptom due to conditions of childhood.

The purpose and mechanism of a conversion hysteria are very clearly seen in a common form of conversion hysteria we call occupation neurosis, like writer's cramp and telephone girl's deafness. A telephone girl, having all day to say 'Number please,' and being cursed at for the wrong number may get wearied to death of it but has to stick it because it is her living. One day she has wax in the ear and is deaf. This satisfies her unconscious wish and this solves her problem, for no one can expect her to carry on when she is deaf. Another girl is a violinist, but she is poor. Her uncle pays for her training on condition that she does not marry. She wanted to marry. She then developed a painful organic neuritis in the right arm from over-practising so that she can't use the bow. It 'solved' her problem. The pain started as an organic neuritis; it persisted as a hysteric pain. Hysteric symptoms are often suggested by organic illness, present or past, so that it exactly reproduces an organic illness. (See p. 52)

Yet it must be clearly remembered that in all these cases the whole process is subconscious: the patient has no idea that is why he has the disability.

These occupational neuroses used to be put down to physical causes such as fatigue. But if a clerk has writer's cramp (which is so often put down to fatigue of the hand muscles), and changes over to the other hand, he immediately gets writer's cramp in that hand, which proves that it is not due to fatigue, but is centred in the mind. The cause lies deeper in that he loathes doing a job which he nevertheless must do. The subconscious, to escape, says, 'I will get you out of this by paralyzing your hand.' 'Very well,' says the other side, 'I will use my other hand.' 'Oh no,' says the first, 'you don't get out of it that way,' and promptly paralyzes the other hand.

Fugue states, as we have seen (p. 55) have the same mechanism and purpose to escape from an intolerable situation by flight. The symptom is purposive: it is an attempt to solve the problem but a most unsatisfactory way since it does so at the cost of an illness.

Dependence. The main characteristic of hysteria as we have said, is the sense of dependence. This applies to all forms of hysteria. In hysterics the patient faced with difficulties beyond his control throws his hand in and gives way to uncontrolled emotion; in anxiety hysteria, such as the phobia of travelling or being alone, the patient clings to others for help; in conversion hysteria the patient, by means of an illness or pain, makes a mute appeal for sympathy and help.

Dependence is a natural and innate propensity of human life: it is most characteristic of the child, who is helpless, so that the feeling of dependence is necessary to its safety. It is also characteristic of social life in the form of interdependence, being an ingredient of the social or herd instinct. Its basis is the need for security: in the infant the security is provided for in the love of the mother.

In many cases there is a persistence of dependence, the reasons for which are various. It is natural to assume that it is due merely to the mother keeping the child too dependent on her. Curiously enough this is rarely found to be the case, for the ordinary healthy child is more likely to rebel against such restrictions and breaks away from the bondage of his mother's apron strings. Then the mother says, 'What have I done to deserve this?' What she has done is to try to keep her child dependent to gratify her maternal instincts, whereas true love should encourage this development. The usual cause is insecurity and deprivation of love.

Differential diagnosis
From hysterics. Conversion hysteria, as already stated, differs from hysterics, for as we have said, hysterics is an explosion of pent-up feelings whereas in conversion hysteria that is repression of the emotions, so that they are forced to emerge as physical symptoms, but usually without any 'show' of emotion. Janet calls this lack *la belle indifférence.*

From malingering: A hysterical symptom is to be distinguished from malingering, for the malingerer pretends to have a pain which he has not got. His 'pain' is consciously faked: whereas the hysteric's pain is a real one. Malingering amongst soldiers and sailors in the wars I found to be very uncommon. On the other hand 'skrimshanking' was common: it consists of making the most of a pain or disability one has got—a pain in the back being 'awful'; a slight injury to the foot making it 'impossible to walk'. Skrimshanking is different from hysteria because, like malingering, it is a conscious process, whereas hysteria is a disability unconsciously produced; it comes from a dissociated complex. Skrimshanking is 'swinging the lead', to see, as with a ship coming inshore, 'how far he can go.'

From psycho-somatic disorders. Both conversion hysterics and psychosomatic disorders are of a physical nature, and both psychogenic; but they must be clearly distinguished. Conversion hysteria is a disorder of the central nervous system, like pain and paralysis, as distinct from disorders of the autonomic nervous system such as palpitation and indigestion.

But that is not the only difference, for psychosomatic disorders like nervous indigestion may be the result of worries of which we are perfectly conscious, but about which we can do little. Conversion hysteria is always the result of dissociation, of repressed complexes of which we are quite unaware. Further, hysteric conditions are purposive, directed towards an end of getting sympathy, whereas psychosomatic conditions are usually the mere result of frustrated emotions, the emotion of bottled up anger, for instance directly affecting our digestion.

But, as we have seen, a psychosomatic condition may be transformed into a hysteric one, since, once formed, it may be used purposively as a means of getting sympathy or escaping responsibilities (p. 287), and it may be due to deep unconscious inhibitions to the emotions of which the patient is quite unaware.

From Anxiety hysteria. In both conversion hysteria and anxiety hysteria there is the sense of helplessness and dependence: but whereas the conversion hysteric resorts to illness as a means of getting the care he wants, the anxiety hysteric gets into a panic and calls out for help. To this we turn.

ANXIETY HYSTERIA: PHOBIAS

There are many people who suffer from odd fears. Some are 'chronic worriers', always nervous, always anxious, always tense, always with a fear of some disaster that never happens. These generalized fears of anything and everything we call 'anxiety states'. It is 'free-floating' anxiety—anxiety without an object, without our knowing what we are anxious about. But that is very unpleasant because we cannot cope with an unseen foe. So the mind overcomes that difficulty by fixing the fear on some object or situation, which is not the real object of fear, but only a projection of it. So we develop a phobia of open spaces, of meeting strangers, or travelling (separation anxiety), of knives (a repressed impulse to kill). This fixation of the anxiety serves a purpose; by telling ourselves that it is travelling by train that we are afraid of, we can avoid it by not travelling. But that does not cure the anxiety. We side-track the fear from the real object of fear of which we are unaware and so produce a bogus peace of mind—but only temporarily for it has not dealt with the real problem.

Origin. These phobias are mainly revivals of infantile fears (a) Their infantile origin is obvious from the nature of the symptoms, for in these panics the patients behave like one-year-old children, which is in fact what they are while in that state; for they are reviving infantile experiences of being alone, or separated from their mother. (b) Moreover, these panics are absolutely overwhelming, far greater than any present-day fear. This exaggeration also reveals their infantile origin.

One of the commonest experiences giving rise to these phobias is a bad birth; for if an infant has a prolonged birth it suffers from suffocation from pressure on the umbilical cord, and a lack of oxygen, which is most distressing. This is the prototype of the claustrophobia, the feeling of being shut in and stifled. When at last the infant is freed, half dead, it is resuscitated and put aside, the attention of doctor and nurse being required by the mother who has now the greater need. The infant then suffers a different kind of fear, the dread of separation, of lack of contact. It has been flung out into an inhospitable world, so unlike the safe cosy comfort of inter-uterine life. You may see it waving its arms for something to hold on to—but there is nothing to cling to. That is the prototype and a primary cause of agoraphobia.

I have frequently found in analysis that both these phobias go back to birth, and that is why we so often find that the same person suffers from both a claustrophobia—fear of suffocation, and an agrophobic fear of space, which in essence is a fear from loss of contact. In analysis the patient revives and actually re-lives these experiences, and is cured of his phobia by releasing the pent-up infantile fear and realizing that the causes of fear no longer exist.

It may be objected that many infants have a bad and prolonged birth but do not suffer from phobias later. That is quite true. For if a child has some such experience, it usually gets over it *provided it is given reassurance from the mother*. In other circumstances the fear may persist through early childhood, but passes away as the child develops greater confidence in himself. So he gets over it without treatment, for as we know any conditioned reflex has to be re-inforced for it to persist; without re-inforcement it disappears in time.

If, on the other hand, the child in its state of fear does not receive reassurance from the love and affection of the mother (perhaps because it is an unwanted child or another child is favoured or because the mother is ill), since there is no-one else to give it the protection it needs, it has to fend for itself. It must be self-sufficient, independent and stand on its own—yet without the resources in itself to do so. It develops a 'power psychology' very like 'Adler's fictitious goal' yet due, not to organ inferiority, but to the feeling of insecurity and lack of protective love.

This self-sufficiency and urge for power and success is set up as a barrier against fear. At all costs he must succeed for as long as he is successful he can keep his fear at bay. He must never relax, he must always get to the top. 'I *must* get on!' is his one motto in life. In broad terms we may call this his Ego-ideal, the standards he consciously adopts. Though false, it constitutes his character.

The result is that he is often a successful man because of this urge to succeed.

But it is a grim struggle, so that he is always tense, always anxious, always strained, and the struggle is exhausting. Added to this he begins to sleep badly and has to face a new day physically exhausted.

Then some adverse circumstance occurs; his business is failing, he feels his power is waning, his memory is worse, he cannot do things as he used to. He begins to fear failure and the more he fears failure the harder he must work. Then suddenly the strain snaps, the barriers of self-sufficiency break down and all the old fears that he has kept at bay for so many years come surging back and overwhelm him. He has a nervous breakdown, taking the form of these infantile fears.

The nervous breakdown is usually said to be due to overwork; in point of fact the overwork is due to over-anxiety; and the anxiety is due to the strain of keeping up the barriers against the infantile fears. It is not really present-day circumstances that have got him down; it is the fight against his own fears. As already stated, the neurosis is, as Freud taught, always an endo-psychic conflict, a conflict between a man and himself, in the same way as the house that is divided against itself cannot stand.

The 'power psychology' which he has set up as a barrier against his fear explains why, as a rule, you find that the people who have such breakdowns are not the weaklings: they are often 'the last-person we should expect to have a breakdown'. It is their anxiety which drives them to success; it is anxiety which finally catches up with them and overwhelms them.

These breakdowns often occur in men of fifty to sixty who are beginning to feel the strain of life and find that younger men have more initiative and brighter ideas than they have, which acts as a threat to their personality.

The *precipitation* of the breakdown in later life comes either from the breakdown of these barriers of independence and success, or on the contrary, the arousal of the repressed emotions which burst through and overwhelm the barriers, flooding the personality with dread. Or both at once. A successful businessman may come up against difficulties too great for him to solve. This is a threat to his self-sufficiency which he has set up as a barrier. These infantile fears then surge up, break down the weakening barriers and he has a breakdown of agoraphobia, a fear of isolation, of lack of contact, or a claustrophobia, fear of being shut in, or some other fear which he has actually experienced in the recent or distant past.

A simple illustration of this spontaneous revival is the soldier who always had a fit when he happened to be in a road between a ploughed field and a grass field, this being the situation he was in when blown up by a shell. Another case was that of the patient who could not stand people being cheerful because in childhood she was let down by a doctor who was cheerful with her, and then hurt her in opening an abscess. Thereafter she had a phobia about all cheerful people. She also lost confidence in her mother for allowing it and, therefore, could not look for comfort from her.

This is also well illustrated in our Case 1 (p. 225). The circumstances of the breakdown in adult life, namely the dentist's anaesthetic and being let down by his girl friend, revived the very similar circumstances of the tonsil operation when he was let down by his mother who 'deserted' him, and was suffocated (to death he thought), by the doctor. So the old terror was revived and once revived, persisted. The phobia of leaving home was a call for help from his mother, as he called for her when she left him in hospital: so that in his breakdown he could not go out without his mother.

But as a rule we do not find that the mere occurrence of a similar incident stands alone; in such cases we nearly always find that at the time the patient was having difficulty with some basic problem which he could not solve so that he called for help by developing the phobia. Case 1 illustrates this also. The girl he was courting was herself a neurotic and he was trying to help her with her problem. It is a common thing for people who themselves have psychological problems which they cannot solve, to try to solve other people's problems. Without realizing it, they are trying to solve their own problems in other people. If they succeed it is a boost to their self confidence. In this case he failed; the girl mocked him as did other people in the hostel where they both lived. This completely shattered his confidence in himself and revived his old sense of failure. There was another reason: this sense of responsibility which he was projecting on to the girl derived from the fact that his father died when the patient was aged four, and his aunts and others all said, 'Now you must look after your mother. You are the head of the house.' To one already suffering from a lack of self-confidence this was too great a task, and it put too great a strain upon him: yet he had to try. In any case his bossy mother was quite capable of looking after herself. He then transferred his sense of being responsible to the girl—with disastrous results. For what with this rebuff to his morale and the experience at the dentist coming at the same time, he completely lost confidence in himself: his barriers broke down and all his old fears from the tonsil operation came surging up to complete his breakdown.

Anxiety hysteria must also be distinguished from obsessional anxiety, which may however take the same *form*. In anxiety hysteria the symptom is a mere revival and reproduction of an infantile fear when the barriers break down. Obsessional anxieties are fears of our own forbidden desire. In Case 1 there was no forbidden sexual wish it was only a revival of infantile fears from similar circumstances and problems.

Anxiety and conversion hysteria. These phobias are rightly described as hysteria, for hysteria is characterized by dependence on others. How then does anxiety hysteria compare with conversion hysteria? For both are manifestations of dependence.

(a) It differs in the first place in that in conversion hysteria there is a *wish* to be ill in order to get sympathy or escape responsibility: in anxiety hysteria there is a *dread* of illness or other disaster, just as there was in infantile life.

(b) They are, however, both purposive, both an escape from life; but whereas the conversion hysteric in his helplessness says, 'I am ill, take care of me,' the anxiety hysteric says, 'I am afraid, take care of me.'

(c) They arise at different stages in childhood. Anxiety hysteria reverts back to an earlier phase than conversion hysteria. A child of two or three is sufficiently sophisticated, if he feels unloved, to stage an illness to get the sympathy and the attention he wants by illness: the infant in the first year of life, if subjected to situations of danger, can do nothing else than get into a panic. Thus it is that we usually find that the phobias found in anxiety hysteria go back to the first year of life, whereas conversion hysteria more usually originates at two or three.

(d) In conversion hysteria, therefore, there is a more personal attachment and a personal appeal for help. This occurs after the child has become attached to a person (Freud calls it the Oedipus phase, but it is usually dependence, not necessarily sexual). The infant in the first year of life is not attached to any particular person; any bosom will do. That was demonstrated in the evacuated children in the war. An infant in the first year of life would take to any motherly person: the three-year-olds were very choosey and screamed for their mothers. In some cases they preferred an unkind mother who beat them, to a kind foster mother: it was their mother they wanted. Anxiety hysteria thus goes back to infancy and is a state of sheer panic. When these infant horrors are revived they are added to the present fear. The child is then subjected to a double dose of fear which is exaggerated far beyond the demands of present circumstances a fear that is greatly exaggerated and is, therefore, recognized to be abnormal. This constitutes a neurosis.

In treatment it is as necessary to analyze out the objective fears of infancy which originally gave rise to the unresolved problem, as to analyze the subjective problem as it presents itself at the present day. It was not enough to discover in Case 1 that he was trying to help that girl with her neurotic problems and failed. Why should this be so disastrous, and why should going to a dentist call forth those terrors of going out alone. These were only the precipitating causes. It was necessary to discover where his fears originally came from, and why they were revived. When we discover the basic cause of his fear in infancy, which are revived in his symptom, the whole neurosis automatically disappears; for the patient realizes that there is no need to be afraid nor indeed to strain himself as a barrier and an off-set against these fears. He de-bunks his fear so that he is more relaxed, he can work with far less strain, and his work is more efficient.

Prevention. It is obvious, however, with the thousands of people who suffer from these disorders that analysis for all is impossible, and the only way to cope with these distresses is by prevention. It was with that purpose that I wrote my *Child and Adolescence.* Every infant should be protected from all excessive fears but if such fears are inevitable as by operations, then every care should be taken to give the child all possible reassurance, whereupon the fear passes. Fear is very contagious—for biological reasons—the flight of one bird or the running of one rabbit sets all the lot going. So the anxious mother will produce anxiety in the child, whereas if the mother is calm and reassuring in a crisis, the child will be reassured. That was observed in London during the air raids: if the mother was calm the children were calm: they feared a frightened mother more than they did the bombs.

DEPRESSION AND THE USE OF DRUGS

Depression is often classed with anxiety states: but the two are different. Depression is a stage worse than anxiety. In anxiety you may be worried that you will not come through successfully, but you still hope: in depression you have lost all hope and give way to despair.

Depression may belong to any one of the four classes mentioned under behaviour disorders. Many cases of depression are of a physical constitutional type like involutional melancholia which often comes on at mid-life and is probably caused by chemical changes in the body the nature of which is unknown. It is more typical of women because it is often combined with psychological depression coming from the fact that their work in life is done now that their children are growing up, and they feel themselves to be less attractive. The treatment for that constitutional condition is electric convulsive therapy (E.C.T.) which was originally used for schizophrenia, but turned out to be even more useful in these depressive states. There are also a number of anti-depressive drugs like imipramine which are also very effective. These conditions do not concern us for while they are mental disorders they are not treated by mental means or psychotherapy. These methods are fully dealt with by Sargant and Salter in *Physical Methods of Treatment*.

Apart from depression of a constitutional or temperamental type there are many cases due to psychological causes.

Anyone is liable to be depressed if circumstances in life go sufficiently against him, though some are more prone to it, being defeatist, than others who battle through. This condition is usually called 'reactive depression'. It corresponds to what I have called simple traits due to circumstances. Suggestion treatment is most effective for such forms of depression.

But many are of a neurotic type being the emergence of deep-seated depressions going back to experiences of early childhood, which have for some reason been revived. I find that such primary depression almost invariably goes back to the first year of life, and is often connected with malnutrition and feeding troubles. That is to be expected; for if things go wrong for an infant, say with the distress of rickets, there is nothing at all it can do about it but fall into a state of depression. Reviving these infantile experiences is enough to cure such a patient of his depression. (Case p. 345.)

It is not surprising that drugs are tried for the psychoneuroses: but while they may have a temporary effect (so may alcohol) they are no use for deep-seated cases. Amphetamine (Benzedrine) may give you a temporary boost to tide you over a difficult time but is little use otherwise. Its effects last only eight hours.

Sargant and Slater discourage the use of such drugs in cases of hysteria and anxiety neuroses, saying that, 'Most patients with "anxiety neuroses" who benefit from convulsive therapy are those who are wrongly so called.'

I personally never use drugs in my treatment at all, for, treating only psychoneurotics, my aim is to get to the cause of the trouble; and as for tranquillizers like drinamine and stelazine are concerned they tend to check free association. I find by far the best tranquillizer, if a patient is in such a state of anxiety that he cannot carry on treatment, is relaxation and suggestion to produce peace and calmness of mind: and the best stimulant is the hope of cure. If, however, the patient requires sleeping pills I leave that to the G.P., but that is rarely acquired.

CHAPTER XXXVI

SEXUAL IMPOTENCE AND PERVERSIONS

Sexual impotence and frigidity

These are disorders productive of much unhappiness not only to the individual but in married life: for the non-consummation of a marriage is grounds for separation, even when the partners are otherwise suited to one another and love one another.

Sometimes the patient is devoid of sex feelings altogether; at other times he may have strong sex feelings, but is entirely incapable of effecting sex relations. The frigidity of the female does not prevent sexual intercourse, but robs it of much of its pleasure to both partners. The female may also suffer other disorders which are not perversions, such as vaginismus, in which there is such contraction of the genitals in sex intercourse that penetration is impossible.

(i) Frigidity and impotence may have a physiological or a psychological origin. (a) Sex feelings are dependent on the gonadotropic hormone of the pituitary gland. Frigidity from this cause is particularly found in women, many of whom (some say most of whom) never have an orgasm. After all, looking at it biologically, sex feelings in a woman are not so necessary for the procreation of the species as in the male who is the aggressor. (b) In other cases the impotence is acquired. In the male, an attack of mumps, especially about puberty may give rise to inflammation in the testicles (orchitis) with resulting impotence and infertility. In a hospital ship (H.M.S. *Agadir*) in the first World War I had numerous cases of mumps to deal with, and our chief concern was this inflammation of the testicles.

(ii) But a great deal of sexual impotence and frigidity has no physical basis but is due to psychological causes, the main factor being repression of sex, usually by threats of punishment, such as castration in childhood. These threats are particularly effective when the little boy is found to be masturbating and is then subjected to circumcision, which he regards as a punishment. Later although he may naturally desire sex relations, this inhibition may automatically prevent him from having them.

In such cases there is usually a normal desire for sexual intercourse, and no concious fear at all, but it is an unconscious fear which prohibits it, to the disappointment of both parties.

In cases of vaginismus there may be a strong desire for intercourse, but this is prevented by the contraction. This is often found to be due to a sexual assault of some kind in childhood which produces physical pleasure, but at the same time pain and horror,

316

which therefore accompanies any further attempt at intercourse.

In other cases male or female persons may be sexually impotent as regards normal sex relations, because their sex feelings are attached to other objects or activities. A man may fail to have intercourse with his wife because his sex feelings are attached to fetichistic objects like corsets, or to those of his own sex, homo-sexuality, and other sex perversions. Such people may, however, overcome this by imagining and having phantasies of these perverse objects while having intercourse with the partner. In this way a wife frigid towards her husband, may enjoy sex relations with him by imagining a former lover.

Treatment. Sexual impotence of psychological origin in the male, and frigidity in the female, may often be cured by suggestion treatment designed to get rid of the basic fear produced by the original repression. Men suffering from sexual impotence become subject to a morbid auto-suggestion; as they have so often failed they expect to fail at any new attempt at intercourse. If by suggestion you give them confidence and they once succeed it breaks the vicious circle. 'Once aboard the lugger and the girl is mine.' Conditional therapy may also be successful.

In other cases more radical analysis is necessary to discover and eradicate the original repressing fear.

Sexual perversions are the emergence of repressed infantile activities. Let us consider how they develop.

I have already mentioned (p.165) that the infant has many physiological activities, like sucking and defecation, which are associated with strong sensuous pleasure, the biological function of this pleasure being to enhance and encourage the activity. If sucking were unpleasant as it sometimes is from the taste of the milk with an infected breast or because it is hard to get, the activity itself is discouraged and the infant suffers harm.

I have also made it clear, I hope, that these physiological activities as such are essentially egoistic in their aims, being concerned with the self-preservation of the child and have nothing to do with sexual or reproductive functions. Sucking is pleasurable, but to call it sexual as Freud does is to confuse the sensuous with the sexual (p.165).

Nevertheless these physiological pleasures often give rise to sensuous feelings so strong that they spread to the sex organs; so that the infant at the breast can often be observed to have an erection and even an orgasm.

Wooing. When these physiological functions, such as defecation or sucking, thus encouraged by their sensuous pleasure, become established as habits, the sensuous pleasure associated with them normally passes, and becomes transferred to the uses of adult sexuality. These constitute the wooing or love-making activities. Kissing for instance is nothing else but sucking. We kiss with protruded lips, we make the same noise, and we like kissing the rounded parts of the body like the cheeks which are reminiscent of the breasts in infancy, and still more the lips, which are reminiscent of the similar membrane of the nipple, which arouses far greater sensuous and even sexual pleasure. In brief these infantile sensuous activities are used to increase adult sexuality.

The attraction to the breasts may then be transferred to the buttocks which are also sexually attractive in adult life (as Marilyn Monroe made us realize, if we were not aware of it before), for the buttocks are reminiscent of the breast—with the dual lobes and the cleft in between.

Perverse activities. Things, however, may not turn out so happily. Normally in infancy the infant's first love object is the mother's breast, which it craves for when hungry, and then this transfers to the mother herself who provides the infant with all this pleasure and comfort. The infant may then continue to give itself the same sensuous pleasure by sucking its thumb or stimulating its sex organs. There is no particular harm in that unless these activities are fixated or repressed.

Sometimes, however, they become definitely 'perverse'. If, for instance, the infant is suddenly deprived of the breast, or feels deprived of his mother's love, it will produce a reaction against her and resort to masturbation as a solace, repressing his love for her. It says 'I don't want her love, I can do without.' For it now has a pleasure which it can give itself at any time, without the mother. In such a case there is a definite conflict and dissociation in the infant's personality.

These activities we may call 'perverse', though they are not 'sex perversions.' They are abnormal for several reasons:

First, such activities are auto-erotic: the child finds pleasure in itself instead of in its mother. Self love is substituted for object love. Secondly, it means that the whole of the love life is concentrated on its sexual aspect, which is therefore greatly exaggerated. Thirdly, being exaggerated, it is much, much more likely to be repressed. Finally, such sexual excesses are not satisfactory, since whilst giving the child sexual pleasure it does not give the child the sense of security as it has definely excluded the mother. It is unhappy. These perverse activities are the beginning of perversions. The real damage comes when these perverse habits are themselves repressed.

Sexual repressions. This repression may come from threats from the mother that he will have his penis cut off, especially if followed by circumcision, or that she will not love him if he does that. These threats, however, may merely have the effect of increasing his sense of insecurity so that he masturbates the more as a needed solace. He is thrown into a terrible state of conflict and dread.

But threats are not the only cause of repression. For the masturbation may lead to an orgasm, which frightens the child because it is so overwhelming. Moreover, this appears in nightmares, which take the form of overwhelming monsters, of vampires which suck his blood, of crabs and spiders which symbolize the spread of his sex feelings over his body in an orgasm. This is not surmise but comes from our patients. (Dreams and Nightmares p. 194.)

These terrors may be so great that he is compelled to repress his sex activities. Thus sexuality in infancy may become the cause of its own repression.

The results of the repression. This repression means that the child's sexuality is arrested in development and fixated at an infantile level.

Nothing further may happen, for the question of sexuality does not arise: but in adolescence, when the sex feelings are more strongly developed for physiological reasons, the repressed sexuality forces its way into consciousness, but emerges in the form in which it was originally repressed, that is to say in the infantile form.

Thus sex perversions are the emergence of infantile sex activities. One or two further comments.

All sex perversions are due to repression of sex. I agree with Freud that sex perversions are the persistence, or I would prefer to say, the revival of infantile sex activities. But with my experience in analyzing dozens of these cases of sex perversion I entirely disagree with Freud that they are due to the *mere* persistence of these activities, such as the boy's fixation to his mother producing homosexuality (p.160). In every case I have analyzed by free association the cause of the arrest of development was repression as I have described. It is on account of that repression that the sexuality is fixated at an infantile level. Homosexuality, for instance, as I shall illustrate later, far from being a fixation and identification with the mother, often arises from a fear or hatred of the mother, which puts the child off women for good.

The other comment I would make is that these perversions start at a very early level, very commonly in the first year of life. The reason for this seems to be that this is the sensuous period of life when the infant gives itself over to sensuous pleasure without restraint or taboo, so that it is at this period of life that its sexual pleasure, whether in getting an erection at the breast or in masturbation is most likely to be scolded by the shocked mother, who may, for instance, remove the infant from the breast which the child experiences as a punishment.

There are, it is true, later precipitating factors which are often taken for the true cause: but these alone would not have produced a perversion had there not been predisposing causes in infancy. A boy does not become a homosexual merely because he is seduced by a bigger boy or man, or else homosexuality would be far more rife than it is. But such a seduction may be the precipitating factor without which he might not have become an active homosexual To cure such patients it is usually necessary to analyze out both precipitating causes and the predisposing causes in early childhood.

Sex perversions and sex aberrations

The characteristic of sex perversions is that the abnormal activity is desired *to the exclusion* of normal sex desire. Thus the homo-sexual is attracted entirely to his own sex and may be completely indifferent to the opposite sex: he could sleep all night with a most seductive female who attracts him no more than the bolster. In sex aberrations as distinct from perversions, there is a *preference* for the perverted object or activity, but not to the complete exclusion of the other sex. Thus many homosexuals are quite capable of begetting children, but prefer sex relations with a man. Another can have sex relations with a woman provided she first beats him. In two cases I know, the husband, though quite sexually inclined to sexual intercourse with his wife, must play the feminine role and be under his wife, overmastered by her, which was most unsatisfactory to her. This arose because his mother, romping in bed with him as a child, played the dominant masculine role in arousing his feelings.

Types of Perversion: Sadism.

Let us illustrate from actual cases: Here is a man who has the sadistic impulse to strangle any girl towards whom he is sexually attracted. So strong is the urge that on several occasions he has rushed off to see a psychiatrist. Tracing this back in analysis, he revives an experience in infancy when he was at his mother's breast, which aroused in him both sensuous and sexual feelings. But the milk gave out, which made him furiously angry so that he 'strangled' and bit the breast. For this he got a smack and was put off the breast. The sex feelings were associated in his mind with the smacking, and the whole experience repressed for fear of punishment. His sexuality was consequently arrested in development. Thus was formed in his mind a complex in which sex feelings, rage and fear were all combined. That complex was latent for some years, since the problem of sex did not arise; but when he became adult and his sex feelings forced their way into consciousness, they appeared in the form in which they were originally repressed, namely as an impulse to strangle the sexually loved object. Thus a sadist may murder a girl without assaulting her sexually (Case p. 352)

Masochism. In the case just mentioned the sex feelings were associated with rage and anger, and so persisted as sadism. But it might well have been that the boy was smacked say for an erection at the breast, or for masturbation, in which case *the sexual feelings would be associated with the infliction of pain.* Not only so, but if the beating were on the buttocks, that in itself might reflexly arouse sex feelings. At the same time since the beating is painful, that would repress the sex feelings, and thus fixate them at this infantile level as a complex. In that case he might suffer later from the emergence of this complex in the form of masochism, the sex pleasure in having pain inflicted on one. The desire to be sexually overmastered is a natural pleasure in the female who loves the he-man. But there are cases, both male and female, in which, as in the circumstances mentioned, the sex pleasure is fixated to the pain and this may persist *to the exclusion* of normal sexuality, in which case it is a perversion.

Fetichism. Many men (curiously enough not women) suffer from sexual fetichisms. Just as primitive man kept inanimate fetichistic objects like stones to represent spirits, so some men's sexual feelings are aroused only towards inanimate objects like corsets, shoes, the buttocks of trousers, or mackintosh capes. Why this odd choice? On analysis taking these perversions back to their origin, I have invariably found that they reverted back to infantile breast substitutes. (Perhaps that is why women, who have breasts, do not require a substitute.) An infant is sucking voraciously at the breast, has an erection which scandalizes the mother who thinks her infant must be a monstrosity. He is 'punished' by being smacked and removed from the breast and so comes to regard it as an object of evil omen; he must repress his desire for it. He then transfers this unconscious desire on to objects *like* the breast. Corsets is an obvious choice. Shoes? because shoes put together have the same shape as the breasts; they are both soft, and leather has the same body smell. So his sexuality becomes fixed on to that, but anything sexual to do with a woman is taboo. You commonly see a child fondling a quilt or silk handkerchief while sucking his thumb. This is obviously a substitute for breast feeding, the fondling of the silk being a reproduction of the fondling or squeezing movements an infant makes on the softness of the breast, and the thumb taking the place of the breast itself. This may be quite simple and harmless, being a mere substitute when the breast is no longer there. But if it is accompanied by repression and fear of the mother then the whole of the sexual interest may be concentrated upon it to the exclusion of the normal sexual interest—just as a fetich or graven image may itself be worshipped instead of the god which it represents.

Homosexuality. Some authorities consider homosexuality to be a constitutional disorder—that these people are born homosexual. No physiological cause, however, has been found to account for this; nor has glandular treatment so far had any effect. On the other hand the fact that many homosexuals have been cured by psychological treatment implies that some at least, perhaps most, are psychogenic. I have quoted a number of such cases in my *Psychology and Mental Health* (p. 377); and also in an article in the *British Medical Journal* (12/3/66) on 'The cure of homosexuality'.

That does not altogether rule out the constitutional factor; for we often find that homosexuals are of a youthful adolescent type, physiologically immature, in fact 'the Nancy boy.'

There is an age in puberty when homosexuality is a natural propensity, in the gang phase, before they develop towards heterosexuality. (See *Childhood and Adolescence*, p. 206f.) Some adolescents seem not to pass beyond that phase of maturation and so remain, or have inclination towards, homosexuality. Others remain half and half both homosexual and heterosexual, preferring neither to the other. Most of us leave homosexuality far behind.

Such homosexuals are often regarded as 'feminine'. That is hardly correct: it is not that they are feminine, but they are more youthful, boy-like: they have not developed into men, but remain adolescent. It is the same with some lesbians; they are not so much 'masculine' as boy-like, they are less fully differentiated into the matured feminine type.

Constitutional factors, therefore, particularly immaturity, may be regarded as a contributory factor; but even in these cases we find the psychological factor the most important—for many immature males, very young and boy-like marry and are quite happily married: it is merely that people of their type are more prone to become homosexuals whereas the fully developed and mature person often drives through to normal sexuality even though subject to the same psychological disturbances in childhood. The physiologically immature homosexual is, however, more difficult to treat than the fully matured.

Homosexuality is self-love once removed. If an infant is deprived of its mother's love, it often resorts to masturbation. This is self love: it can now do without its mother: it represses its desire for her, for now it has something it can have at any time it wants. Masturbation may give it sexual pleasure but it does not give it real love. So from loving himself he passes to love of someone like himself, that is to say, someone of the same sex.

I have often also found in cases of homosexuality a negative factor, namely that there was also a fear of women, and especially of female sexuality; such as from a seduction by a nurse. Being inherently afraid of women's sexuality, when he grows up he has no outlet for his sexuality except to resort to those of his own sex. He may be very good friends with women, but sexuality? Definitely no.

The most recent case of homosexuality I have treated, was a schoolmaster dismissed from his post on that account, and put on the Home Office 'black list' forbidding him to teach. Taking the case chronologically (which is the opposite of the way we proceed in analysis); he was an illegitimate child of a schoolmistress. She was dismissed from her job and, being penniless, she attempted on two occasions to suffocate her infant, but she could not bring herself to do so. In analysis the patient experienced those suffocations, on one occasion with the mother's body on another with a pillow. It is interesting to find that later in childhood he used to have a compulsion to bring his pillow over his head to suffocate himself and then to release himself. That is a typical reaction in childhood, reviving a situation in order to solve the unsolved problem—just as the children in a Bristol Hospital which got a direct hit from a bomb, afterwards played at bombing. These suffocations gave him a fear of women. Later, in a home for abandoned babies, the domineering of the matron, and the indifference of everyone as he was just a number, did nothing to destroy that fear. This fear of domination by women meant he would never marry. There followed an episode in which he was seduced by a man, but in that case he stated definitely that he was more intrigued by the affection and attention than by the sex. But this turned his sex impulses in that direction, so that he inevitably became homosexual. This analysis cured him completely and he became quite heterosexual, both in conscious life and in his dreams. One of which is given on page 260. The outcome was interesting. Now that he had become heterosexual, he was taken off the Home Office 'black list', but the bright lads at the Home Office now gave him permission to teach, provided it was in a girls' and

L*

not a boys' school. However, he preferred to keep out of teaching.

Sodomy or buggery (a legal term) is a perversion taking the form of a desire for intercourse by the back passage of another, whether male or female. The attraction of the buttocks is a common substitute for the breasts, when the latter are denied in infancy; there is also, of course, a natural sexual attraction since in animal life the approach is from behind. It is a perversion when sex intercourse by the anus is to the complete exclusion of the normal direction. The giving of enemas which arouse a child's sexual feelings by reflex action is commonly found to be at the root of the condition, the woman desiring the continuance of it, and the male wanting to do to another what gave him such pleasure in childhood.

Exhibitionism is of course a natural propensity in a child to call attention to itself for protection and security. It is, of course, a natural wooing tendency to arouse the sexual attention of the other sex. Where a child feels deprived of love it tries to attract the attention of others by exposing that part of the body which gives him or her pleasure and presumably will give pleasure and attract others. When, as is so often, the only result is punishment, the exhibitionism is repressed and sexuality in general is arrested in development so that it later emerges in that arrested infantile form of exhibitionism, sometimes to the complete exclusion of any normal sex desire, but only to expose oneself. (See p.192)

Sadism is the sexual pleasure in inflicting pain on the sexually loved object. I have often found it to originate in rage at the breast, the first sensuous object in infancy, associated with biting. This fixates sexual feelings with attack. A case is given on page 352.

A consideration of the origin in infancy of these sex perversions prove that these individuals are in no sense responsible for having these inclinations, though it may be said that they are responsible for giving way to them, in the same way as the heterosexual has to curb his desires in the public interest, and not to pervert others.

Differential diagnosis. Why does the repression of sex in one case produce sex impotence and in another sex perversions? The difference as far as I can gather is that in the perversions the child's sexuality has been excessively developed first, and so strongly that it will not be repressed altogether and so emerges in the perverted form. This occurs particularly when the child deprived of love concentrates its whole love life on its sex aspect (p. 318).

The differences between conversion hysteria, anxiety hysteria and the sex perversions may be expressed thus: all these are reactions due to the feeling of deprivation of love (chap. XXXIV). But the convertion hysteric when feeling deprived of love [says, 'I've got a pain,' in order to get the love; the anxiety hysteric says, 'Oh, I am afraid,' in order to get the attention; the sex pervert turns his back on others and resorts to sex as a solace, saying, 'I want no one's love; I have my own,' and loves himself.

Again, sexual perversions differ from sexual obsessions, like a fear of raping, in that they are pleasurably desired and consciously sought after. They are not compulsions. Indeed, their gratification may be the greatest pleasure in life. So while the sex perversion is consciously desirable, the sex obsession is only unconsciously desired. The man who has the fear of raping certainly does not desire it consciously, but does desire it unconsciously. Sex perversions, have an unconscious origin, but the desire is fully conscious.

But there is a very close connection between sex and the propitiatory obsessions, for it is mainly on account of infantile threats to sexual sins that the propitiations have to be made.

Treatment. When in analysis we go back to the original sexual experience, discover the cause of the fear and raise the siege, the repressed sexuality is released and develops as it would have developed if it had never been repressed. So the person becomes normal. But it is a long process, and the only adequate way to deal with this problem, which is a social as well as a psychological and medical one, is prevention.

Prevention. Unfortunately with the comparatively few cases it is not yet possible to dogmatize as to what the basic cause is, applying to all cases. In general it may be stated that the sex perversions arise from the excessive stimulation of sex, followed by its repression. Both of these can be avoided by the parent with common sense and intelligence. In particular, severe threats must be avoided. Even so, quite apart from parents' threats, an orgasm in infancy often leads to terrifying nightmares, which repress sex. That can be avoided only by preventing the masturbation which produced the orgasm, by removing its cause. Excessive masturbation is not as innocuous as some psychologists would have us believe.

The parent must, therefore, discover how to deal with the excessive masturbation which is often the result of fear, inferiority, or lack of affection. All these can be got rid of by the mother's reassurance and love.

It keeps the child's affection towards her instead of being auto-erotic; and it gives the child the sense of security so that it does not need to turn to sex as a solace.

CHAPTER XXXVII

OBSESSIONS

Psychopathology

Obsessions are morbid mental compulsions. They may be *compulsions to act* in certain ways like hand-washing or constantly returning to see that the back door is locked, that the gas is turned off, or that one has put everything tidy: to scrub everything in case of infection when there is no necessity to do so; to put knife, fork and spoon exactly straight as soon as one sits down at table; or to say 'Wakey! Wakey!' first thing on waking in the morning, accompanied by, 'Dash it, why do I keep on saying that?'

Compulsive feelings and emotions, like compulsive fear when there is nothing to be afraid of, compulsive outbursts of temper, or feelings of self-deprecation, a persistent need to apologize for oneself, or a feeling of inferiority when there is no reason to feel so are common.

Or they may be *compulsive thoughts*, being obsessed with the thoughts of death, of millions and billions, of how the universe came to be when one is not in the least interested to know how, or it may be merely a tune ringing in the head.

Or they may be *moral compulsions*, to be over-conscientious, over-punctilious as to religious exercises, scrupulously honest in every stupid detail.

All these are *compulsions:* they force themselves unwillingly upon the mind, being quite beyond the control of the will. They are *mental* in so far as they are all motivated by complexes in the mind. They are *morbid*, and recognized to be so by the patient who has no wish to do these things or have these thoughts; indeed they hamper him in life and in getting on with the things he wants to do.

As the characteristic feature of hysteria is helplessness and dependence with a need to be cared for; and the characteristic of sex perversions is sensuous and sexual pleasure; so the main characteristic of obsessions is that of obstinacy, aggressiveness and self-will.

The main characteristic of obsessions is aggressiveness and self-will. It is that which gives to the obsessions their compulsiveness and obsessional drive. The obsessional patient is motivated by a strong power urge, he must get what he wants, he must have his own way. But that urge to power is frustrated by his fear of consequences, so that the aggressiveness comes out in the form of a morbid obsession. Thus he *must* go back to see that the back door is locked, or he is compelled to wash his hands fifty times a day. This aggressiveness accounts for the so-called 'obsessional drive'.

The quality of assertiveness, and even its exaggeration which we call aggressiveness, is of great value in life. It enables us to fight our foes, to get the food we need and to make our way in the world.

It is, moreover, the raw material of the will. For what we call the will is the direction of our assertiveness towards the ends and aims of the personality as a whole. It makes for a strong character.

If the aggressiveness is frustrated it is subject to perversions such as obstinacy, resentment, revenge, sulkiness, sullenness and other *abnormal character traits* which may persist through life. If repressed it leads to *obsessional neurosis*.

The conflict between self-will and fear of consequences is of course common to everyday life, especially in children in the tantrum age at two or three. The individual subjected to it tries to solve the situation in various ways.

(a) If the child is of a docile and gentle temperament or of an amiable disposition, he will abandon his self-will and conform. He yields to the fear voluntarily. It is not worth risking and nothing more is heard of it. If the threat of consequences is too strong, it may have the effect of crushing his will altogether, so that he is robbed of the wherewithal to face the problems and fight the difficulties of life. He becomes good but sapless, devoid of will and character and lacking in initiative. Parents of sensitive children need to be particularly careful not to crush their will. For such a child finding himself handicapped in life, unable to cope with the difficulties of life, resorts to neurotic illness as a means of getting the help he needs.

(b) A child of more aggressive temperament or one whose assertiveness has been more strongly developed may, on the contrary, become defiant in spite of the threats: he takes the risk, and if he finds that the threats are not carried out, as so often is the case, he gets away with it. He may become a rebel against authority, perhaps a delinquent. Under better circumstances he may direct his aggressive tendencies to good purpose, strike out a new line of his own and become a thorough success in life.

(c) In other cases neither the fear nor the self-will will give way.

The essential conflict in the obsession is therefore between exaggerated self-will and exaggerated fear of consequences. One part of the personality says, 'I'm going to have my own way.' The other part says, 'If you do, disaster will follow.' It is the irresistible force against the immovable object. The irresistible force is the self-will; the immovable object is the fear of consequences.

The self-will refuses to give way; but the fear of consequences is so great that it dare not assert itself. In some people this conflict is never resolved, with the result that the patient is in a state of permanent anxiety.

How then does such a situation arise?

The *exaggerated aggressiveness* may arise from two sources; one physiological, one psychological. Some children are temperamentally highly aggressive by nature, inherited from father or mother, which is all to the good if directed in right channels. But such a child cannot bear to be thwarted and must have his own way.

In other cases the self-will comes from psychological causes. (i) A child who is spoilt and given his own way, (Says the mother, 'He's such a darling, I can't deny him anything'), when he is thwarted, gets into tantrums and rages. He cannot bear frustration. (ii) In other cases it is the opposite: a child who is always told not to becomes exasperated and rebellious. (iii) Still more exaggerated is the aggressiveness felt by the child who feels left out and unloved, perhaps with the coming of another baby, especially when previously he has had all the attention. He gets furiously angry, jealous, hates the baby and the mother, and becomes thoroughly 'difficult', obstinate and bloody-minded.

The *exaggerated fear* arises sometimes from the actual consequences of the forbidden desire, such as where sexual masturbation produces an orgasm which then is objectified as a terrifying threatening monster which forces the child to repress his desires. Or from threats of the parents, that mother won't love him, being shut up in a room when he is naughty, the fear of loneliness and isolation, none of which the child in its helplessness can bear. The result of such fear is that the forbidden desires are repressed and the child adopts a 'moral' attitude of conformity—its Super-Ego. It comes to heel and the mother is pleased at her good management, but she may be laying up a neurosis in the child, for the essential conflict is not really solved, since the hate, though repressed, is still there and active to return as an obsession.

The precipitation of the obsession comes as a result of this conflict (a) when either the forbidden desires are strongly aroused, it may be merely in the order of growing up and being more independent; or (b) when with growing confidence the fears are passing away, which encourages the forbidden impulses to emerge and have their way. This often occurs in adolescence when repressed sexual or aggressive impulses are aroused.

Thus the whole conflict of earlier days is revived and resurrected producing in the patient a breakdown due to a re-activation of a basic problem he has never solved. The result is that a panic will come on, (a) whenever there is something in the present circumstances such as loneliness, illness, open space, close space, which reminds the patient of the original threat; (b) whenever the forbidden impulses of aggression or sex are aroused, even normally. In such circumstances the patient gets into a panic, yet may have no idea as to why he should fear, nor is he aware of what are the forbidden impulses of which he is afraid or of which he feels guilty. Nor indeed is there necessarily any present day cause for his panics. The whole process is unconscious: all that he is aware of is a state of dread, or the compulsion to perform some stupid act. Nor can he, as a rule, solve the problem himself because he does not know what it is. Only analysis can reveal this.

In some mild fortunate cases the symptoms cure themselves. Many girls in adolescence, for instance, with the arousal of their sex feelings, have revived within themselves the conflict of early childhood regarding sex, and many suffer from propitiatory acts or religiosity to propitiate for these impulses; but when the desires continue and no disaster happens, the conflict is resolved and the patient recovers automatically. In mild cases also, suggestion treatment to abolish the fear may be sufficient to resolve the conflict and cure.

Sometimes the problem is far too deeply rooted and is precipitated into consciousness to produce permanent breakdown.

There are then three phases in the obsessional complex.

(a) The exaggerated aggressiveness and self-will, (b) the fear of consequences which represses the aggressiveness, (c) the moral Super-Ego of being good to avoid these consequences.

Each of these phases may appear as the dominant feature of the obsession.

(a) In some cases it is the fear and nothing but the fear which appears as the symptom. Those are the obsessional anxieties.

(b) In other cases the forbidden desires appear alongside the fear, as in an obsessional fear of hurting, or fear of raping, which are obsessional aggressions and sexual obsessions respectively.

(c) In the third group it is the moral attitude, the Super-Ego, which dominates, so that the obsession takes the form of compulsive religious practices or other rituals such as hand-washing. These are the propitiatory obsessions designed to avert the consequences of the forbidden desires.

Obsessional anxiety and fear
Such fear is aroused in this way. Whenever the patients' aggressiveness or self-will is aroused even normally, with it comes the fear of consequences, which represses it. He may have no awareness of this aggressiveness, all that he is aware of is a sense of

terror, of impending doom, of something dreadful going to happen. Obsessional fears are the fears of the consequences of our forbidden desires. They differ, therefore, from hysterical phobias which may take the same form but which are merely the revival of infantile fears, when the barriers to these fears break down.

Long before the breakdown a practised eye can see the break-down coming. This man is always anxious, always strained. He can never leave his work to others; he must do it himself or it will not be properly done. An obsessional woman is the chronic worrier: if she has nothing to worry about she must find something to put it on to. She is worried about the laundry, the children's schooling or the future. If she is awake for two hours in the night, she reports she has had an 'awful night', when her husband returns tired at night she has a dramatic story to tell him of the 'terrible' hold up in the traffic. Any trifle or mishap is a disaster.

Another form of obsession is indecision: no sooner has the patient decided on one thing than he wonders if he has decided correctly and so decides the opposite—which is equally wrong.

The origin of this is obvious; it relates to the original conflict between self-will and fear of consequences. The decision was never made in the original conflict. Any decision necessitates being assertive: and this is immediately followed by the fear. The original unsolved problem being forgotten is projected on to every decision of the present; for any decision is dangerous.

Obsessional phobias

Since it is intolerable to be in a state of chronic anxiety without any apparent cause or object, the patient fixes his fear on some object, usually an object or situation connected in some way with the original experience. The reason for this projection is that it is easier to combat a known fear than an unknown: so he develops a phobia, say for travelling in tube trains, for if that is his fear he can avoid it by not travelling in such trains or by not going to the theatre. So his fear is projected on to some concrete object or situation; that he can deal with. But of course it is not the real object of the fear, and therefore does not resolve the problem.

Stammering is an obsessional compulsion: and is due to the same basic conflict. One part of the personality says, 'I'm *going* to have my *say*'—the other part (coming from some early experience) says 'If you do disaster will follow'—you will be snubbed, pun-ished or humiliated, so that whenever the patient has the impulse to have his say it brings up with it the old fear which was so closely associated with it. It usually comes from some humiliating experience in childhood concerned with his saying something. In war cases it is usually found that the soldier was actually speaking when he was subjected to the trauma of being blown up (p. 51).

Why the specific phobia? That depends mainly on the fear with which the child has been threatened for its forbidden desires. The phobia may take the form of insanity if the child has been so threatened for masturbation; a fear of death may result from threats of hell: a fear of isolation and loneliness if the threat was that 'mother won't love him unless he loves the baby of whom he is jealous,' and yet he can't love at will, so that the problem is unresolved and the fear perpetuated.

In other cases the fear is derived from an actual objective experience of dread in infancy, for if the patient is simply obsessed with generalized fear but is quite unaware of why he is afraid, he looks around for the cause of his fears. What is more natural than that he should select some fear he has already experienced: so his mind naturally revives the infantile fear. 'It must be suffocation, or isolation, that I fear', and this becomes his phobia. '*That* must be what I am afraid of.'

This corresponds to some extent with Jung's idea that the patient goes into the past to borrow a symptom, something on which to put his fears (p.183).

These phobias therefore may be precisely the same as appear in anxiety hysteria: but apart from the distinction already mentioned, the motives of the phobias are quite different. In anxiety hysteria the symptom is unconsciously wished as an appeal for sympathy and help on account of one's insecurity: in obsessional anxiety far from being a wish, it is a threat: a fear of the consequences of forbidden desires.

Obsessional aggressions

In the obsessional anxieties which we have so far discussed, there is a fear of our forbidden desires, but only the fear comes into the phobia, and the fear is always of some harm coming to oneself, such as in agoraphobia or fear of death. The obsessional aggressions are conditions in which the forbidden impulses themselves are so strong that they emerge in the symptom itself. This may take the form of a compulsive *impulse*, as in one patient who felt the impulse to strangle every baby she saw in a pram (a throw-back to her jealousy of her baby sister in childhood). Or it may take the form of a *fear* of injuring without any conscious impulse to do so. Or it may take a milder form of simply a *thought* of bashing someone on the head without any fear that she will; or of some accident happening to a husband on his way back to work. A patient of mine with a negative transference said, 'The thought came to me of taking up that bronze statue on the mantle-piece and bashing it on your head.' I have already described one case (p. 250) in which a mother had the fear that something she did would mean that her son, to whom she was devoted, would get T.B. The fear in all these cases, as Freud points out, is the fear of a forbidden desire, but in these cases what one fears comes into the picture, so that we call them obsessional aggressions.

To take a case I have recently treated. It is the case of a mother who had a fear and even an impulse, that in bathing her infant she might accidentally drown it. It was a horrifying thought. Owing to childhood experiences she had never had any confidence in herself and found her housework and children too heavy a task, although it was nothing more than many women have. She got frantic about her incompetences. One might interpret her symptom merely as a fear of her own incompetence. It was far more.

She traced the impulse back to her jealousy of her younger brother in childhood, which she now transferred to her own child, since her husband was paying more attention to the child than to her, as originally her mother paid more attention to her brother. The precipitating cause? At the time of the outset she had a minor nervous breakdown and was in a mental hospital, and then found herself pregnant. Another child was the last thing she wanted. The thought came to her, if she accidentally drowned the baby in the bath that would solve the problem. She immediately repressed the horrible idea, but it haunted her. But if the drowning were accidental she could not be blamed. This is an unconscious wish: it is an obsessional aggression disguised as a fear.

With the realization of the cause of the phobia, she lost it, and bathed her baby without fear. Not only so, but having got rid of her fear she was able to release her natural assertiveness in normal channels. Her confidence restored, she took up sculpture in addition to running her home with success and happiness.

It will be observed that there is nothing sexual about such cases: it is purely a matter of repressed aggression.

Sexual Obsessions

Similar in development to the obsessional aggressions, are the sex obsessions, in which it is repressed and forbidden sex desires which appear in the symptom. Thus one man has the obsession that he will sexually assault a small girl: a father has the obsession that when he is carving the joint, he will plunge the carving knife into his adolescent daughter. This was not an obsessional aggression due to an unconscious hostility to the girl as it might have been, but an obsession symbolic of forbidden sex desires towards the girl, the knife of course being here a phallic symbol. A similar case was that of a woman who feared she might go mad in a public place. She was asked what she would do if she did go mad. She replied that she might tear off her clothes and run about naked—a repressed sexual exhibitionist tendency. The wish was expressed as a fear. Why madness? Because nobody of course could blame her for doing so if she was mad. Her symptom was a compromise between the desire and her moral inhibitions.

The forbidden desires may thus be of a sexual nature. But it is self-willedness which turns it into an obsession and makes it compulsive. It is simply that it is with regard to sex that the child must have his own way. Without the aggressive self-will element, the repression of the forbidden repressed sex impulse might produce sex perversion of exhibitionism but not an obsessive compulsion.

Differential diagnosis. What then is the essential difference between these three sexual abnormalities—sex impotence, sex perversions and sex obsessions?

In sexual impotence the sexual impulses are not very strongly developed before they are repressed, so that if the child innocently masturbating is threatened with castration, it just gives it up, represses sex, and that is the end of the matter. In later life, the unconscious fear completely dominates and inhibits any sexual intercourse, even if the person consciously desires it: there is always the threat within, 'Take care.'

The sex obsessions are quite different from the sex perversions—even in their overt forms: whereas the sex obsessions, like plunging a knife into one's daughter, are horrible and terrifying to the patient, the sex perversions are anything but horrible; they are consciously desired, perhaps the most desirable on earth.

In both, the sex impulses were strongly developed before repression, but in the perversions while sex in general is arrested in development, it is permitted expression in other forms: thus if sex pleasure at the breast is denied (perhaps because the infant bit), it is permitted in the form of a substitute such as a fetishism for a silk quilt: in sex obsessions it is feared.

Propitiatory obsessions are designed to avert the dreaded consequences of our own forbidden desires. They take two distinct forms:

(a) Obsessional character traits, like over-conscientiousness.

(b) Propitiatory acts and rituals like hand-washing, or continually going to see that the back door is locked when we know we have just looked at it.

In both these types of obsession the fears are so terrifying and the threats so inevitable, that the patient must at all costs take measures to avert their consequences. And the first obvious measure is to re-inforce the Super-Ego or moral attitudes which all these years have kept the fears at bay. If the patient cannot keep the impulses at bay he must do something to avert their threats.

Obsessional character traits. The patient must become over-conscientious, over-scrupulous, in everything he does; punctilious in his religious exercises, strictly honest in every detail. He becomes in fact what the Scots call 'unco-guid'. A child placed in this dilemma of self-will and fear often makes a pact with himself or with God, that he may continue with his forbidden desire but be good in everything else. Such a child is always asking, 'Am I a good boy?' because he isn't, but wants reassurance that he will not meet with the threatened consequences of being bad. The more guilt, the more the necessity for propitiation; yet the patient may have no idea of the connection between the two. Religiosity and excessive religious practices are often the result of an unresolved guilt.

Propitiatory acts. In other cases the obsession takes the form of propitiatory acts or rituals: the compulsion to make sure you have locked the office or the compulsion to return to see that you have turned off the gas fire although you know perfectly well that you have; or the compulsion to be scrupulously clean to avoid microbic infection when it is your soul that is unclean.

The classic instance of the obsessions is, of course, found in *Macbeth*. Macbeth himself suffered from obsessional anxiety. He was 'Cabin'd, cribb'd, confin'd, bound in by saucy doubts and fears!' Lady Macbeth suffered from propitiatory obsessions. She too was full of guilt, but refused to admit her guilt and repressed it; but although repressed it was there and it made her feel unclean for her complicity in the murder of the King and of Banquo. She therefore transferred her guilt of soul to her hands, 'Out! damn'd spot! out I say!' Why does it take this form? Because it is far easier to wash your hands than to cleanse your soul. But this gives only temporary relief for it does not solve the real issue of her guilt: so the propitiatory act has constantly to be repeated.

No wonder the gentlewoman remarked, 'I would not have such a heart in by bosom for the dignity of the whole body!' and the doctor, wise man, said, 'This is beyond my practice!'

Propitiatory acts have the semblance of morality, but in fact they are the opposite. They are substitutes for moral behaviour; for the individual avoids being moral by bluffing himself with these substitutes, to pretend that he is clean or pious. One patient was compelled, whenever he passed a church to take off his hat in order to propitiate God. But he never went in. As a small boy he was robust and normally aggressive; but when once he disobeyed and went out on a winter day and got pneumonia, he became delirious, and with the heat of temperature thought he was in hell with hallucinations of the devils pitchforking sinners into the fire. He recovered, and took it that God let him off this time, but never again. He developed a strong moral Super-Ego. Later he had very mild sex adventures, but guilt of this was enough to arouse the old fears. But as he was unwilling to give up these sex pleasures, he must do something to appease God; so took off his hat. This gave him the feeling that he was reverent, but avoided the need to be reverent.

Indeed, quite often the propitiatory act takes the form of gratifying the very impulses for which the propitiation has to be made—as in the case of the woman patient who, when she went up the stairs, had to press her hand up between the banisters to propitiate for masturbation; but of course this act was itself a form of substitute masturbation.

What of the patient who has to go time after time to see that he has locked the back door; or to see that he has not left the gas turned on; or that the books in the office are straight?

Analysis shows the obvious cause of these acts which are symbolic: the patient must return to see that the back-door is locked symbolically to make sure that his forbidden impulses, like burglars, did not break through surreptitiously. He must see that the gas is turned off lest there should be an explosion: but the real explosion he fears is from the bursting out of his forbidden impulses. He must see that his desk is tidy, not for common-sense reasons, for he knows it is already tidy. It is not his desk that needs tidying but his soul.

They are all symbolic—not the real issue.

It is no use telling these people that it is silly to carry out these acts, for they know that as well as you do. They may feel guilty but they will tell you they have no idea why. That is because they have repressed both the guilt and the reason for their need to propitiate.

Moreover, if you tell them to force themselves to stop doing these propitiatory acts it puts them into a panic, for these propitiations are designed to avert disaster, and if they are neglected that leaves them open to suffer these dreaded consequences.

In analysis. In my experience practically all the propitiatory obsessions I have analyzed have a sexual origin: the guilt is a sexual guilt. But it is usually found that the 'sin' in childhood about which the child is made to feel guilty is something quite trifling but the excessive threats of punishment compel the child to repress such impulses.

In these obsessions, not only are the impulses repressed but also the sense of guilt. It has therefore been said that we not only have a conscious conscience, but an unconscious conscience. It is this unconscious conscience of guilt which perpetuates the obsession. Such patients may have no conscious sense of guilt about sex at all; the sense of guilt is from an unconscious complex.

Treatment of these obsessional propitiations is extremely difficult. For as already mentioned, if you try to stop an obsessional patient performing one of these compulsive acts it will throw him into a state of fearful anxiety. He therefore resists getting rid of his fears. Furthermore, according to the patient you are attacking his moral character (his false Super-Ego), which is what he stands for. He comes to be treated for his obsessions, he says, not to have his morals questioned. Yet it is his 'moral' inhibitions that are at fault.

Another reason for the difficulty in treating obsessional patients is that they are always very self-willed and therefore obstinate, refusing to co-operate or sometimes determined to do the analysis in their way and not in yours. Further, there is always the risk of a negative transference, anger and hate against the analyst, a revival of the anger towards the forbidding mother in childhood. Lastly, the patient's symptoms arise from the Super-Ego, which is the person's adopted moral character, an attitude of mind, and such an 'attitude' is much more difficult to move than a repressed impulse (as in conversion hysteria or sex perversion), where you have the help of the impulse itself which is already trying to emerge.

They can, however, be cured by psychotherapy with patience and persistence in delving into the causes of the obsession in each case. The patient comes to see the cruel threats of the mother or nurse for the lies that they are. He also sees that the 'sins' for which these threats were made are trifling. He comes to see why he had to adopt the 'unco-guid' over-conscientiousness, and why he had to adopt these propitiating acts: and comes to see the false motives and stupidity of his excessive 'morality'. He defies these threats and his fear goes, with a return to confidence. But let no one think this is an easy task.

Prevention is ultimately the only adequate way of dealing with such disorders; and in the main prevention means avoiding all excessive threats to the child. After all it is no morality that is based on fear: true morality in early childhood should be based on identification with a parent he loves and admires. In bringing up children discipline is necessary to guide and direct their native impulses in good and healthy activities; but no child should be put under the strain of being so terrified by threats that his personality is paralyzed by fear.

Macbeth says to the doctor.
'Cans't thou not minister to a mind diseased,
Pluck from the memory a rooted sorrow,
Raze out the written troubles of the brain
And with some sweet oblivious antidote
Cleanse the stuffed bosom of that perilous stuff
Which weighs upon the heart?'
The answer now is, we can, but it is not easy.

CHAPTER XXXVIII

ARE THESE INFANTILE MEMORIES TRUE?
THERAPEUTIC RESULTS

The whole problem of reductive analysis by free association revolves round this question. Are these visualizations and reproductions of infantile experiences true? What evidence have we that the child in fact had these experiences, which we have taken to be the basic causes of the neurotic personality? Freud, as we know found that the 'memories' of sexual assaults in infancy which he at first took to be the cause of hysterical symptoms were largely fictitious; and partly for that reason he—I think too precipitately— abandoned the direct reduction method. To this problem we now turn. It is not a purely academic question; nor indeed is it concerned only with treatment: it affects also the whole question of the upbringing of children, and how we are to prevent these disorders. It is a question of truth.

In the present state of things, owing to the length and therefore the costliness of analytic treatment, which merely a fraction of those needing treatment can get, the only adequate way to deal with the problem of psychoneuroses is by prevention, which means right parenthood. There is distinct hope along these lines. This question of prevention and the principles of parenthood is the main theme of my book 'Childhood and adolescence' (Penguin). I have come to the conclusion that about nineteen out of twenty neurotic disorders could be prevented with right parenthood. This is not pure guesswork but is based on a study of the specific causes found to be at the root of the neuroses in my patients. A study of these causes reveals that they could have been avoided in the large majority of cases with right parenthood. There are some cases, however, which, humanly speaking, could not have been avoided, but these are few.

I have for many years, therefore, paid particular attention to the question of the truth of these experiences which emerge in analysis. Indeed over thirty years ago, as Chairman of the British Psychological Society, Medical Section, I gave as my Chairman's Address a paper on 'The Reliability of Infantile Memories,' published in the *Lancet* of June 10th, 1928, and also published in the *British Journal of Medical Psychology*, Vol. VIII, part 2, 1928. In the intervening years I have had numerous cases in which such infantile memories, even to the first year of life, have been recovered, and many of them confirmed. Indeed, there are few cases in analytic treatment of the neuroses in which it has not been found necessary to recover experiences in the first year or two of life, in order to effect a radical cure of the patient. As we have seen, cases of claustrophobia for instance are frequently found to be reproductions of infantile suffocation at birth; cases of agoraphobia or separation anxiety from a child's removal from the mother at birth and left exposed to the outer world, and later by removal to hospital for an operation. When these experiences have been revived, the patients have become cured of their symptoms.

Many illustrations have been given in my *Psychology and Mental Health*, and more recently in two articles in the *British Medical Journal* of June 7, 1958 and on 'The Cure of Homosexuality' of February, 1966, in which patients suffering from this condition (often regarded as incurable) have been cured by the recovery of the basic cause in infantile life.

A PRIORI ARGUMENTS

Inconceivability. The main argument against the acceptance of these infantile memories seems to be that of inconceivability. It is said that it is inconceivable that a person can revive what happened to him in the first year of life. So it might seem. Yet what evidence is there for the dogmatic statement that these experiences cannot be revived? What grounds have we to declare that it is impossible?

We agree that we do not remember these experiences in the full meaning of memory, as having happened. But there is no *a priori* reason why a person cannot retain and later revive such experiences, although he does not remember them happening. Most people cannot spontaneously recall what happened further back than, say, three years of age. But that does not mean that we cannot by special methods revive such experiences. If we can fully remember what happened to us at the age of three or four, as many people can, is there any reason why we should not be able to reproduce what happened when we were one or two? In the same way neurotic symptoms *are* spontaneous revivals of infantile experiences.

The miracle is not that we can recall what happened to us at the age of one or two; the mystery, which has never been solved, is how we can remember past events at all. But we can, in both cases.

If the critic dogmatically declares that such experience cannot be recalled, it is up to him to prove that they cannot, and why they cannot be recalled. On what does he base his confident assertion?

The argument from inconceivability is the weakest of all arguments. It means only that the objector cannot conceive it, which proves nothing. Many things like rockets to the moon were inconceivable a few years back, yet have been demonstrated as possible.

But, of course, the fact that there is no evidence to prove that these experiences cannot be recalled is no proof that they are re-called. We need more positive evidence that we can and do retain infantile experiences, and that they can be revived.

PHYSIOLOGICAL EVIDENCE

(i) *Experimentally*, if the temporal lobe of the brain is stimulated, flashes of memory from the distant past come back into conscious-ness. This implies (a) that they have been retained, and (b) that they can be reproduced.

(ii) Lysergic acid (L.S.D.) is frequently used in analytic treat-ment, since under its influence, it is said, memories of infancy are reproduced, without the patient losing ordinary consciousness. From my little experience of L.S.D., however, I am inclined to doubt whether what emerges are real reproductions. Is it not merely that the L.S.D. has activated the more primitive centres of the brain so that the patient is for the time being simply living in a lower infantile level, with infantile reactions? He is behaving like an infant, but his baby feelings are not necessarily reproductions of past baby experiences. By excision of certain centres of the brain we can produce 'sham rage', but that does not mean that such rage is a reproduction of early rages. More confirmation is required.

All the same, most of those who have used lysergic acid more than I have, are convinced of the reality of these past revivals.

(iii) If, as some people think, memory consists in circuits of electrons set going by an experience and retained, there is no telling how long they may last, nor why at any time they should not be reactivated into consciousness. Incidentally this hypothesis of the electrons explains not only the functions of memory, but the so-called 'unconscious mind'. It is a purely physiological process and itself, therefore, non-conscious; but it is capable of giving rise to consciousness and to reproduce what originally produced it—in the same way as a gramophone record, itself a purely material thing, can under certain conditions produce beautiful music.

(iv) *Conditioned reflexes.* Further evidence of the possibility of retention and reproduction of infantile experiences comes from a study of conditioned reflexes. Anyone may observe an infant even in the first few weeks of life getting excited when its mother is preparing to undo her dress to feed it. On the other hand such an infant feeding contentedly at the breast, if suddenly terrified by a loud noise, or choked with too much milk, may thereafter refuse to take the breast. Both are acquired reflexes which imply retention of the previous experience, of feeding in the first case, and of the terror in the second, and its reproduction.

Furthermore, such conditioned reflexes can be experimentally produced in the earliest weeks of life. Arnold Gesell, the greatest of all observers of child behaviour, tells me in a private letter that 'the normal infant may acquire conditioned reflexes during the first few weeks of life'. A striking instance to which he referred was that reported by Aldrick in an article in the *American Journal of Diseases* (January, 1928, p. 36). An infant of three weeks showed no signs of responding to any sounds, and as it was an adoption case, the question arose, 'Was it deaf?'. Aldrick devised an experiment in which he sounded a dinner bell, and then scratched the infant's foot with a pin, which made the child cry out. After twelve to fifteen applications the bell was rung without the foot being touched, and the child cried out, proving that the child could hear. It also proved that the child must have retained the previous experience (the sound of the bell), and was able to reproduce the response of crying. This child was three weeks old.

Conditioned reflexes, it is true, do not necessarily imply consciousness; but, however it is to be explained, they do imply retention in some form of past experiences and modification of behaviour as a result of such experiences; but crying, we must assume, must be associated with consciousness. I have heard it argued that an infant has no consciousness and, therefore, the patient could not remember what happened in infancy. That is pure assumption. Is there any evidence whatever that an infant is devoid of consciousness? True, we cannot prove that an infant is possessed of consciousness; but equally there is no proof that the man we are talking to is possessed of consciousness. Nevertheless we assume it as a result of an awareness of our own consciousness. So why deny it to a child?

Such evidence from physiological facts, from experimental reproductions and from conditioned reflexes all tend to dispose of the dogmatic assertion that the revival of infantile experiences is 'inconceivable'. The evidence all goes to prove that even the infant has a memory in the sense of retention and reproduction of past experiences.

But of course it is one thing to advance evidence that the infant is possessed of a memory and quite a different thing to assert that what our patients recount are true reproductions of actual infantile experiences. What more positive evidence have we of their truth?

Positive Evidence of the revival of the infantile experience

(a) *Spontaneous reproduction*. That the brain has phenomenal powers of retention and reproduction can be demonstrated by such cases as the well-known case mentioned by S. T. Coleridge, in his *Biographica Literaria* (1847, Ed. I, p.117) of the maid who in a delirium quoted passages of Hebrew, a language of which she was completely ignorant. It transpired that her former employer, an old Protestant pastor, was a great Hebrew scholar, and was accustomed to read aloud from his books passages of Hebrew. He did this walking up and down a passage into which the kitchen opened. Many of the passages spoken by the girl were identified with those read by the pastor. Other similar anecdotes are given in Prof. W. B. Carpender's *Principles of Mental Physiology*, 1874, p. 437. Another case is quoted of a man in Paris who was hypnotized during a lecture and who afterwards repeated the lecture word for word, including the slips of the tongue. Such cases illustrate the capacity of the brain to retain and to reproduce most detailed impressions. So there seems no reason why the brain of the infant, which presumably is more impressionable than that of an adult, should not be able to retain—and reproduce—impressions of the same nature. Old people recall incidents of their early years which they have previously long since forgotten. This means that the 'memory' was there all the time, though in abeyance.

We may recall what McDougall mentioned (p. 71) that a post-hypnotic suggestion may be spontaneously acted upon months after it was given, showing both retention and reproduction to be automatic processes.

Another instance of spontaneous recollection was given me by a medical colleague who tells me that at the age of six or seven he recalled a fire which occurred when he was eight months old. He says, 'In the course of a conversation with my parents, I was told that the house in which I was born had caught fire and had been completely destroyed when I was eight months old. Immediately that was mentioned, I said 'Oh, yes, I remember.' This was ridiculed by my parents who informed me that, as I was only eight months old at the time, this memory was quite impossible. However I said, 'But I do remember and can tell you something about it.' I then proceeded to describe a circular staircase coming round a circular wall, and at the top of the staircase was a landing lit by a window. The window had frosted glass in the centre with coloured panels at the sides. I described the whole place lit up— flames licking the glass panels which were cracking with a noise like the report of a pistol. These details were corroborated by both my parents who said that the fire had reached considerable proportions by the time we had reached the landing, and that within five minutes the whole staircase and floors of the house had collapsed.'

It may be objected that he had at some time heard it mentioned. Maybe, although there is no evidence of this. In any case, anyone mentioning the fire would hardly go into such precise details as the stained glass window, or the circular staircase, which would be taken for granted. Nor, he assured me, was there extant any photo of the house from which the patient could have got these details.

But, it may be objected, how could a child of eight months know what a 'window' was or that it had 'frosted glass', or that the crackling noise was like the 'report of a pistol' since it is unlikely he had ever seen a pistol. Agreed. The infant does not know them, as such. But what occurs in such cases is that the infant retains a photographic image or picture of the whole scene which imprinted itself upon his impressionable mind (or brain); and later when the image is revived in the adult mind he is now able to describe what he sees in the light of his present-day knowledge and experience and puts into words what he now sees them to be—as pistols or frosted glass. In brief, the sensation and image are there and is revived; the perception and interpretation come later.

(b) That is what happens also in analysis, when, in free association, the patient visualizes the original experiences of what caused his illness. One patient visualizes herself at birth 'held upside down' and smacked. How does an infant know what is up and what is down? It does not. But try holding an infant upside-down and it soon lets you know it. 'I felt I was dying,' says another patient of infancy. How does an infant know what dying is? He does not, but he can feel his strength ebbing away, and re-live this feeling in analysis. So when he recounts it, he describes it in terms of dying. Thus a patient, reviving a feeding episode in infancy says he had bad 'indigestion'. Absurd. How does an infant know what indigestion is? He does not, but he can have indigestion as an infant and in reproducing the experience he recognizes and describes it for what he now knows it to be, as indigestion. Not only so, but as he recalls it he actually feels the pain and the nausea, and may ask for a receptacle in case he is sick.

(c) Other evidences of spontaneous revival are found in eidetic images and in dreams which carry us back to long-since-forgotten infantile images.

Eidetic images are those glimpses and momentary pictures which flash into our minds—'a child lying on the ground', 'horses jumping', 'a lovely scene', 'being overwhelmed by a wave'—and are as soon gone. These images if traced back are found to be memory traces of actual past experiences. (One patient I analyze entirely by his eidetic images which are more reliable as actual experiences than his dreams which are symbolic.)

(d) Dreams also, far more often than is recognized, relate to actual experience of the past, leaving residual problems which by the law of perseveration persist in coming into consciousness for solution. Always to give dreams a symbolic interpretation is to miss their real significance and the problems requiring solution. (See case on page 252.) Even if symbolic they often relate to facts of experience. As we have seen, the common dream of passing through a long and dark tunnel with great anxiety is usually traceable back to the experiences of birth, passing through the vaginal passage. The German word *angst* (anxiety) means a narrow space. Such experiences can surely be impressed on an infant's brain—why not? And if it is retained why should it not be reproduced as indeed it is in dreams, as well as in symptoms of suffocation (claustrophobia) and again most fully in analytic revival.

OBJECTIVE CONFIRMATION

What objective confirmation can we find for such infantile memories? It will be readily understood that it is not by any means easy to get confirmation of these infantile experiences. There may be no-one to whom we can refer who is likely to know: the mother may have long since died. In other cases the mother may have no idea of what is happening; for nurse-maids can do a lot to the child which the mother knows nothing about, such as sexual experiences or punishment, and the child is either too young to speak or is threatened with dire consequences if it tells.

In other cases, experiences which are of tragic importance to the child may be of little importance to the mother—as in the case of the tonsil operation (p. 225) in which the child lost all faith in the mother who deserted him. In spite of these difficulties there are a number of cases in which it has been possible to get objective confirmation.

(a) *In analysis*. A Jewish young man suffering from an anxiety neurosis revives his circumcision in infancy, as usual on the eighth day. But he also visualized and felt that something went wrong and it had to be done by the doctor a second time. He afterwards asked his mother whether anything of this sort happened and she replied, 'Nonsense, it went perfectly all right.' I think it will generally be conceded that her boy's circumcision, being a religious ceremony, is of considerable moment to a Jewish mother, and she is not likely to make a mistake about such a matter. Nevertheless, about three weeks later she came with her son, said that she had been clearing out some old private drawers and had come across a diary which she had kept of her son in infancy, and to her astonishment found that what he had visualized was perfectly correct. There was documentary evidence of the truth of the incident which no one could remember happening but which was revived in analysis. Nor was it likely that he had heard of it since his mother herself had entirely fogotten it.

A patient who had severe asthma visualized himself under hypnosis as a small child with a bad cough and his mother putting something near his face which choked him. As he revived the experience he choked and coughed violently. He had no 'memory' of his experience as having occurred; it was merely a 'reproduction' of his asthmatic symptoms and the horror of the experience associated with it. The mother, however, corroborated the story saying that as a child he had whooping cough and she put some friar's balsam on a hot shovel to ease the cough, but overdid it and nearly suffocated him. She 'thought she was going to lose him.' She added that 'the same green bottle was still standing on a kitchen shelf.' There is nothing 'inconceivable' about such an experience; nor is there any need to doubt that this was the cause of the asthma. For (a) the patient re-lived the experience vividly and emotionally, which left no doubt in his own mind as to the truth of the incident; and (b) the uprooting of the experience produced an immediate and complete cure of his asthma.

A more striking case of corroborative evidence is that of a middle-aged woman suffering from deep depression with two serious attempts at suicide. Involutional melancholia had to be considered but was ruled out. She had an unhappy marriage and was separated from her husband who said he no longer loved her. But that was only the precipitating cause, not the essential one. She had had seven years previous analysis of a Freudian interpretive type but only got worse. In fact, one of the suicidal attempts was during that treatment owing to a hopeless transference. Tracing the symptom back to its source she ultimately revived with emotional vividness an experience in infancy. Asked to visualize when first she had this depression, she says, living in the past, 'I am feeding quietly on my mother's breast. Now I suddenly got a slap on the right side of my face—I can feel it now—then I got dropped on the floor and my mother rushes out of the room. I want to get up but only succeed in rubbing my face on the floor, and the more I do that the more painful it is. (She felt that pain in her face and held her hand to her face as she described it). I always told my previous analyst that I should never get well till I'd slapped him in the face—although I had no idea why—it must have been retaliation against my mother. My face is all hot and sweaty and wet and terrible. There was no living person in the world to help. Now I see the maid or someone come in and I get lifted up or propped up in a chair or couch and she then leaves me. I am no longer crying; I have got beyond that. I am in a state of deepest depression, just like the depression and despair which comes over me now.' All this was recounted with great emotion.

A most improbable story. Mothers feeding their babies don't slap their faces, drop them on the floor and walk out on them. Improbable, it is true, but not so incredible when we discover that the mother in the patient's infancy suffered from gall stones, for which she was operated on in the first year of the patient's life. But that is not all; as it happened, the nursing home in which she was operated upon belonged to my patient's grandmother, and there the patient was fortunate enough to find the very day-book (which I saw), in which was entered the mother's operation for gall stones. This was dated October 1917, the very year in which the patient was born in the previous April, making the infant six months old when the mother was operated upon, and when the incident occurred.

While it therefore may be 'inconceivable' that a mother should drop her baby in this fashion, it is not at all inconceivable that she should do so with the sudden excruciating pain of passing a gall stone; and that the infant should be left there for a long period while the mother was being attended to by the one maid, if only temporarily, since the mother's need was the greater. Further corroboration of the truth of this revival was that the re-living of this experience cured the patient of her acute depression.

(b) In the following case the infantile experience was revealed at first, not in free association but by an automatic drawing of a ghost-like woman in a long fluttering dressing gown. The drawing of the picture and the picture itself horrified the patient, although she did not know why, for the picture itself was innocent enough. She was in her forties and suffered from panic of thunderstorms. Associating on the picture—and the feeling of horror—the patient visualized herself a small child asleep in bed, when the mother, screaming and hysterical, snatched her up and rushed downstairs with her to the accompaniment of loud bangs, which she now presumed to be an air raid. (See p. 188)

She was not aware of having been in an air raid and it seemed improbable, as there was no evidence of a raid where they lived in the country in Yorkshire. On enquiry, however, the patient had the story corroborated by an aunt; who told her that when she was a toddler her mother took her to stay at Scarborough. Now Scarborough did not have an air raid in the First World War, but it was twice shelled from the sea—once in December 1914 and once in December 1917, this latter time by a German submarine which damaged the Grand Hotel next door to where mother and child stayed, and killed three people. The patient was born in February 1916 and therefore would be a year and ten months when this took place—a 'toddler' as her aunt described. The experience left her with a terror of loud noises, especially thunderstorms of which her mother was also terrified. She was cured by the revival of this experience. The dissociated experience was brought into consciousness and therefore under control.

(c) Dreams, which, as we have said, are far more factual than is generally supposed, can sometimes be objectively verified. Such was the following: the patient dreamt of himself about the age of two with a dark-haired nurse-maid; of her being half naked and seducing him (the mother being out working all day): of a man coming in and there being a 'hell of a row'. (An uncle lived in the flat below.) If you straight away resort to a symbolic interpretation you might see in the nurse-maid an 'anima' figure, or a mother figure (Jung) and the man the revengeful father figure (Freud). The patient, at my instance, asked his mother if he had a nurse-maid and she said, 'Yes, Betty.' The patient remembered Betty but she was fair haired, not dark as the girl of the dream. The mother then recalled Ethel—a previous girl of fourteen who nursed him from infancy, and whom the mother said she dismissed. He was interested to know how far the story was true and in his provincial town advertised for the whereabouts of Ethel. He found her (now having married three times), and she was thrilled to see him. Asked if she ever remembered a row with the uncle, she said, 'Oh, don't I? It puts a shiver down my back when I think of it.' She also spoke of 'the naughty things I did'. He did not pursue the matter then, but arranged to see her again one afternoon, to get more details. But when he arrived, the husband being out, the woman was so tarted up with low neck, &c., that he feared a repetition of the infantile experience and, deciding that discretion was preferable to scientific investigation, he pursued the matter no further. The 'naughty' things she did do not appear to be confined to the past. So unfortunately we did not get complete corroboration; but we must certainly regard that as enough circumstantial evidence. The girl was in fact sacked after the row; but the episode left the child with a fear of sex and a distrust of women. The girl leaving also gave him the impression that she had let him down, 'women get you for sexual purposes, and then desert you.' Later, therefore, he was attracted but never married; for to him women in their sex relationship were dangerous. There is no reason to doubt the story and its effects.

These are some of the cases which have been objectively verified. They are by no means isolated cases.

EMOTIONAL REVIVAL

Further corroboration of the reality of these experiences is found

M

in the vivid emotions they revive. When these experiences are revived, the patient re-lives them with great emotional outbursts, as though they were actually occurring. He feels the terror: he goes through the suffocation; he chokes, he struggles and kicks with rage: he suffers an acute pain in the shoulder, gets actual stomach-ache, has spasms in his legs; he suddenly bursts out crying: after his ten minutes feed he lies back with a contented bloated look on his face. Patients re-live these experiences with what Freud calls 'hallucinatory vividness'. They are not hallucinations, but revivals of actual experiences. Anyone who has seen a man, suffering from war neurosis, going through the experiences of being blown-up, with his 'fits', his fighting and struggling for breath, cannot but be convinced of the reality of the experience he is going through. So it is with these infantile experiences.

A case was mentioned in my article in the *British Medical Journal* on 'The cure of homosexuality'. This patient revives an infantile experience of being choked at his mother's breast with a surfeit of milk. In reviving it he choked and choked for a dozen treatments or so till he 'got it out of his system'. This experience gave him a fear of his mother, and, since a child universalizes its experience he fears all women, especially in their sensuous and sexual aspect (as at the breast). Had he had an affectionate mother, he would have overcome this, for the conditioned reflex would in time have disappeared for lack of re-inforcement. But unfortunately he had a selfish and unloving mother, and so the fear persisted. He was completely cured of his homosexuality as a result of this repro-duction of the infantile experiences and married happily with children.

There was no objective corroboration of this story, his mother having died, but the realistic emotional revival of the choking and suffocation was sufficient evidence of the truth of the repro-duction—not to speak of the fact that its revival and his re-adjustment to the experiences cured him of his homosexuality.

Another instance of homosexuality has been given on page 323, when the patient revived the experience of being suffocated by the mother.

Frequently, the liberated emotions may be very violent—anger, fear, misery, sexual feelings and the need of love surges up uncontrollably. One man visualizing being unjustly treated by his father, bursts out, 'My God, if I saw him again, I'd strangle him.' Another patient, a professor of philosophy with a loveless child-hood, (which made him curious as to the meaning of life, so that he became a philosopher) pictures himself in adolescence, meeting a strange but attractive girl in the street and bursts out weeping. 'I want her to hold me in her arms and be kind to me'—not, mark you, wanting to hold her in his arms, for the feeling was an infantile one, the need of affection, which he never had from his mother. The emotions released are not of course always so violent as in the instances given, for many patients are temperamentally more reserved by nature. Even so there is still some emotional response if only a passing feeling of resentment or an infantile feeling of want of affection.

These experiences were in no way suggested; indeed one had no idea what they were till they emerged. Nor is it acting, for the feelings are deeply felt. They emerged spontaneously; they were reproductions of actual infantile experiences.

The revival of the original emotion not only corroborates the truth of the experience, but as we have said (p. 233) is necessary to cure.

REVIVAL OF UNEXPECTED EXPERIENCES

Further evidence of the reality of these infantile memories is the fact that the patient often visualizes infantile experiences, which he did not know could happen, but which we know can and do happen.

A striking case in point was that of a woman who re-lived her birth, and being held after birth by her legs upside down and smacked. She ridiculed the idea that they would do such a thing. I said, 'Don't you know how they sometimes revive infants when they are not breathing after birth?' She replied 'I have no idea.' 'They sometimes take them by the feet upside down and smack them.' She said, 'Surely that is very cruel.' I replied, 'But they think it does not matter because the child of that age has no cutaneous sensations of pain.' She said, 'But this is what I experienced; there was no pain at all, but there was a terrible shock, which made me feel dreadful terror.' She suffered from protopathic though not epicritic sensibility.

There was a certain amount of corroboration of this. She was born on a cold Christmas Day in Sweden and was put aside in a basket as dead, until her grandmother saw some movement and called out, 'Good gracious, the child is alive!' and saved her. In reviving the experience in analysis she felt bitterly cold and went blue even on a hot summer day. It was the worst case of anxiety hysteria I have ever treated. Another patient with claustrophobia re-lived the experience of birth. He suddenly asks, 'You can't be born legs first, can you? I thought babies were always born head first.' What seemed to him to be impossible was not only possible, but was later confirmed to be so in his case by his mother; and proved the reason for his claustrophobia.

M*

Most striking in this category are those cases in which infants have a circumcision in the first few days of life, and without an anaesthetic. In case after case the patient re-lived the experience with great horror and shock, but without experiencing any pain. In reviving the experience one man spontaneously remarks, 'Curiously enough I can feel no pain. Why is that?' Another said, 'As he cuts I feel a sudden shrinking in my genitals and stomach but no pain.' Another, 'I don't feel anything in my genitals but only a feeling of great shock in my chest and in my head, but no pain.' Another patient described 'No pain but I have a grating feeling when he cuts—I can feel it now. I have a dryness in my mouth, sunk-in cheeks, of being pale, which is odd, and pain in my eyes. My whole body becomes unfeeling.' These are obviously symptoms of physiological shock. Indeed, I cannot recall any instance of circumcision in the early days of life without anaesthetic, in which the patient did describe a feeling of pain. None of these patients had been aware of the fact of the absence of cutaneous sensation in early infancy; nor was there any suggestion on my part to that effect.

Another curious fact here emerges. While they do not feel any pain at the actual cutting, the patients in several cases have described pain afterwards during the dressing of the wound—in one case when he kicked and struggled in anger. Why they should have no pain at the cutting, but pain and soreness from the wound afterwards I do not know. But perhaps a physiologist would have an explanation.

This revival of the lack of pain acts as a 'control' of the early memory, for if a patient were inventing the story or simply imagining it, he would certainly associate such an experience with pain, for it would be 'inconceivable' to him that an infant would not feel pain if cut. But we know it to be a fact.

EXACT CORRESPONDENCE

Further evidence of the reality of these infantile experiences is the exact correspondence between the present-day symptom and the original visualized experience. This is in keeping with Freud's dictum that 'the hysteric suffers from reminiscences—a most important pronouncement. Indeed, the symptom often is a pure reproduction of that experience, in a most uncanny way.

This exact correspondence was well illustrated in the Case 1 mentioned (p. 225) of separation anxiety resulting from the tonsil operation. Both the causes and the symptoms suffered were almost identical. As to the circumstances the predisposing cause was that his mother deserted him and he was put under the anaesthetic; the precipitating cause was being given gas by the dentist and being let down by his girl friend. The recent combination of experiences was enough to arouse and revive the original experience with all its horror.

As for symptoms, his later symptom was a fear of 'passing out' which corresponds to his 'going over' with the anaesthetic at the operation: his separation anxiety which made him incapable of going out alone, to his being separated from his mother. He could not bear to sit in a dentist's chair, nor in a hairdresser's chair where he had to 'stay put', reminiscent of his being held down struggling on the operating table. From the same circumstances he could not bear anyone to touch him on the chest or to put an arm on his shoulder even in a friendly fashion, corresponding to his being pushed to lie down on the operating table. He got into a panic at the sound of any sizzling noise such as a running tap, the electric clippers at the barber's, a coffee machine, or the starting of a tube train, all of which reverted to the noise of the gas cylinder when he had the operation. The incident was forgotten, but every time he heard the sizzling noise afterwards, the panic came over him. 'There it is again!' although he did not know why or what 'it' was. There was also that patient who had a constant buzzing in the head as his main symptom, which was a revival of a motor bike accident in which he got 'concussion', during which he heard only the buzzing of the engine which kept running. In all these cases the patient re-lived the early experience in his neurosis. In all these cases, when the cause was revealed the patient lost his symptom.

A curious case was the following: A patient had an obsession against any unbuttoned buttonhole; he must immediately button it up. It was a nuisance to him because so strong was the compulsion that if he is in bed and sees his dressing gown with such an unbuttoned buttonhole he has to get up and attend to it: indeed he felt the same embarrassing impulse towards someone in the train whose coat was unbuttoned.

On a Freudian interpretation the urge to put the button in the button hole would be symbolic of sexual intercourse. I wonder whether being given that interpretation the patient would have been cured of this obsession, as he was by the revival of the actual fact of the origin? I suspect his reply would be, 'So what?'

When we took the symptom back by free association to its origin the patient spontaneously goes back to infancy, when at his mother's breast he had an erection, was smacked and so developed a horror of her breast, which he now regarded as dangerous. Thereafter when his mother approached with her dress undone to feed him, he couldn't bear it. 'Take it away! Button it up!' were his unexpressed feelings. The exact correspondence between his symptoms and his infantile 'memory' was good evidence of the truth of the revival. This was no interpretation of mine but what the patient visualized in free association: and by the revelation he was cured of the compulsion.

Another patient had a horror of hanging, which obsessed his waking life and haunted his dreams, in which he is tried, condemned and hanged. This reverted back to an experience at the age of three when he first went to kindergarten school. He was too afraid to ask for the lavatory and so in the break made do with a waste paper basket. In class the teacher asked the culprit to own up. He was too afraid to do so, with the result that another boy who suffered from incontinence was accused and punished. Returning home the patient, somewhat distressed at the outcome, asked his grandmother what happened to anyone who did something wrong and let someone else get the blame and punishment. She replied very gravely that it was very wicked; that people like that grew up to be criminals and in the end were hanged. Of course this made him still more terrified of owning up. The experience was too painful to think of and so was repressed. But the guilt remained, for the problem though repressed was still unresolved and so it kept cropping up in his dreams and also in his symptom. The fear of hanging was a reproduction of the original guilt fear. When the patient realized the cause of his fear he was cured of both symptoms and dreams; the only residue being an opposition to capital punishment, which is understandable.

A more complicated but most interesting case of sex perversion, but one clearly establishing the detailed correspondence between symptoms and event, is that of a man of thirty-five who has two main symptoms, a sadistic urge to overpower and strangle any woman towards whom he is sexually inclined, and a fetichism for a rubber mackintosh with which he is impelled to suffocate her. So violent is this sadistic impulse that he tried strangling himself to see how far he could go, lest he have a murder on his hands.

There were other details in his perversion; in strangling the woman he must first blindfold her so as not to see her eyes; he also must put the mackintosh against his face and chest, but it must always be back to front and inside out. It is not enough for us to say 'Oh! obviously a case of sadism', and dismiss the case. Why did his symptom take these strange specific forms? Scientifically speaking each symptom must have a cause and each of them had to be explained. In free association there emerged an infantile visualization of himself at his mother's breast and the milk giving out. He is angry and attacks it, squeezing (strangling) it to make it give him what he wanted, which gave him a great sense of power and satisfaction at his achievement; it also gave him sex feelings. This combination of aggression and sex is what constitutes 'sadism'. Finally he bit the nipple in anger and to make it give him more; but when he did this his mother angrily removed her breast. This put him in a quandary: in order to get more milk he must attack the breast, but if he did so he lost it altogether. Furthermore his mother's disapproval was registered in her eyes and frown. So he had to come to heel and repress his aggressive and sexual feelings, but with deep resentment against his mother, his unsolved problem.

Then he was weaned and given the bottle, which also he resented. But in feeding him with the bottle his mother rightly held him on her knee, where he made contact with her waterproof apron as he nestled against her covered breast. The breast itself was taboo; the waterproof over her breast was obviously not taboo, so was now adopted as a permitted substitute for the breast itself. Thus a rubber waterproof became his love object, a fetichism. (See page 321). As we have mentioned, many children are seen to suck their thumbs whilst fondling something soft like a silk handkerchief or quilt—a breast substitute. These conditions normally pass like all conditioned reflexes unless reinforced by later circumstances. If they persist or are revived the patients suffer from fetichisms. In every case of fetichism I have analyzed the fetichistic object was a breast substitute (*Psychology and Mental Health*, p. 376).

At the age of five this patient's father was taken acutely ill in the night and had to be hurried to hospital. Bewildered and frightened at the commotion, the child, wanting reassurance, kept asking his mother what was the matter, but she, poor woman, was too flustered to answer and was impatient with him. Another rebuff. Standing in the hall in misery and fear he saw his mother's waterproof hanging there; so to comfort himself he wrapped himself in this as a substitute for his mother, to give him comfort and security. His symptoms were a reproduction of each and all of those early experiences.

His sadism, attacking the woman 'to get what he wanted' was equivalent to his attacking his mother's breast to get what he wanted, by strangling in both cases; his putting the waterproof over his lover recaptured the feeling of his mother's rubber apron and later her mackintosh. The waterproof had to be held right over the woman's chest; that was to hide the breast itself because that was taboo. The cape had to be inside out; that was so that his face could come against the smooth rubber, like the smoothness of the breast, whereas the cotton outside was rough. Rubber is a common fetichistic object—not only on account of its smoothness, but because the smell of rubber recalls the body smell at the breast.

Why must the loved woman be blindfolded? It was lest she should show disapproval as his mother did when she frowned. Let me repeat that all this was not surmise, an ingenious explanation on my part of his strange variety of symptoms, but his spontaneous discovery in his visualizations, the significance of many of which in relation to his fetichism he did not realize until after they had arrived; and certainly I would not have guessed such an explanation.

The obvious criticism in all these cases is first of all that these visualizations were purely imaginary; but as we have pointed out in our last section, the patient would not imagine these things taking place which he did not know could happen, such as having a circumcision without pain. Secondly, purely imaginary pictures would not have produced such violent emotions such as we see in many cases. Thirdly, it is naturally objected that the patient was simply reading his present-day symptoms into imaginary experiences of the past. That is not in fact how it happens. In the last case we started off with the symptom of the rubber cape. That took him to the five-year-old incident in the hall. That took him spontaneously and without prompting to the infantile scene with all its concomitants in breast-feeding such as his anger, his mother's disapproving frown and his sexual feelings. When these pictures first arrived there was no recognizable connection between them and the symptoms. The symptoms were therefore not read into some imaginary incident, but they nevertheless led to the cause of the symptoms. It was only after the infantile experiences were revived, that he realized they corresponded precisely to the feelings and symptoms he felt at the present day, and were quite obviously the cause of these symptoms. It was only after the patient had visualized his distress at his mother's frown and his turning away from it that he saw the connection between that and his covering his lover's eyes.

The process is the same as in automatic drawings. In conventional drawings, you have in mind what you intend to draw, and draw it. In automatic drawing you do not know what you are drawing; only afterwards do you see the significance and meaning of what you have drawn. So these patients spontaneously and automatically revive these infantile pictures and only then see their connection with their present-day symptoms.

THERAPEUTIC RESULTS

The most striking evidence of the reality of these infantile experiences is the therapeutic result. When these infantile experiences are revived, the symptom immediately disappears, 'never to return',

Freud says—somewhat optimistically! In all the cases I have mentioned the patient was cured by these revivals. Such results are evidence not only of the reality of these experiences, but of their importance as causative factors in the production of the neurosis; also of the necessity in many cases of discovering them if we are to cure our patients radically. If these visualizations were simply imaginations they could certainly not produce such therapeutic results.

Nor was the cure coincidence. It was when and only when the patient discovered and re-lived this experience at the tonsil operation that he lost his claustrophobia and agoraphobia. It was when, and only when, the man with asthma (p. 345) re-lived his choking with friar's balsam that he lost his symptoms. It was when, and only when, the homosexual traced his symptom back to his erection and subsequent suffocation at his mother's breast (p. 348) which left him with a fear of women, that he lost his fear of women and his homosexuality, and married happily. It was when, and only when, the woman experienced being let fall by her mother in infancy that she lost her acute depression. So when the patient realized why he could not tolerate an unbuttoned buttonhole from the experience in infancy (p. 351), he completely lost his symptoms; and the patient with the fear of hanging (p. 352) lost it when he recovered the cause of it in the episode at school and his grandmother's warning.

A woman patient complains of unpleasant eidetic images of faeces, which greatly distress her. In free association she revives a childhood picture of having messed herself and of the mother scolding her, calling her a 'nasty dirty filthy little thing'. She is humiliated, and at the same time furious with her mother, but even more afraid of her. So she must repress the whole experience, including her anger and humiliation. Her 'complex' consisted of the association of all these feelings with faeces. The result was that whenever she felt like being even normally angry, the anger was automatically repressed, but the associated eidetic image of faeces would emerge as a symbol or representation of her defiance. She was cured of this in one treatment. (She was, however, under treatment for other symptoms, so that free association came easily to her). The immediacy of the cure on recovery of these infantile experiences leaves no doubt in our minds and in the mind of the patient (a) of the reality of the infantile experience, (b) that it was a causal factor in producing the neurosis; (c) of the recoverability of such experiences and (d) of the clinical importance of discovering them if we are radically to cure the patient. It also makes nonsense of the common criticism that these patients would have got better anyway. Some had twenty and thirty years to do that, and only when the infantile cause was discovered did they recover, and that almost immediately.

SPONTANEOUS CURE

Still further therapeutic evidence is found in cases of spontaneous cure—that is to say cure resulting from the spontaneous revival of infantile experiences. Cases are reported from time to time in the press, of people suffering from aphonia suddenly getting their speech back with some shock. A soldier patient who suffered severe headaches: in the street he saw a huge crane and the thought came to him, 'Suppose it fell down on me'. That night he dreamt of the time he was buried by a shell, remembered all about it in the morning, and was spontaneously cured of his headache. Nature shows the way to cure: our method is to follow nature's method in recovering forgotten experiences to effect a cure, just as we take a thorn out of the body to cure an abscess.

I shall conclude with the most striking case I have met with, of spontaneous cure—in a child of three years. (She was not my patient, but her mother was and I knew the child.) From the age of three days after birth the infant had screamed and struggled with nightmares every night, sometimes for as much as five hours. As a rule if the mother came she screamed worse, crying for 'Daddy' and the father could sometimes comfort her. She could never say what her nightmares were. Curiously enough these nightmares did not affect the child's health which was robust— perhaps because of the exercise of her lungs. It was the parents who suffered. At the age of three years, (1961), she had the most terrifying nightmare she had ever had, and wakened up screaming: 'The chain broke—the chain broke—the water was everywhere and I was frightened.' The following day she was asked if she remembered the dream and for the first time she was able to do so. She said, 'There was a snake round the baby's leg, right round the baby's leg'—and she touched her own leg—'a snake round the baby's leg!' Later she asked for a cup of water and for more still; and said to her mother, 'Come and see, and I will tell you all about it. Bring me scissors; come and sit down and I will show you!' On the desk in a saucer was the water. 'I'll show you what happened! Listen! Look!' She then took an empty cigarette packet, making a long strip which she said was Mummy. Another smaller strip she called the baby. She said, 'There was a snake round the baby', and wanted to 'play snake' with it. She asked for and was given some wool which she tied round the 'baby'. All this was done with great seriousness and purpose, and with a lot of emotion. Tearing up pieces of cardboard and tying wool round them she said, 'Plenty of babies. All in the water with plenty of snakes round them. Frightened!' Carried away by emotion she cried, 'A lion came and got the snake away; a bear came. Daddy came. The baby screamed and then couldn't scream!' With this she gripped her throat, thereby cutting off the scream, her eyes staring with terror. She was holding her breath and struggling frantically against 'the snake'. Just as suddenly it was over, and she said quite matter-of-factly, 'Then Daddy came and cut the snake away.' She unwound the wool from the bits of cardboard and thereafter continued the game composedly. She got two dolls and tied the same string tightly round the dolls' necks. The she cut away the 'snake' with scissors saying calmly, 'Daddy came and cut the snake away.' She then buried the 'snake' in the garden and said, 'It will grow to be a flower,' and was very delighted. All this took several hours.

As for objective corroborations: the child was born in Nigeria. Her birth was precipitous—'She almost bolted into the world,' but with the cord tight round her neck. The father ran to the telephone exchange whilst a friend put her finger under the cord to relieve the pressure on the baby's throat. On his return the father (who had been a medical student and had been present at native births) got artery forceps and scissors and cut the cord and the child was born in a state of shock—apparently dead.

The child's nightmares corresponded exactly with her birth experiences; indeed like many nightmares (e.g., passing through a narrow tunnel with great anxiety) it was an exact replica of it.

Most striking was the therapeutic effect; she had previously screamed every night since she was three days old. When at the age of three years, she recovered this experience with the nightmares coming into consciousness, her nightmares suddenly ceased, not to return. It was a complete cessation. She has since (the experience was five years ago) had what she described as 'little dreams—I wasn't frightened', and these dreams were such as any child may have. She now sometimes gets up in the night for a drink of water without any fear and without disturbing anybody; moreover for the first time in her life she has begun to show affection to her mother of whom she was previously afraid. The mother reports that 'she is now a happy child, very healthy with a sort of blazing serenity'. I can confirm this as I have seen her with her parents camping on my place in the country.

The obvious criticism is that the child had heard talk of the birth. The mother declares that she has never told her of her birth—there was no cause to do so. She cannot guarantee that she never spoke of it to someone else in the child's hearing, but cannot recollect ever having done so nor seen any reason to have mentioned it to anyone.

In any case we must remember that what the child was describing was not what happened at birth, but what happened in her nightmare; and these nightmares were certainly not the result of being told of her birth experiences, for they had been going on since the child was three days old—long before she could have heard anything about it from her mother. The nightmares which the child was describing were obviously an exact reproduction of her birth of which the child remembered nothing, but which she had been obviously reproducing nightly. Yet only now had it come into full consciousness, with the result that she was cured.

To the child, what she told her mother obviously had nothing to do with the birth; for when, on my suggestion, the mother asked her if she remembered anything about her birth, she replied 'Yes! I was born in Africa and came out of my mummy's tummy.' That was all. In her mind there was no connection between the nightmares and birth, so she could not have been making it up nor does it look as if it was something she had been told.

But let us suppose that by some chance the mother had spoken of the birth in the child's presence, the possibility of which we cannot exclude, that could not possibly produce such violent emotional reaction unless it were a revival of a real experience, which was now being revived. Nor would it have produced such dramatic therapeutic results since the nightmare which had occurred nightly for three years suddenly ceased with its revival, never to return. In any case the nightmares, as we have said, dated back to three days old.

As corroborative evidence, it is worth noticing that the child recounting the nightmare first mentioned the 'snake' (the cord) being round her leg, which the mother knew nothing about and therefore could not have reproduced, but which the child recalled vividly, touching her leg as she did so. Only afterwards it choked her round the throat.

There is further objective corroboration, which explained another symptom. The mother now recalled that prior to this revelation, whenever the child had a piece of string or a cord like a skipping rope, she would always put it round her neck, as though to strangle herself, a habit which could now be explained. This is in conformity with the fact that a great deal of a child's play is the subconscious effort to solve her problems. Just as the children in Bristol Hospital (as already mentioned), which got a direct hit in the war, afterwards played at bombing!

It may be further objected. How could she distinguish her mother from the father who 'got the snake away'? Every parent knows that an infant does distinguish them. A tiny infant very soon distinguishes mother from father; she may snuggle into one and cry when lifted by the other. Dogs lost in a crowd find their master by smell not by sight. The Parisian perfume expert can with his eyes blindfolded pick out persons in a group by their individual smell; why then should an infant not do so? Smell is a very primitive sense indeed. Her father she took for something hostile at first, 'a bear, a lion,' but then as something giving her release. The smell of the mother in this case may have been associated with terror: the smell of the father with relief from the terror: no wonder she went to him for protection thereafter.

All the evidence of the reliability of infantile neurosis may not convince the sceptic who has already made up his mind. But in doing so he may be missing a most important means of cure, for many cures, as in this case, depend on the revival of experiences in infancy. The evidence is, however, sufficient to convince those of us who witness the recovery of these experiences day by day in our patients, and the acceptance of the evidence enables us with confidence to seek for the causes of neuroses in infantile situations. After all the real test is the cure of our patients.

With all these varied and often contradictory theories and methods of treatment the question naturally arises: how is it that they all seem to get good results? The answer is that all analytic systems agree on several points. First, that the patient is led to look into himself, to examine himself and his motives; also to unburden himself and to talk about himself. That in itself is a valuable therapeutic measure. He discovers himself, and reveals things about himself, which he did not know about himself, and therefore fulfils the first injunction of the Delphic oracle 'Know thyself'.

Secondly, all systems are at one in this: they all set about liberating potentialities in the personality, however these are conceived.

Thirdly, the patient, misunderstood and misunderstanding himself, at last meets with someone who is interested in him, takes his symptom seriously and so far gives him affection. This personal interest is what the patient has craved all his life and is a great relief.

Prevention. If it can be substantiated that the original cause of neurotic disorders lies in infantile experiences it gives us some hope that by the avoidance of such experiences most neurotic conditions can be prevented (p. 338). If they are unavoidable, by taking special care to give to such a child the sense of security and it will thereby be reassured.

To my mind the great contribution which analytic treatment has made towards human happiness is that by delving down to discover the deep-seated causes of neurotic and behaviour disorders it may find the way to right parenthood. This is the task I set myself in my *Childhood and Adolescence* which deals not with the treatment of disorders, but how to prevent them and so open the way to health and happiness.

That is why it is necessary to know what in fact are the true causes of neurotic disorders, and this is my reason for bringing forward the facts of their origin.

As we have seen, when we examine the actual experiences which caused the neurotic conditions in our patients in early childhood, we see clearly that the vast majority of them could have been prevented by right parenthood.

INDEX

GEORGE ALLEN & UNWIN LTD
London: 40 Museum Street, W.C.1

Auckland: P.O. Box 36013, Northcote Central N.4
Bombay: 15 Graham Road, Ballard Estate, Bombay 1
Barbados: P.O. Box 222, Bridgetown
Beirut: Deeb Building, Jeanne d'Arc Street
Buenos Aires: Escritorio 454–459, Florida 165
Calcutta: 17 Chittaranjan Avenue, Calcutta 13
Cape Town: 68 Shortmarket Street
Hong Kong: 105 Wing On Mansion, 26 Hancow Road,
Kowloon
Ibadan: P.O. Box 62
Karachi: Karachi Chambers, McLeod Road
Madras: Mohan Mansions, 38c Mount Road, Madras 6
Mexico: Villalongin 32–10, Piso, Mexico 5, D.F.
Nairobi: P.O. Box 4536
New Delhi: 13–14 Asaf Ali Road, New Delhi 1
Ontario: 81 Curlew Drive, Don Mills
Philippines: P.O. Box 4322, Manila
Rio de Janeiro: Caixa Postal 2537-Zc-00
Singapore: 36c Prinsep Street, Singapore 7
Sydney, N.S.W.: Bradbury House, 55 York Street
Tokyo: P.O. Box 26, Kamata

PSYCHIATRY FOR STUDENTS
DAVID STAFFORD CLARK

'. . . very much to be welcomed . . . an excellent book . . comprehensive, reliable and vivid; and should be read (and will be read
easily) by all seeking some knowledge of psychiatry. Though
designed presumably for medical students and general practitioners,
there is much in it that the more experienced psychiatrist will
learn from: and yet the intelligent non-medical student will also
learn from its balance and simplicity.' *British Journal of Psychiatry*

'This is an excellent book and is valuable not only for the student
but also for the general practitioner who, whether he likes it or
not, has to cope with more psychiatric patients than ever before'
The Practitioner

'. . . one of the best of the recent books on psychiatry for medical
students' *Proceedings of the Royal Society of Medicine*

PSYCHOSOMATIC MEDICINE
FRANZ ALEXANDER

'This, in spite of the relative brevity, is the soundest general
work on the subject yet published by a psychiatrist . . . should do
much to bridge the gulf of misunderstanding which has so long
delayed the psychosomatic era in medicine. It is suitable for
trainee and mature physician alike, attractively printed and with
an excellent bibliography.' *The Practitioner*

'A very useful account of the underlying theory and practical
therapeutic results in this field . . . clearly and sensibly written.'
Lancet

'Should make a general appeal to senior medical students and
general practitioners as well as young psychiatrists and specialists
in the fields covered.' *British Medical Journal*

GEORGE ALLEN & UNWIN LTD